Captive Hearts

Shojo Beat

Story & Art by
Matsuri Hino

Vol. 1

Captive Hearts
Vol. 1

CONTENTS

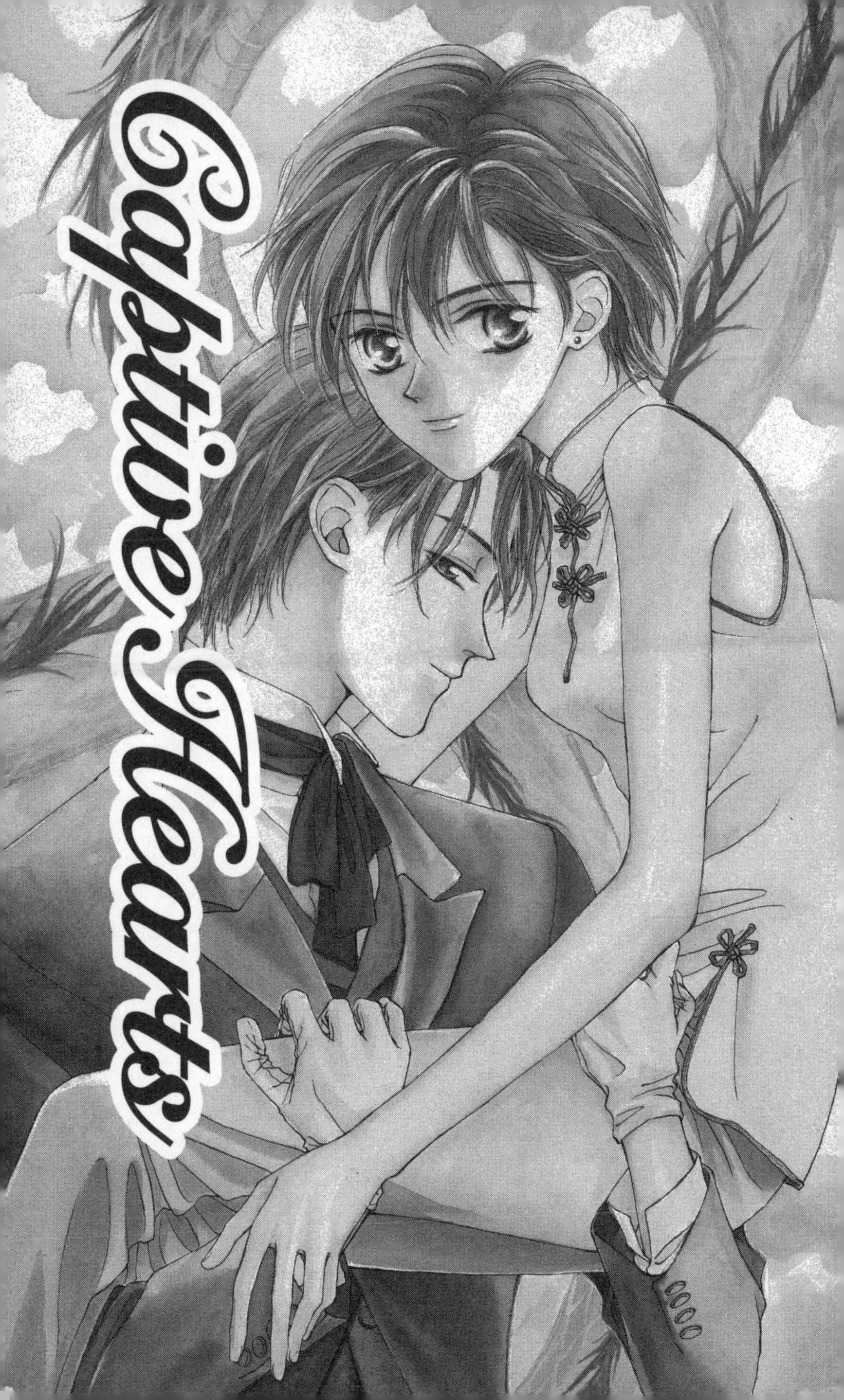
Captive Hearts

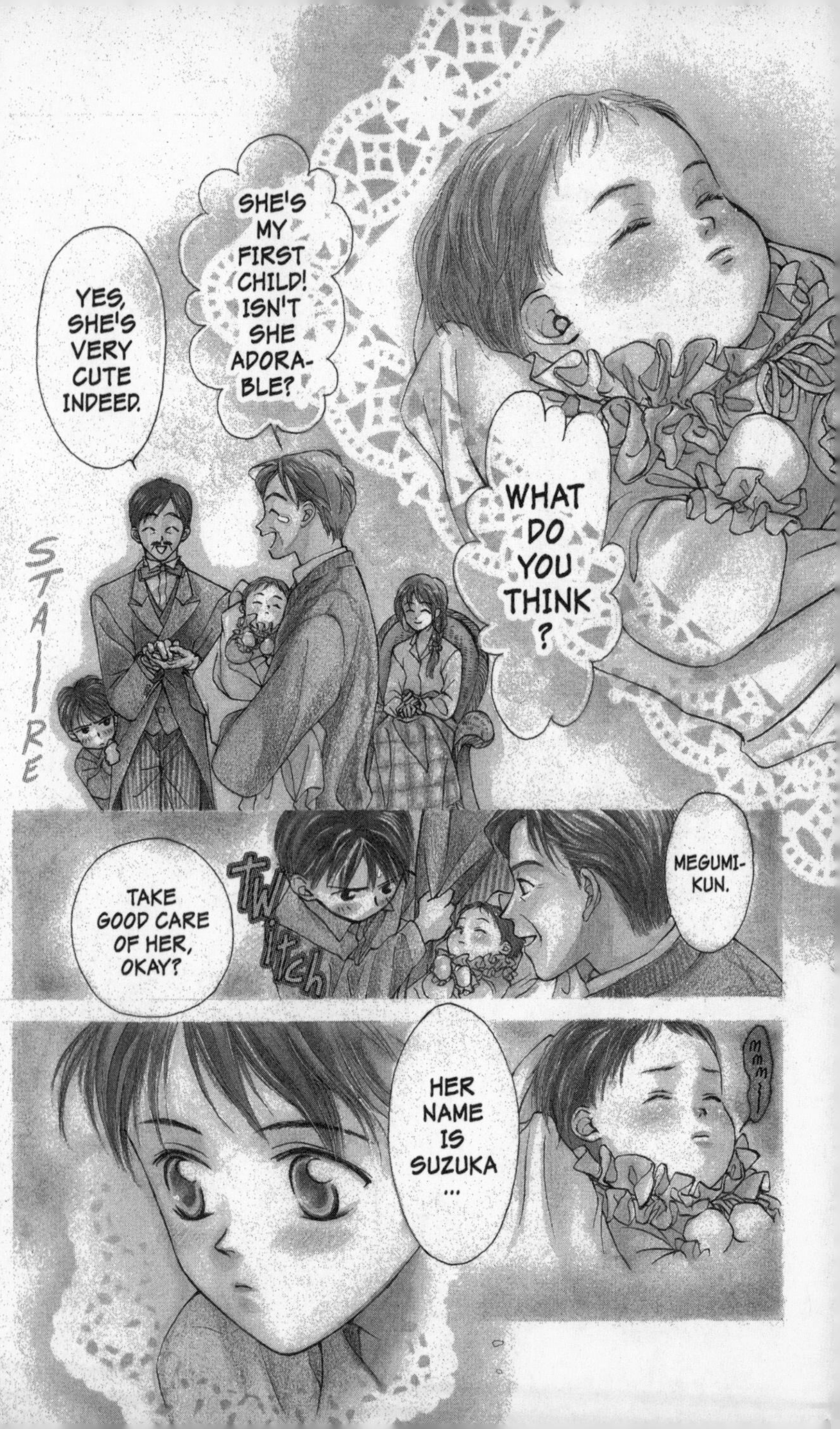
WHAT DO YOU THINK?
SHE'S MY FIRST CHILD! ISN'T SHE ADORABLE?
YES, SHE'S VERY CUTE INDEED.
STAIRE
MEGUMI-KUN.
TAKE GOOD CARE OF HER, OKAY?
twitch
mmm...
HER NAME IS SUZUKA ...

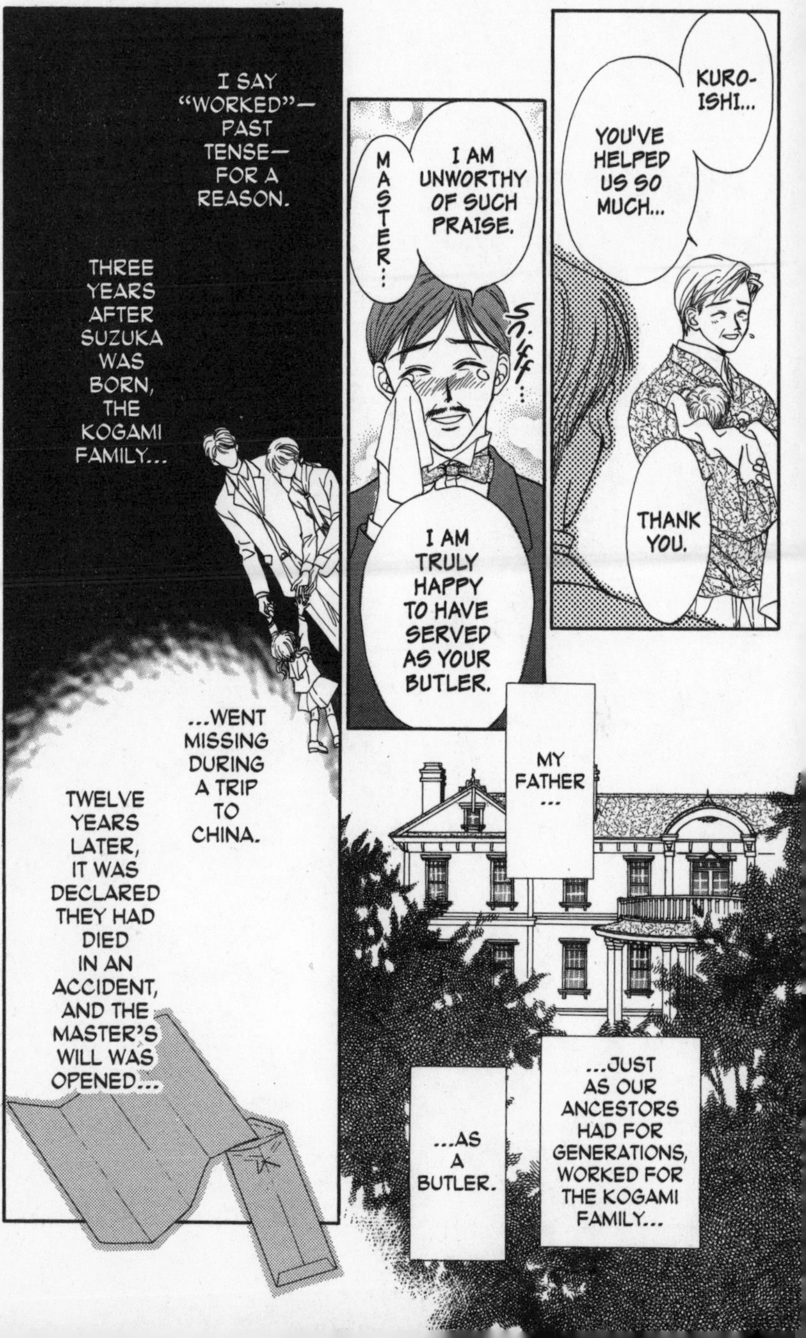
KURO-ISHI...
YOU'VE HELPED US SO MUCH...
THANK YOU.
I AM UNWORTHY OF SUCH PRAISE.
MASTER...
SNIFF...
I AM TRULY HAPPY TO HAVE SERVED AS YOUR BUTLER.
MY FATHER...
...JUST AS OUR ANCESTORS HAD FOR GENERATIONS, WORKED FOR THE KOGAMI FAMILY...
...AS A BUTLER.
I SAY "WORKED"—PAST TENSE—FOR A REASON.
THREE YEARS AFTER SUZUKA WAS BORN, THE KOGAMI FAMILY...
...WENT MISSING DURING A TRIP TO CHINA.
TWELVE YEARS LATER, IT WAS DECLARED THEY HAD DIED IN AN ACCIDENT, AND THE MASTER'S WILL WAS OPENED...

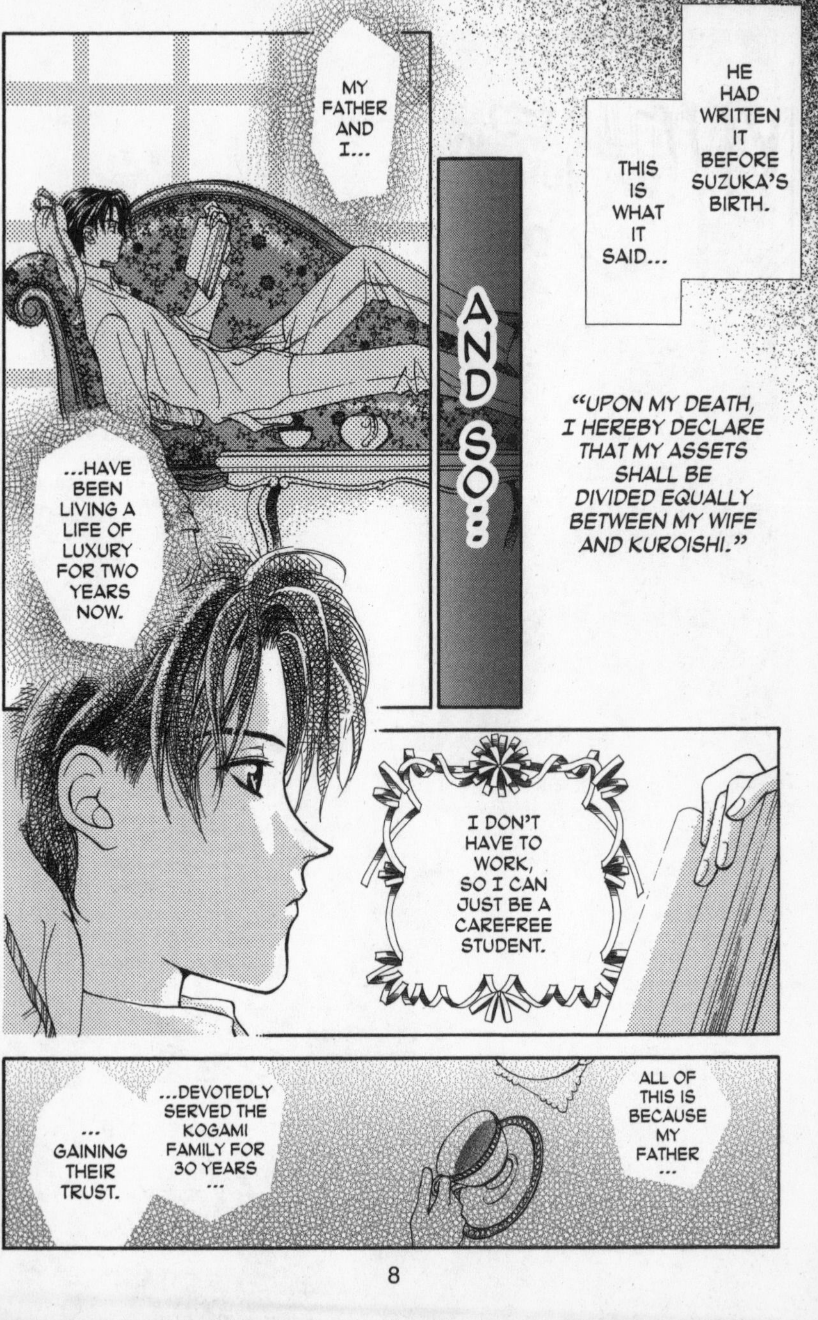
HE HAD WRITTEN IT BEFORE SUZUKA'S BIRTH.
THIS IS WHAT IT SAID...
"UPON MY DEATH, I HEREBY DECLARE THAT MY ASSETS SHALL BE DIVIDED EQUALLY BETWEEN MY WIFE AND KUROISHI."
AND SO...
MY FATHER AND I...
...HAVE BEEN LIVING A LIFE OF LUXURY FOR TWO YEARS NOW.
I DON'T HAVE TO WORK, SO I CAN JUST BE A CAREFREE STUDENT.
ALL OF THIS IS BECAUSE MY FATHER...
...DEVOTEDLY SERVED THE KOGAMI FAMILY FOR 30 YEARS...
...GAINING THEIR TRUST.

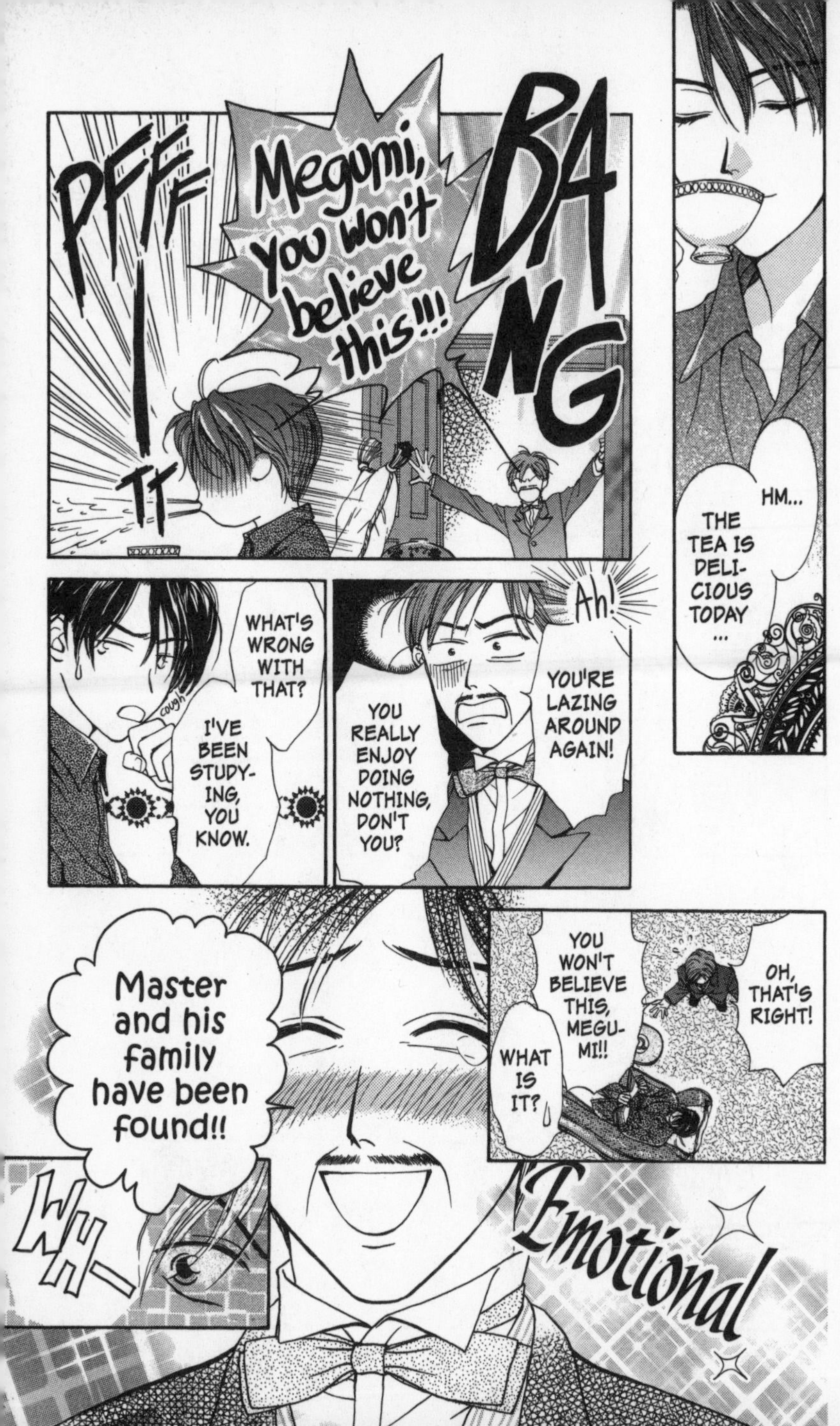
HM...
THE TEA IS DELICIOUS TODAY...
BANG
Megumi, you won't believe this!!!
PFFFT
Ah!
YOU'RE LAZING AROUND AGAIN!
YOU REALLY ENJOY DOING NOTHING, DON'T YOU?
WHAT'S WRONG WITH THAT?
cough
I'VE BEEN STUDYING, YOU KNOW.
OH, THAT'S RIGHT!
YOU WON'T BELIEVE THIS, MEGUMI!!
WHAT IS IT?
Master and his family have been found!!
Emotional
WH-

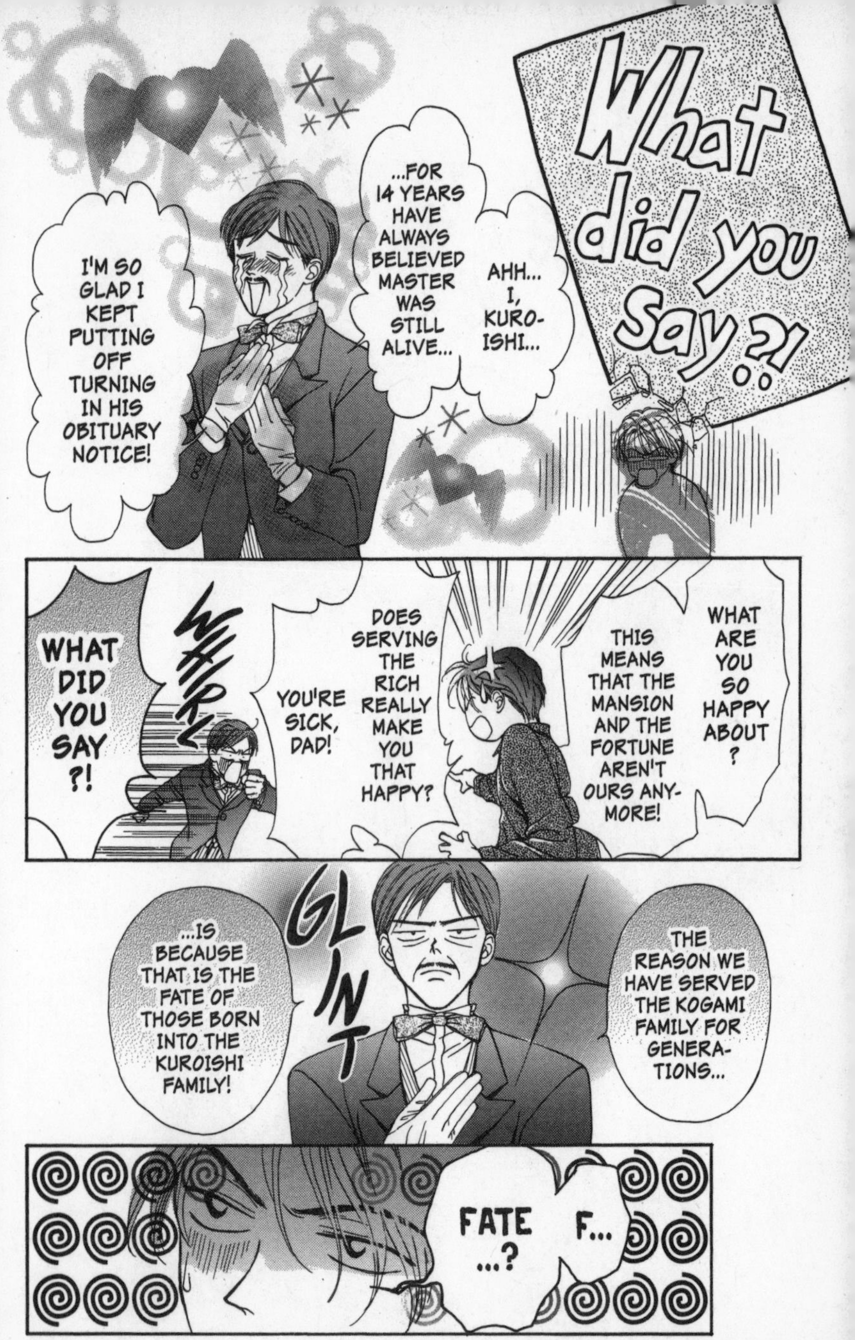
What did you Say?!
AHH... I, KURO-ISHI...
...FOR 14 YEARS HAVE ALWAYS BELIEVED MASTER WAS STILL ALIVE...
I'M SO GLAD I KEPT PUTTING OFF TURNING IN HIS OBITUARY NOTICE!
WHAT ARE YOU SO HAPPY ABOUT?
THIS MEANS THAT THE MANSION AND THE FORTUNE AREN'T OURS ANYMORE!
DOES SERVING THE RICH REALLY MAKE YOU THAT HAPPY?
YOU'RE SICK, DAD!
WHIRL
WHAT DID YOU SAY?!
THE REASON WE HAVE SERVED THE KOGAMI FAMILY FOR GENERATIONS...
GLINT
...IS BECAUSE THAT IS THE FATE OF THOSE BORN INTO THE KUROISHI FAMILY!
F...
FATE ...?

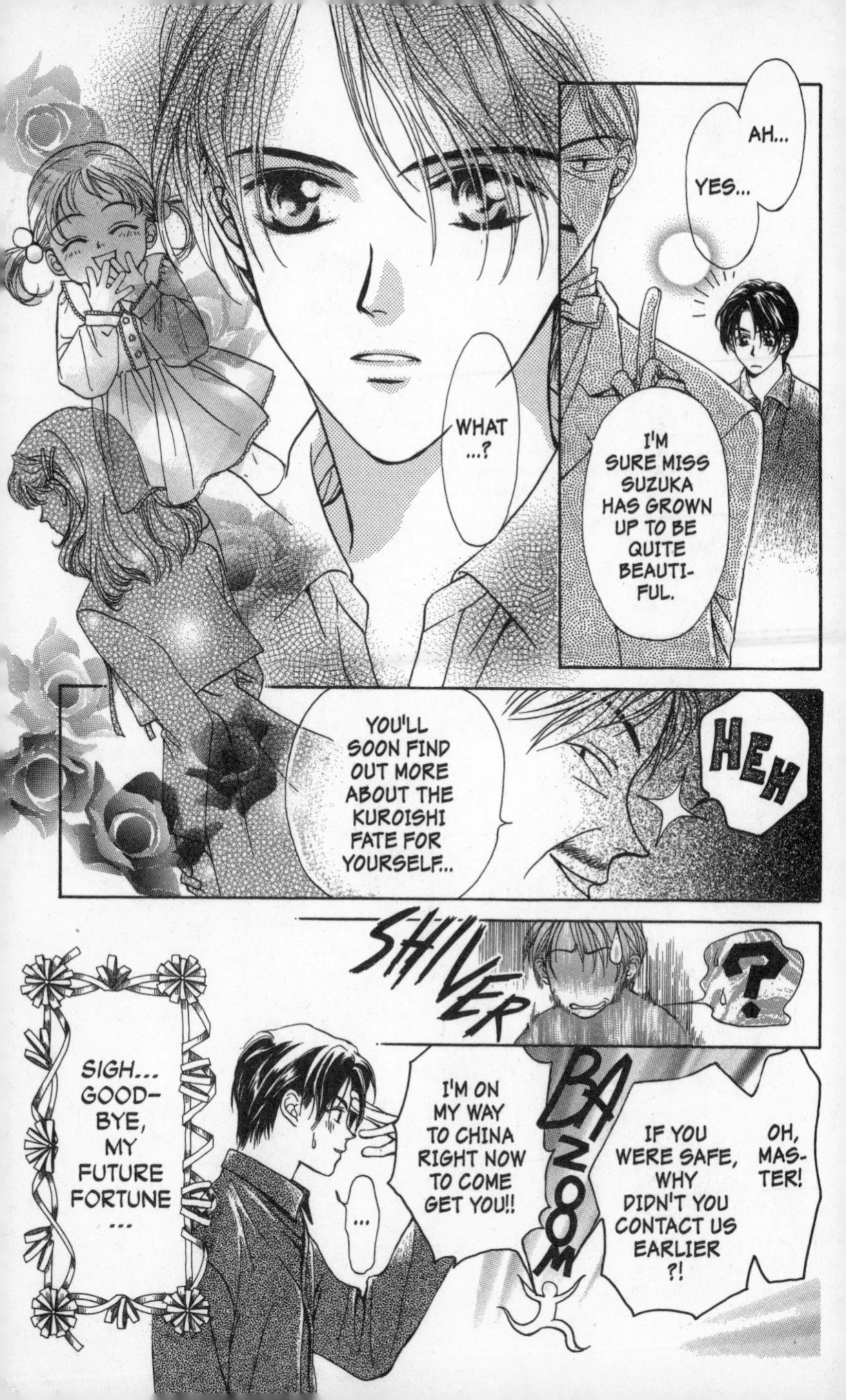
AH... YES...
I'M SURE MISS SUZUKA HAS GROWN UP TO BE QUITE BEAUTI-FUL.
WHAT ...?
HEH
YOU'LL SOON FIND OUT MORE ABOUT THE KUROISHI FATE FOR YOURSELF...
?
SHIVER
OH, MAS-TER!
IF YOU WERE SAFE, WHY DIDN'T YOU CONTACT US EARLIER ?!
BAZOOM
I'M ON MY WAY TO CHINA RIGHT NOW TO COME GET YOU!!
...
SIGH... GOOD-BYE, MY FUTURE FORTUNE ...

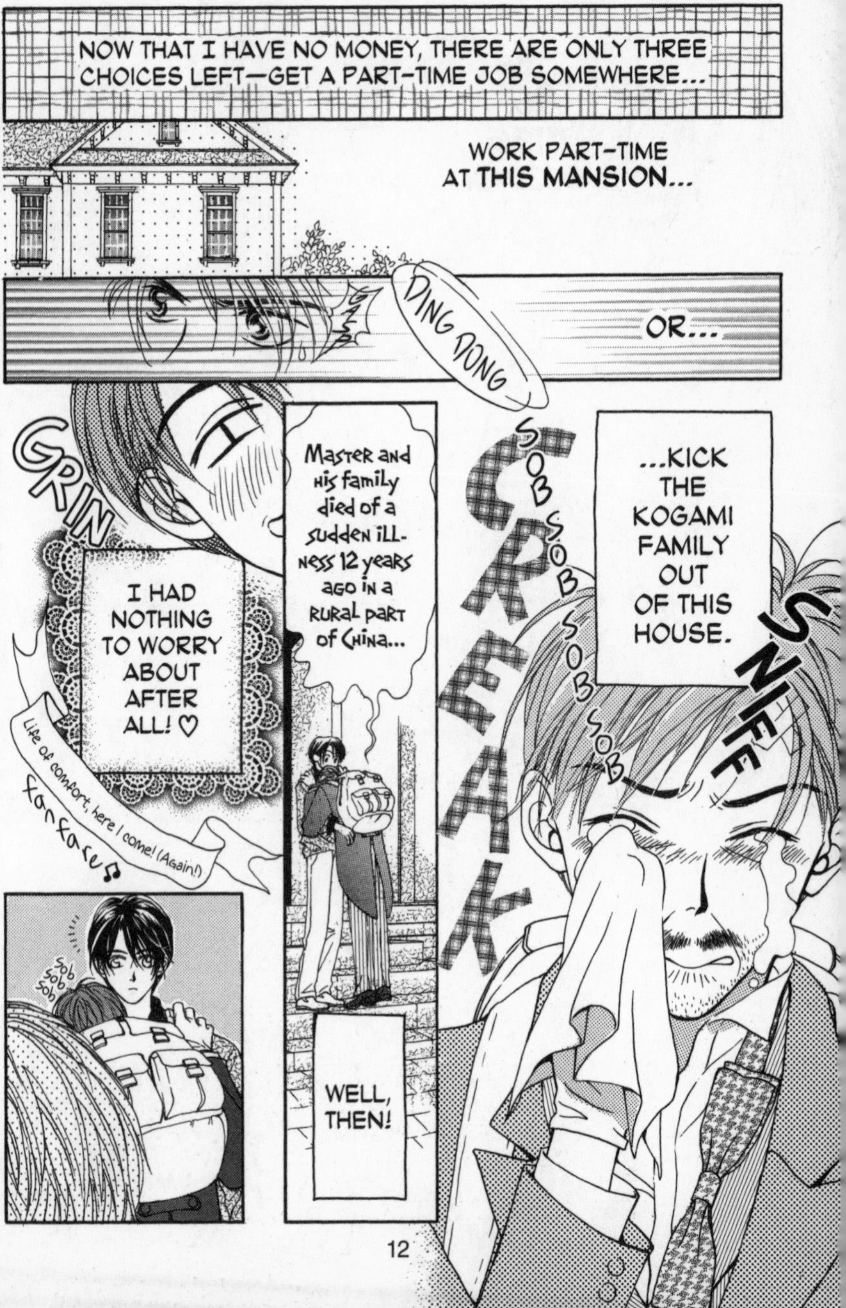

NOW THAT I HAVE NO MONEY, THERE ARE ONLY THREE CHOICES LEFT—GET A PART-TIME JOB SOMEWHERE...
WORK PART-TIME AT THIS MANSION...
DING DONG
OR...
...KICK THE KOGAMI FAMILY OUT OF THIS HOUSE.
SNIFF
SOB SOB SOB SOB
CREAK
Master and his family died of a sudden illness 12 years ago in a rural part of China...
WELL, THEN!
GRIN
I HAD NOTHING TO WORRY ABOUT AFTER ALL! ♡
Life of comfort, here I come! (Again!)
fanfare♫
Sob sob sob

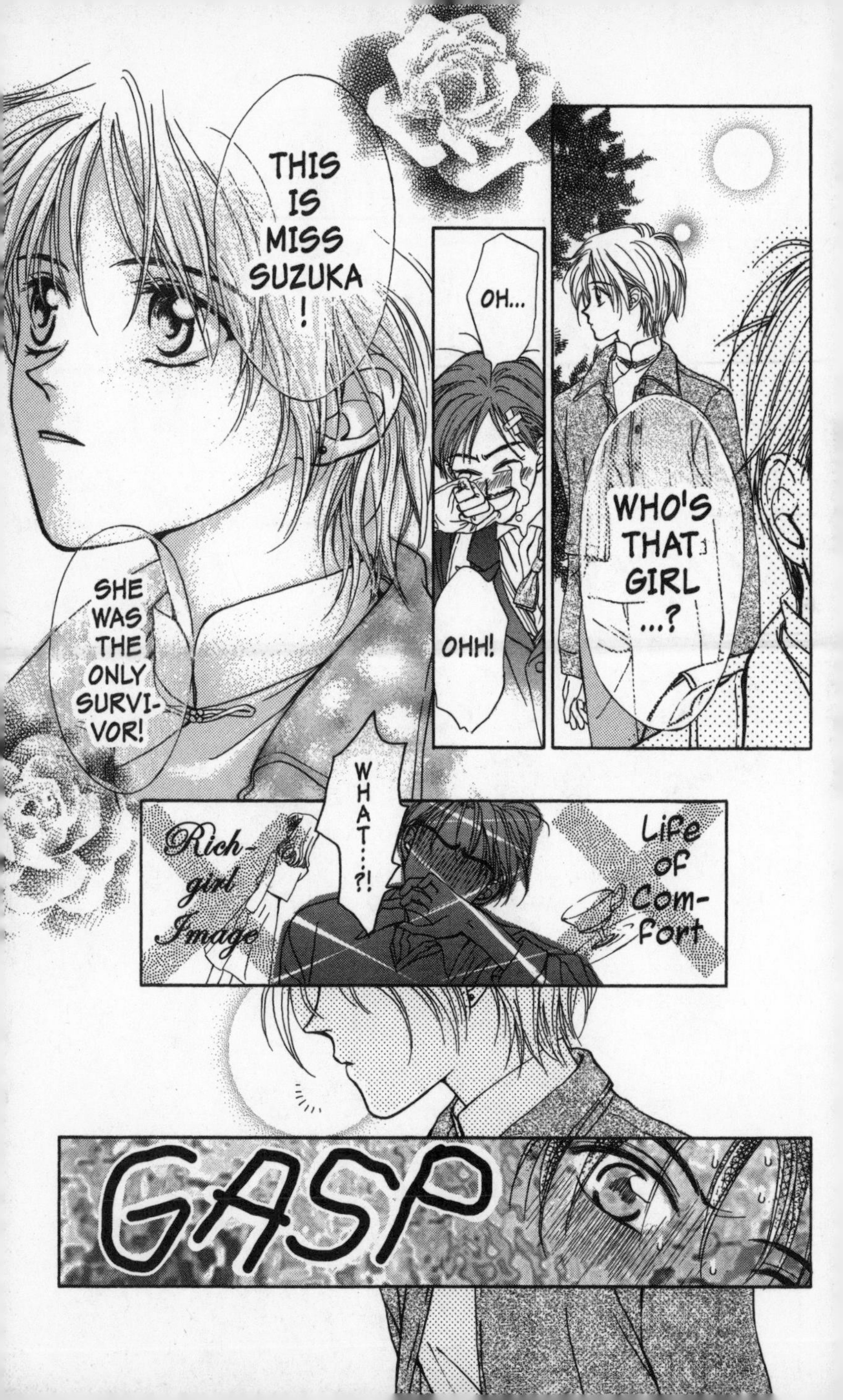
WHO'S THAT GIRL ...?
OH...
OHH!
THIS IS MISS SUZUKA!
SHE WAS THE ONLY SURVI-VOR!
Life of Com-fort
WHAT...?!
Rich-girl Image
GASP

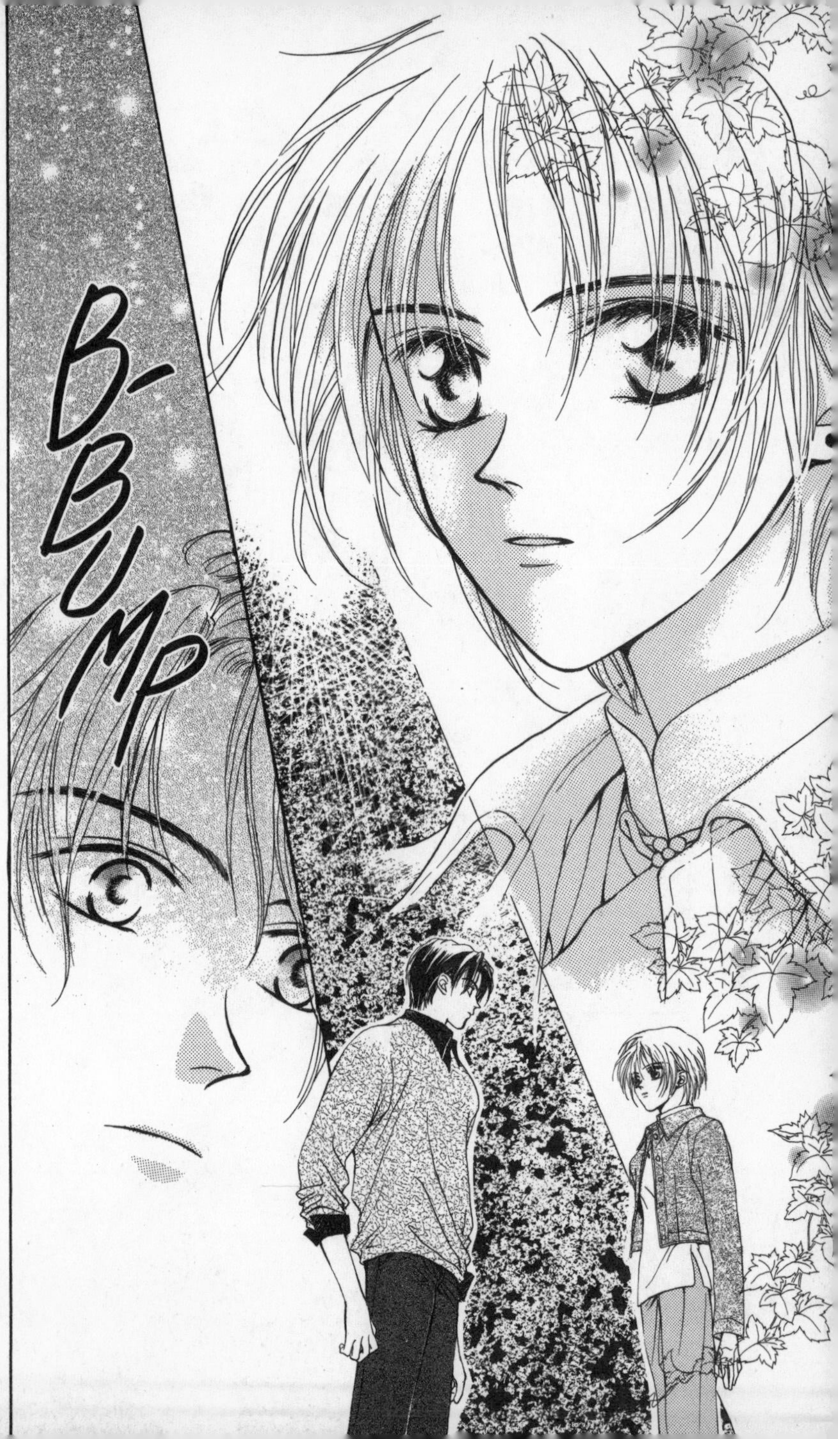
B-BUMP

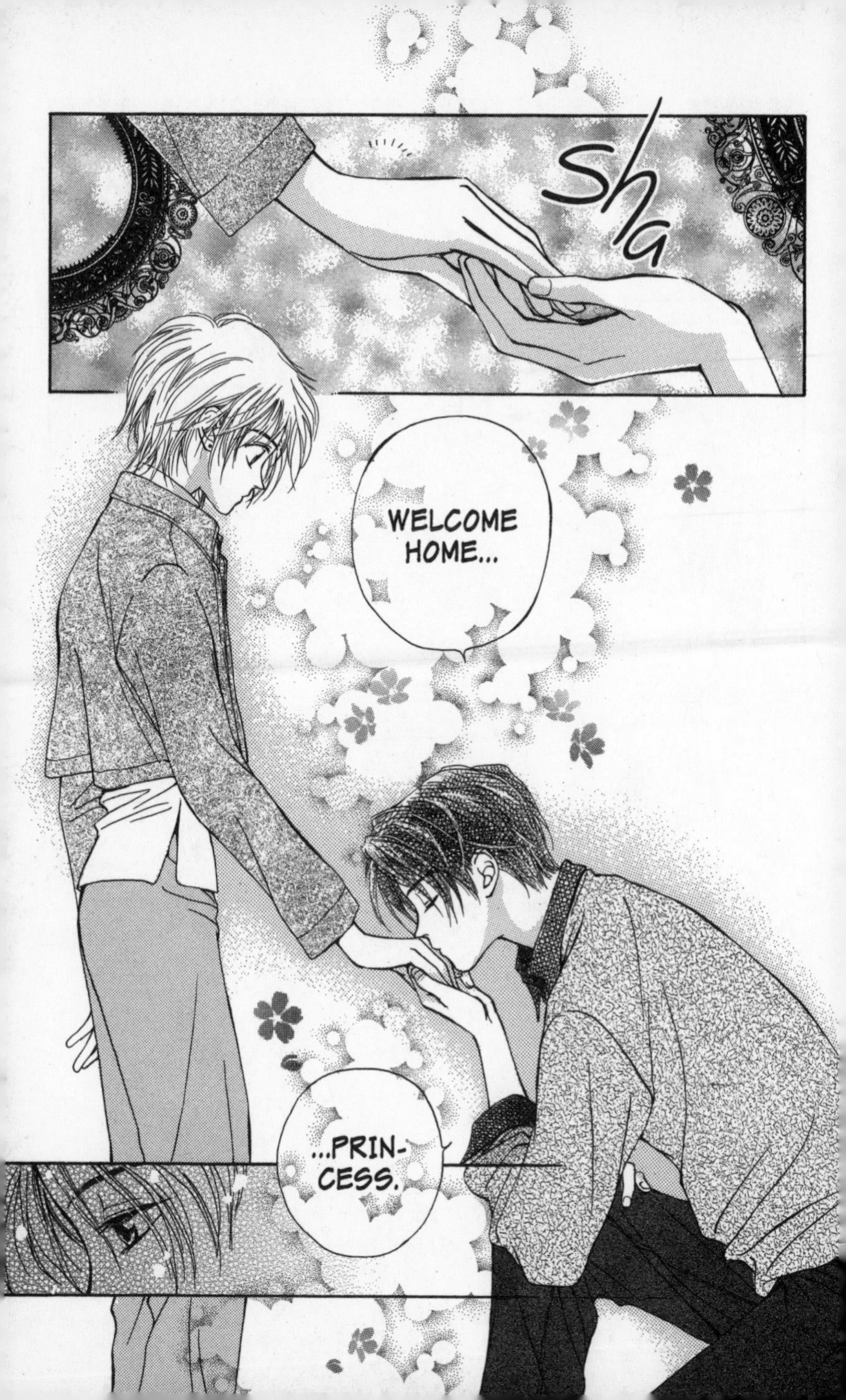
SHA
WELCOME HOME...
...PRIN-CESS.

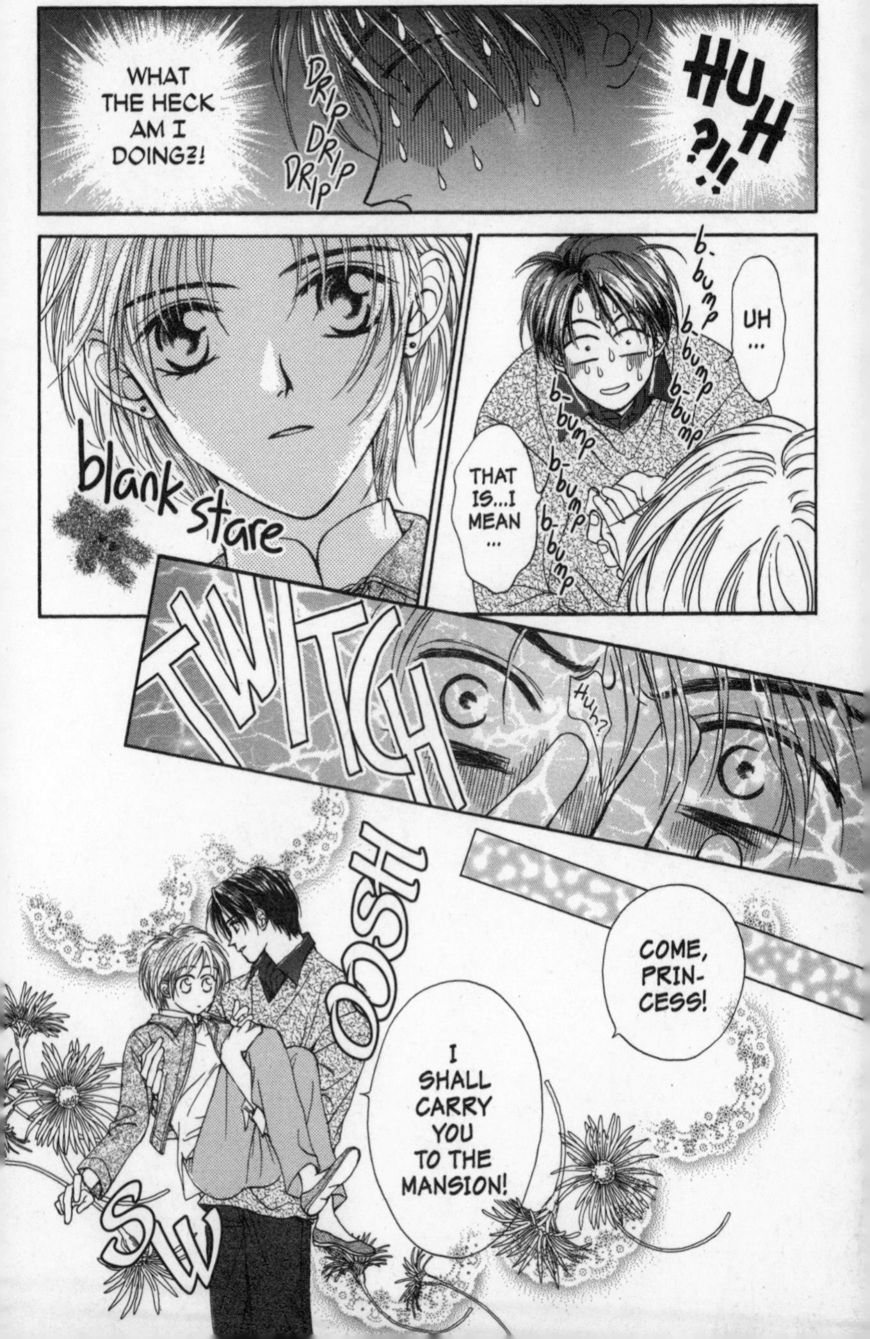
HUH?!!
DRIP DRIP DRIP
WHAT THE HECK AM I DOING?!
b-bump b-bump b-bump b-bump b-bump b-bump
UH ...
THAT IS...I MEAN ...
blank stare
TWITCH
Huh?
COME, PRINCESS!
I SHALL CARRY YOU TO THE MANSION!
SWOOSH

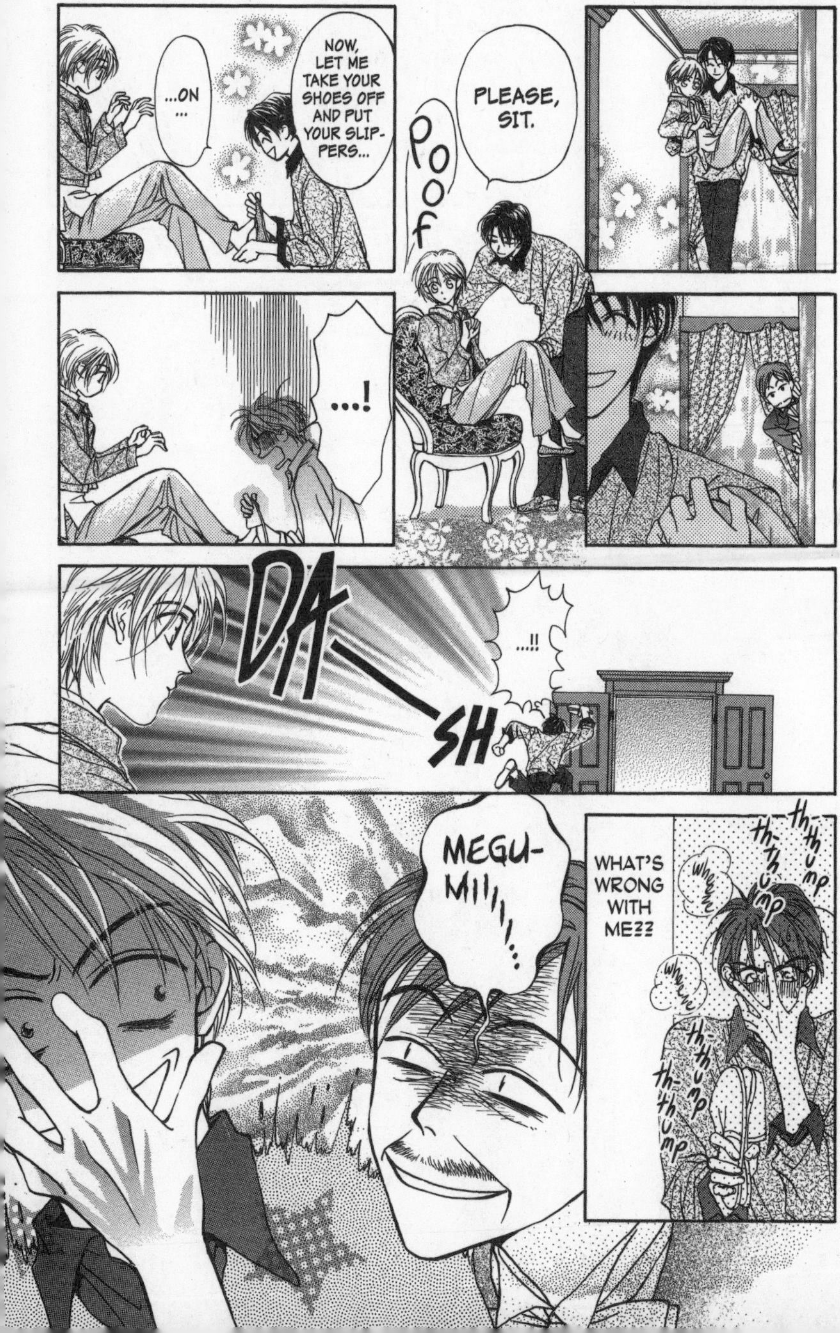
POOF
PLEASE, SIT.
NOW, LET ME TAKE YOUR SHOES OFF AND PUT YOUR SLIP-PERS...
...ON ...
...!
DA—SH
...!!
WHAT'S WRONG WITH ME??
th-thump th-thump
wheeze
wheeze
th-thump th-thump
MEGU-MI!!!!!...

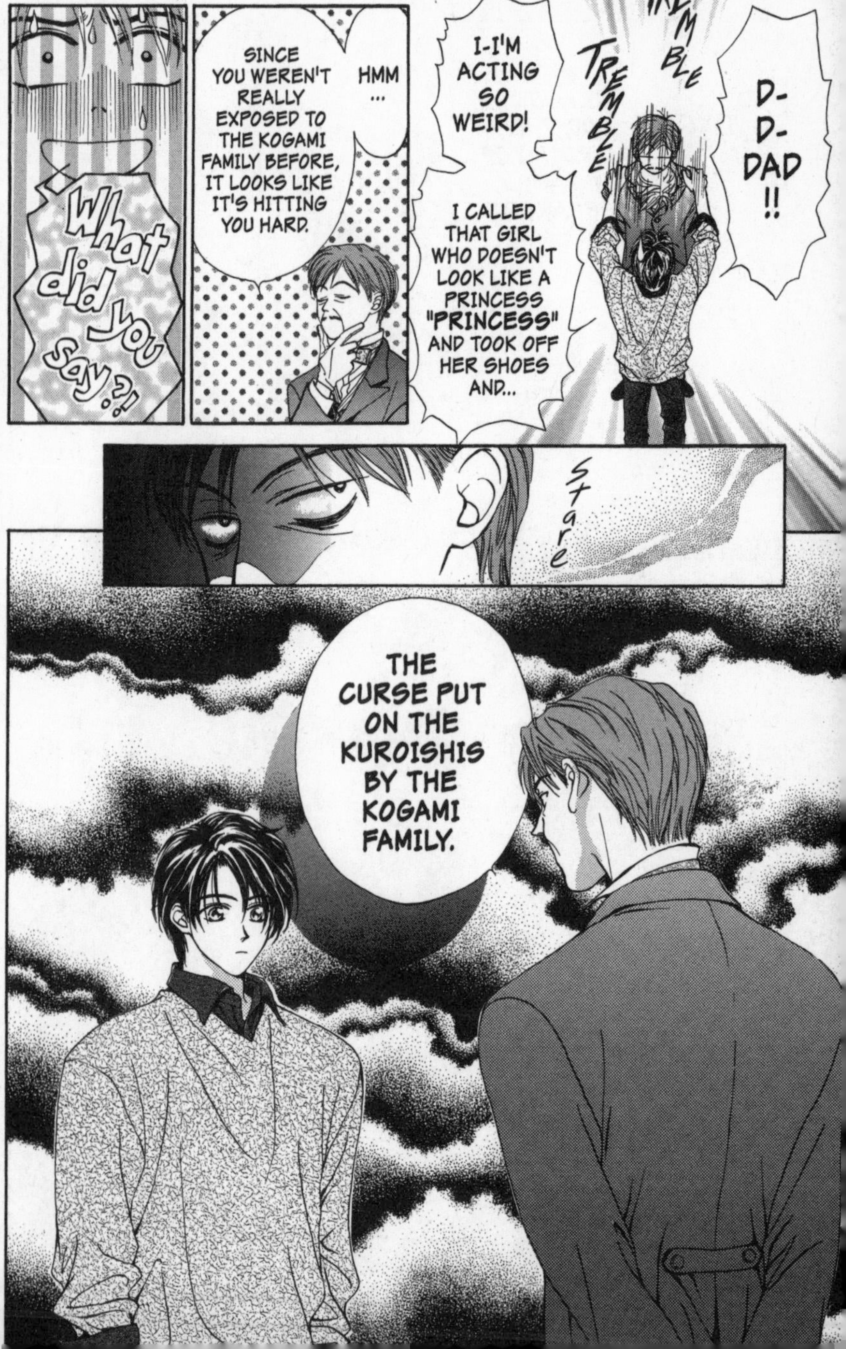
D-D-DAD!!
TREMBLE
TREMBLE
I-I'M ACTING SO WEIRD!
I CALLED THAT GIRL WHO DOESN'T LOOK LIKE A PRINCESS "PRINCESS" AND TOOK OFF HER SHOES AND...
HMM...
SINCE YOU WEREN'T REALLY EXPOSED TO THE KOGAMI FAMILY BEFORE, IT LOOKS LIKE IT'S HITTING YOU HARD.
What did you say?!
Stare
THE CURSE PUT ON THE KUROISHIS BY THE KOGAMI FAMILY.

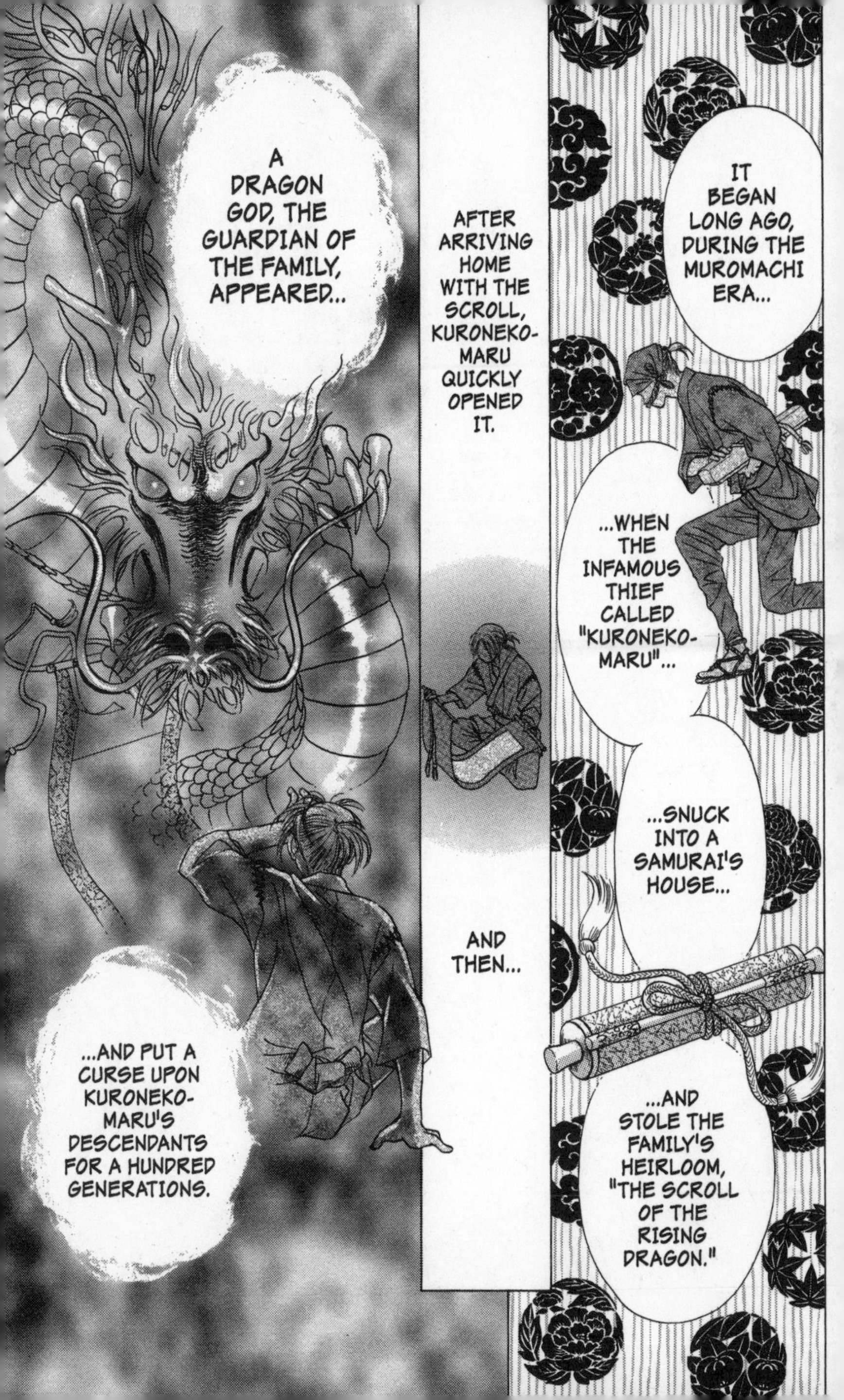
IT BEGAN LONG AGO, DURING THE MUROMACHI ERA...
...WHEN THE INFAMOUS THIEF CALLED "KURONEKO-MARU"...
...SNUCK INTO A SAMURAI'S HOUSE...
...AND STOLE THE FAMILY'S HEIRLOOM, "THE SCROLL OF THE RISING DRAGON."
AFTER ARRIVING HOME WITH THE SCROLL, KURONEKO-MARU QUICKLY OPENED IT.
AND THEN...
A DRAGON GOD, THE GUARDIAN OF THE FAMILY, APPEARED...
...AND PUT A CURSE UPON KURONEKO-MARU'S DESCENDANTS FOR A HUNDRED GENERATIONS.

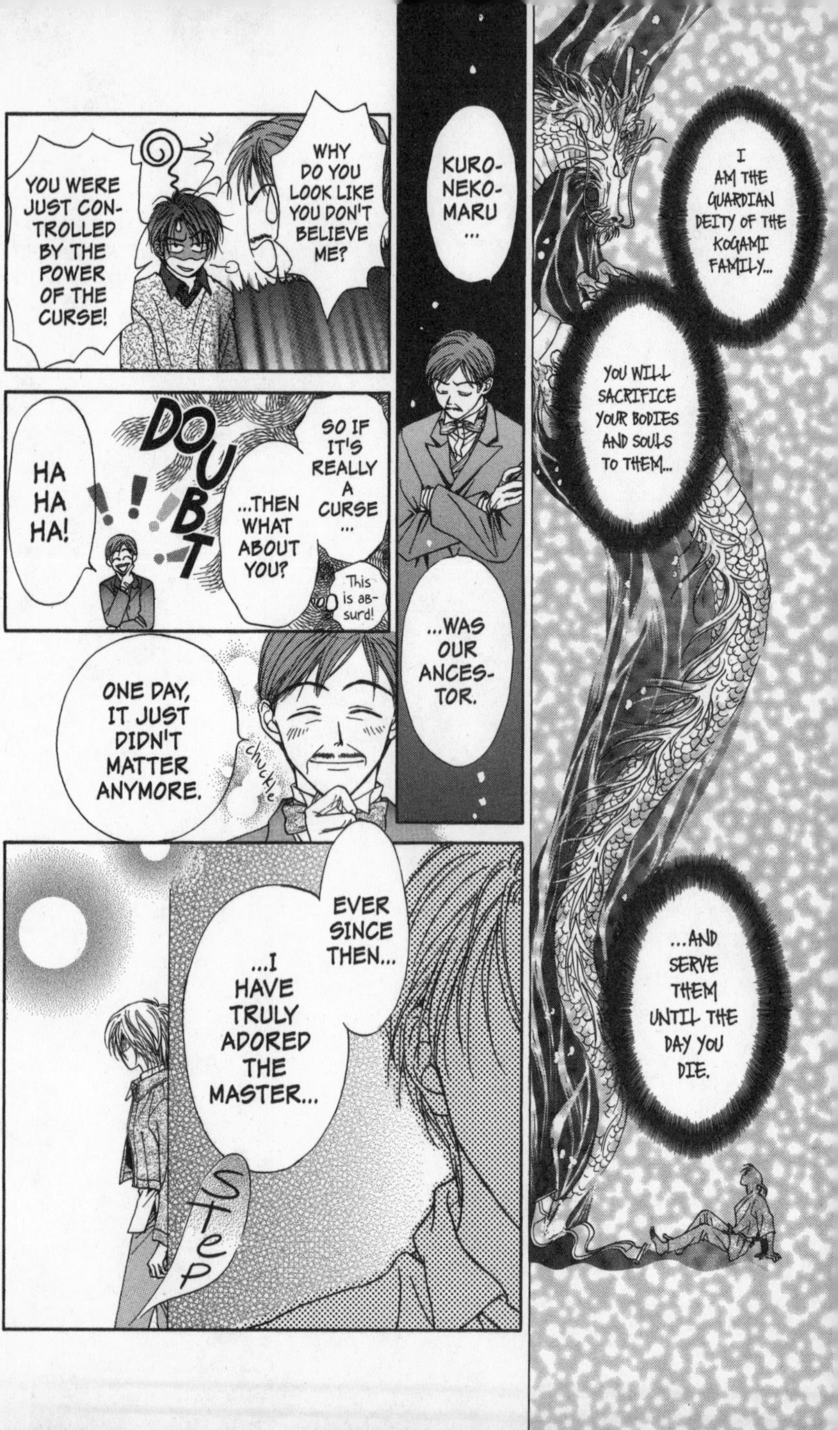
I AM THE GUARDIAN DEITY OF THE KOGAMI FAMILY...
YOU WILL SACRIFICE YOUR BODIES AND SOULS TO THEM...
...AND SERVE THEM UNTIL THE DAY YOU DIE.
KURO-NEKO-MARU...
...WAS OUR ANCES-TOR.
WHY DO YOU LOOK LIKE YOU DON'T BELIEVE ME?
YOU WERE JUST CON-TROLLED BY THE POWER OF THE CURSE!
SO IF IT'S REALLY A CURSE...
...THEN WHAT ABOUT YOU?
This is ab-surd!
DOUBT
HA HA HA!
ONE DAY, IT JUST DIDN'T MATTER ANYMORE.
chuckle
EVER SINCE THEN...
...I HAVE TRULY ADORED THE MASTER...
STEP

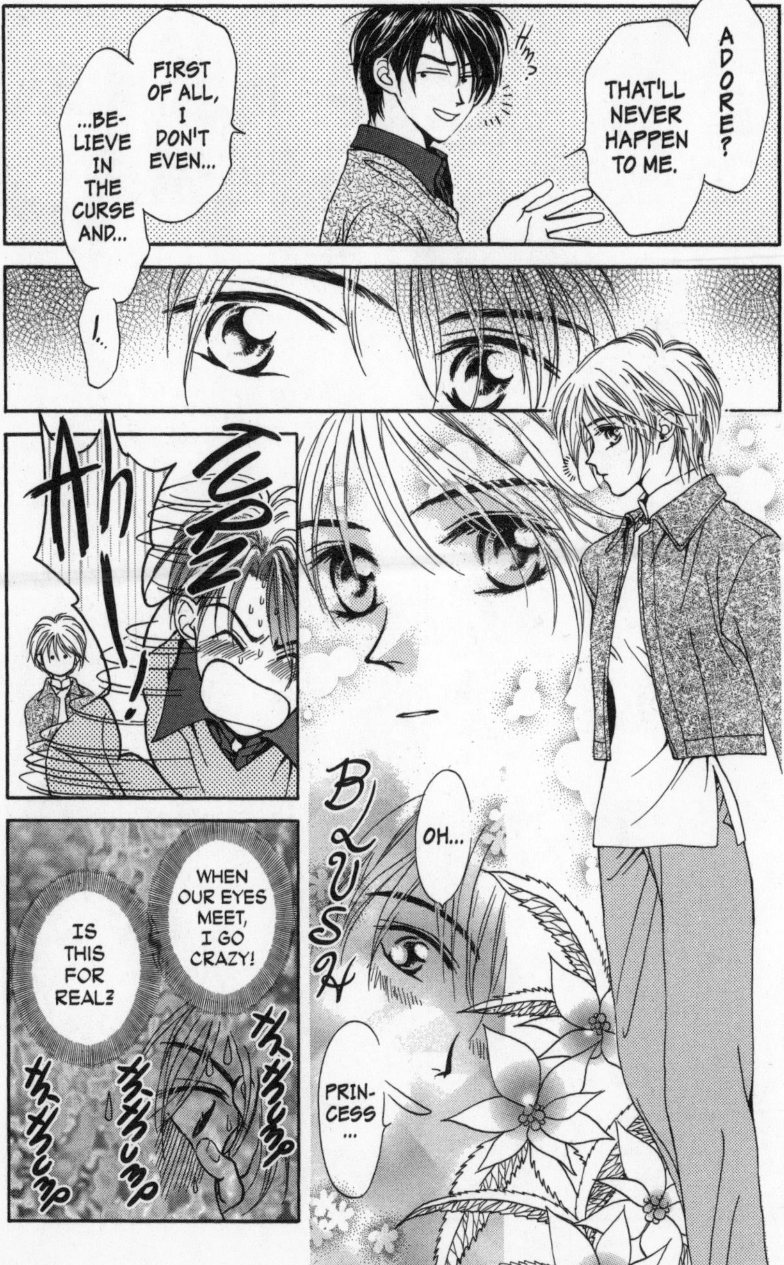
ADORE? THAT'LL NEVER HAPPEN TO ME.
Hm?
FIRST OF ALL, I DON'T EVEN...
...BE-LIEVE IN THE CURSE AND...
I...
OH...
BLUSH
PRIN-CESS...
Ah-!
TURN
WHEN OUR EYES MEET, I GO CRAZY!
IS THIS FOR REAL?
thump thump thump

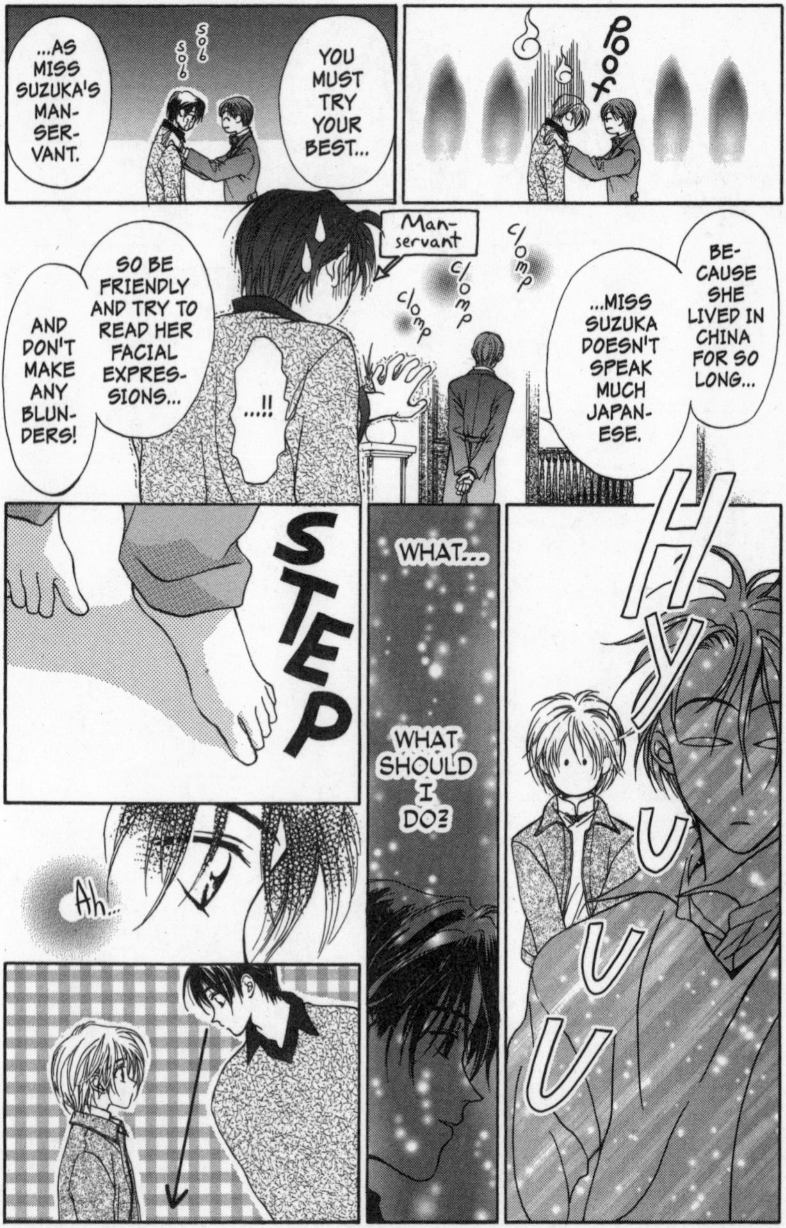
POOF
YOU MUST TRY YOUR BEST...
sob sob
...AS MISS SUZUKA'S MAN-SERVANT.
BE-CAUSE SHE LIVED IN CHINA FOR SO LONG...
...MISS SUZUKA DOESN'T SPEAK MUCH JAPAN-ESE.
clomp clomp clomp
Man-servant
SO BE FRIENDLY AND TRY TO READ HER FACIAL EXPRES-SIONS...
...!!
AND DON'T MAKE ANY BLUN-DERS!
HYUUUU
WHAT...
WHAT SHOULD I DO?
STEP
Ah...

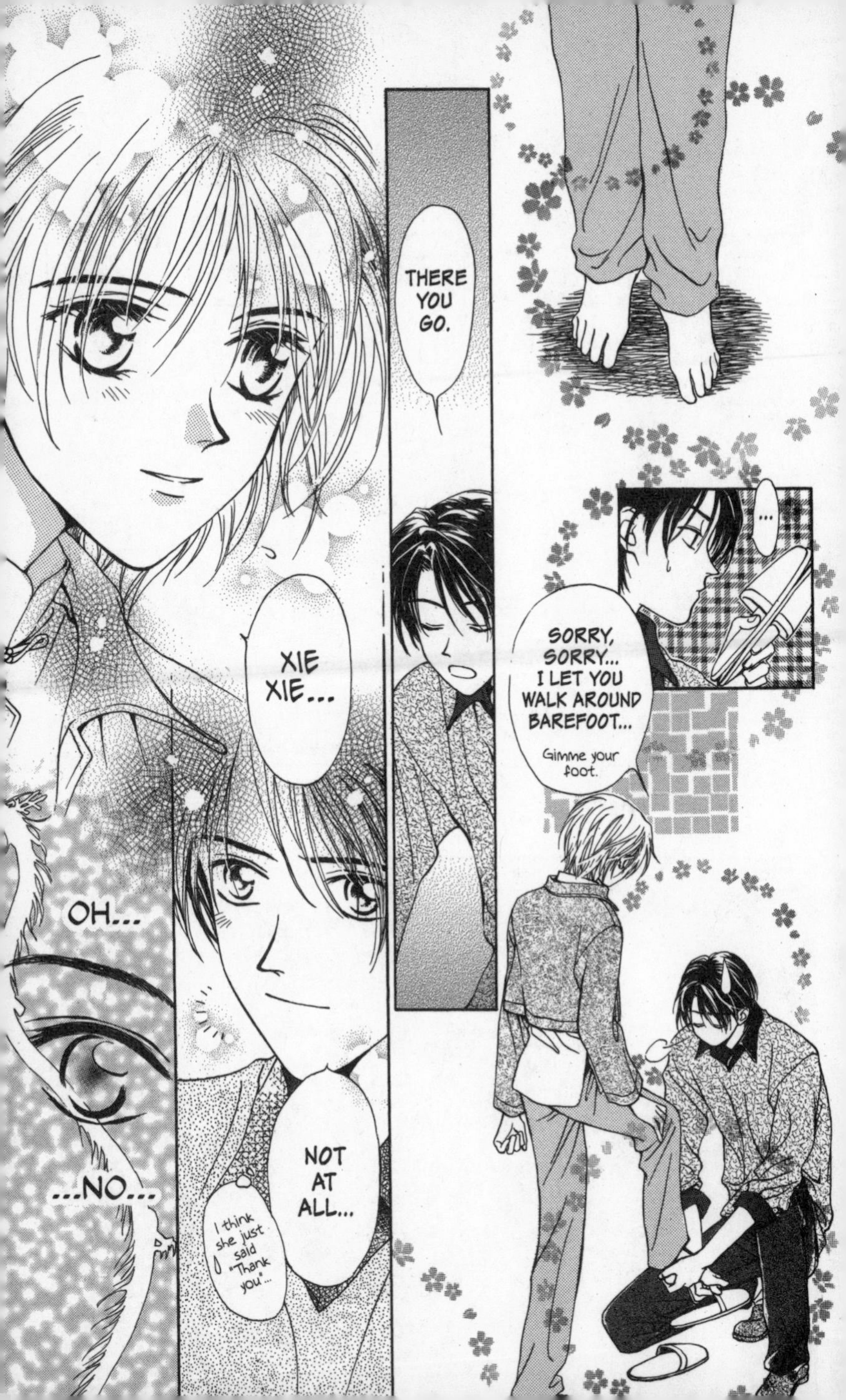
...
SORRY, SORRY... I LET YOU WALK AROUND BAREFOOT...
Gimme your foot.
THERE YOU GO.
XIE XIE...
NOT AT ALL...
I think she just said "Thank you"...
OH...
...NO...

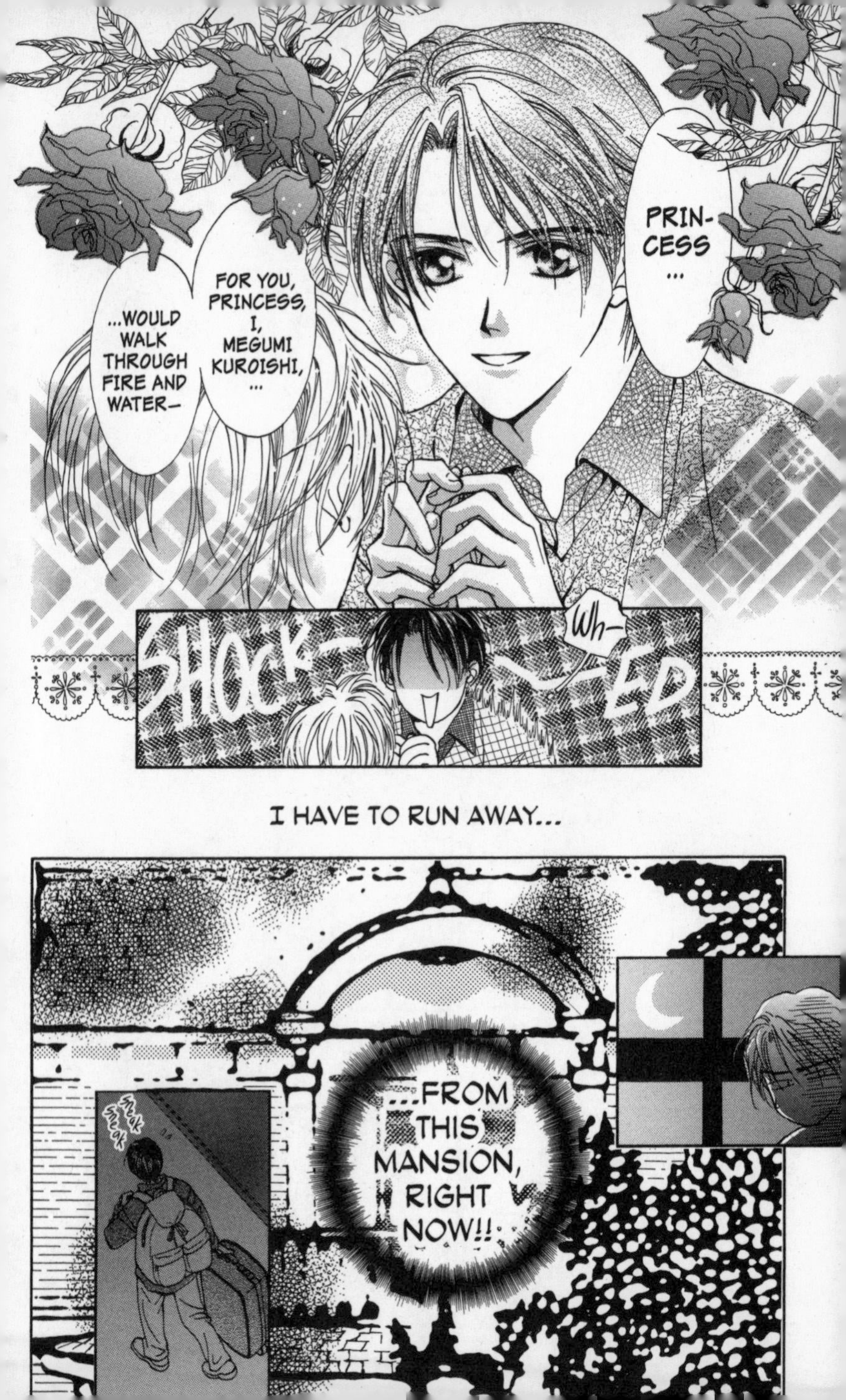
PRIN-
CESS
...
FOR YOU, PRINCESS, I, MEGUMI KUROISHI, ...
...WOULD WALK THROUGH FIRE AND WATER—
Wh—
SHOCK—
—ED
I HAVE TO RUN AWAY...
...FROM THIS MANSION, RIGHT NOW!!

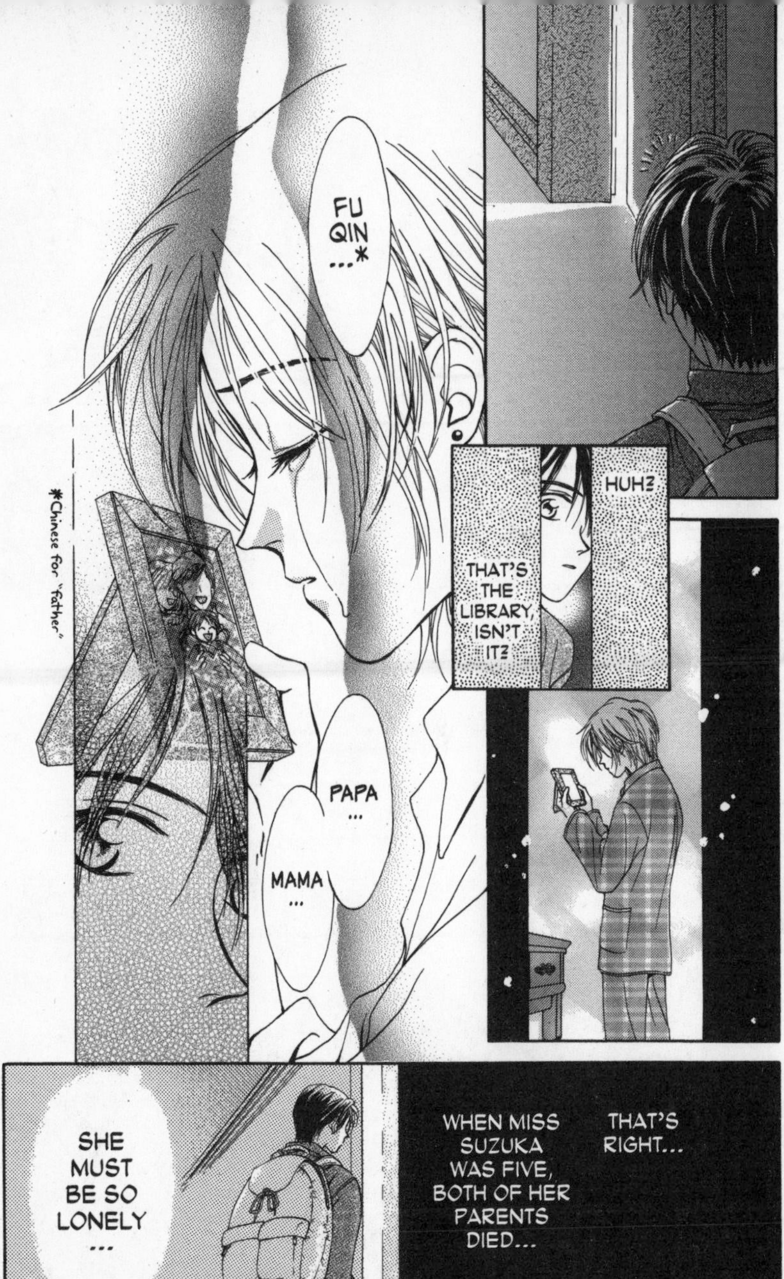
HUH?
THAT'S THE LIBRARY, ISN'T IT?
FU QIN ...*
PAPA ...
MAMA ...
*Chinese for "father"
THAT'S RIGHT...
WHEN MISS SUZUKA WAS FIVE, BOTH OF HER PARENTS DIED...
SHE MUST BE SO LONELY ...

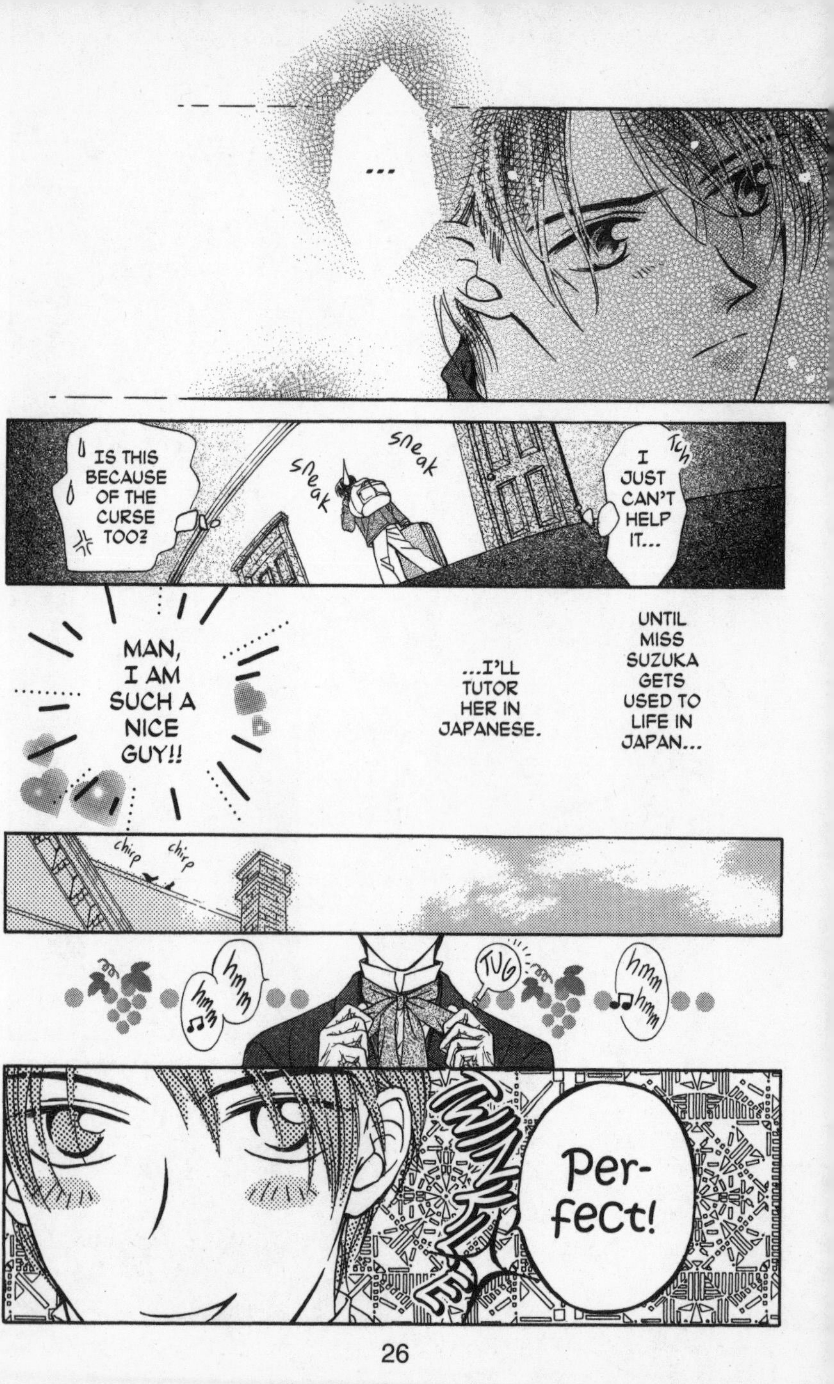
...
Tch
I JUST CAN'T HELP IT...
sneak
sneak
IS THIS BECAUSE OF THE CURSE TOO?
UNTIL MISS SUZUKA GETS USED TO LIFE IN JAPAN...
...I'LL TUTOR HER IN JAPANESE.
MAN, I AM SUCH A NICE GUY!!
chirp
chirp
hmm hmm
TUG
hmm hmm
Per-fect!
TWINKLE

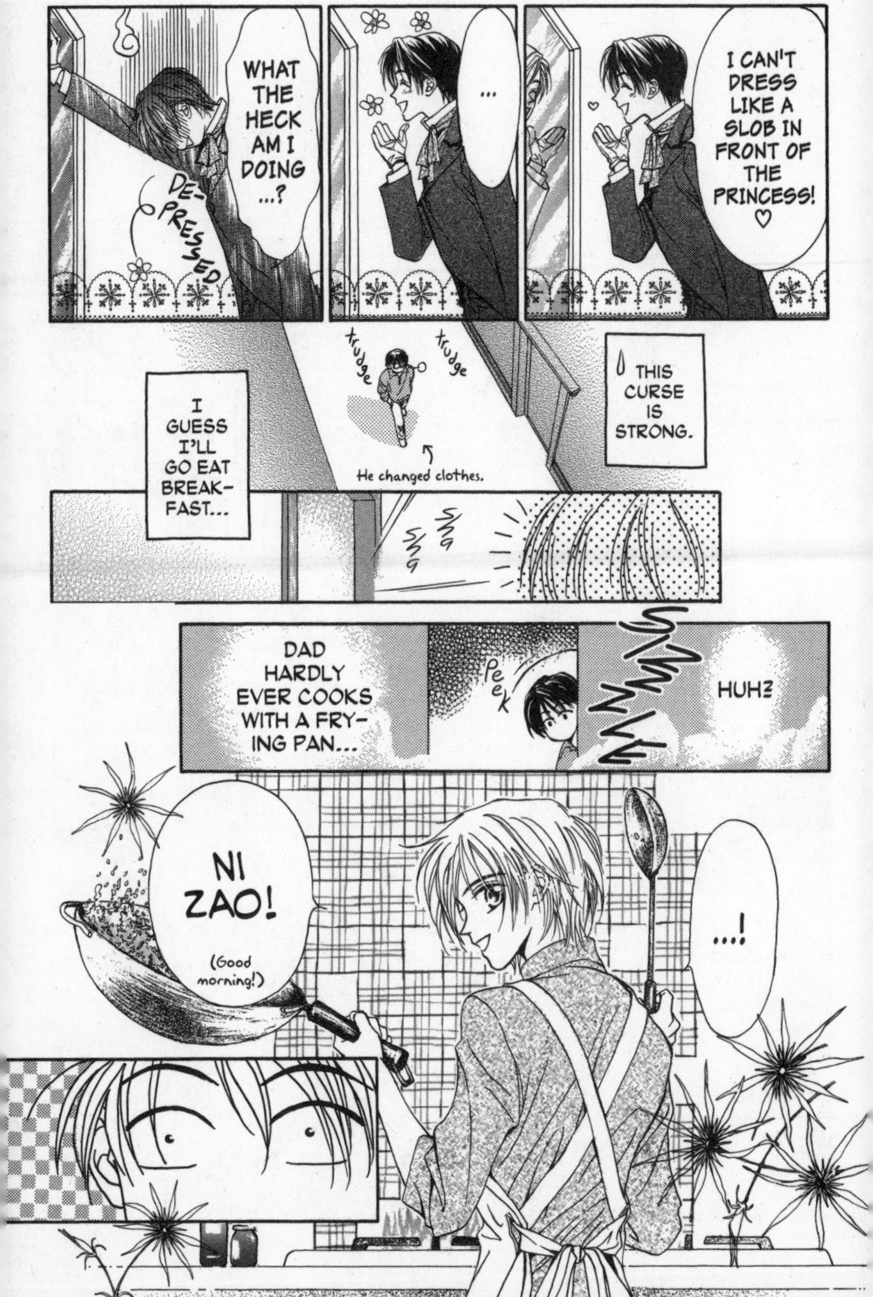
I CAN'T DRESS LIKE A SLOB IN FRONT OF THE PRINCESS! ♡
...
WHAT THE HECK AM I DOING ...?
DE-PRESSED
THIS CURSE IS STRONG.
trudge
trudge
He changed clothes.
I GUESS I'LL GO EAT BREAKFAST...
HUH?
Peek
DAD HARDLY EVER COOKS WITH A FRYING PAN...
...!
NI ZAO!
(Good morning!)

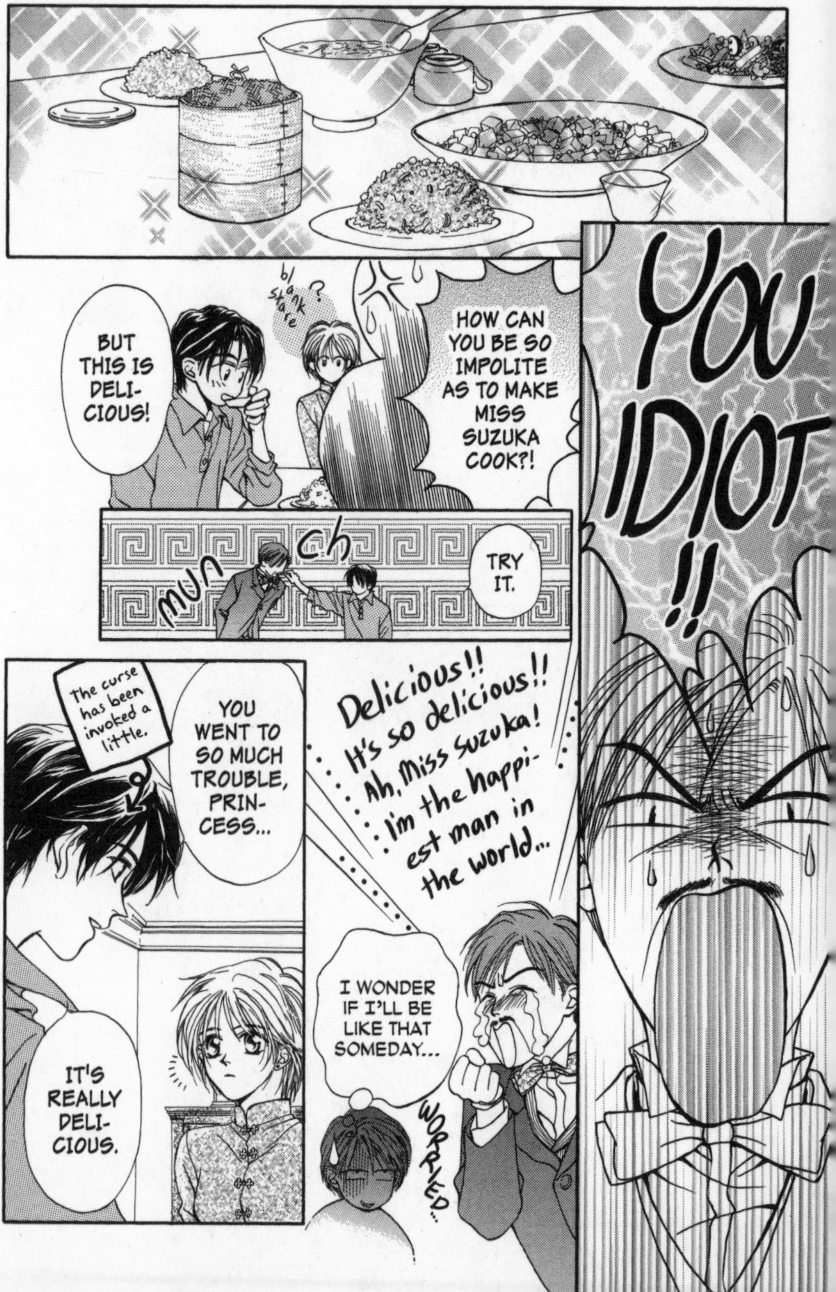
YOU IDIOT!!
HOW CAN YOU BE SO IMPOLITE AS TO MAKE MISS SUZUKA COOK?!
blank stare
BUT THIS IS DELICIOUS!
TRY IT.
munch
Delicious!! It's so delicious!! Ah, Miss Suzuka! I'm the happiest man in the world...
YOU WENT TO SO MUCH TROUBLE, PRINCESS...
The curse has been invoked a little.
I WONDER IF I'LL BE LIKE THAT SOMEDAY...
WORRIED...
IT'S REALLY DELICIOUS.

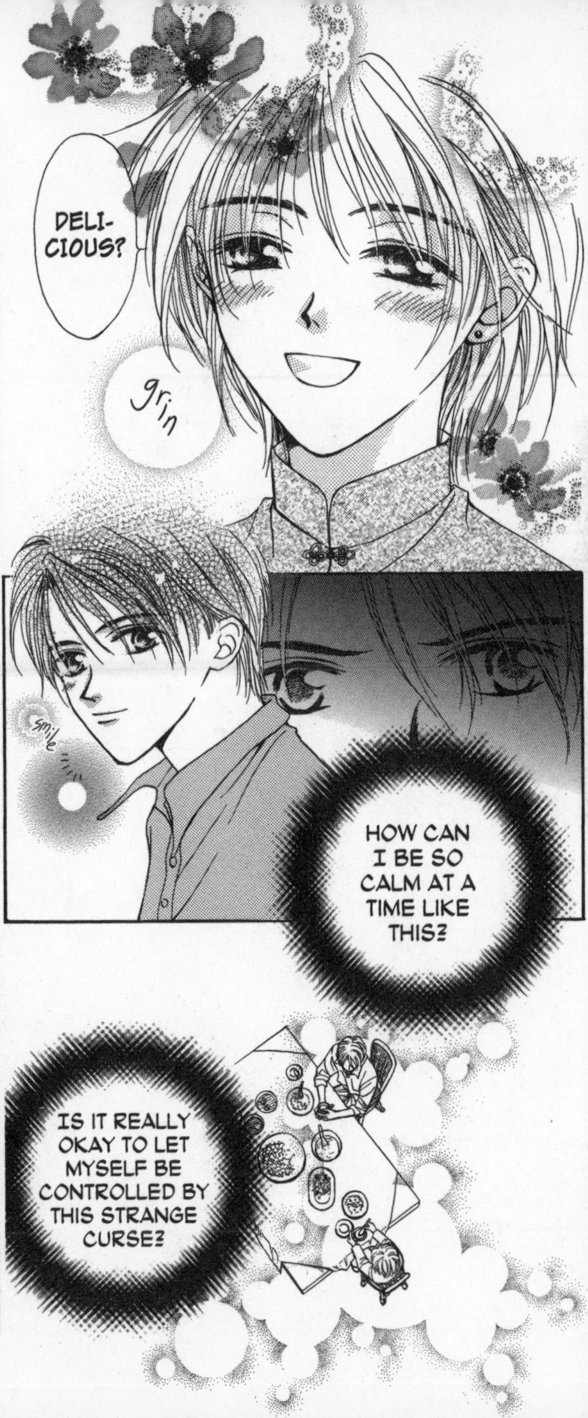
DELI-
CIOUS?
grin
smile
HOW CAN I BE SO CALM AT A TIME LIKE THIS?
IS IT REALLY OKAY TO LET MYSELF BE CONTROLLED BY THIS STRANGE CURSE?

1

In honor of my very first comic...♥

Yahoo! I'm so happy! Congratulations, me!!!

Nice to meet you. ♥

This is "me."

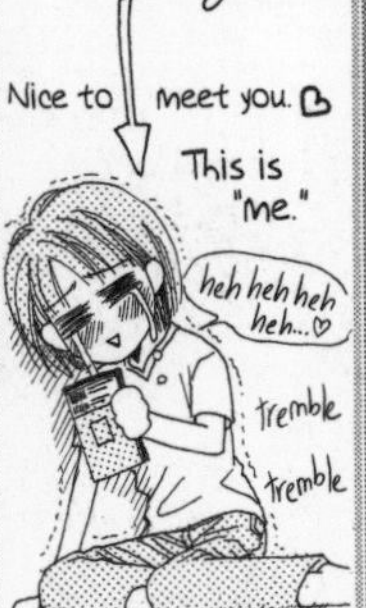
heh heh heh heh...♡
tremble
tremble

...I'll tell you a little bit about myself.

If you don't care, I'm sorry.

Pen Name: Matsuri Hino (It's completely different from my real name)
Blood Type: B
Birthday: January 24, sometime during the Showa Era
Hobbies: Driving (especially at night in the mountains), gardening and taking care of my dog, Pochi.
Things I like: Books, green tea and Pochi ♥

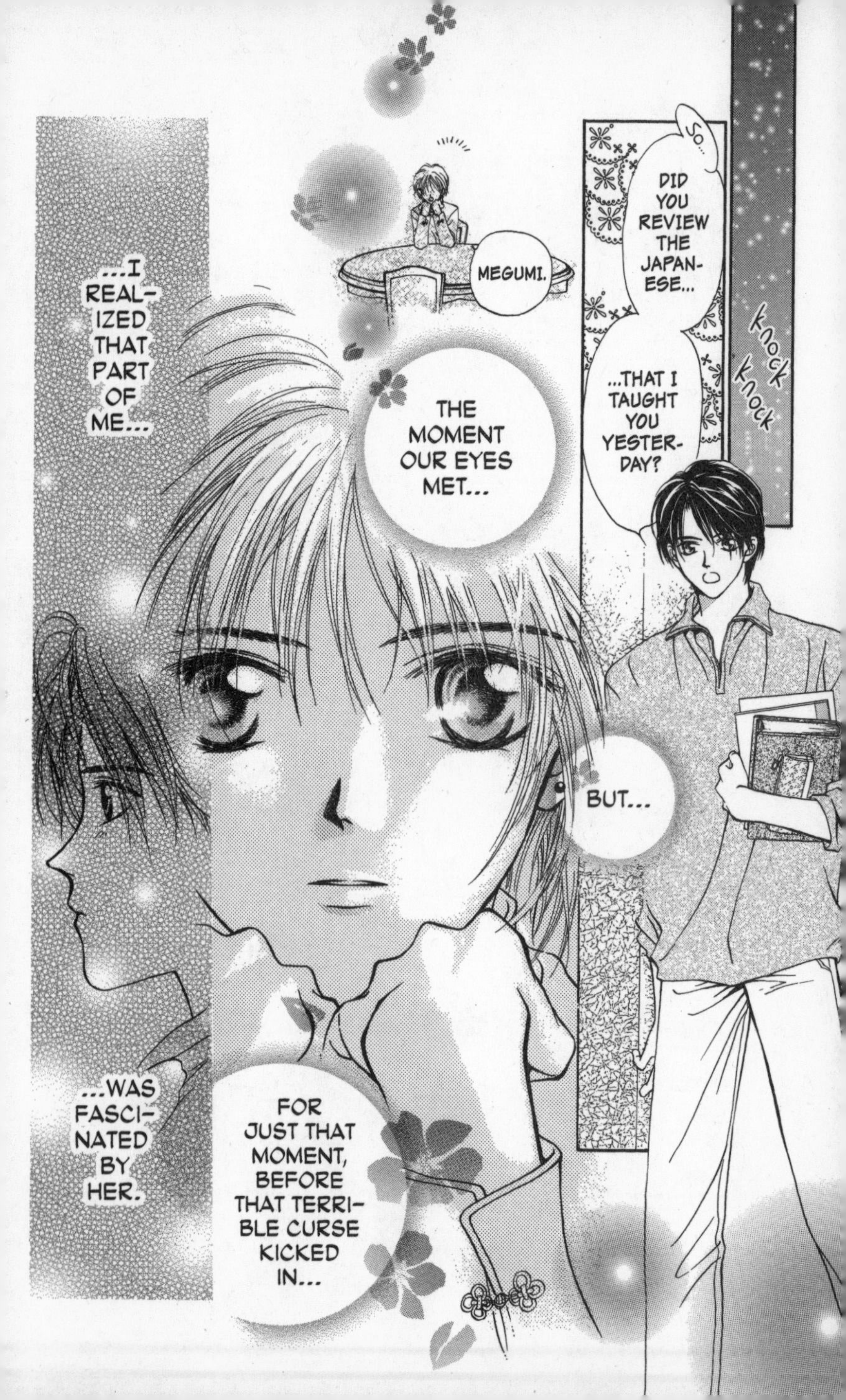
knock knock
So...
DID YOU REVIEW THE JAPANESE...
...THAT I TAUGHT YOU YESTERDAY?
MEGUMI.
THE MOMENT OUR EYES MET...
BUT...
...I REALIZED THAT PART OF ME...
FOR JUST THAT MOMENT, BEFORE THAT TERRIBLE CURSE KICKED IN...
...WAS FASCINATED BY HER.

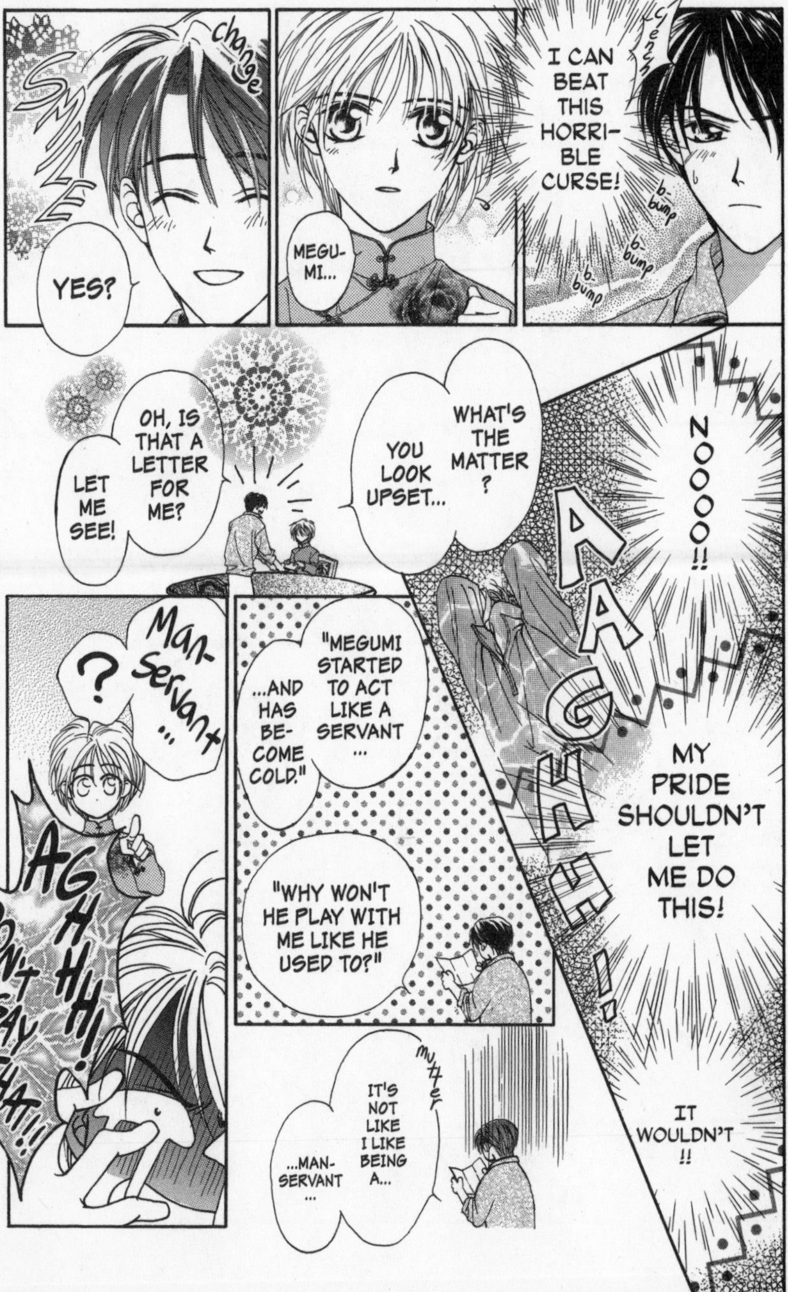
clench
I CAN BEAT THIS HORRIBLE CURSE!
b-bump
b-bump
b-bump
MEGUMI...
change
SMILE
YES?
NOOOO!!
AAGHH!
MY PRIDE SHOULDN'T LET ME DO THIS!
IT WOULDN'T!!
WHAT'S THE MATTER?
YOU LOOK UPSET...
OH, IS THAT A LETTER FOR ME?
LET ME SEE!
"MEGUMI STARTED TO ACT LIKE A SERVANT...
...AND HAS BECOME COLD."
"WHY WON'T HE PLAY WITH ME LIKE HE USED TO?"
Man-servant...
?
AGHHH!
DON'T SAY THAT!!
mutter
IT'S NOT LIKE I LIKE BEING A...
...MAN-SERVANT...

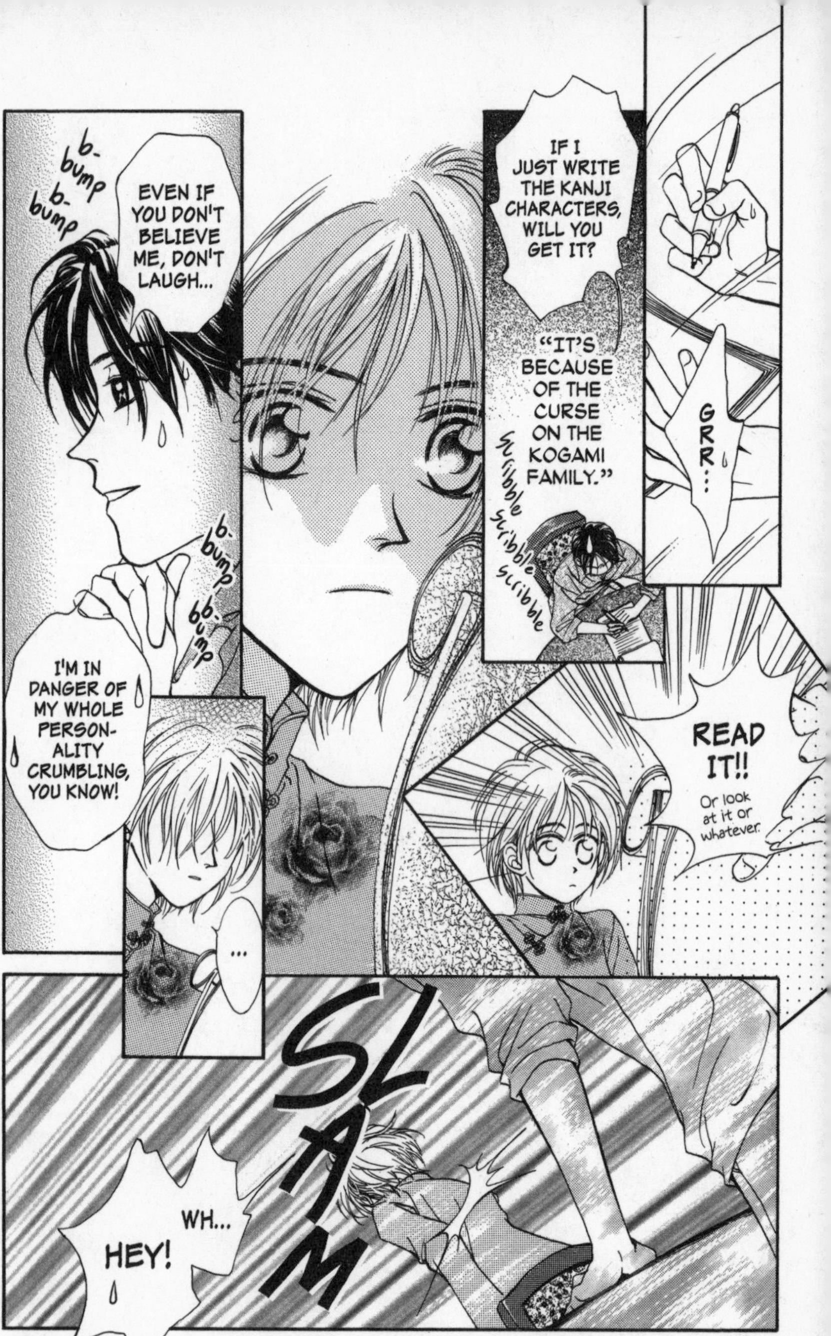
GRR...
IF I JUST WRITE THE KANJI CHARACTERS, WILL YOU GET IT?
"IT'S BECAUSE OF THE CURSE ON THE KOGAMI FAMILY."
scribble scribble scribble
b-bump b-bump
EVEN IF YOU DON'T BELIEVE ME, DON'T LAUGH...
b-bump b-bump
I'M IN DANGER OF MY WHOLE PERSON-ALITY CRUMBLING, YOU KNOW!
READ IT!!
Or look at it or whatever.
...
SLAM
WH...
HEY!

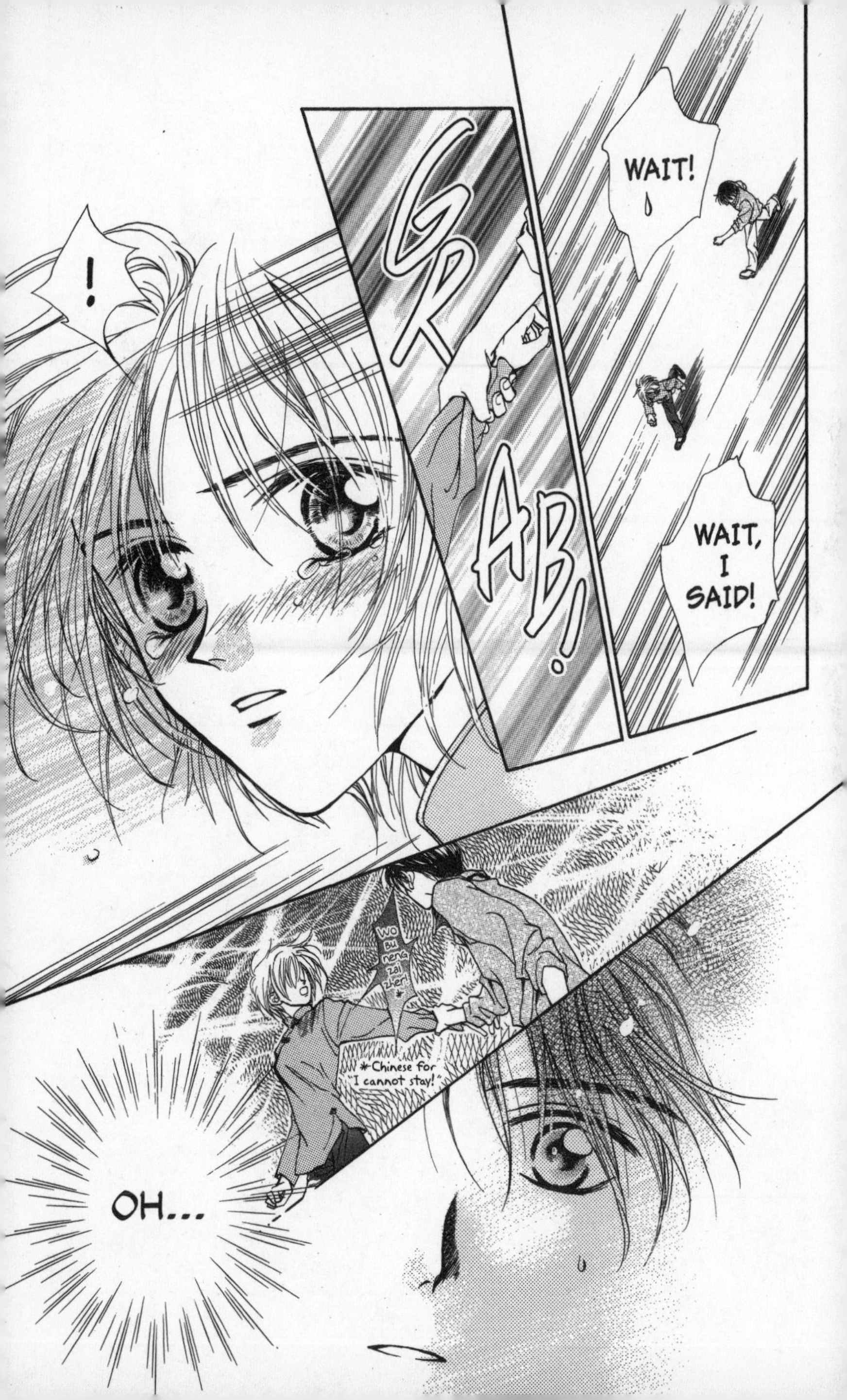
WAIT!
WAIT, I SAID!
GRAB!
!
Wo bu neng zai zher!*
*Chinese for "I cannot stay!"
OH...

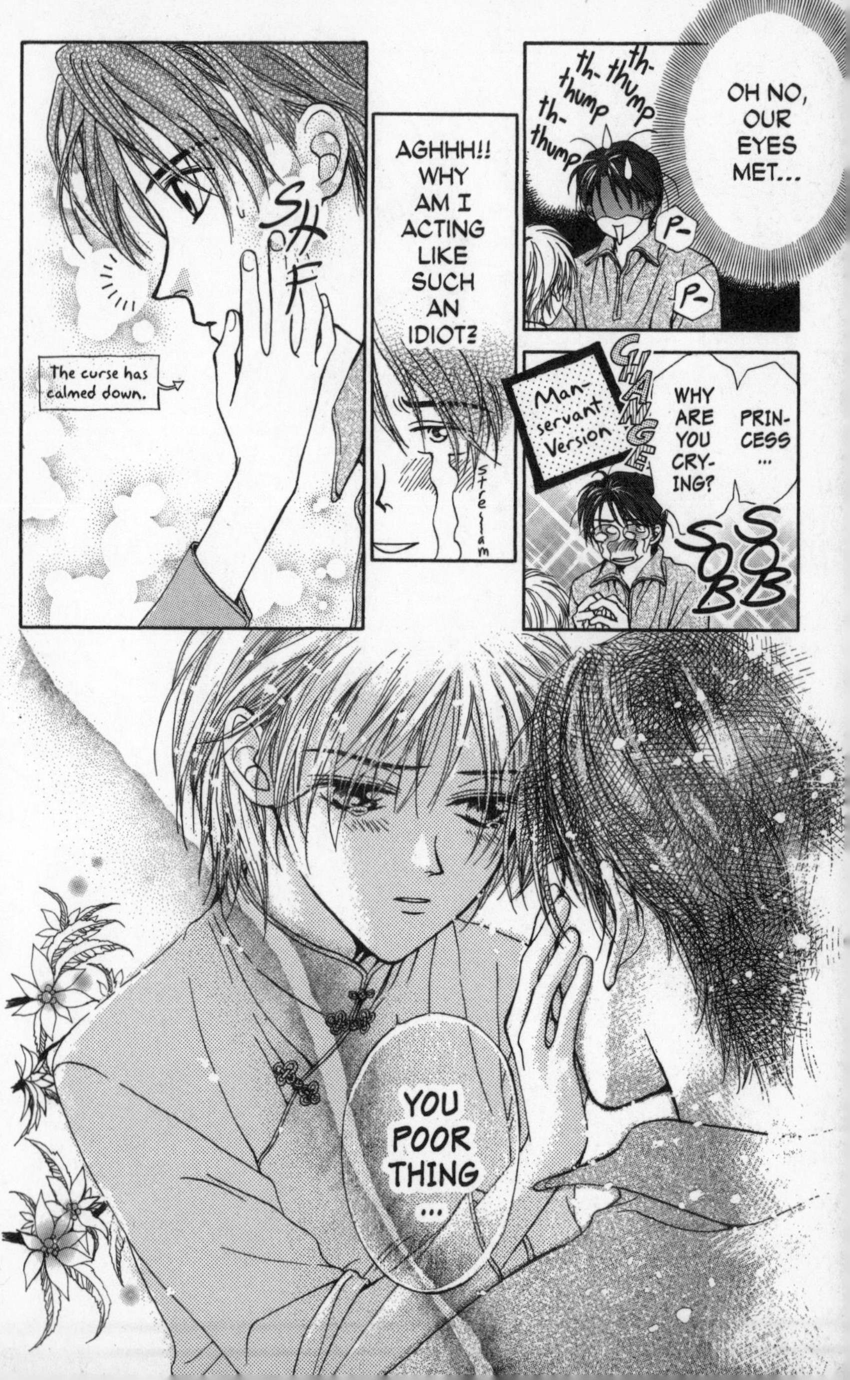
OH NO, OUR EYES MET...
th-thump th-thump th-thump
P- P-
Man-servant Version
CHANGE
PRINCESS...
WHY ARE YOU CRYING?
SOB SOB
AGHHH!! WHY AM I ACTING LIKE SUCH AN IDIOT?
Stream
SHFF
The curse has calmed down.
YOU POOR THING...

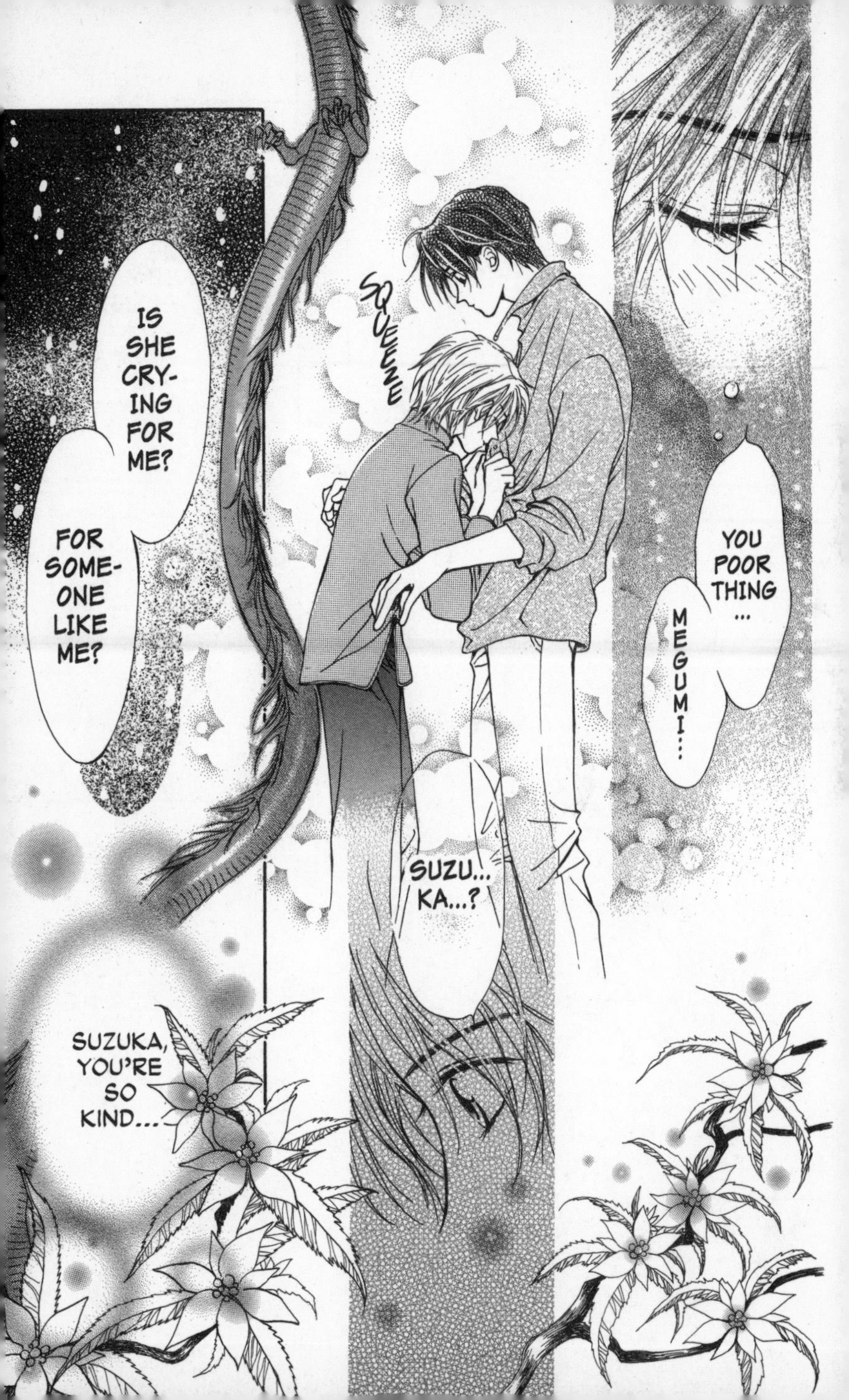
YOU POOR THING...
MEGUMI...
SQUEEZE
SUZU... KA...?
IS SHE CRYING FOR ME?
FOR SOMEONE LIKE ME?
SUZUKA, YOU'RE SO KIND...

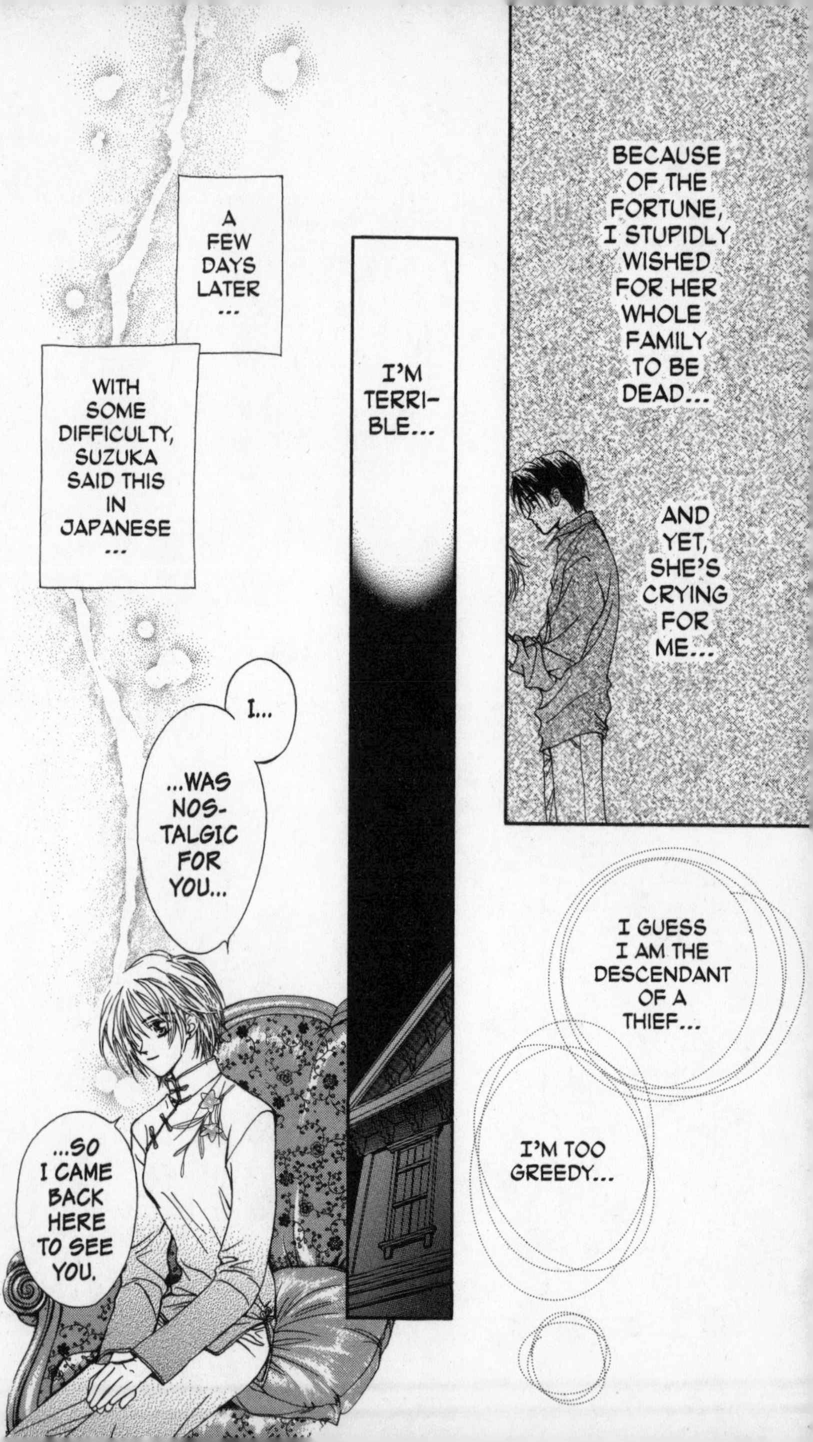
BECAUSE OF THE FORTUNE, I STUPIDLY WISHED FOR HER WHOLE FAMILY TO BE DEAD...
AND YET, SHE'S CRYING FOR ME...
I GUESS I AM THE DESCENDANT OF A THIEF...
I'M TOO GREEDY...
I'M TERRI-BLE...
A FEW DAYS LATER...
WITH SOME DIFFICULTY, SUZUKA SAID THIS IN JAPANESE...
I...
...WAS NOS-TALGIC FOR YOU...
...SO I CAME BACK HERE TO SEE YOU.

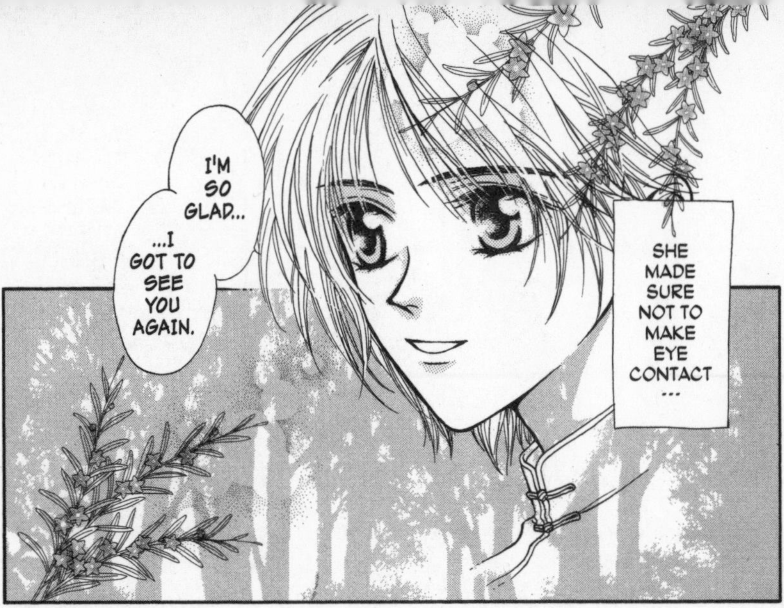
SHE MADE SURE NOT TO MAKE EYE CONTACT ...
I'M SO GLAD...
...I GOT TO SEE YOU AGAIN.

A FEW DAYS LATER, SUZUKA RETURNED TO CHINA...

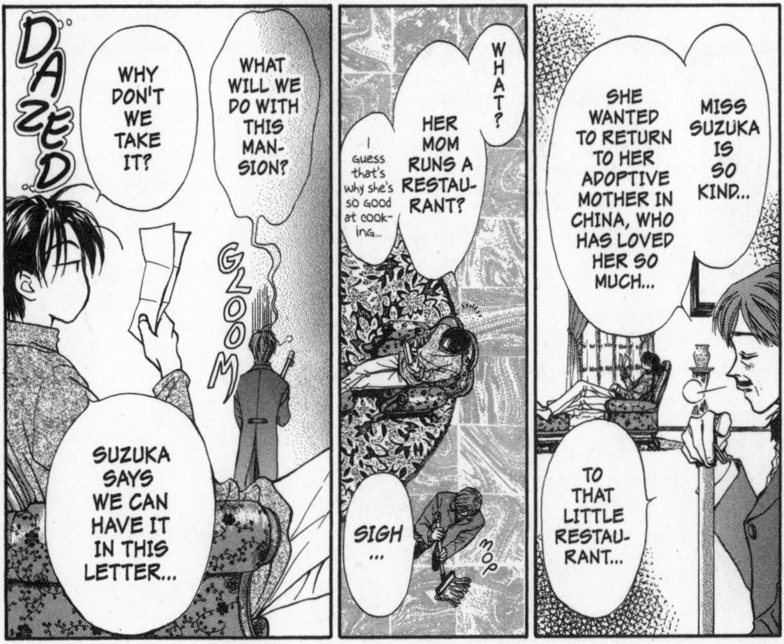
MISS SUZUKA IS SO KIND...
SHE WANTED TO RETURN TO HER ADOPTIVE MOTHER IN CHINA, WHO HAS LOVED HER SO MUCH...
TO THAT LITTLE RESTAURANT...
WHAT?
HER MOM RUNS A RESTAURANT?
I Guess that's why she's so Good at cooking...
SIGH ...
MOP
WHAT WILL WE DO WITH THIS MANSION?
WHY DON'T WE TAKE IT?
DAZED
GLOOM
SUZUKA SAYS WE CAN HAVE IT IN THIS LETTER...

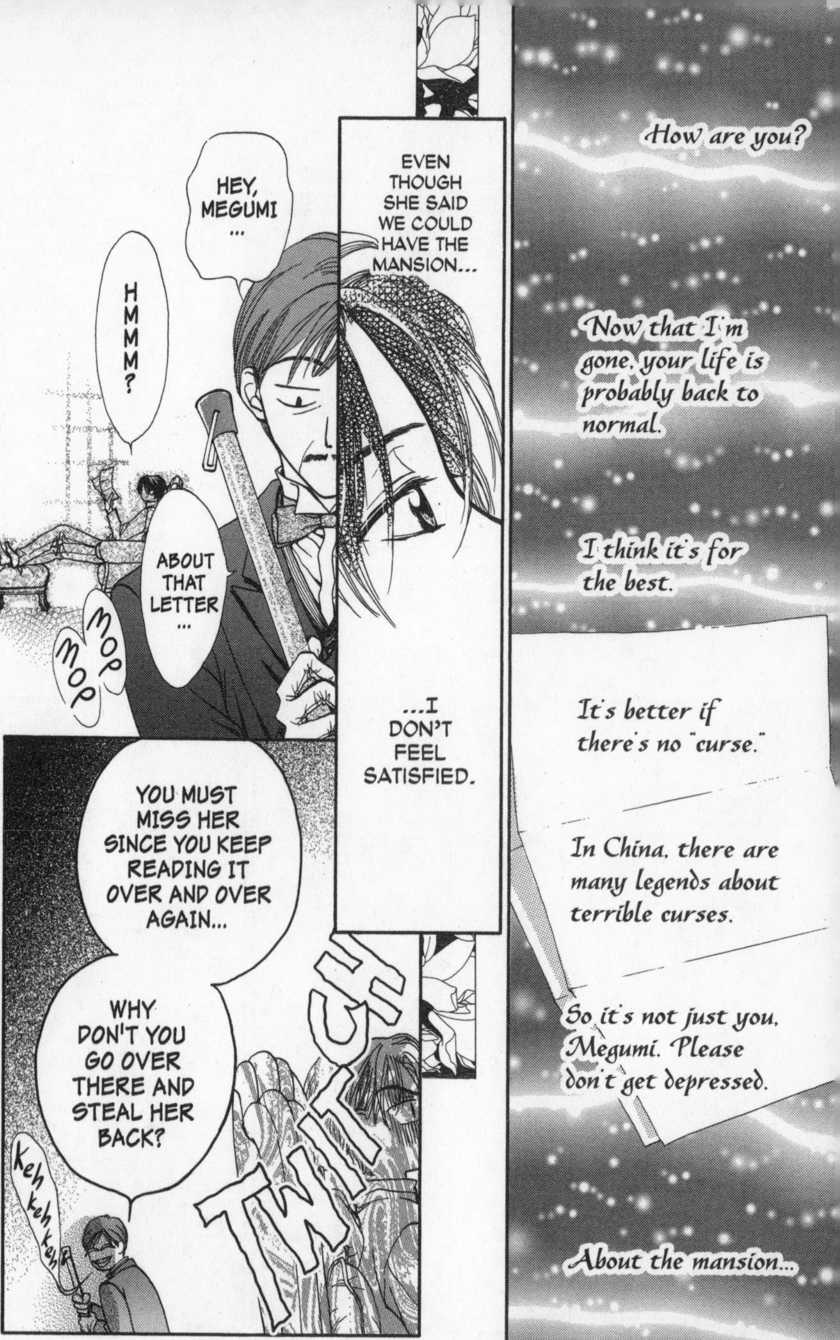
How are you?
Now that I'm gone, your life is probably back to normal.
I think it's for the best.
It's better if there's no "curse."
In China, there are many legends about terrible curses.
So it's not just you, Megumi. Please don't get depressed.
About the mansion...
EVEN THOUGH SHE SAID WE COULD HAVE THE MANSION...
HEY, MEGUMI...
HMMM?
ABOUT THAT LETTER...
MOP MOP
...I DON'T FEEL SATISFIED.
YOU MUST MISS HER SINCE YOU KEEP READING IT OVER AND OVER AGAIN...
WHY DON'T YOU GO OVER THERE AND STEAL HER BACK?
TWITCH
Keh keh keh keh

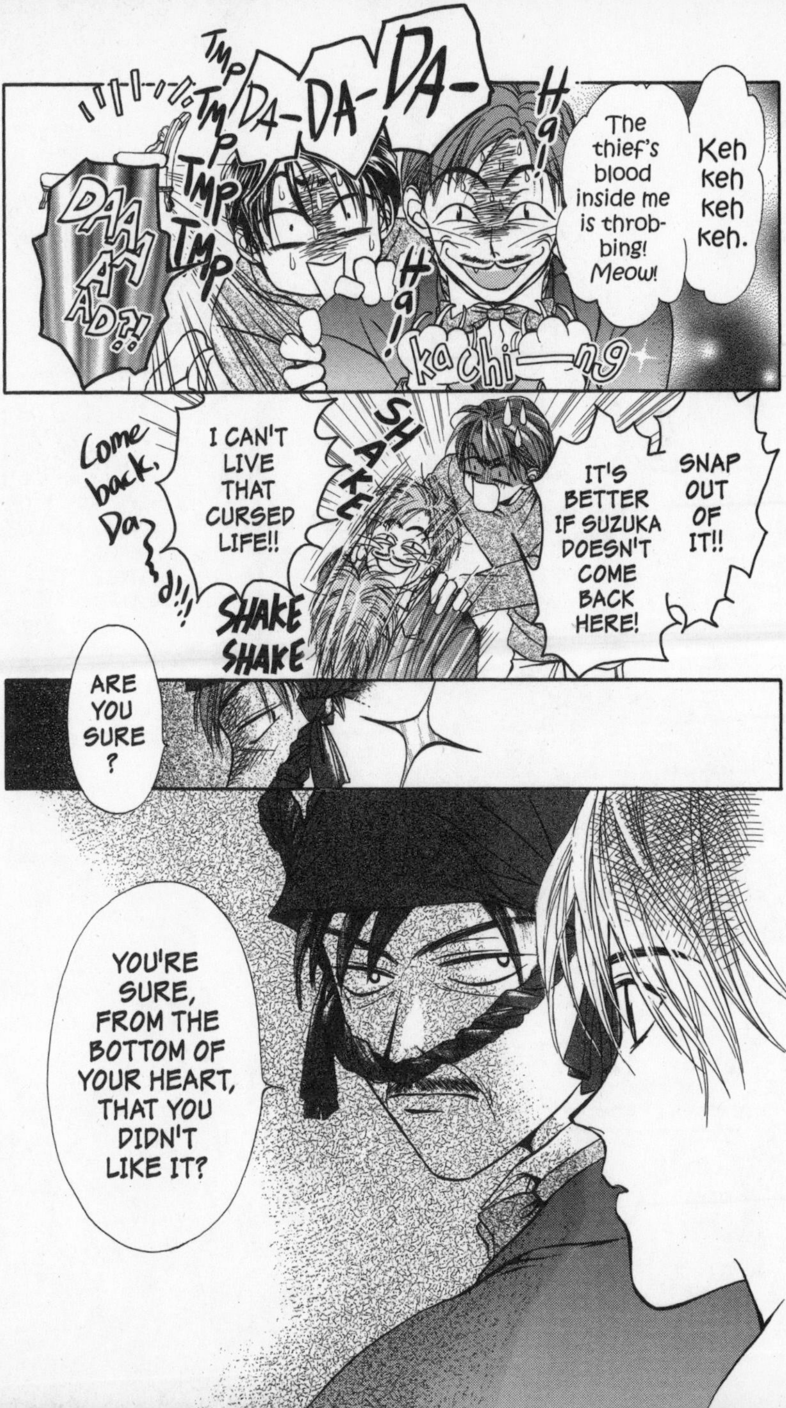
Keh keh keh keh.
The thief's blood inside me is throbbing! Meow!
Hagi! Hagi!
kachi—ng
DA-DA-DA-
TMP TMP TMP TMP TMP
DAAAHAAAD?!!
SNAP OUT OF IT!!
IT'S BETTER IF SUZUKA DOESN'T COME BACK HERE!
SHAKE
I CAN'T LIVE THAT CURSED LIFE!!
Come back, Da~d!!!
SHAKE SHAKE
ARE YOU SURE?
YOU'RE SURE, FROM THE BOTTOM OF YOUR HEART, THAT YOU DIDN'T LIKE IT?

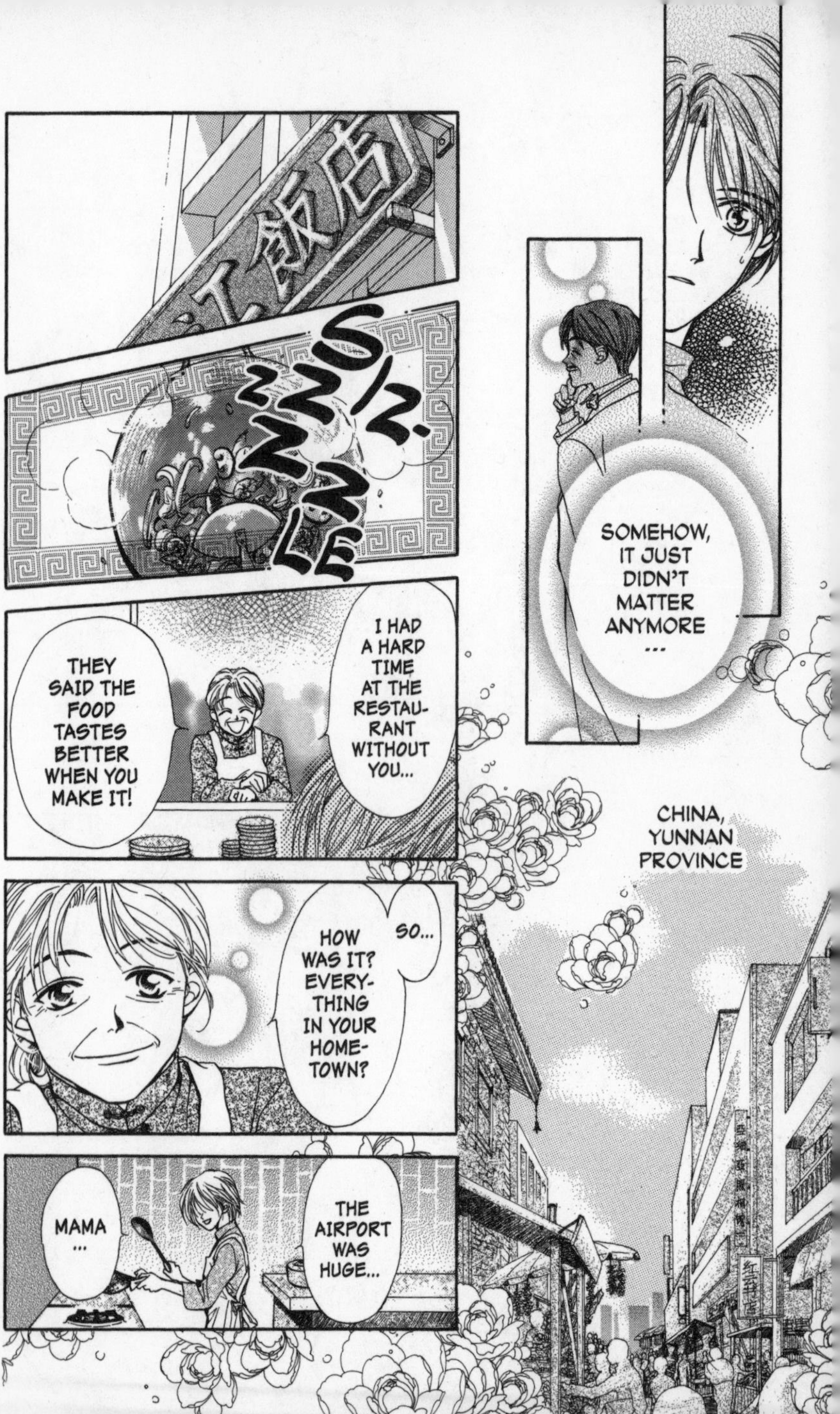
SOMEHOW, IT JUST DIDN'T MATTER ANYMORE...
CHINA, YUNNAN PROVINCE
SIZZLE
I HAD A HARD TIME AT THE RESTAURANT WITHOUT YOU...
THEY SAID THE FOOD TASTES BETTER WHEN YOU MAKE IT!
SO...
HOW WAS IT? EVERYTHING IN YOUR HOMETOWN?
THE AIRPORT WAS HUGE...
MAMA...

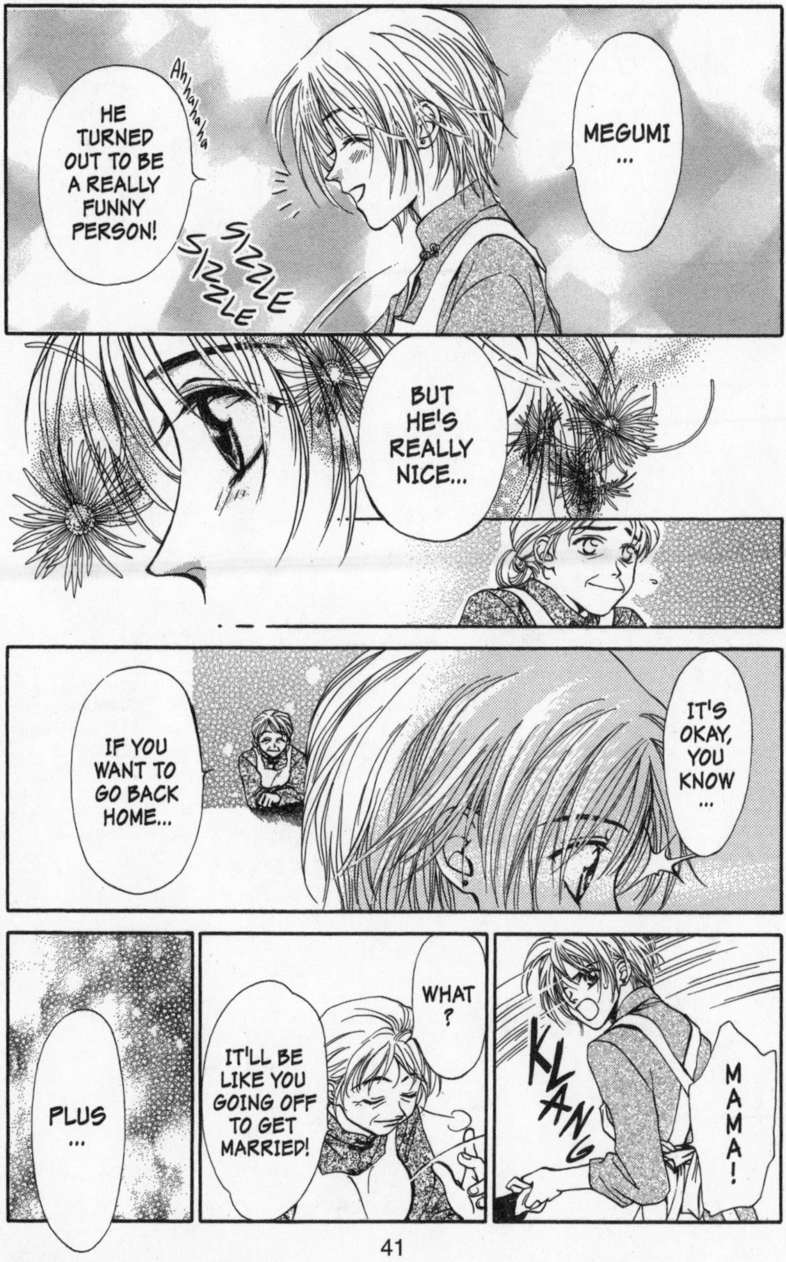
MEGUMI ...
Ah hahahaha
HE TURNED OUT TO BE A REALLY FUNNY PERSON!
SIZZLE SIZZLE
BUT HE'S REALLY NICE...
IT'S OKAY, YOU KNOW ...
IF YOU WANT TO GO BACK HOME...
MAMA!
KLANG
WHAT ?
IT'LL BE LIKE YOU GOING OFF TO GET MARRIED!
PLUS ...

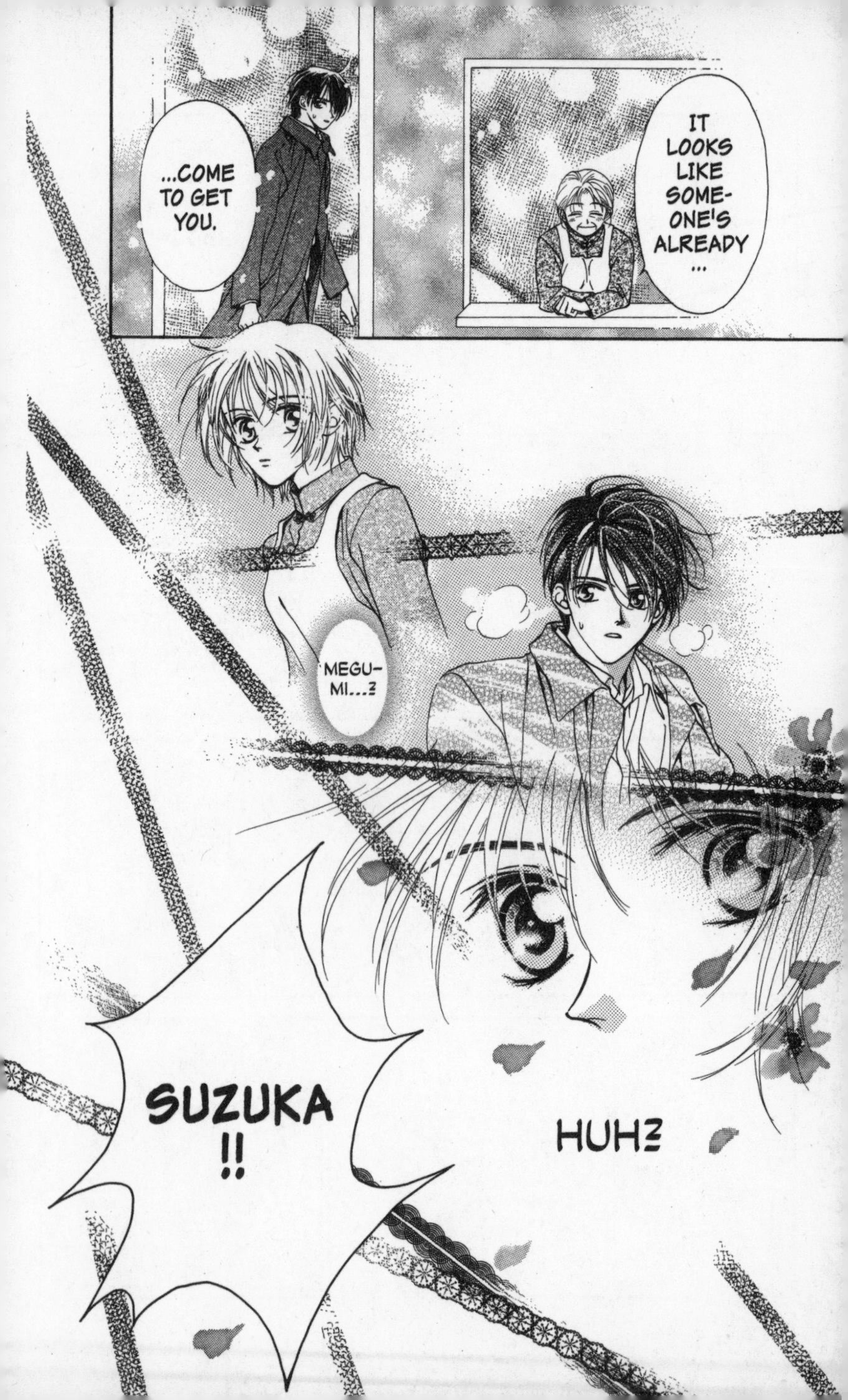
IT LOOKS LIKE SOME-ONE'S ALREADY ...
...COME TO GET YOU.
MEGU-MI...?
HUH?
SUZUKA !!

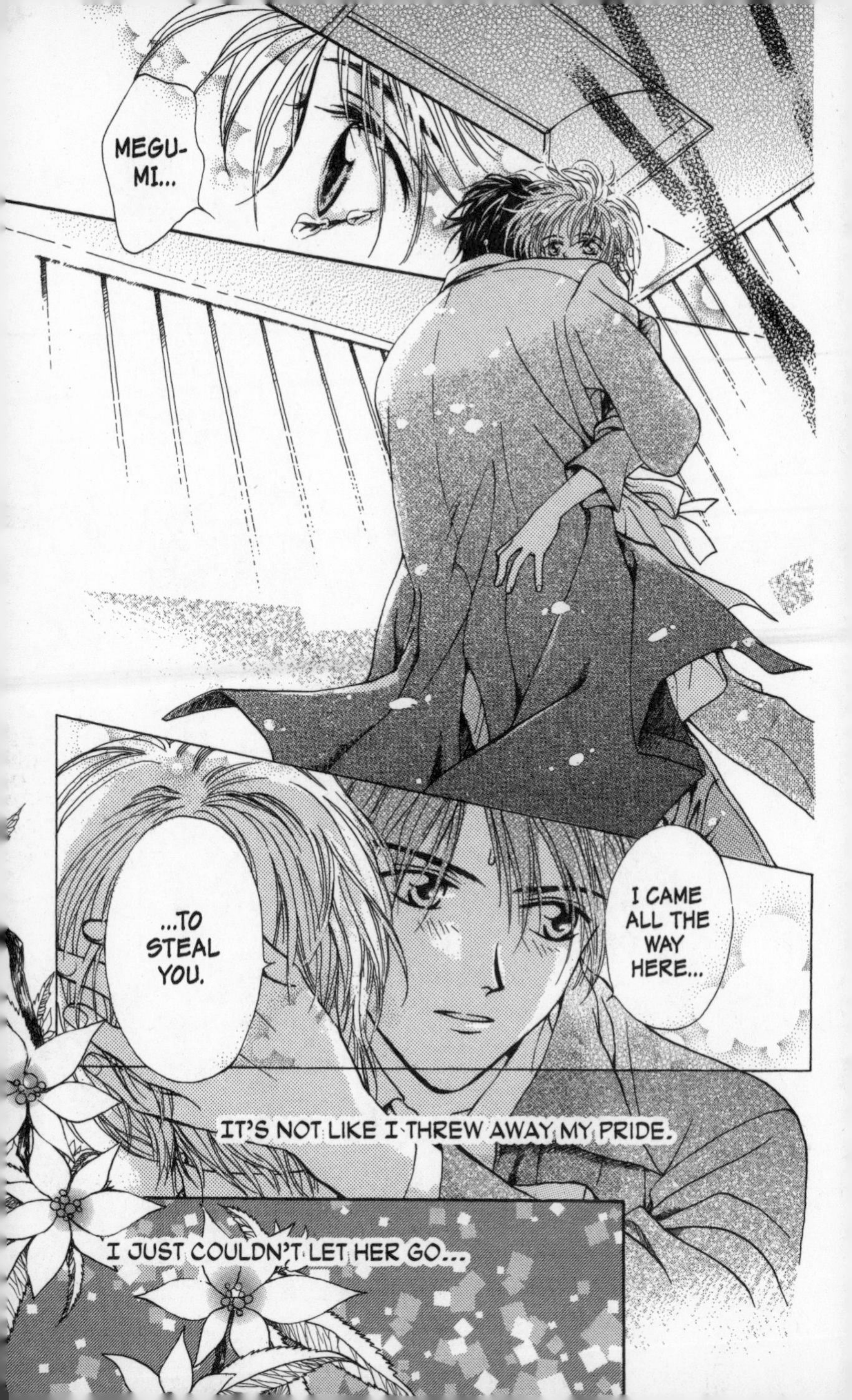
MEGU-MI...
I CAME ALL THE WAY HERE...
...TO STEAL YOU.
IT'S NOT LIKE I THREW AWAY MY PRIDE.
I JUST COULDN'T LET HER GO...

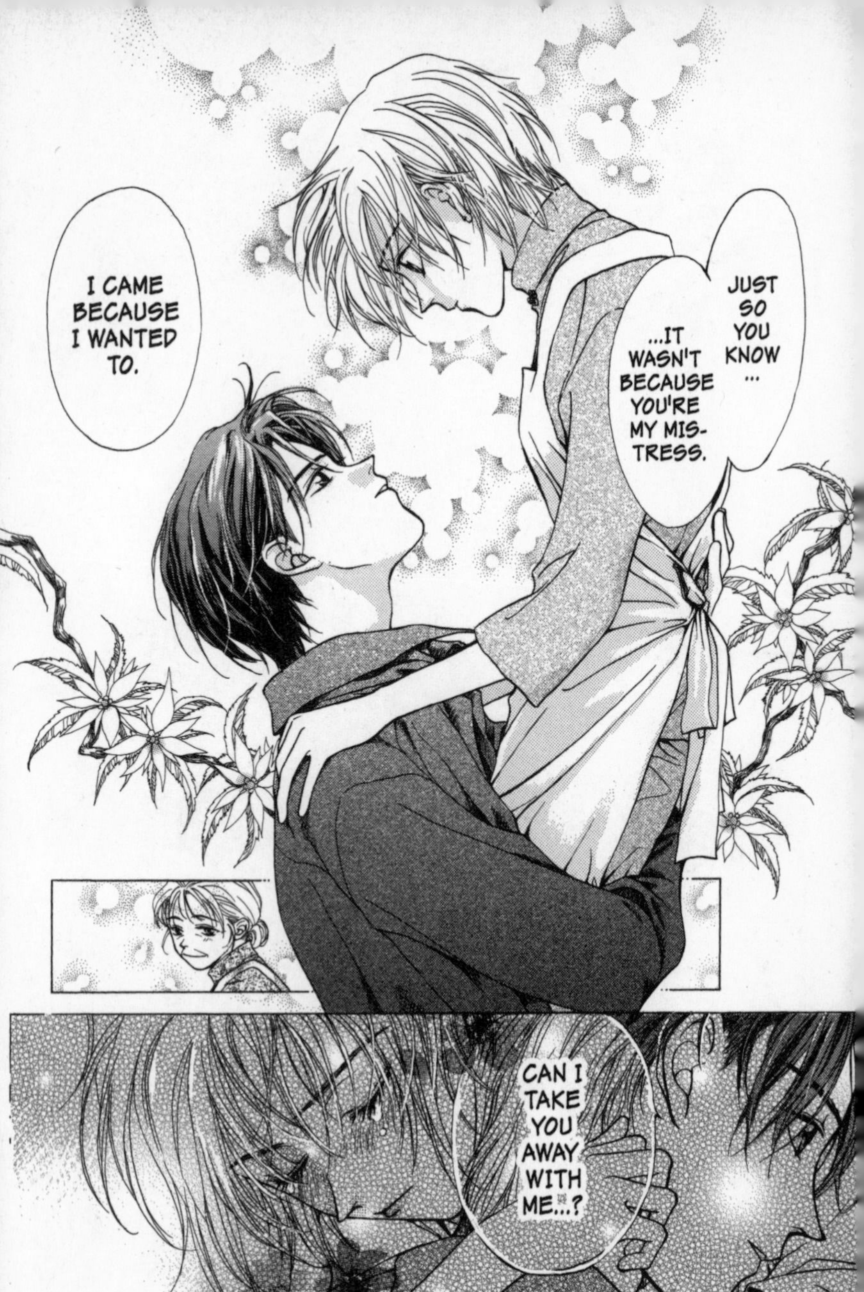
JUST SO YOU KNOW ...
...IT WASN'T BECAUSE YOU'RE MY MIS-TRESS.
I CAME BECAUSE I WANTED TO.
CAN I TAKE YOU AWAY WITH ME...?

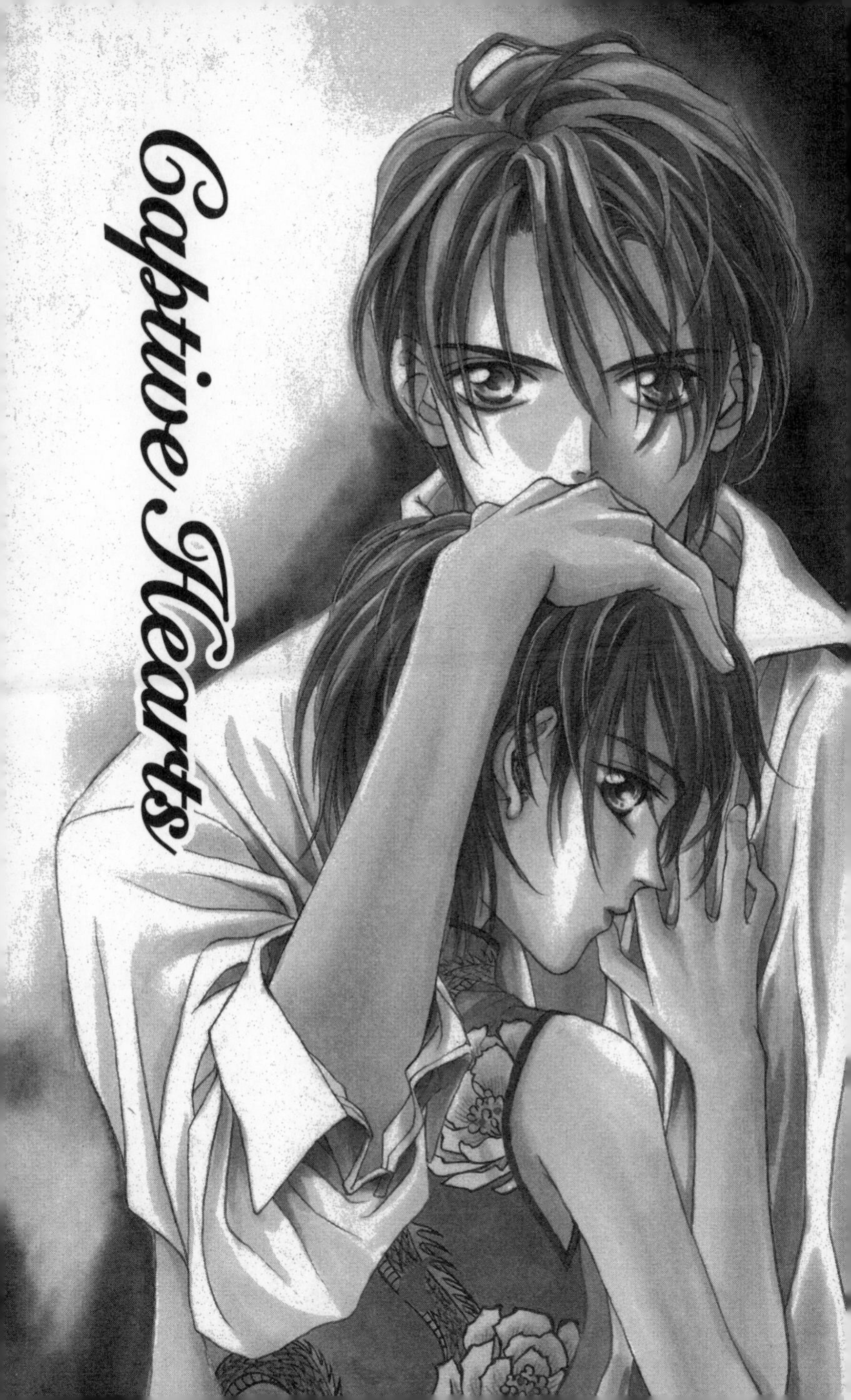
Captive Hearts

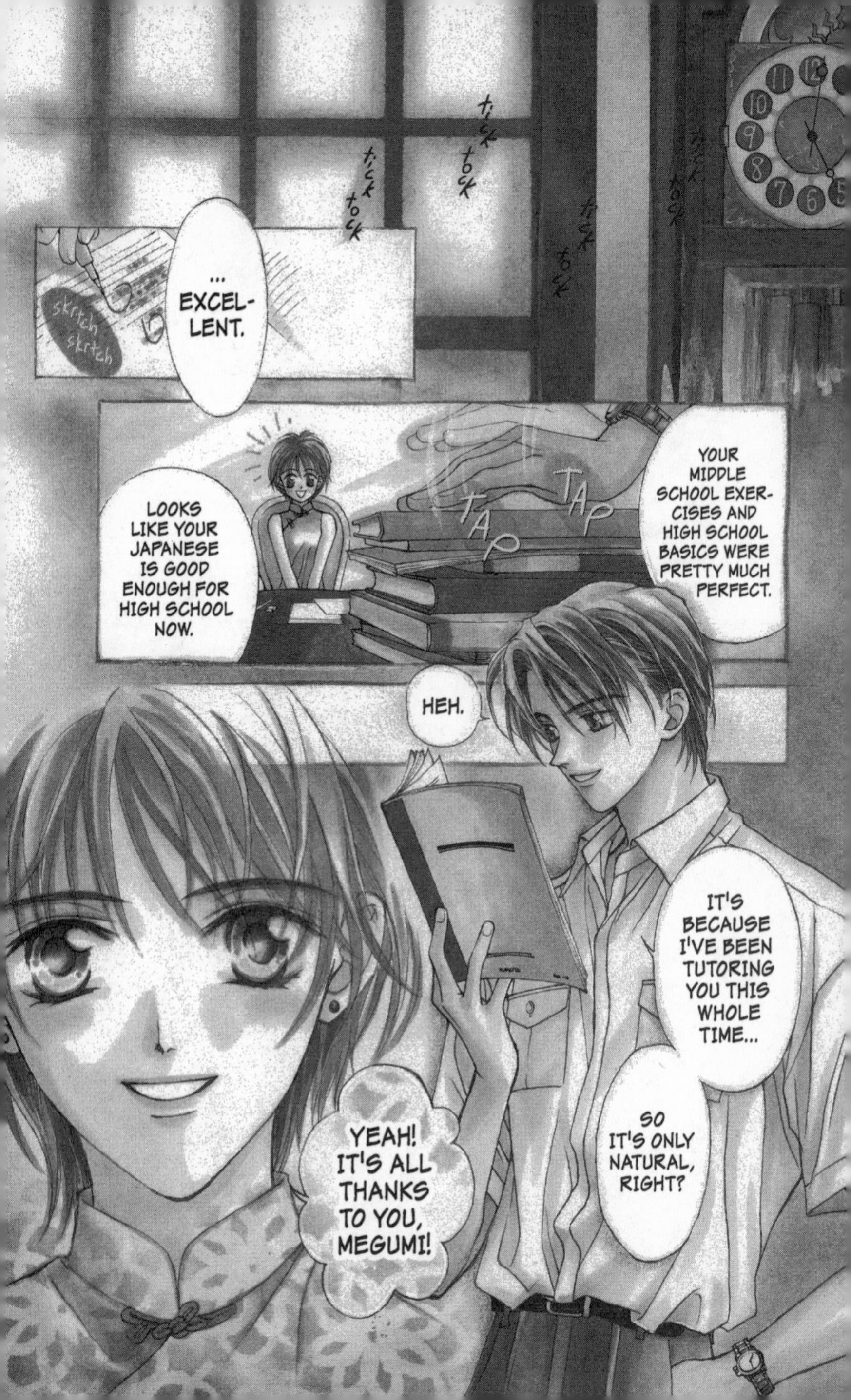
tick tock
tick tock
tick tock
tick tock
skritch skritch
... EXCEL-LENT.
YOUR MIDDLE SCHOOL EXER-CISES AND HIGH SCHOOL BASICS WERE PRETTY MUCH PERFECT.
TAP TAP
LOOKS LIKE YOUR JAPANESE IS GOOD ENOUGH FOR HIGH SCHOOL NOW.
HEH.
IT'S BECAUSE I'VE BEEN TUTORING YOU THIS WHOLE TIME...
SO IT'S ONLY NATURAL, RIGHT?
YEAH! IT'S ALL THANKS TO YOU, MEGUMI!

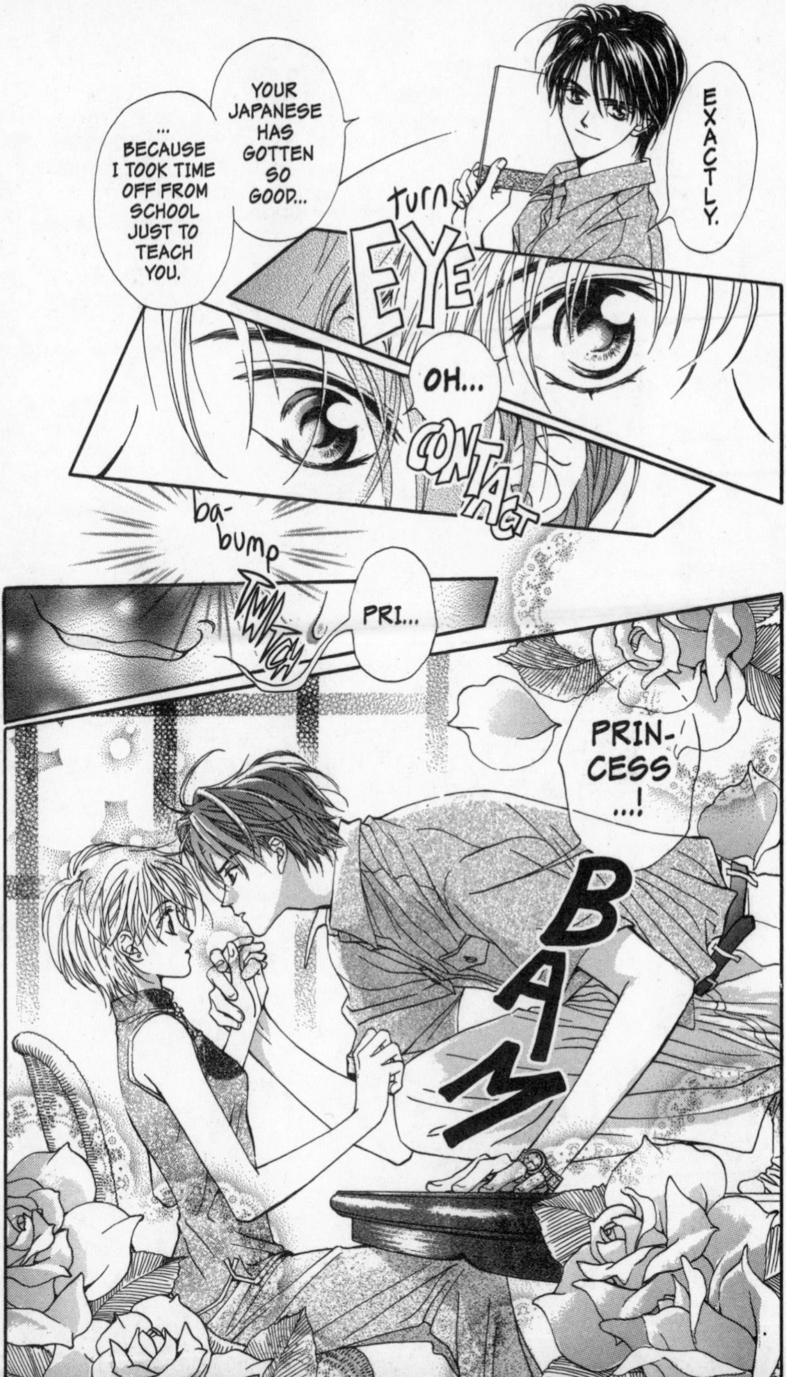
EXACTLY.
turn
YOUR JAPANESE HAS GOTTEN SO GOOD...
... BECAUSE I TOOK TIME OFF FROM SCHOOL JUST TO TEACH YOU.
EYE
OH...
CONTACT
ba-bump
TWITCH
PRI...
PRIN-CESS ...!
BAM

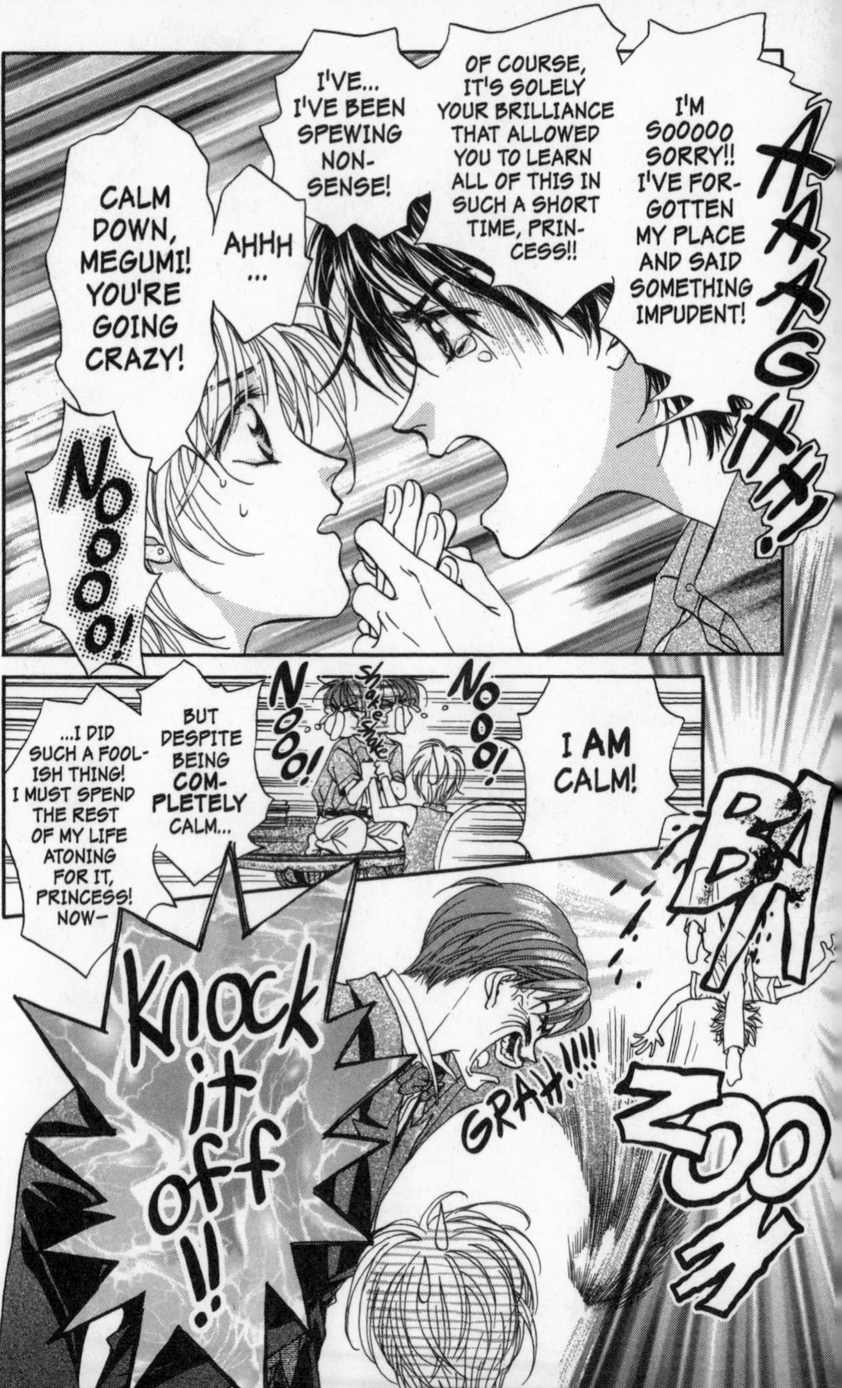
AAAAGHHH!
I'M SOOOOO SORRY!! I'VE FORGOTTEN MY PLACE AND SAID SOMETHING IMPUDENT!
OF COURSE, IT'S SOLELY YOUR BRILLIANCE THAT ALLOWED YOU TO LEARN ALL OF THIS IN SUCH A SHORT TIME, PRINCESS!!
I'VE... I'VE BEEN SPEWING NONSENSE!
AHHH...
CALM DOWN, MEGUMI! YOU'RE GOING CRAZY!
NOOOOO!
I AM CALM!
NOOOO!
shake shake
NOOOO!
BUT DESPITE BEING COMPLETELY CALM...
...I DID SUCH A FOOLISH THING! I MUST SPEND THE REST OF MY LIFE ATONING FOR IT, PRINCESS! NOW—
BADAM
ZOOM
GRAH!!!!
Knock it off!!

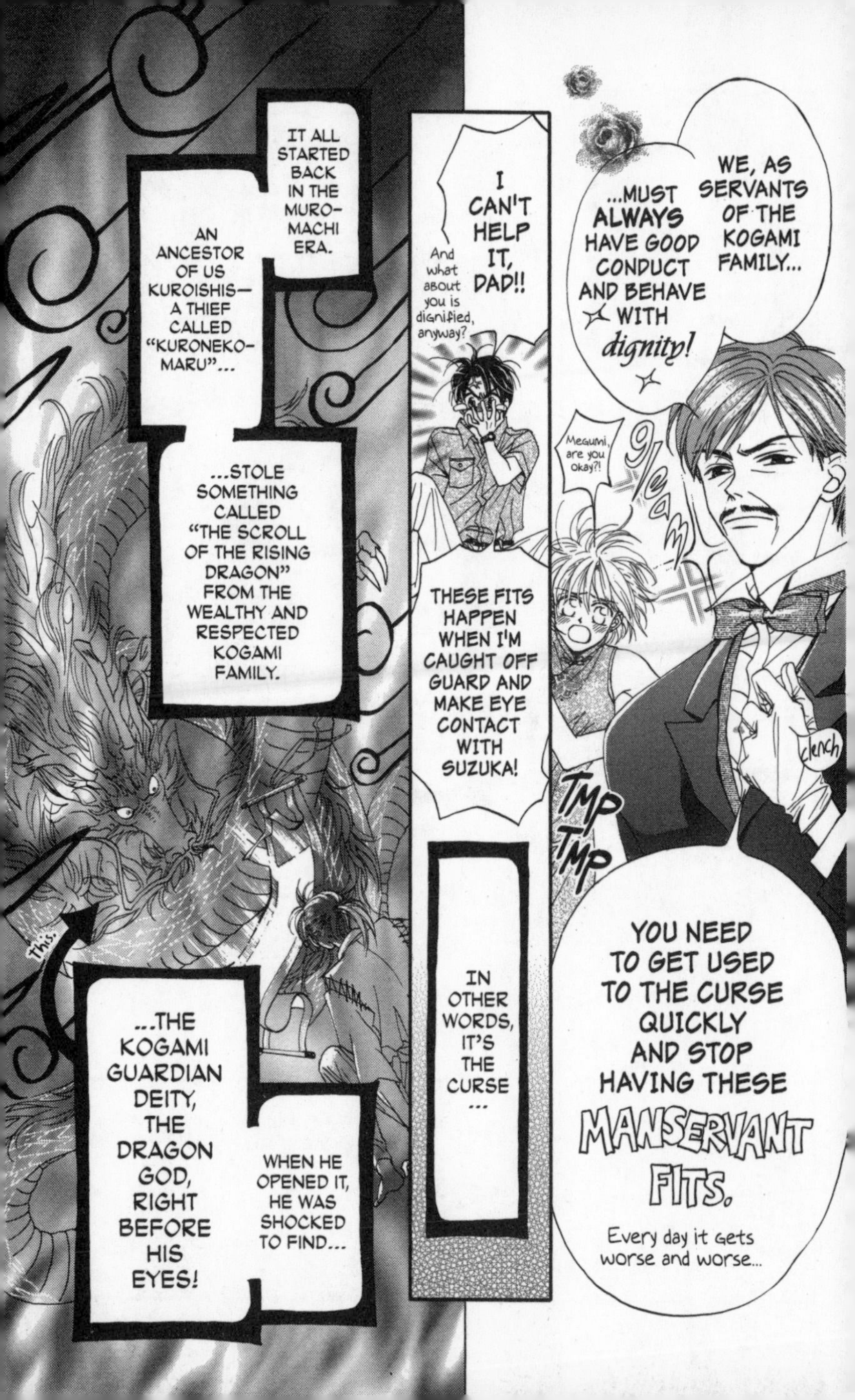
WE, AS SERVANTS OF THE KOGAMI FAMILY...
...MUST ALWAYS HAVE GOOD CONDUCT AND BEHAVE WITH dignity!
gleam
Megumi, are you okay?!
clench
TMP TMP
YOU NEED TO GET USED TO THE CURSE QUICKLY AND STOP HAVING THESE MANSERVANT FITS.
Every day it gets worse and worse...
I CAN'T HELP IT, DAD!!
And what about you is dignified, anyway?
THESE FITS HAPPEN WHEN I'M CAUGHT OFF GUARD AND MAKE EYE CONTACT WITH SUZUKA!
IN OTHER WORDS, IT'S THE CURSE...
IT ALL STARTED BACK IN THE MURO-MACHI ERA.
AN ANCESTOR OF US KUROISHIS— A THIEF CALLED "KURONEKO-MARU"...
...STOLE SOMETHING CALLED "THE SCROLL OF THE RISING DRAGON" FROM THE WEALTHY AND RESPECTED KOGAMI FAMILY.
WHEN HE OPENED IT, HE WAS SHOCKED TO FIND...
This.
...THE KOGAMI GUARDIAN DEITY, THE DRAGON GOD, RIGHT BEFORE HIS EYES!

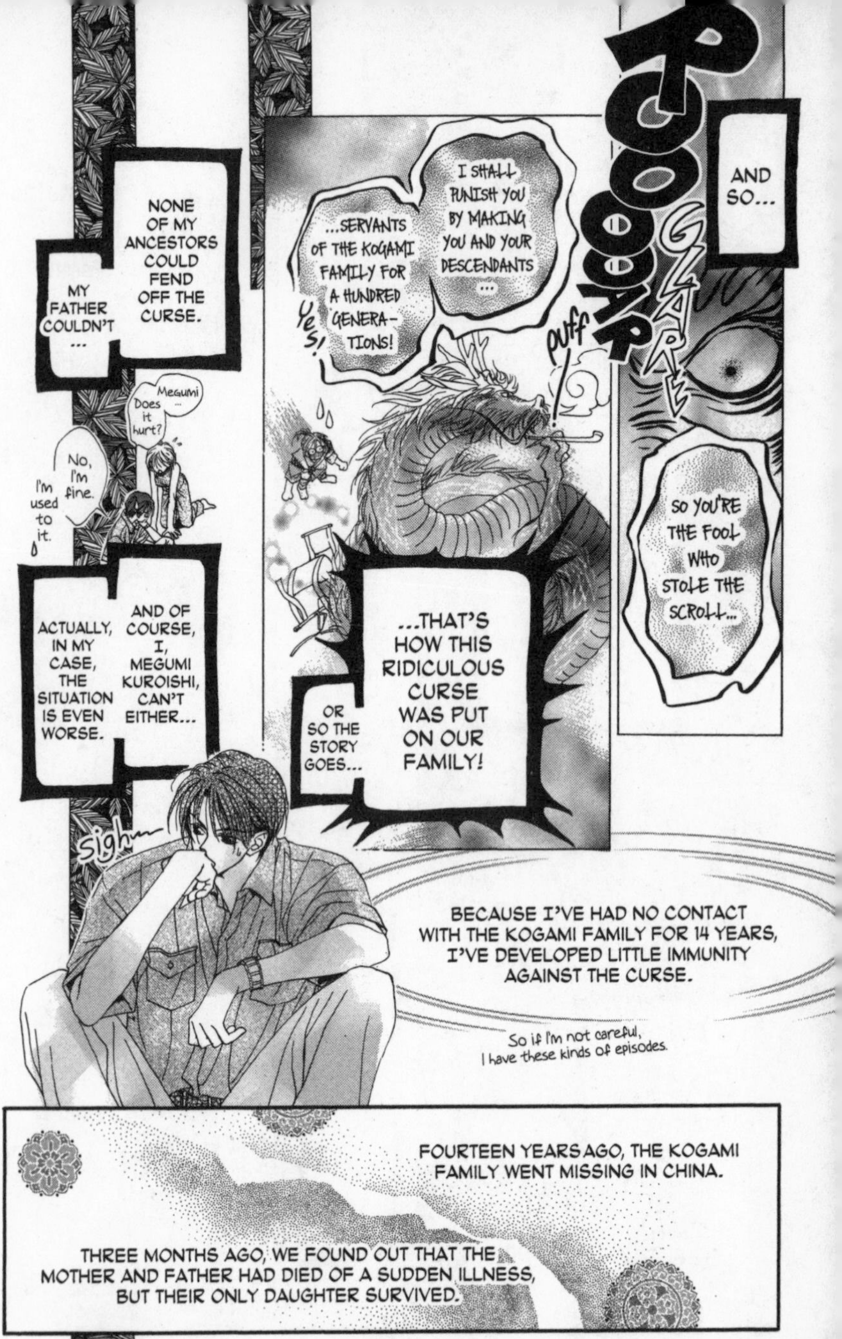

POOOOAR
AND SO...
GLARE
SO YOU'RE THE FOOL WHO STOLE THE SCROLL...
I SHALL PUNISH YOU BY MAKING YOU AND YOUR DESCENDANTS...
...SERVANTS OF THE KOGAMI FAMILY FOR A HUNDRED GENERA-TIONS!
puff!
Yes!
...THAT'S HOW THIS RIDICULOUS CURSE WAS PUT ON OUR FAMILY!
OR SO THE STORY GOES...
NONE OF MY ANCESTORS COULD FEND OFF THE CURSE.
MY FATHER COULDN'T...
Megumi... Does it hurt?
No, I'm fine.
I'm used to it.
AND OF COURSE, I, MEGUMI KUROISHI, CAN'T EITHER...
ACTUALLY, IN MY CASE, THE SITUATION IS EVEN WORSE.
Sigh
BECAUSE I'VE HAD NO CONTACT WITH THE KOGAMI FAMILY FOR 14 YEARS, I'VE DEVELOPED LITTLE IMMUNITY AGAINST THE CURSE.
So if I'm not careful, I have these kinds of episodes.
FOURTEEN YEARS AGO, THE KOGAMI FAMILY WENT MISSING IN CHINA.
THREE MONTHS AGO, WE FOUND OUT THAT THE MOTHER AND FATHER HAD DIED OF A SUDDEN ILLNESS, BUT THEIR ONLY DAUGHTER SURVIVED.

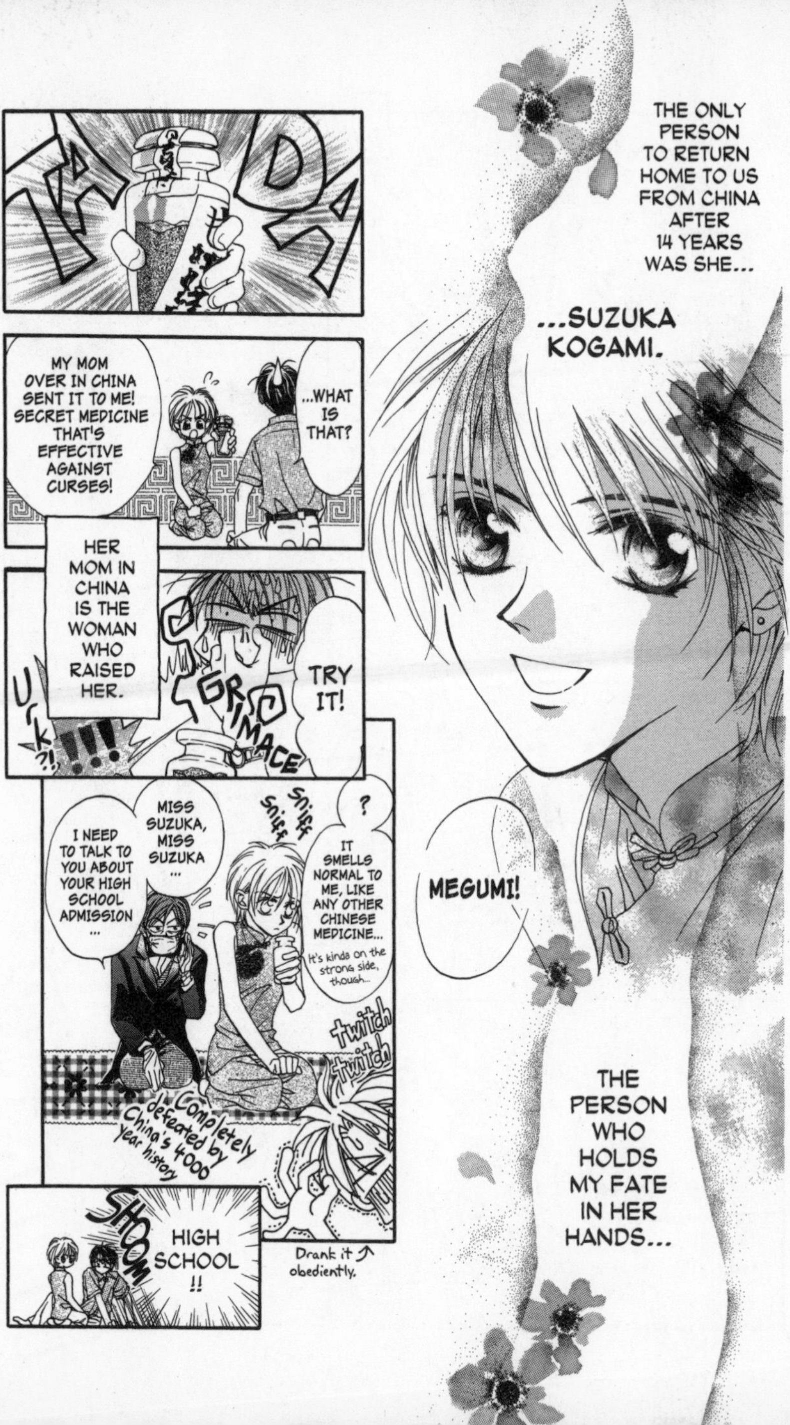
THE ONLY PERSON TO RETURN HOME TO US FROM CHINA AFTER 14 YEARS WAS SHE...
...SUZUKA KOGAMI.
MEGUMI!
THE PERSON WHO HOLDS MY FATE IN HER HANDS...
TA DA
...WHAT IS THAT?
MY MOM OVER IN CHINA SENT IT TO ME! SECRET MEDICINE THAT'S EFFECTIVE AGAINST CURSES!
HER MOM IN CHINA IS THE WOMAN WHO RAISED HER.
TRY IT!
GRIMACE
URK ?!
!!!
?
sniff sniff
IT SMELLS NORMAL TO ME, LIKE ANY OTHER CHINESE MEDICINE...
It's kinda on the strong side, though...
MISS SUZUKA, MISS SUZUKA...
I NEED TO TALK TO YOU ABOUT YOUR HIGH SCHOOL ADMISSION...
twitch twitch
Completely defeated by China's 4000 year history
Drank it obediently.
SHOOM
HIGH SCHOOL !!

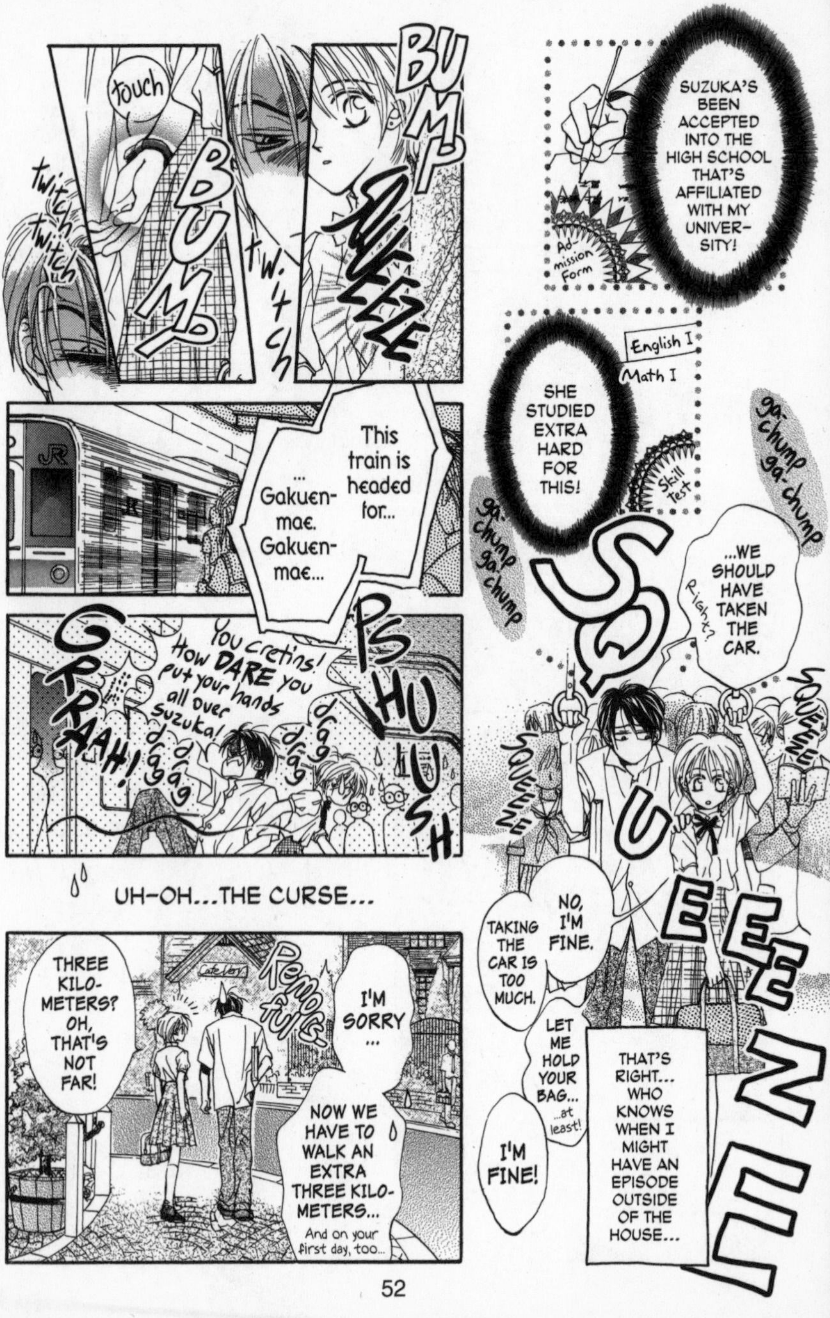
SUZUKA'S BEEN ACCEPTED INTO THE HIGH SCHOOL THAT'S AFFILIATED WITH MY UNIVERSITY!
Admission Form
SHE STUDIED EXTRA HARD FOR THIS!
English I
Math I
Skill Test
ga-chump ga-chump
ga-chump ga-chump
SQUEEZE
SQUEEZE
SQUEEZE
...WE SHOULD HAVE TAKEN THE CAR.
Right?
NO, I'M FINE.
TAKING THE CAR IS TOO MUCH.
LET ME HOLD YOUR BAG... ...at least!
I'M FINE!
THAT'S RIGHT... WHO KNOWS WHEN I MIGHT HAVE AN EPISODE OUTSIDE OF THE HOUSE...
BUMP
SQUEEZE
touch
BUMP
twitch
twitch twitch
This train is headed for...
...Gakuenmae. Gakuenmae...
PSHUUSH
GRRAAH!
You cretins! How DARE you put your hands all over Suzuka!
drag drag
drag drag
UH-OH...THE CURSE...
Remorseful
I'M SORRY...
THREE KILOMETERS? OH, THAT'S NOT FAR!
NOW WE HAVE TO WALK AN EXTRA THREE KILOMETERS...
And on your first day, too...

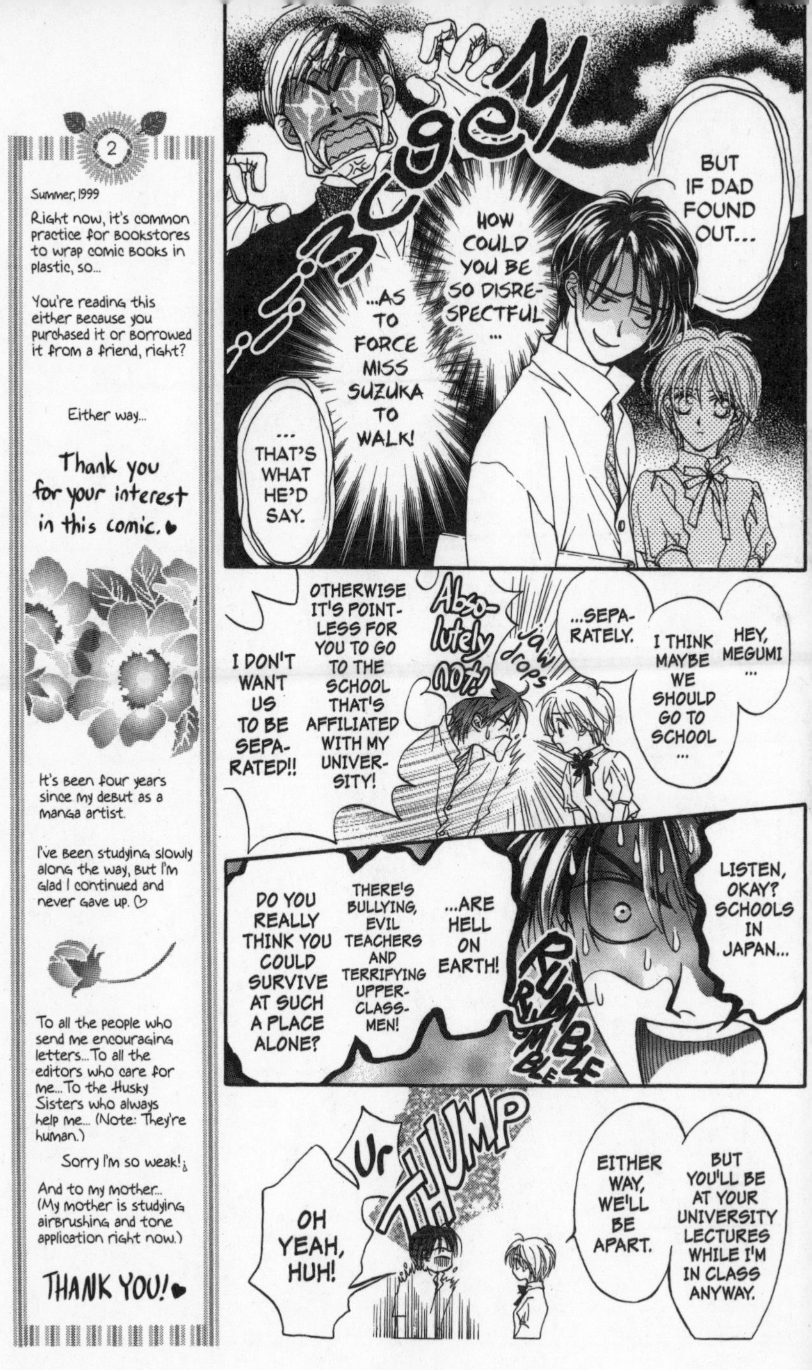

BUT IF DAD FOUND OUT...
HOW COULD YOU BE SO DISRE-SPECTFUL...
...AS TO FORCE MISS SUZUKA TO WALK!
...THAT'S WHAT HE'D SAY.
HEY, MEGUMI...
I THINK MAYBE WE SHOULD GO TO SCHOOL...
...SEPA-RATELY.
Jaw drops
Abso-lutely not!
OTHERWISE IT'S POINT-LESS FOR YOU TO GO TO THE SCHOOL THAT'S AFFILIATED WITH MY UNIVER-SITY!
I DON'T WANT US TO BE SEPA-RATED!!
LISTEN, OKAY? SCHOOLS IN JAPAN...
RUMBLE RUMBLE
...ARE HELL ON EARTH!
THERE'S BULLYING, EVIL TEACHERS AND TERRIFYING UPPER-CLASS-MEN!
DO YOU REALLY THINK YOU COULD SURVIVE AT SUCH A PLACE ALONE?
BUT YOU'LL BE AT YOUR UNIVERSITY LECTURES WHILE I'M IN CLASS ANYWAY.
EITHER WAY, WE'LL BE APART.
THUMP
Ur
OH YEAH, HUH!

2

Summer, 1999

Right now, it's common practice for bookstores to wrap comic books in plastic, so...

You're reading this either because you purchased it or borrowed it from a friend, right?

Either way...

Thank you for your interest in this comic. ♥

It's been four years since my debut as a manga artist.

I've been studying slowly along the way, but I'm glad I continued and never gave up. ♡

To all the people who send me encouraging letters... To all the editors who care for me... To the Husky Sisters who always help me... (Note: They're human.)

Sorry I'm so weak! ¡

And to my mother... (My mother is studying airbrushing and tone application right now.)

THANK YOU! ♥

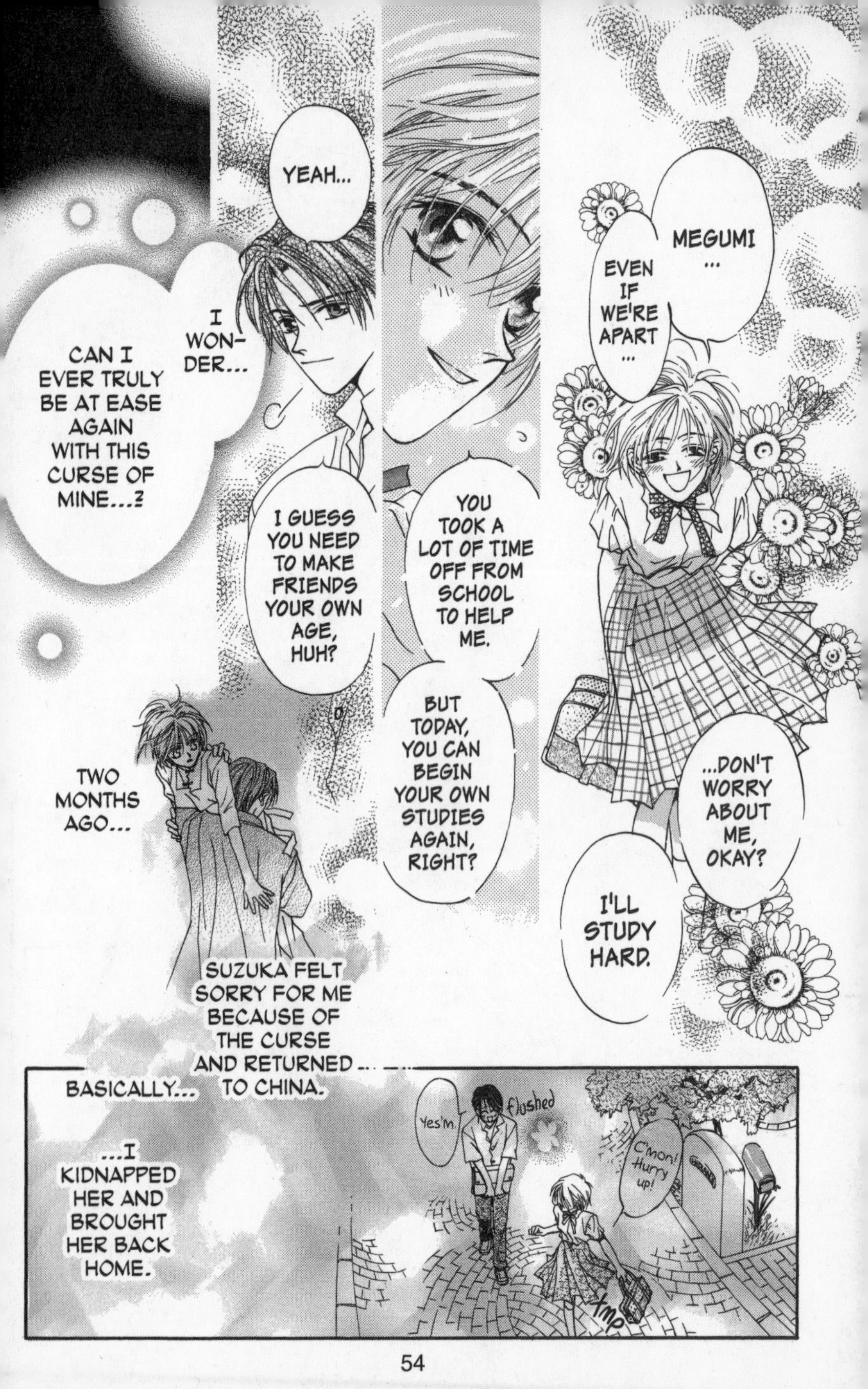
MEGUMI ...
EVEN IF WE'RE APART ...
...DON'T WORRY ABOUT ME, OKAY?
I'LL STUDY HARD.
YOU TOOK A LOT OF TIME OFF FROM SCHOOL TO HELP ME.
BUT TODAY, YOU CAN BEGIN YOUR OWN STUDIES AGAIN, RIGHT?
YEAH...
I GUESS YOU NEED TO MAKE FRIENDS YOUR OWN AGE, HUH?
I WON-DER...
CAN I EVER TRULY BE AT EASE AGAIN WITH THIS CURSE OF MINE...?
TWO MONTHS AGO...
SUZUKA FELT SORRY FOR ME BECAUSE OF THE CURSE AND RETURNED TO CHINA.
BASICALLY...
...I KIDNAPPED HER AND BROUGHT HER BACK HOME.
C'mon! Hurry up!
flushed
Yes'm.
tmp

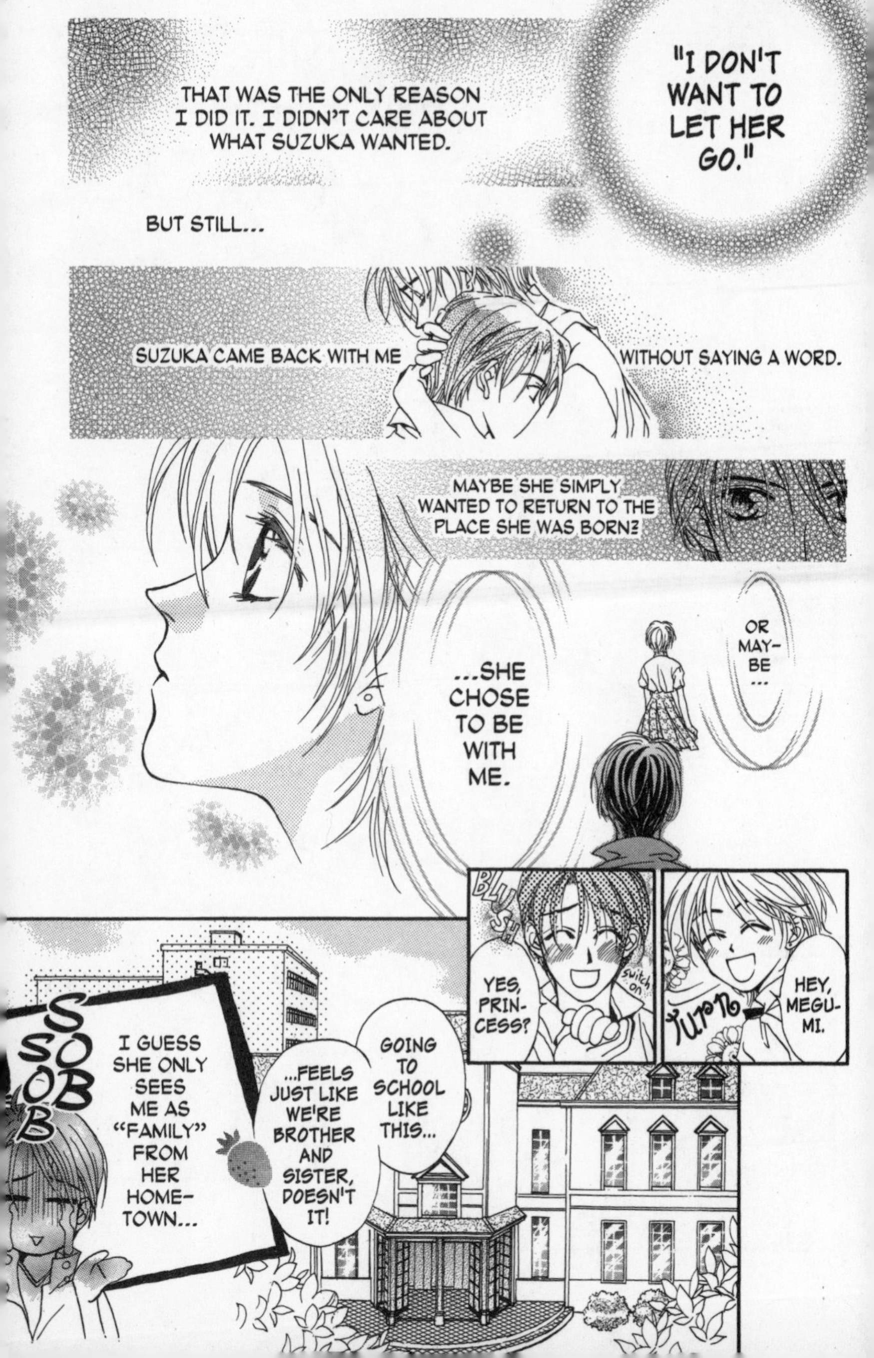

"I DON'T WANT TO LET HER GO."
THAT WAS THE ONLY REASON I DID IT. I DIDN'T CARE ABOUT WHAT SUZUKA WANTED.
BUT STILL...
SUZUKA CAME BACK WITH ME
WITHOUT SAYING A WORD.
MAYBE SHE SIMPLY WANTED TO RETURN TO THE PLACE SHE WAS BORN?
OR MAY-BE...
...SHE CHOSE TO BE WITH ME.
HEY, MEGU-MI.
JUMP
YES, PRIN-CESS?
BLUSH
switch on
GOING TO SCHOOL LIKE THIS...
...FEELS JUST LIKE WE'RE BROTHER AND SISTER, DOESN'T IT!
I GUESS SHE ONLY SEES ME AS "FAMILY" FROM HER HOME-TOWN...
SOB SOB

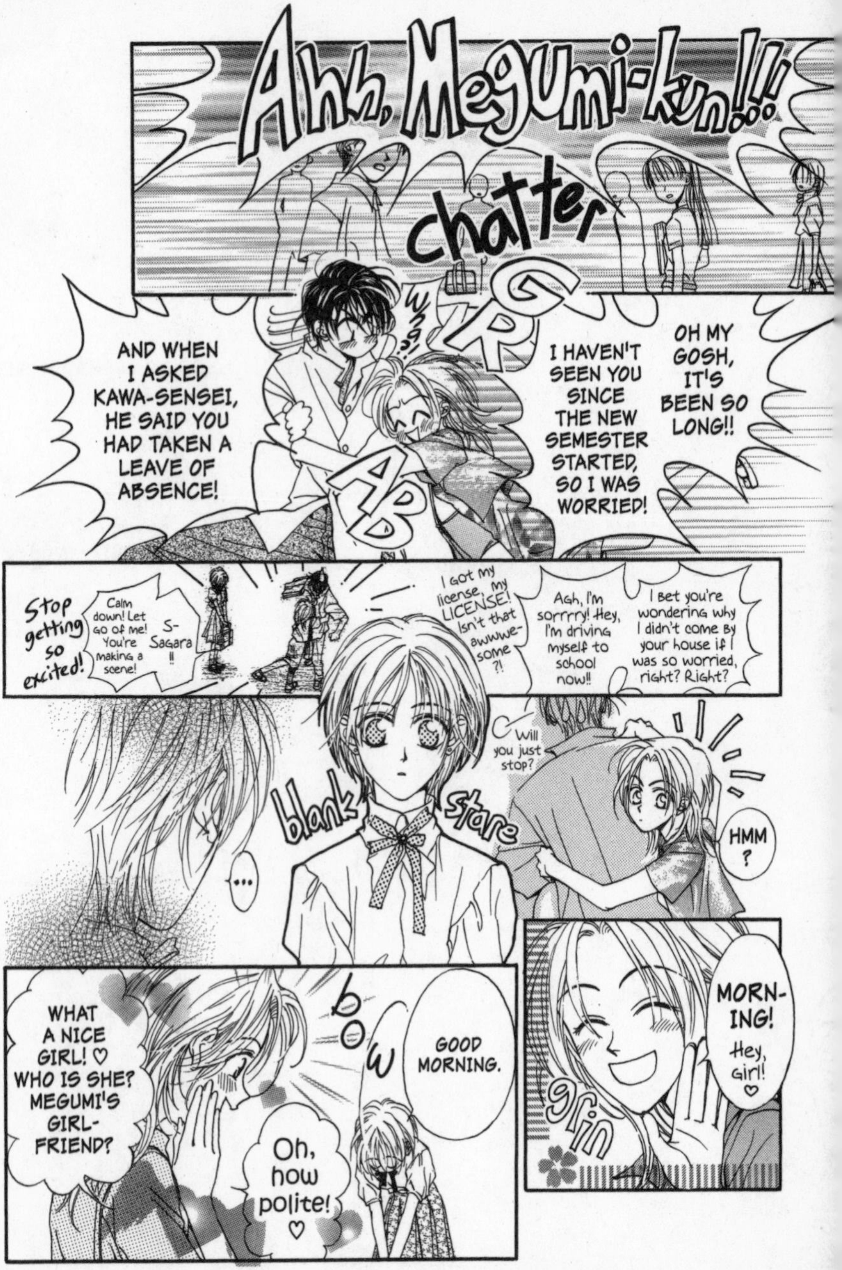
Ahh, Megumi-kun!!!...
chatter
OH MY GOSH, IT'S BEEN SO LONG!!
I HAVEN'T SEEN YOU SINCE THE NEW SEMESTER STARTED, SO I WAS WORRIED!
GR
wha?!
AB
AND WHEN I ASKED KAWA-SENSEI, HE SAID YOU HAD TAKEN A LEAVE OF ABSENCE!
I bet you're wondering why I didn't come by your house if I was so worried, right? Right?
Agh, I'm sorrrry! Hey, I'm driving myself to school now!!
I got my license, my LICENSE! Isn't that awwwe-some ?!
S-Sagara !!
Calm down! Let go of me! You're making a scene!
Stop getting so excited!
HMM ?
Will you just stop?
blank stare
...
MORNING! Hey, girl! ♡
grin
GOOD MORNING.
bow
Oh, how polite! ♡
WHAT A NICE GIRL! ♡ WHO IS SHE? MEGUMI'S GIRL-FRIEND?

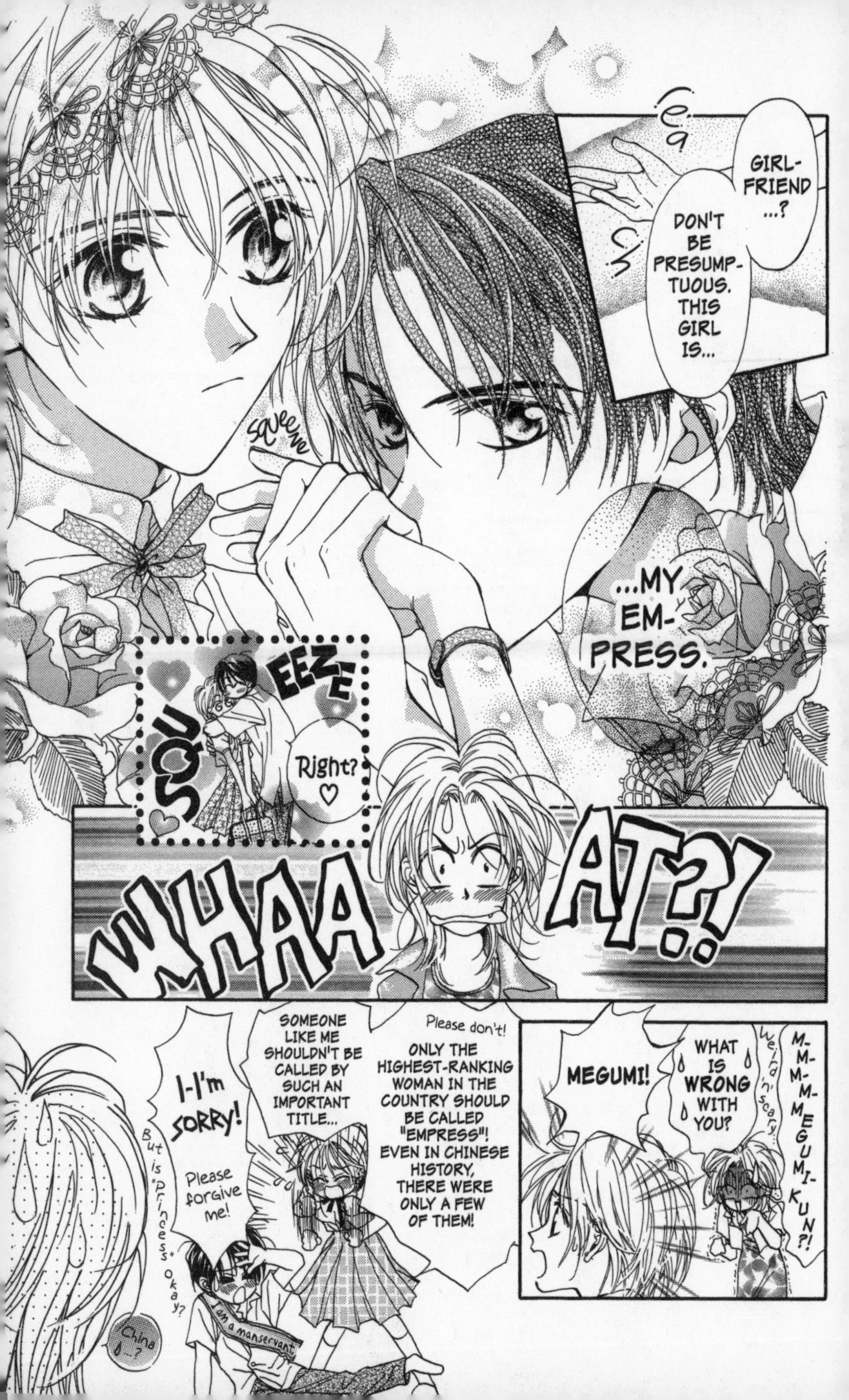
GIRL-FRIEND ...?
DON'T BE PRESUMP-TUOUS. THIS GIRL IS...
...MY EM-PRESS.
SQUEEZE
Right? ♡
WHAAAT?!
M-M-M-MMEGUMI-KUN?!
Weird 'n' scary...
WHAT IS WRONG WITH YOU?
MEGUMI!
Please don't!
ONLY THE HIGHEST-RANKING WOMAN IN THE COUNTRY SHOULD BE CALLED "EMPRESS"! EVEN IN CHINESE HISTORY, THERE WERE ONLY A FEW OF THEM!
SOMEONE LIKE ME SHOULDN'T BE CALLED BY SUCH AN IMPORTANT TITLE...
I-I'm SORRY!
Please forgive me!
But is "Princess" okay?
I am a manservant
China...?

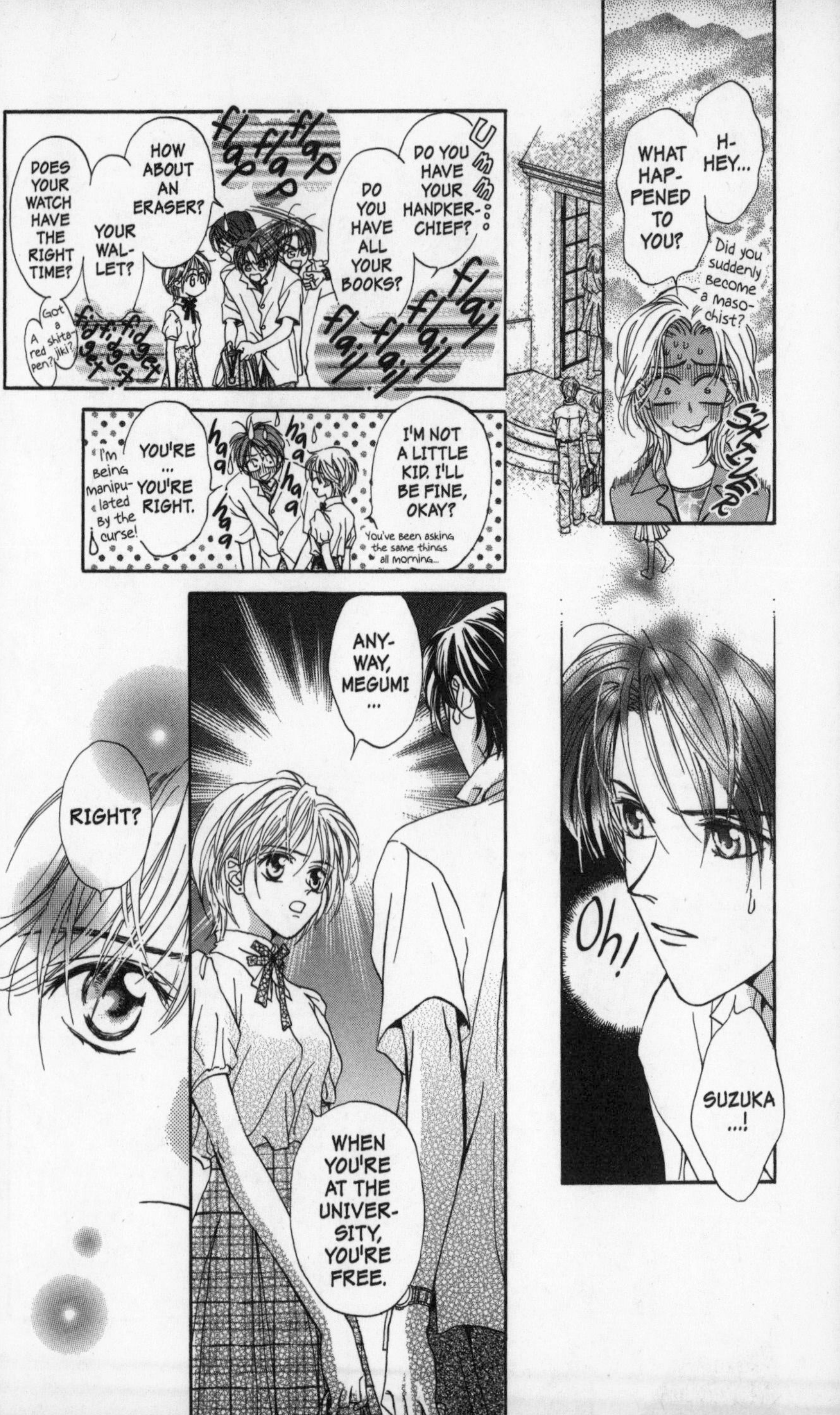
H-HEY...
WHAT HAPPENED TO YOU?
Did you suddenly Become a masochist?
SHIVER
UMM...
DO YOU HAVE YOUR HANDKERCHIEF?
DO YOU HAVE ALL YOUR BOOKS?
flail flail flail
flap flap flap
HOW ABOUT AN ERASER?
YOUR WALLET?
DOES YOUR WATCH HAVE THE RIGHT TIME?
Got a shitajiki? A red pen?
fidget fidget fidget
I'M NOT A LITTLE KID. I'LL BE FINE, OKAY?
You've Been asking the same things all morning...
haa haa haa haa
YOU'RE ... YOU'RE RIGHT.
I'm Being manipulated By the curse!
Oh!
SUZUKA ...!
ANYWAY, MEGUMI ...
WHEN YOU'RE AT THE UNIVERSITY, YOU'RE FREE.
RIGHT?

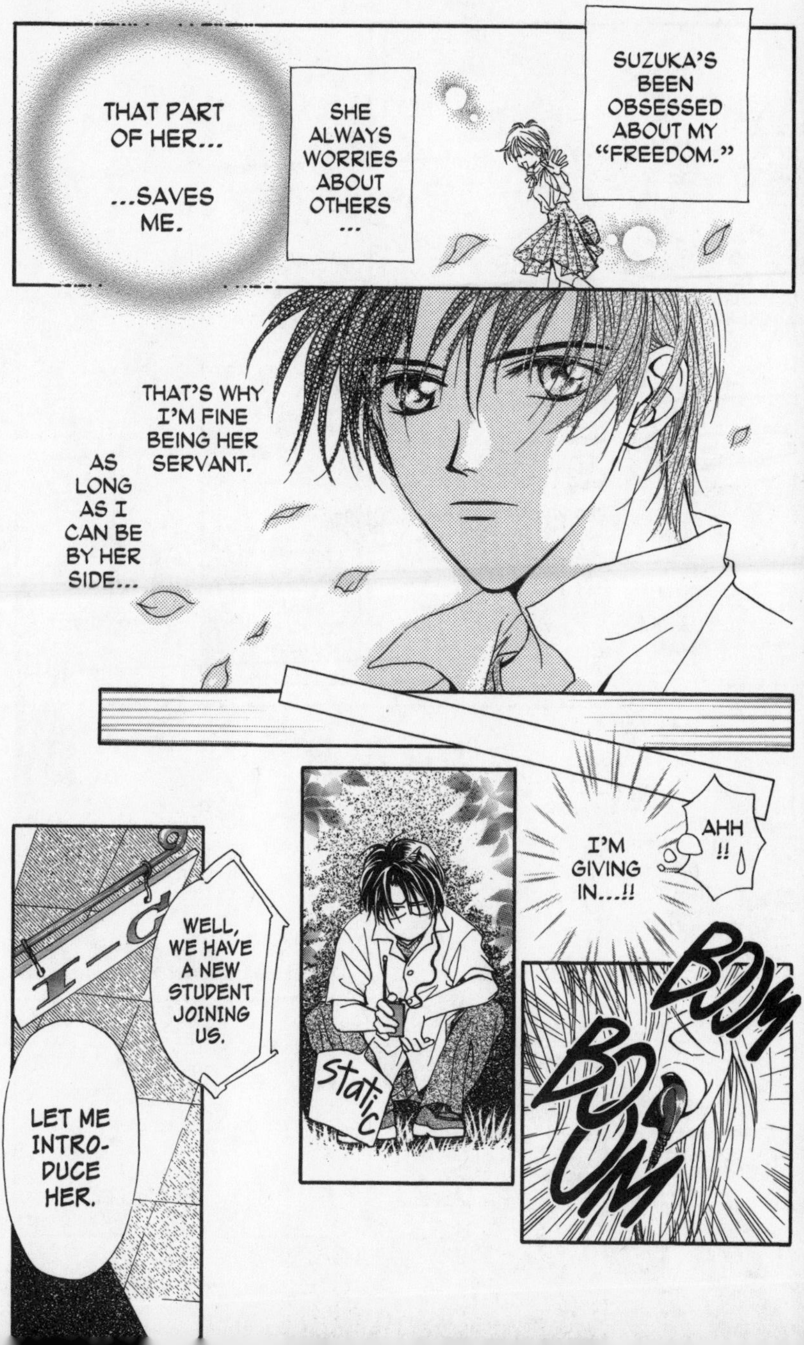
SUZUKA'S BEEN OBSESSED ABOUT MY "FREEDOM."
SHE ALWAYS WORRIES ABOUT OTHERS ...
THAT PART OF HER...
...SAVES ME.
THAT'S WHY I'M FINE BEING HER SERVANT.
AS LONG AS I CAN BE BY HER SIDE...
AHH !!
I'M GIVING IN...!!
BOM
static
WELL, WE HAVE A NEW STUDENT JOINING US.
LET ME INTRO-DUCE HER.

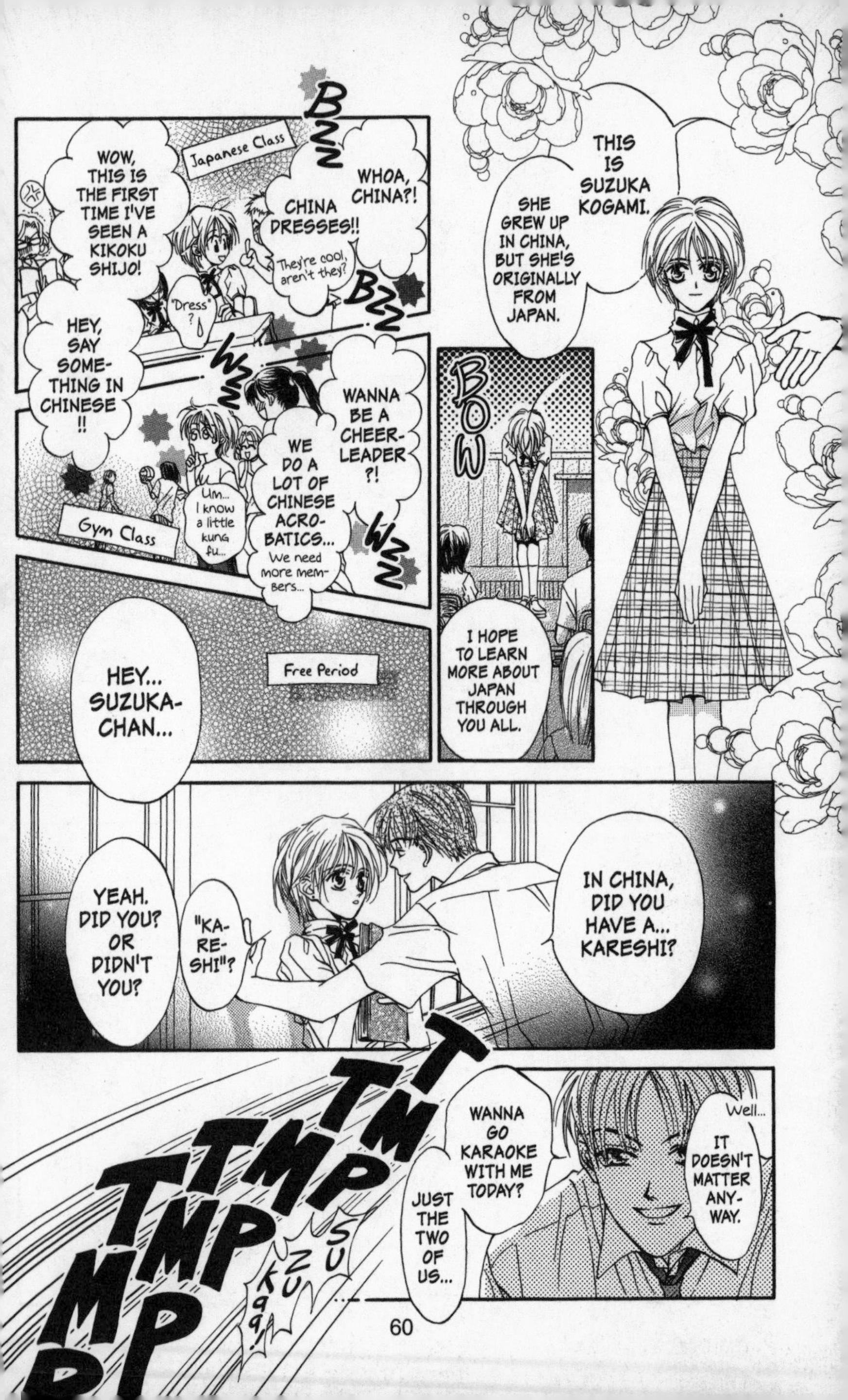

THIS IS SUZUKA KOGAMI.
SHE GREW UP IN CHINA, BUT SHE'S ORIGINALLY FROM JAPAN.
BOW
I HOPE TO LEARN MORE ABOUT JAPAN THROUGH YOU ALL.
Japanese Class
BZZ
WHOA, CHINA?!
CHINA DRESSES!!
They're cool, aren't they?
WOW, THIS IS THE FIRST TIME I'VE SEEN A KIKOKU SHIJO!
"Dress"?
BZZ
WZZ
WANNA BE A CHEER-LEADER?!
WE DO A LOT OF CHINESE ACRO-BATICS... We need more mem-bers...
HEY, SAY SOME-THING IN CHINESE!!
Um... I know a little kung fu...
Gym Class
WZZ
Free Period
HEY... SUZUKA-CHAN...
IN CHINA, DID YOU HAVE A... KARESHI?
"KA-RE-SHI"?
YEAH. DID YOU? OR DIDN'T YOU?
Well...
IT DOESN'T MATTER ANY-WAY.
WANNA GO KARAOKE WITH ME TODAY?
JUST THE TWO OF US...
SU ZU...

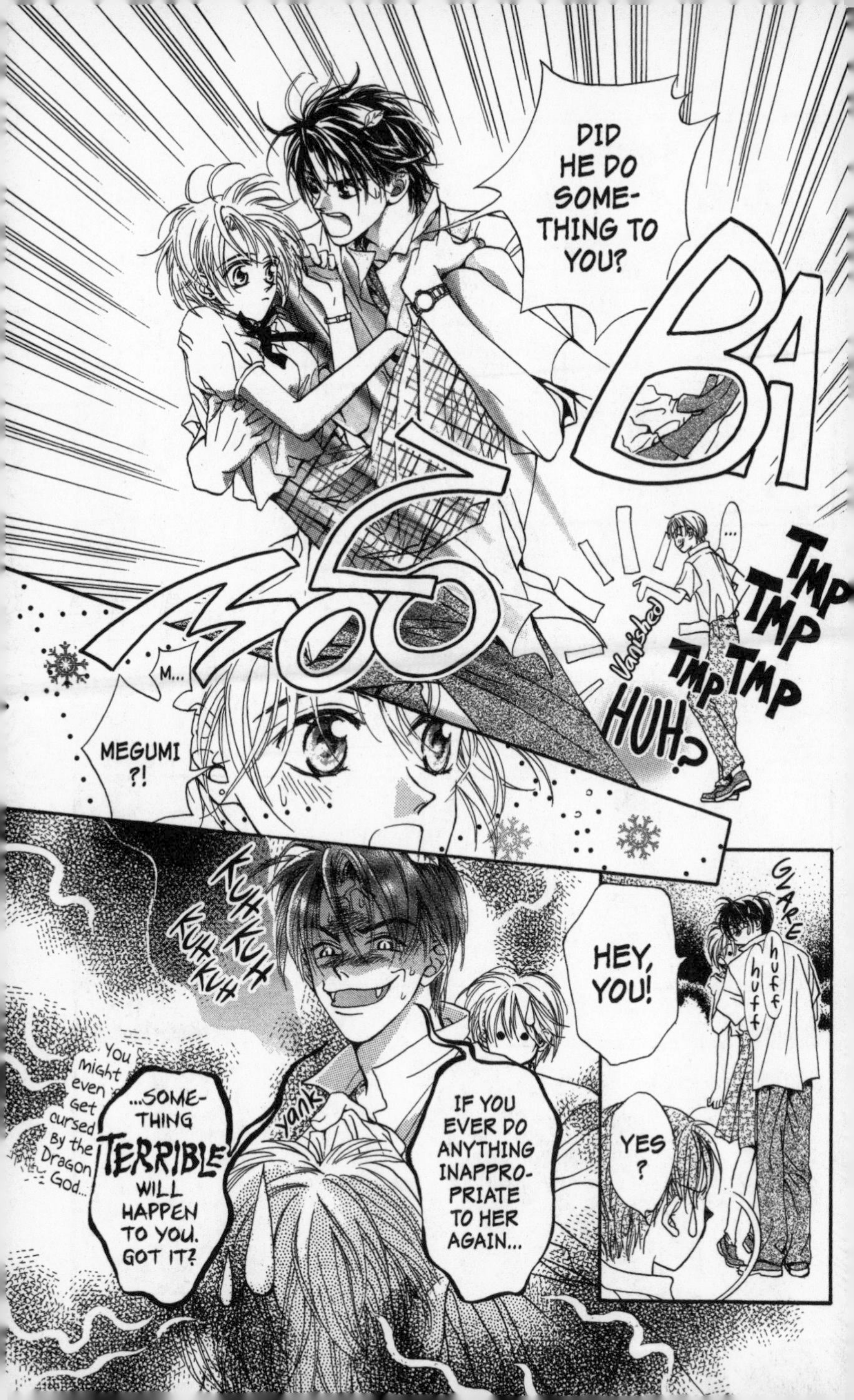
DID HE DO SOME-THING TO YOU?
BA
...
TMP TMP TMP TMP TMP
HUH?
Vanished
M...
MEGUMI ?!
GLARE
huff huff
HEY, YOU!
YES?
KUH KUH KUH KUH
IF YOU EVER DO ANYTHING INAPPRO-PRIATE TO HER AGAIN...
Yank
...SOME-THING TERRIBLE WILL HAPPEN TO YOU. GOT IT?
You might even get cursed By the Dragon God...

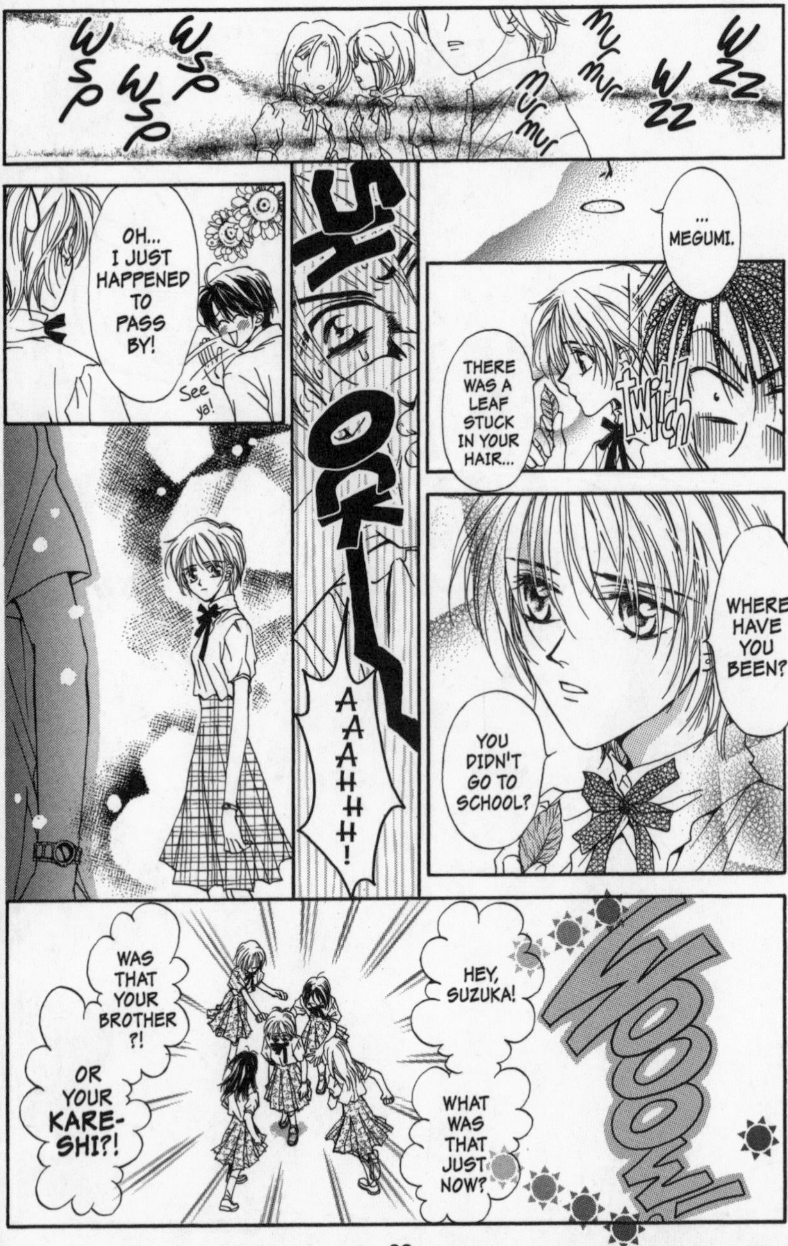

WZZ WZZ
MURMUR MURMUR
MURMUR MURMUR
WSP WSP WSP WSP
... MEGUMI.
THERE WAS A LEAF STUCK IN YOUR HAIR...
TWITCH
WHERE HAVE YOU BEEN?
YOU DIDN'T GO TO SCHOOL?
SHOCK
AAAHHHH!
OH... I JUST HAPPENED TO PASS BY!
See ya!
WOOOW!!
HEY, SUZUKA!
WHAT WAS THAT JUST NOW?
WAS THAT YOUR BROTHER?!
OR YOUR KARE-SHI?!

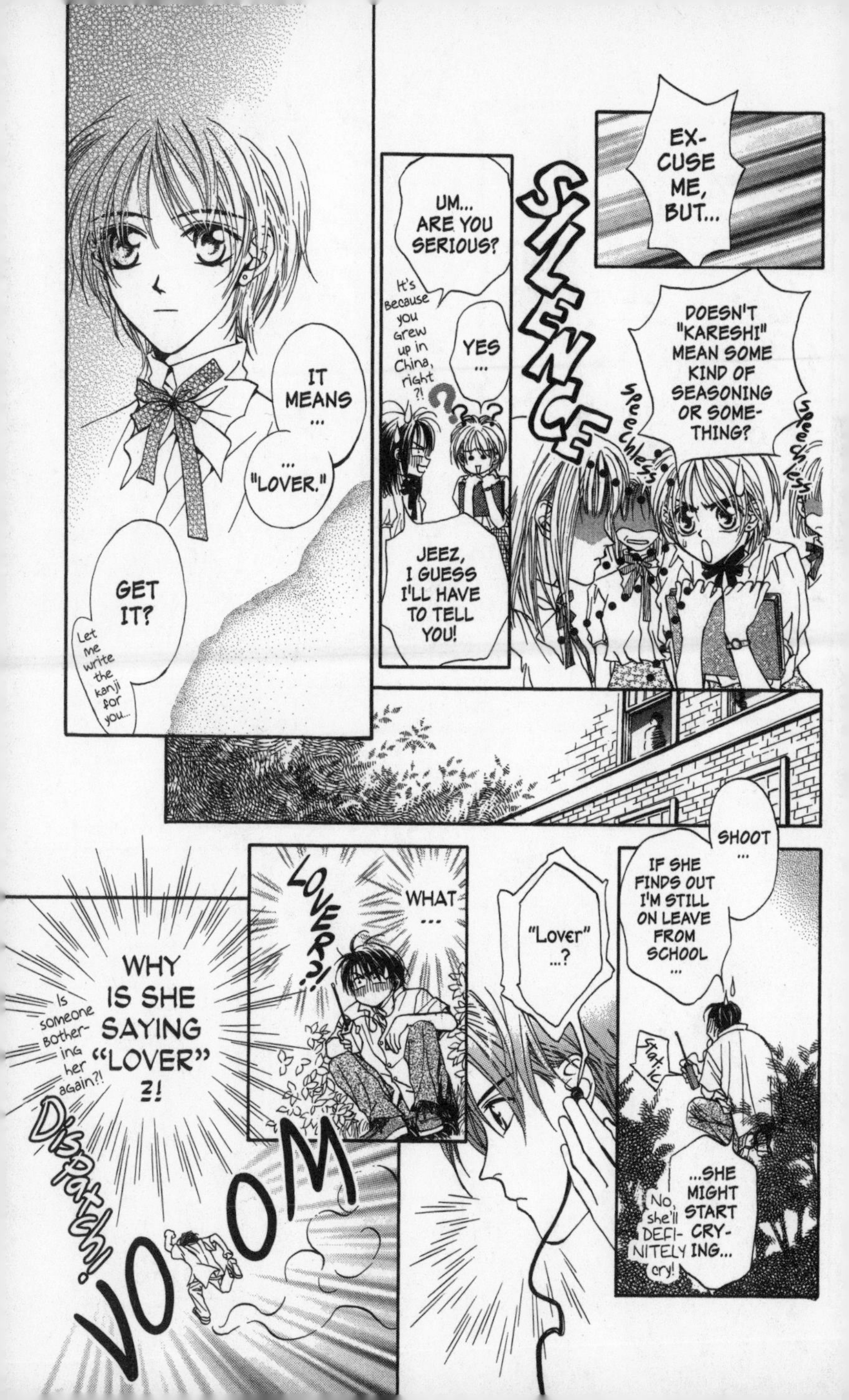
EX-CUSE ME, BUT...
DOESN'T "KARESHI" MEAN SOME KIND OF SEASONING OR SOME-THING?
SILENCE
speechless
speechless
UM... ARE YOU SERIOUS?
YES...
It's because you grew up in China, right?!
JEEZ, I GUESS I'LL HAVE TO TELL YOU!
IT MEANS...
..."LOVER."
GET IT?
Let me write the kanji for you...
SHOOT...
IF SHE FINDS OUT I'M STILL ON LEAVE FROM SCHOOL...
...SHE MIGHT START CRY-ING...
No, she'll DEFI-NITELY cry!
Static
"Lover"...?
WHAT...
LOVER?!
WHY IS SHE SAYING "LOVER"?!
Is someone Bother-ing her again?!
Dispatch!
VOOOM

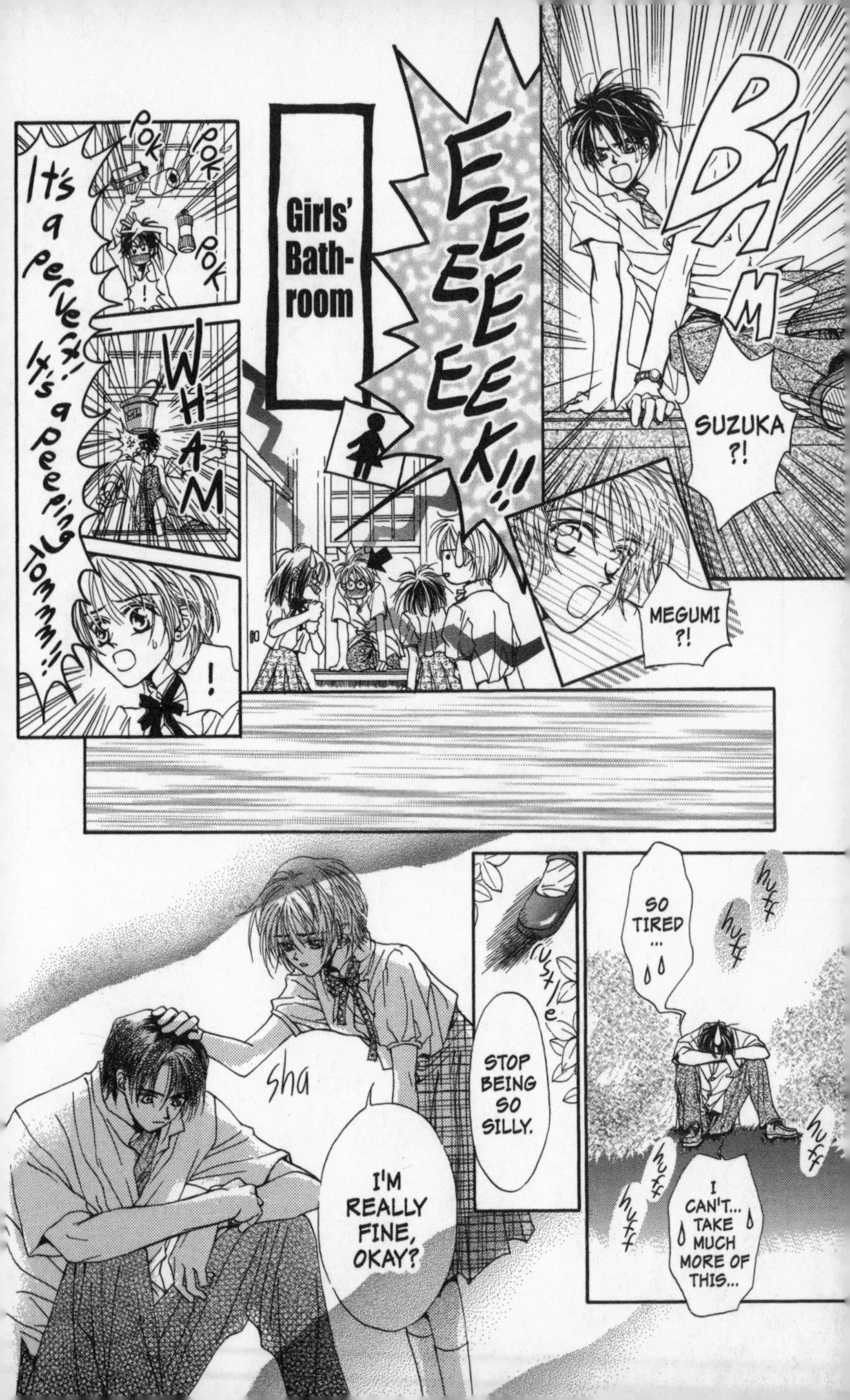
BAM
SUZUKA ?!
MEGUMI ?!
EEEEEK!!
Girls' Bathroom
POK
POK
POK
WHAM
It's a pervert! It's a peeping tommm!!
!
huff
huff
SO TIRED ...
I CAN'T... TAKE MUCH MORE OF THIS...
huff
huff
huff
rustle
STOP BEING SO SILLY.
sha
I'M REALLY FINE, OKAY?

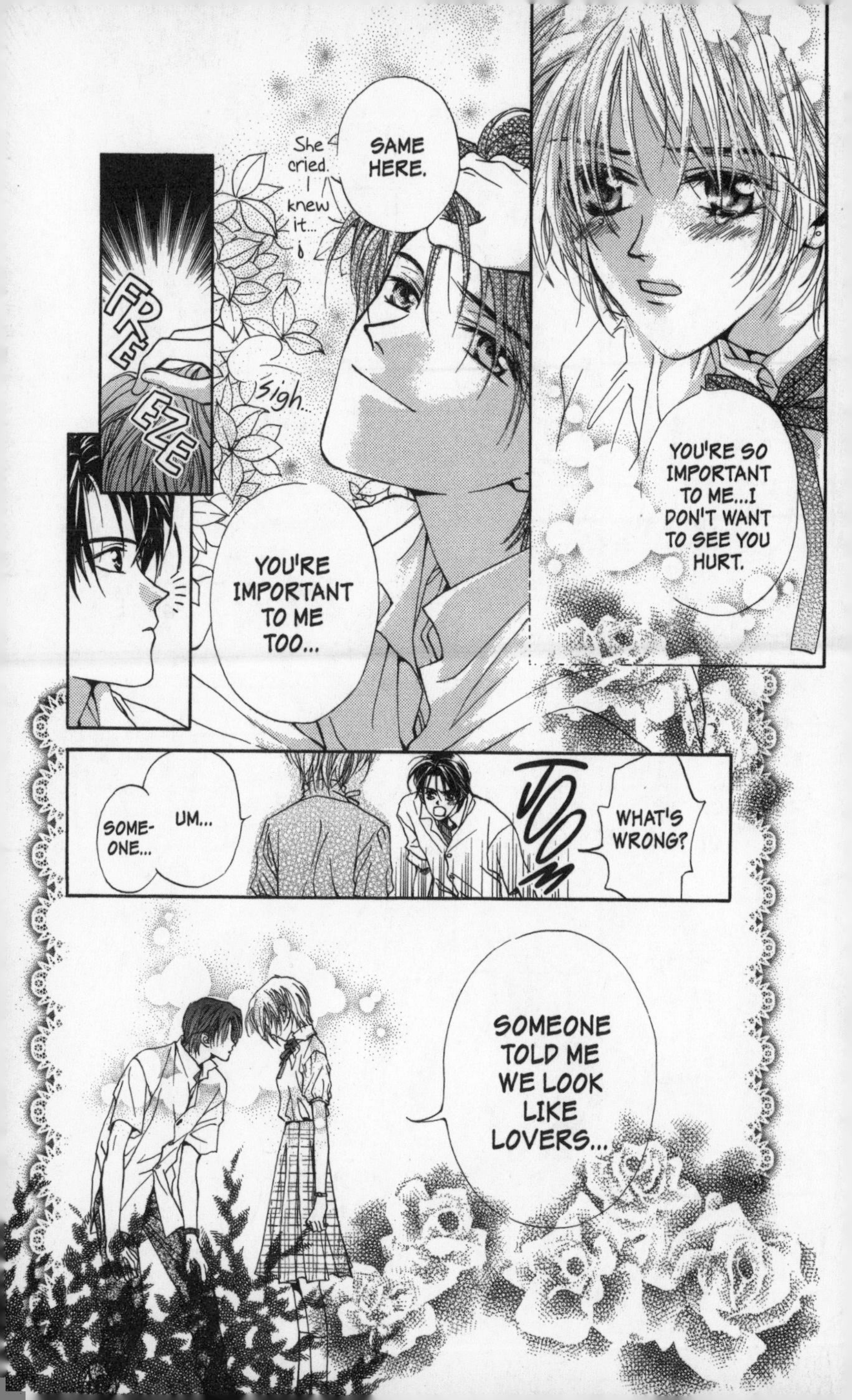
YOU'RE SO IMPORTANT TO ME...I DON'T WANT TO SEE YOU HURT.
SAME HERE.
She cried. I knew it...
sigh...
YOU'RE IMPORTANT TO ME TOO...
FREEZE
WHAT'S WRONG?
JOOM
UM...
SOME-ONE...
SOMEONE TOLD ME WE LOOK LIKE LOVERS...

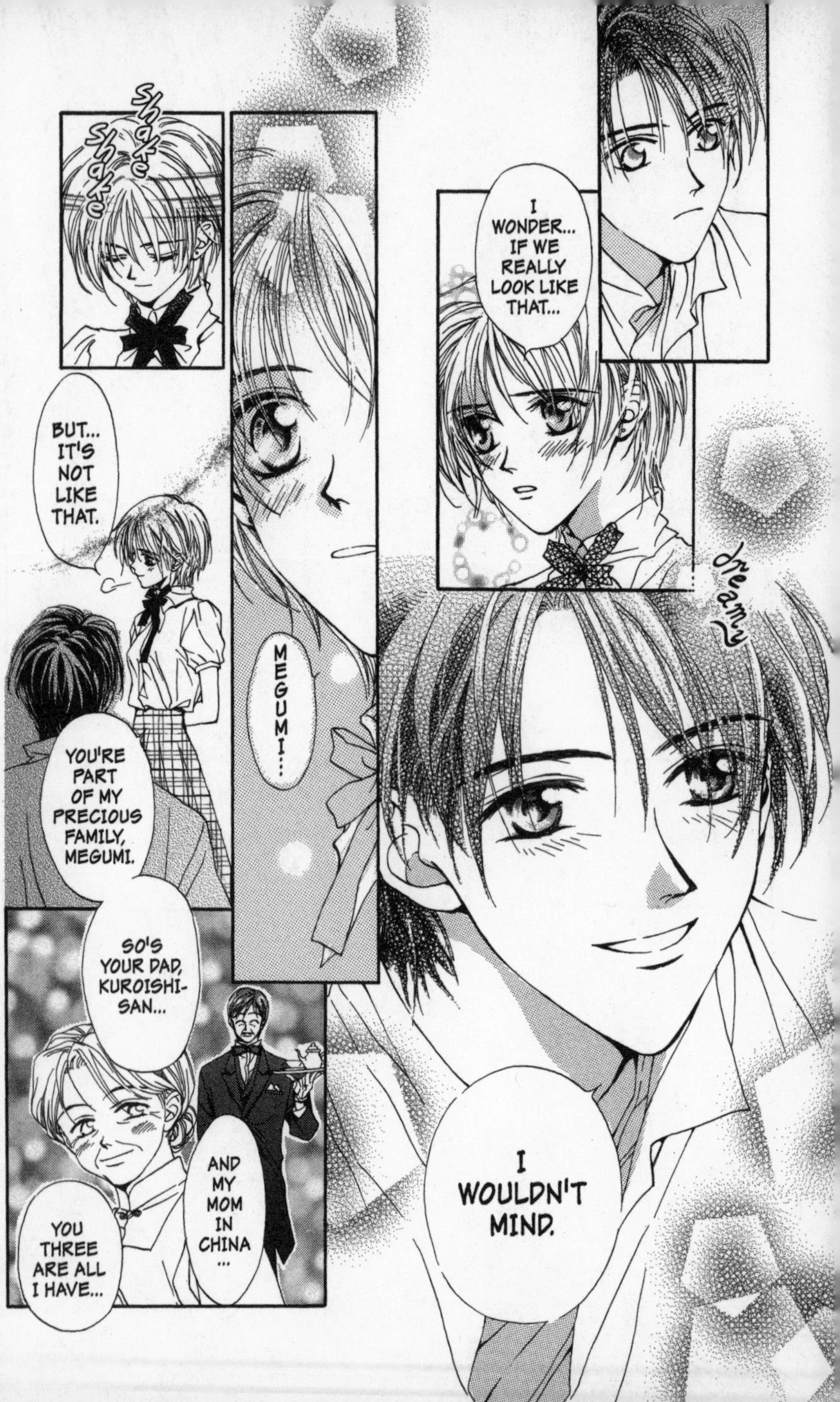
I WONDER... IF WE REALLY LOOK LIKE THAT...
dreamy
I WOULDN'T MIND.
MEGUMI...
Shake Shake
BUT... IT'S NOT LIKE THAT.
YOU'RE PART OF MY PRECIOUS FAMILY, MEGUMI.
SO'S YOUR DAD, KUROISHI-SAN...
AND MY MOM IN CHINA ...
YOU THREE ARE ALL I HAVE...

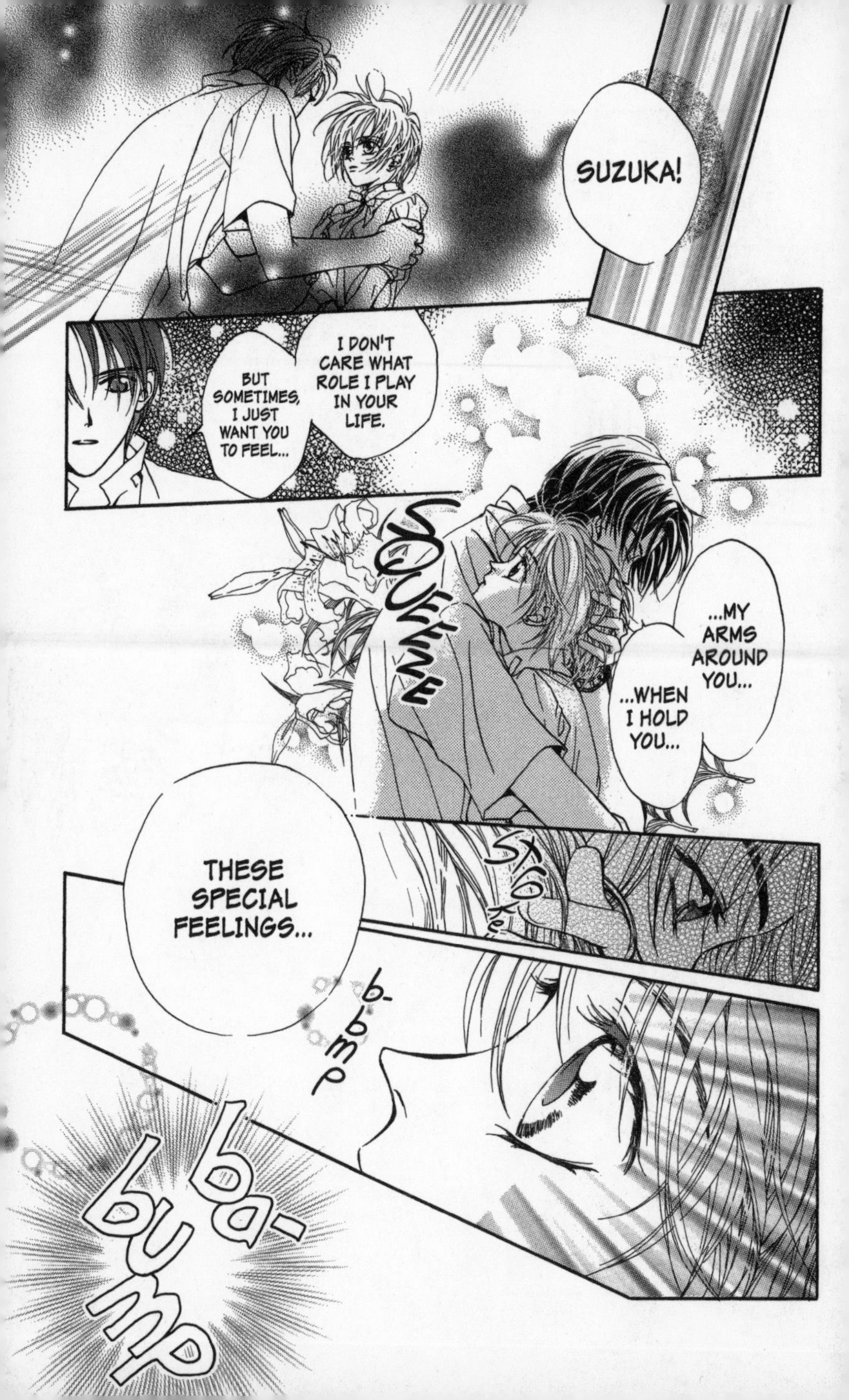
SUZUKA!
I DON'T CARE WHAT ROLE I PLAY IN YOUR LIFE.
BUT SOMETIMES, I JUST WANT YOU TO FEEL...
...MY ARMS AROUND YOU...
...WHEN I HOLD YOU...
SQUEEZE
STROKE
THESE SPECIAL FEELINGS...
b-bump
ba-bump

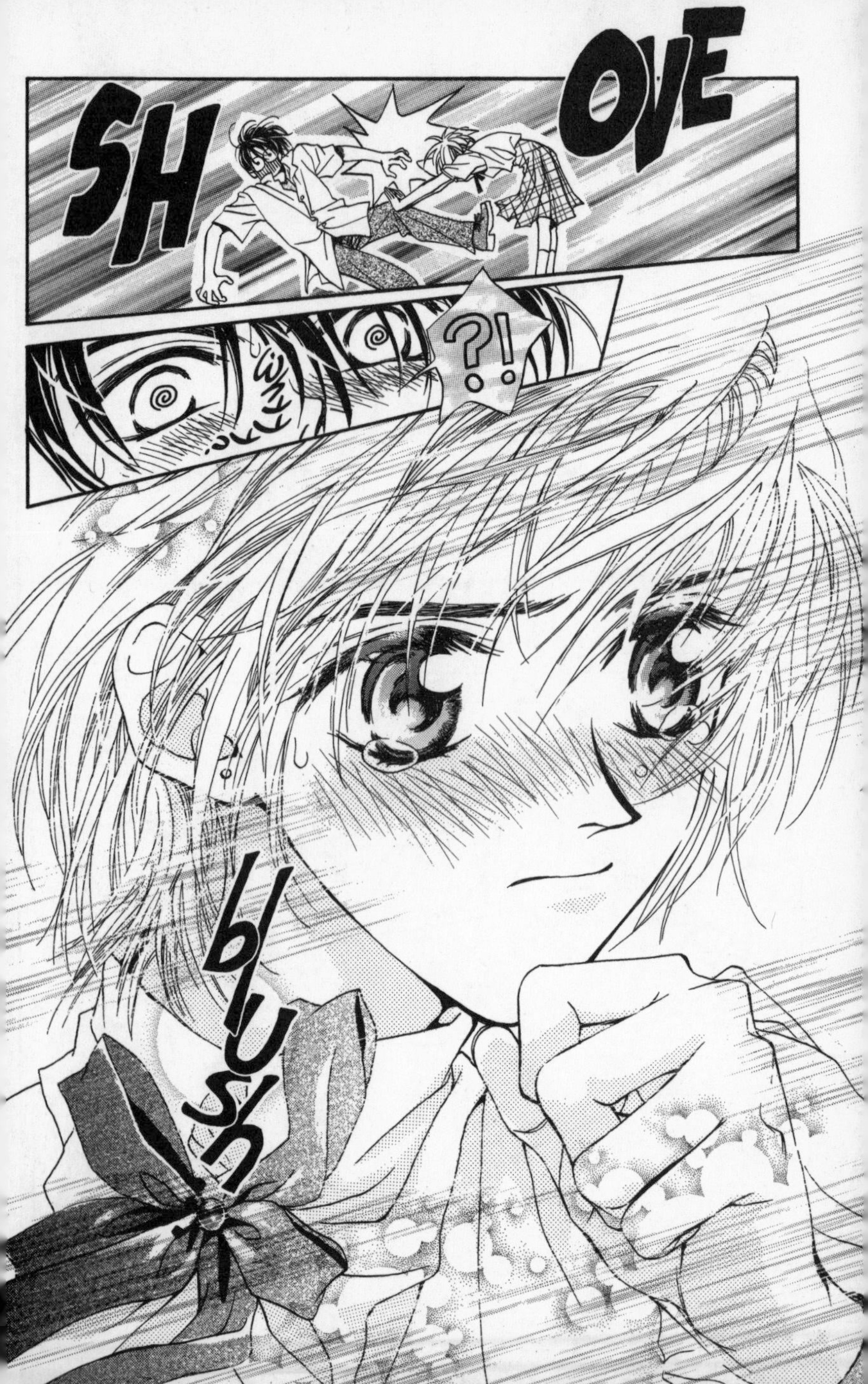
SH OVE
?!
blush

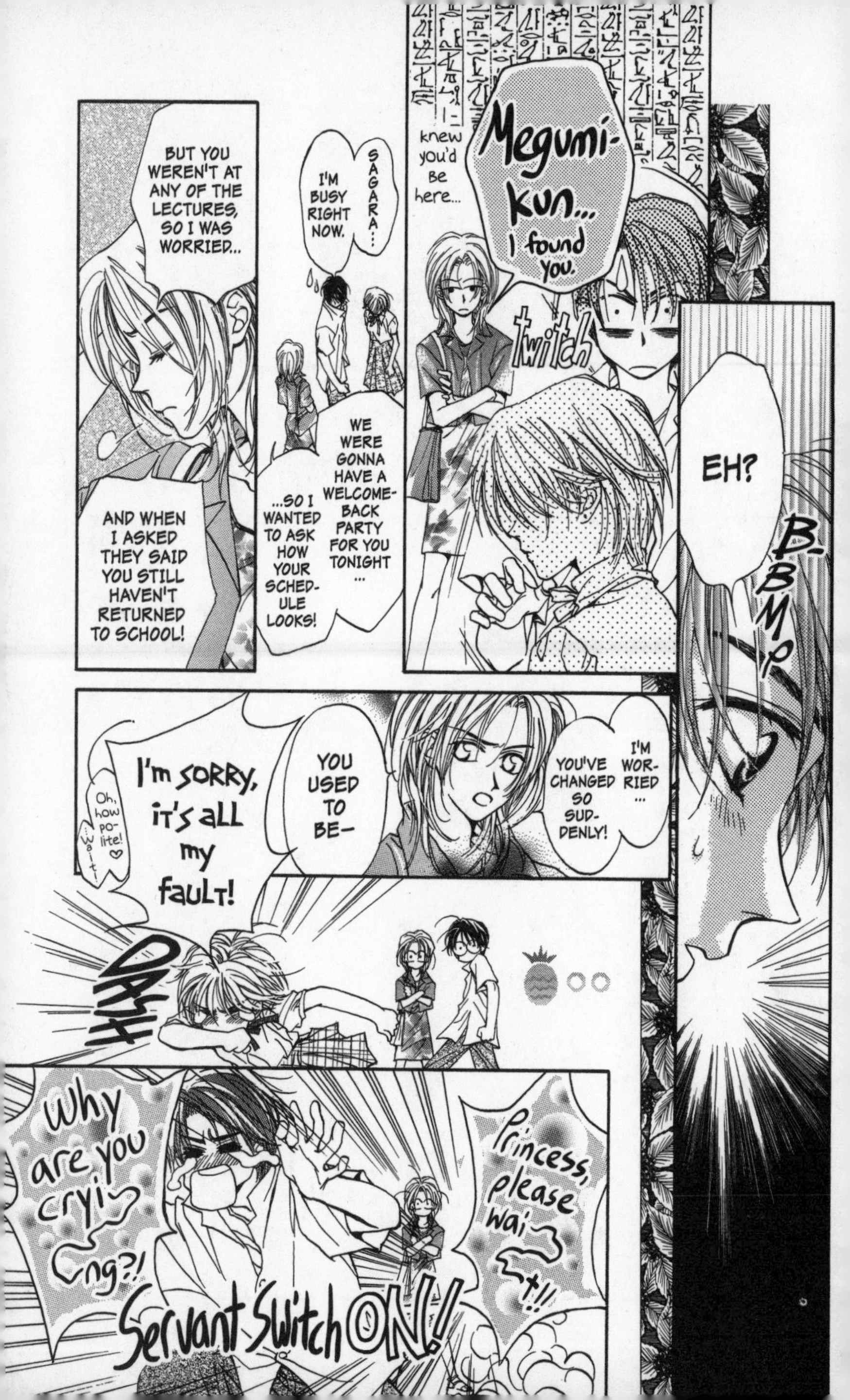
Megumi-kun... I found you.
knew you'd be here...
twitch
SAGARA...
I'M BUSY RIGHT NOW.
WE WERE GONNA HAVE A WELCOME-BACK PARTY FOR YOU TONIGHT...
...SO I WANTED TO ASK HOW YOUR SCHEDULE LOOKS!
BUT YOU WEREN'T AT ANY OF THE LECTURES, SO I WAS WORRIED...
AND WHEN I ASKED THEY SAID YOU STILL HAVEN'T RETURNED TO SCHOOL!
EH?
B-BMP
I'M WORRIED...
YOU'VE CHANGED SO SUDDENLY!
YOU USED TO BE—
I'm sorry, it's all my fault!
Oh, how polite! ♡
...Wait...
DASH
Princess, please wai~t!!
Why are you cryi~ng?!
Servant Switch ON!

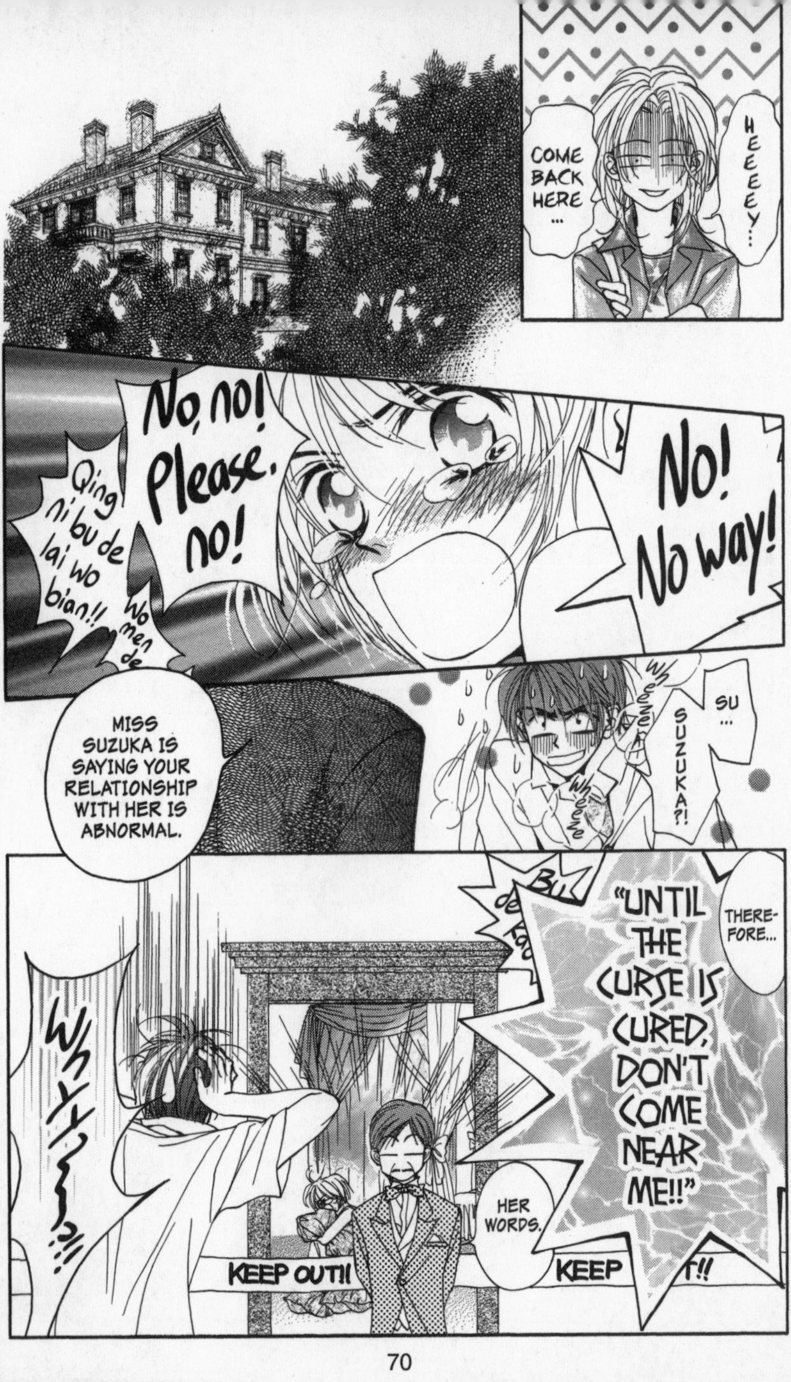
HEEEEY...
COME BACK HERE...
No! No way!
No, no! Please, no!
Qing ni bu de lai wo bian!!
Wo men de
SU...
SUZUKA?!
Wheeze
Wheeze
MISS SUZUKA IS SAYING YOUR RELATIONSHIP WITH HER IS ABNORMAL.
THEREFORE...
"UNTIL THE CURSE IS CURED, DON'T COME NEAR ME!!"
Bu de kao
HER WORDS.
KEEP T!!
KEEP OUT!!
Whyyy?!!

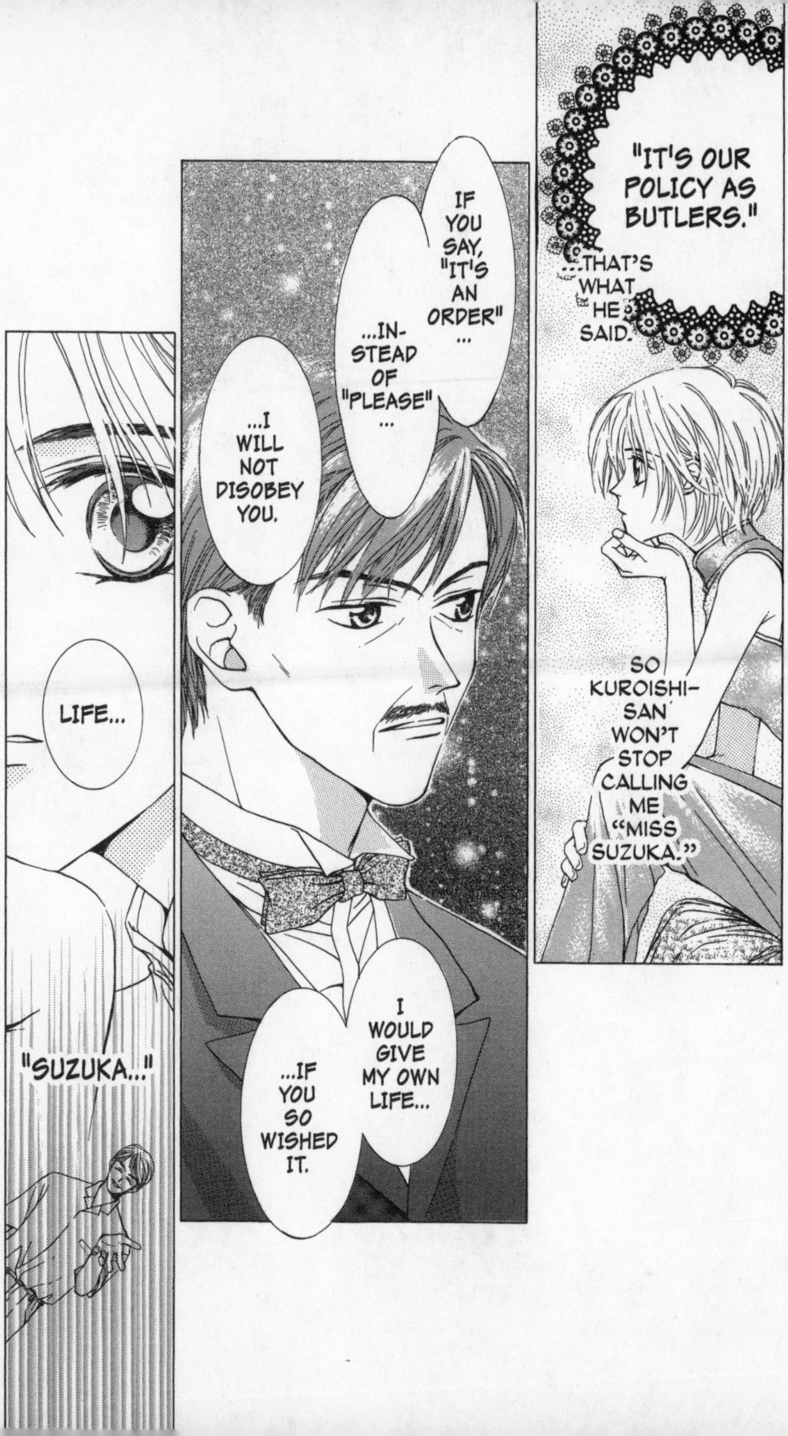
"IT'S OUR POLICY AS BUTLERS."
...THAT'S WHAT HE SAID.
SO KUROISHI-SAN WON'T STOP CALLING ME "MISS SUZUKA."
IF YOU SAY, "IT'S AN ORDER"...
...INSTEAD OF "PLEASE"...
...I WILL NOT DISOBEY YOU.
I WOULD GIVE MY OWN LIFE...
...IF YOU SO WISHED IT.
LIFE...
"SUZUKA..."

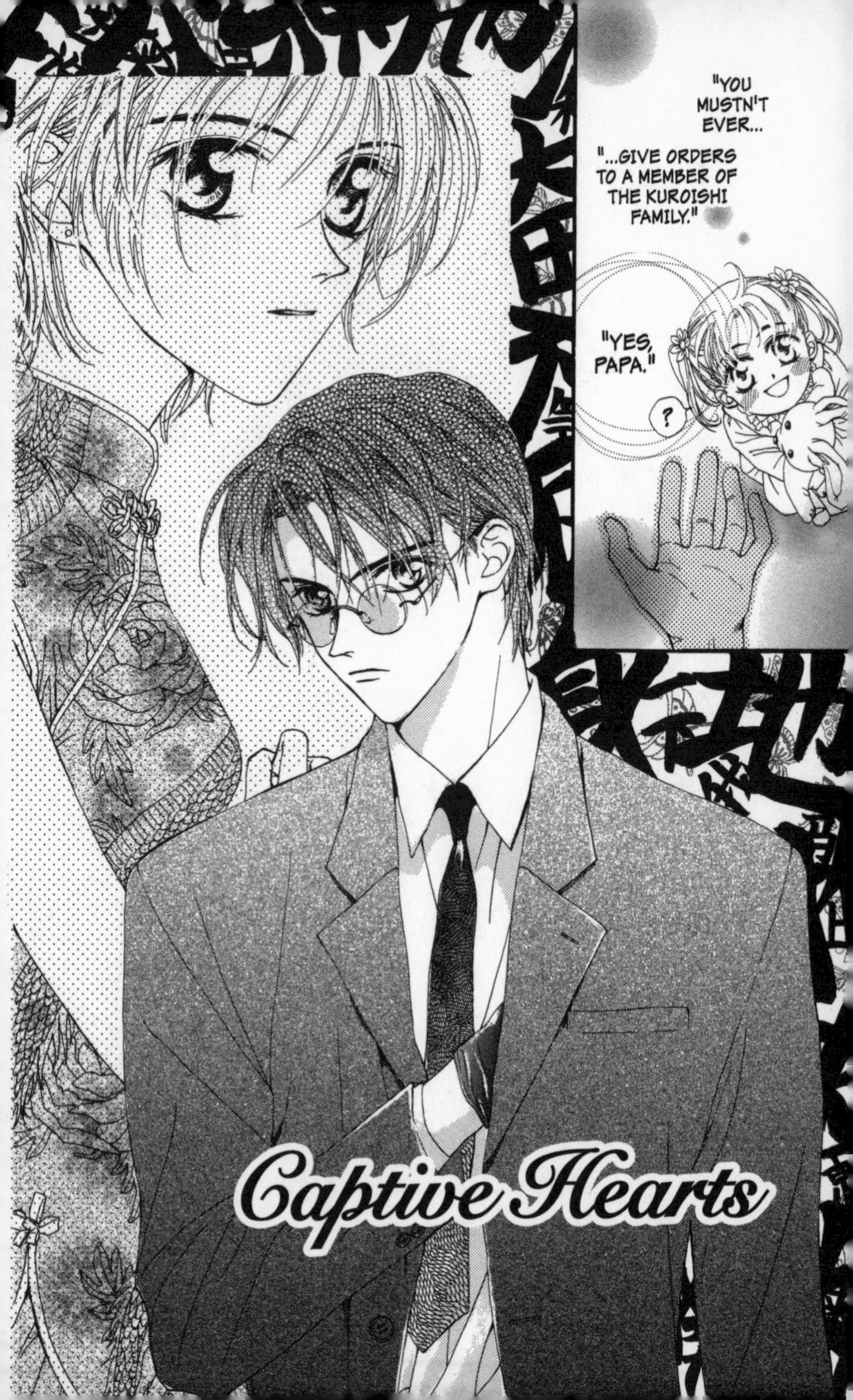
"YOU MUSTN'T EVER...
"...GIVE ORDERS TO A MEMBER OF THE KUROISHI FAMILY."
"YES, PAPA."
?
Captive Hearts

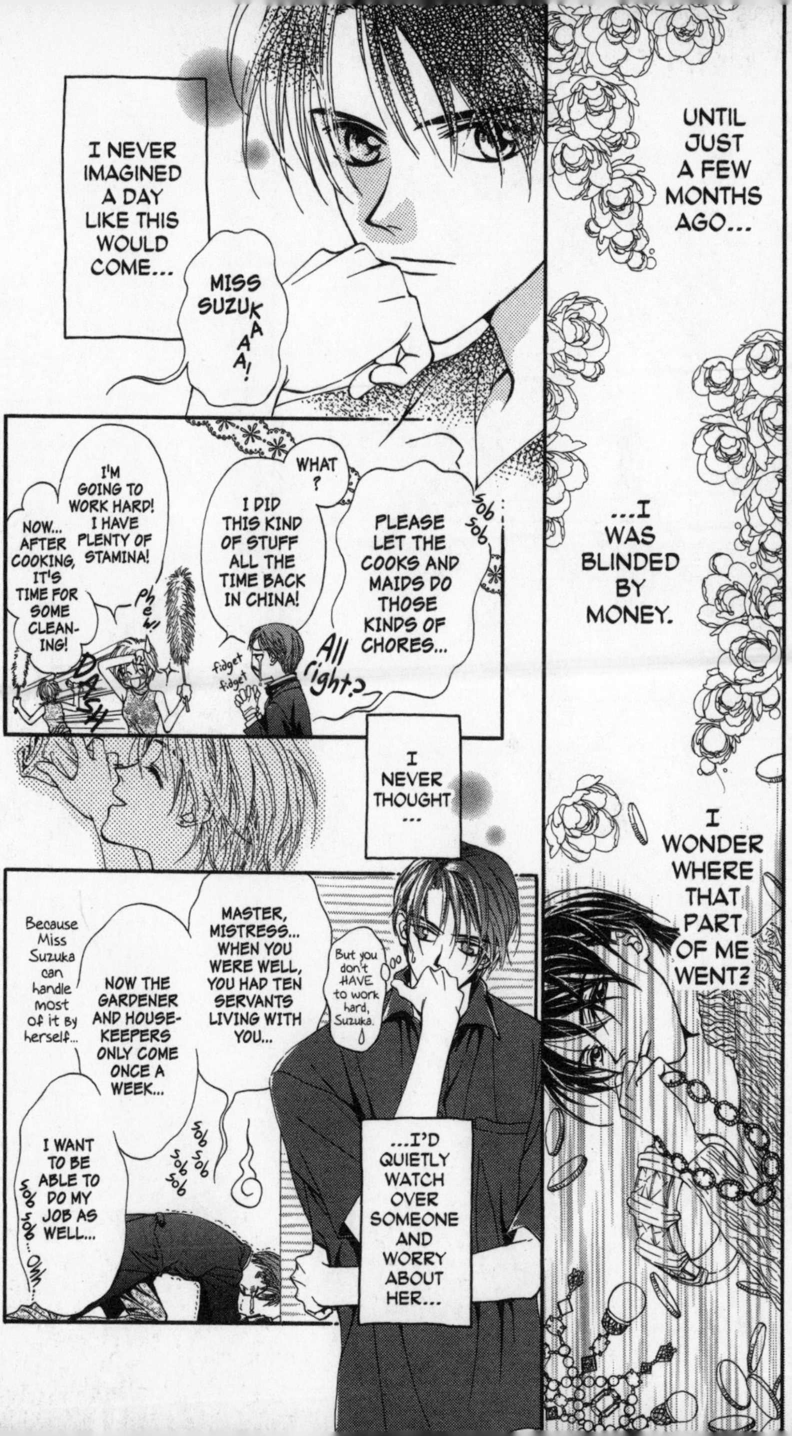
UNTIL JUST A FEW MONTHS AGO...
...I WAS BLINDED BY MONEY.
I WONDER WHERE THAT PART OF ME WENT?
I NEVER IMAGINED A DAY LIKE THIS WOULD COME...
MISS SUZUKAAAA!
PLEASE LET THE COOKS AND MAIDS DO THOSE KINDS OF CHORES...
All right?
sob sob
WHAT?
I DID THIS KIND OF STUFF ALL THE TIME BACK IN CHINA!
I'M GOING TO WORK HARD! I HAVE PLENTY OF STAMINA!
NOW... AFTER COOKING, IT'S TIME FOR SOME CLEANING!
Phew!!
fidget fidget
DASH
I NEVER THOUGHT...
But you don't HAVE to work hard, Suzuka.
MASTER, MISTRESS... WHEN YOU WERE WELL, YOU HAD TEN SERVANTS LIVING WITH YOU...
NOW THE GARDENER AND HOUSEKEEPERS ONLY COME ONCE A WEEK...
Because Miss Suzuka can handle most of it by herself...
sob sob sob sob
I WANT TO BE ABLE TO DO MY JOB AS WELL...
sob sob... ow
...I'D QUIETLY WATCH OVER SOMEONE AND WORRY ABOUT HER...

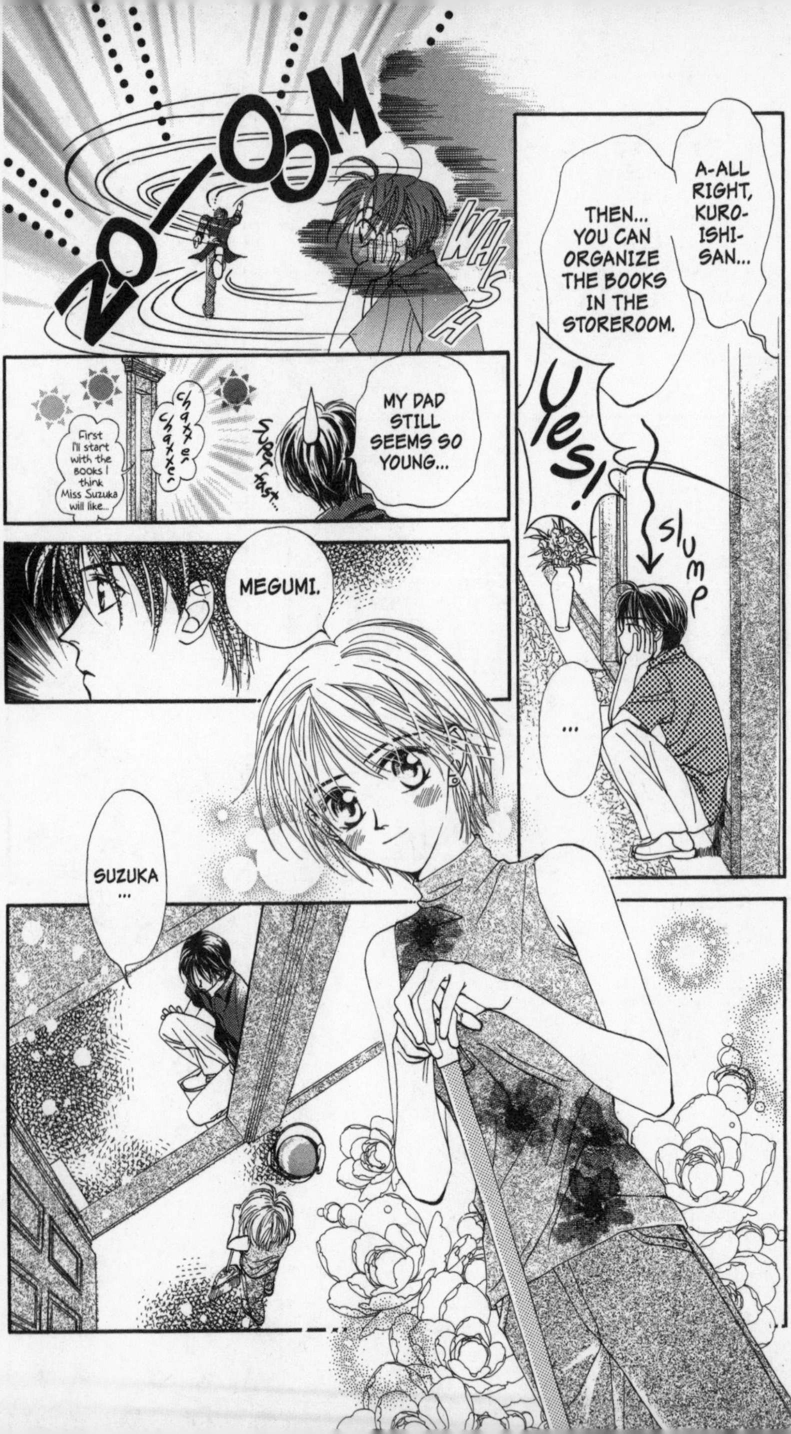
A-ALL RIGHT, KURO-ISHI-SAN...
THEN... YOU CAN ORGANIZE THE BOOKS IN THE STOREROOM.
YES!
ZO-OOM
WHASH
SLUMP
...
MY DAD STILL SEEMS SO YOUNG...
Super fast...
chaxxer chaxxer
First I'll start with the books I think Miss Suzuka will like...
MEGUMI.
SUZUKA ...

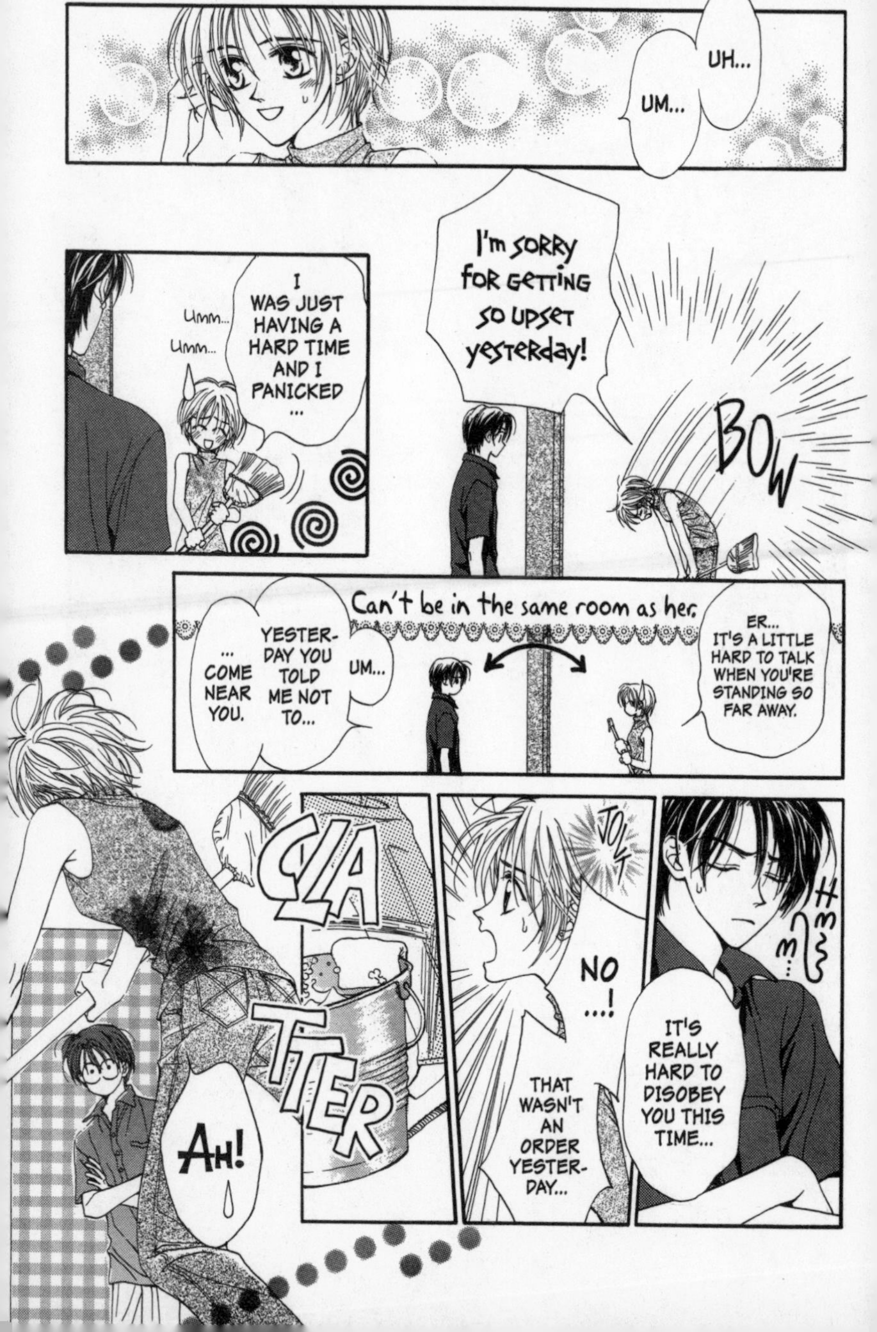
UH...
UM...
I'm SORRY FOR GETTING SO UPSET yesterday!
BOW
Umm...
Umm...
I WAS JUST HAVING A HARD TIME AND I PANICKED ...
ER... IT'S A LITTLE HARD TO TALK WHEN YOU'RE STANDING SO FAR AWAY.
Can't be in the same room as her.
UM...
YESTER-DAY YOU TOLD ME NOT TO...
... COME NEAR YOU.
HMMM...
IT'S REALLY HARD TO DISOBEY YOU THIS TIME...
JOLT
NO ...!
THAT WASN'T AN ORDER YESTER-DAY...
CLATTER
AH!

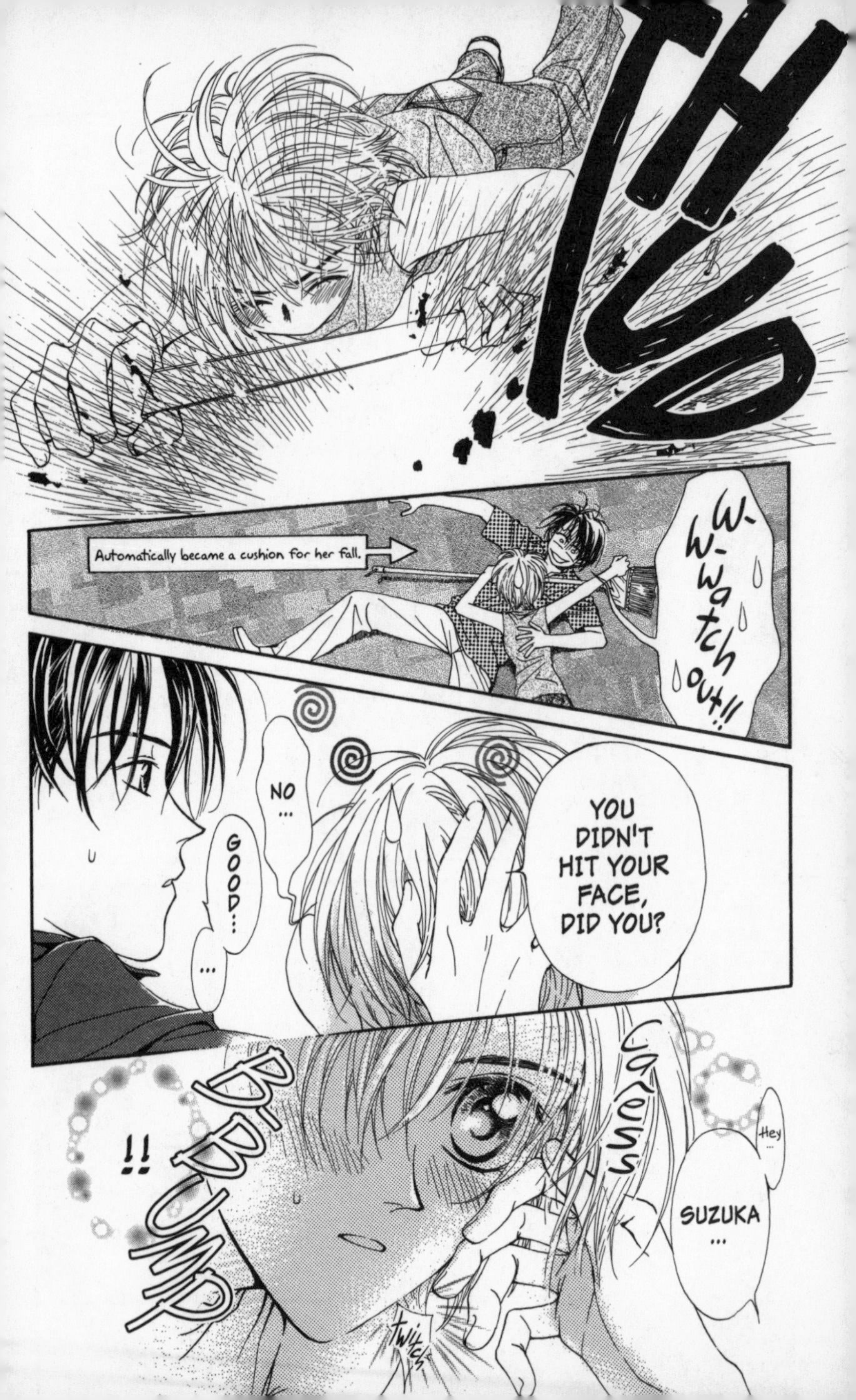
THUD
W-W-watch out!!
Automatically became a cushion for her fall.
YOU DIDN'T HIT YOUR FACE, DID YOU?
NO ...
GOOD...
...
Hey ...
SUZUKA ...
caress
BADUMP
!!
twitch

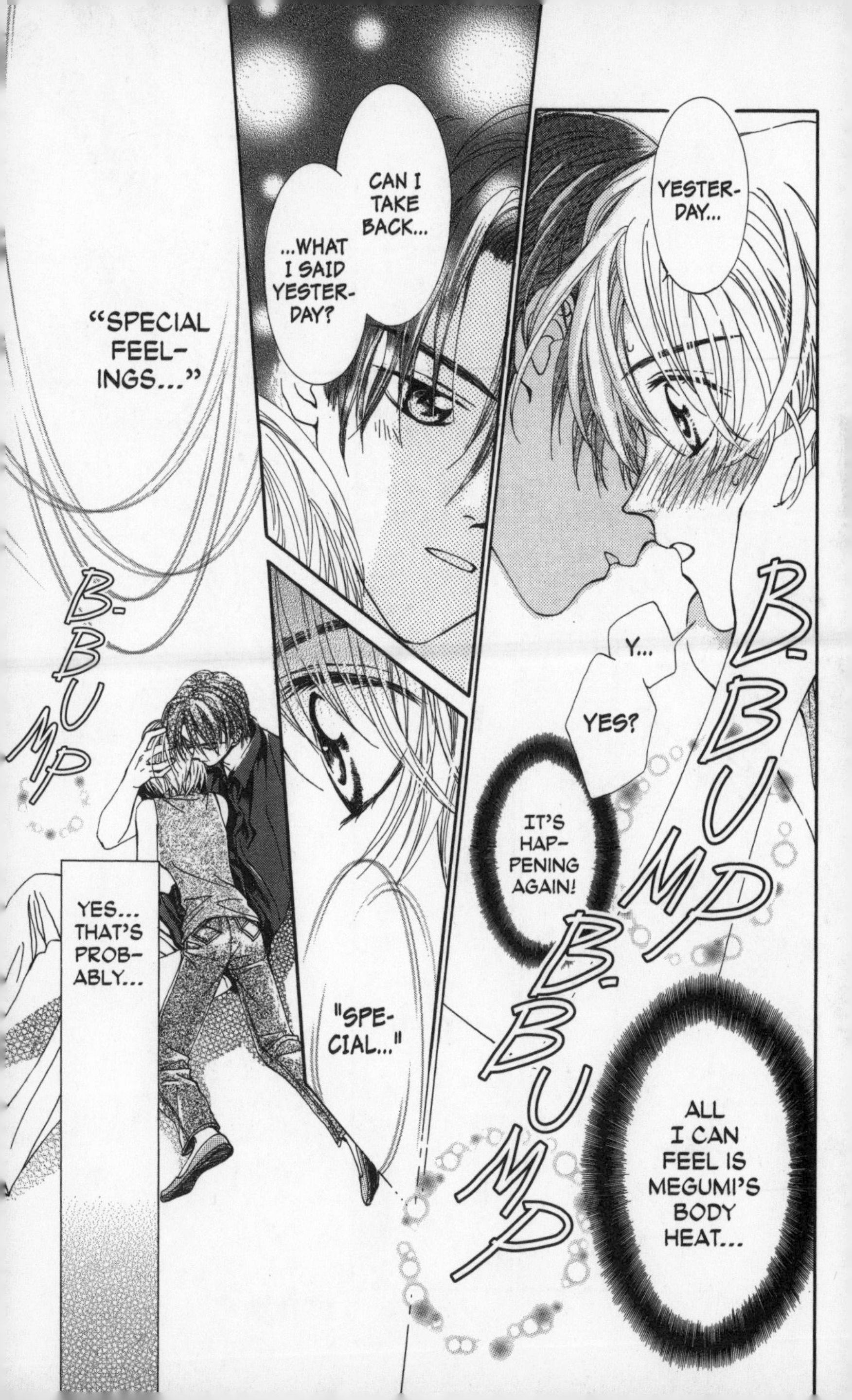
YESTER-DAY...
Y...
YES?
B-BUMP
CAN I TAKE BACK...
...WHAT I SAID YESTER-DAY?
IT'S HAP-PENING AGAIN!
"SPE-CIAL..."
B-BUMP
ALL I CAN FEEL IS MEGUMI'S BODY HEAT...
"SPECIAL FEEL-INGS..."
B-BUMP
YES... THAT'S PROB-ABLY...

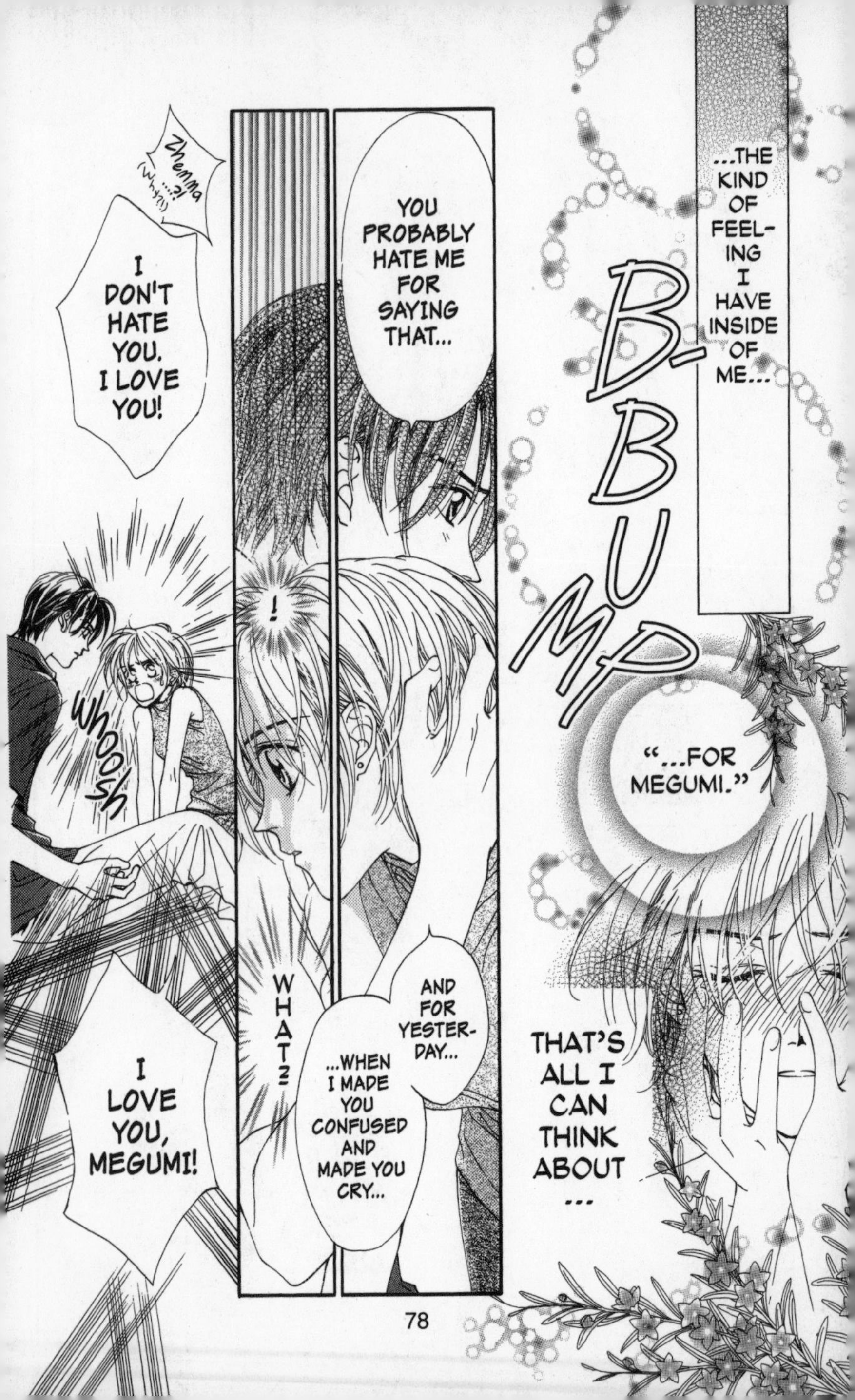
...THE KIND OF FEELING I HAVE INSIDE OF ME...
B-BUMP
"...FOR MEGUMI."
THAT'S ALL I CAN THINK ABOUT ...
YOU PROBABLY HATE ME FOR SAYING THAT...
AND FOR YESTERDAY...
...WHEN I MADE YOU CONFUSED AND MADE YOU CRY...
!
WHAT?
Zhemma ...?!
(Why?!)
I DON'T HATE YOU. I LOVE YOU!
WHOOSH
I LOVE YOU, MEGUMI!

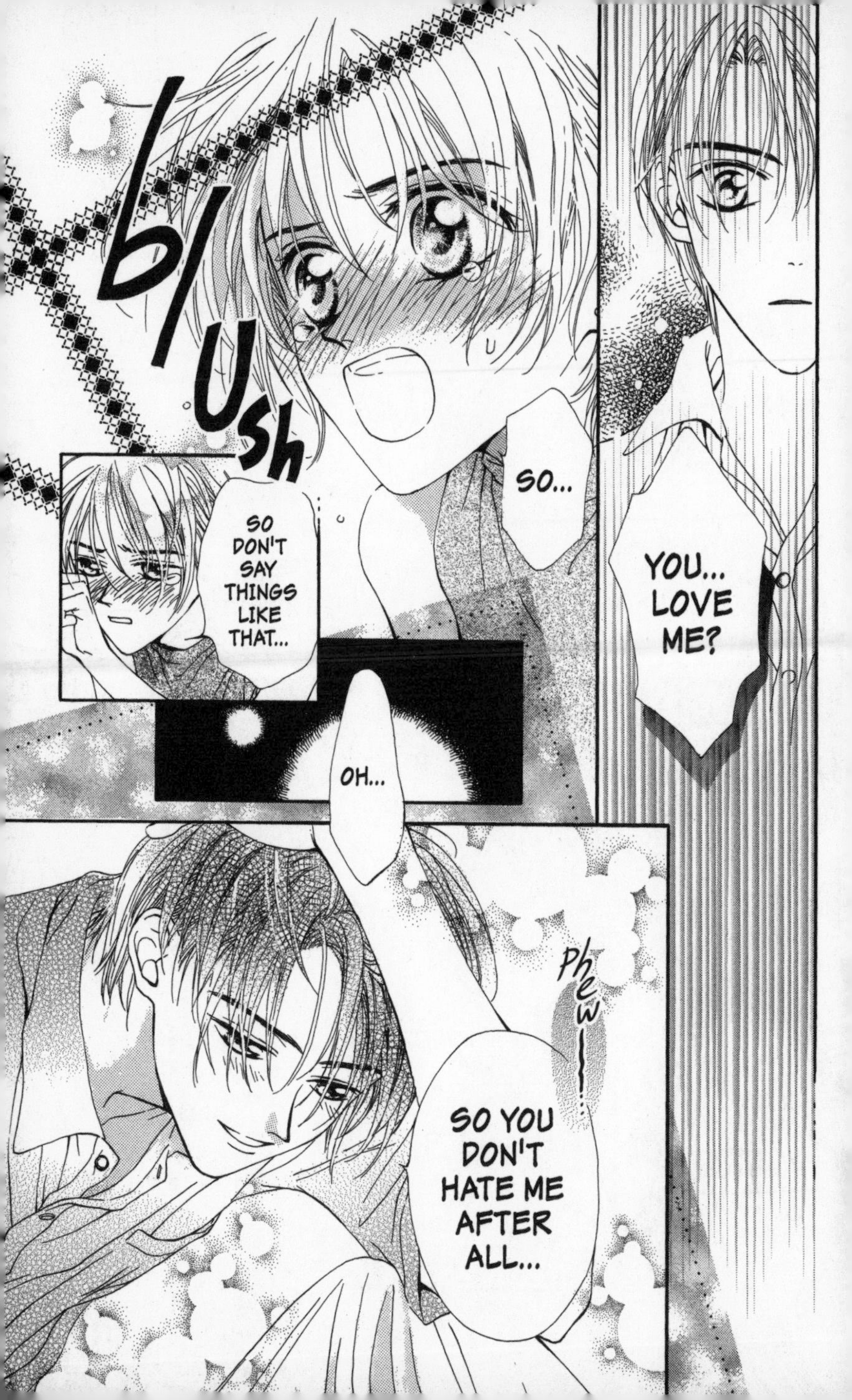
YOU... LOVE ME?
blush
SO...
SO DON'T SAY THINGS LIKE THAT...
OH...
Phew—...
SO YOU DON'T HATE ME AFTER ALL...

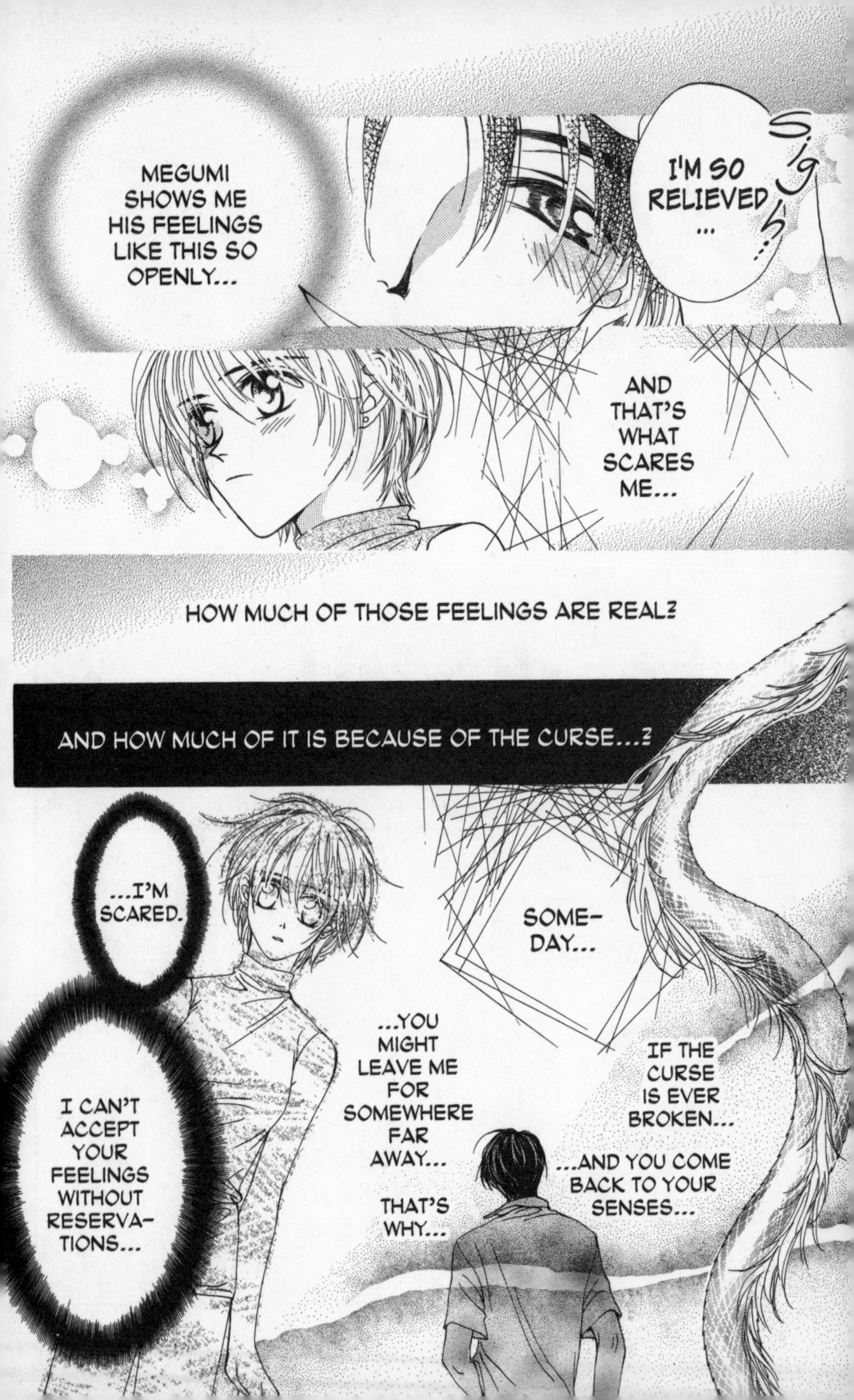
Sigh...
I'M SO RELIEVED...
MEGUMI SHOWS ME HIS FEELINGS LIKE THIS SO OPENLY...
AND THAT'S WHAT SCARES ME...
HOW MUCH OF THOSE FEELINGS ARE REAL?
AND HOW MUCH OF IT IS BECAUSE OF THE CURSE...?
SOME-DAY...
IF THE CURSE IS EVER BROKEN...
...AND YOU COME BACK TO YOUR SENSES...
...YOU MIGHT LEAVE ME FOR SOMEWHERE FAR AWAY...
THAT'S WHY...
...I'M SCARED.
I CAN'T ACCEPT YOUR FEELINGS WITHOUT RESERVA-TIONS...

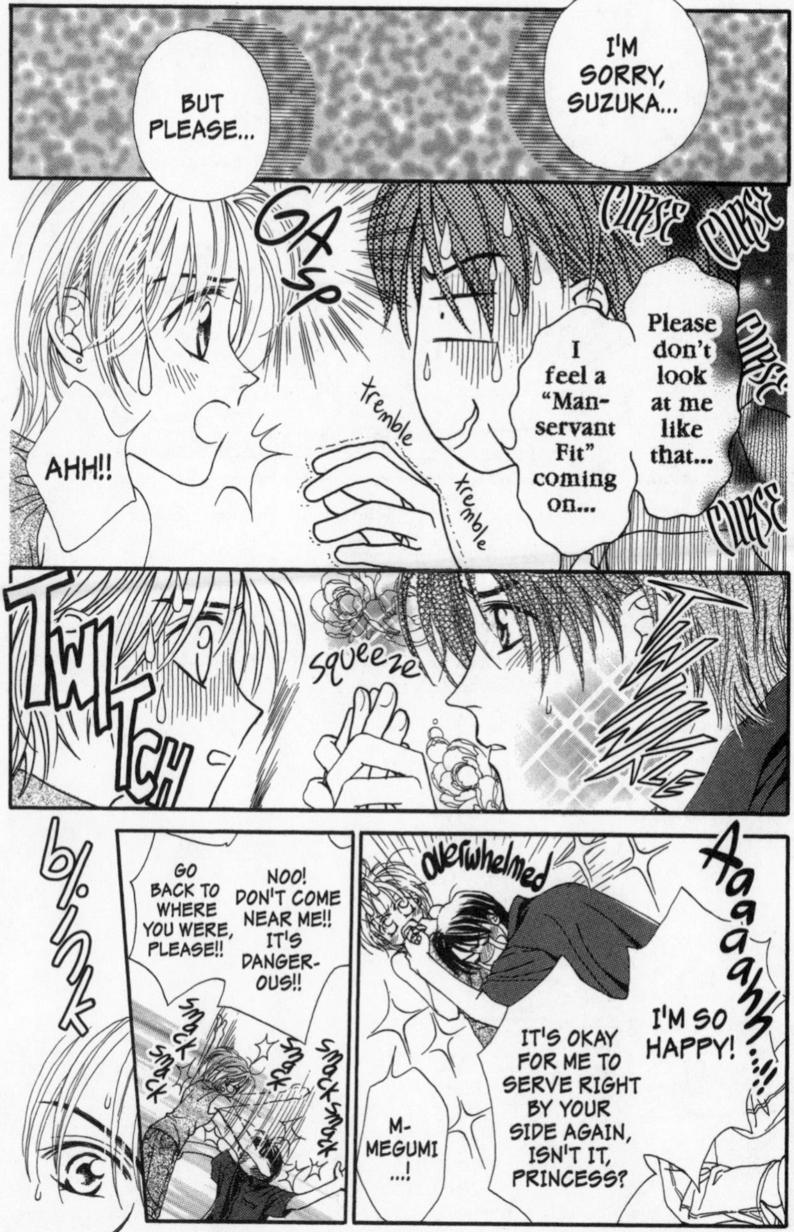
I'M SORRY, SUZUKA...
BUT PLEASE...
CURSE
CURSE
CURSE
CURSE
Please don't look at me like that...
I feel a "Man-servant Fit" coming on...
tremble
tremble
GASP
AHH!!
TWINKLE
squeeze
TWITCH
Aaaaahh...!!
I'M SO HAPPY!
overwhelmed
IT'S OKAY FOR ME TO SERVE RIGHT BY YOUR SIDE AGAIN, ISN'T IT, PRINCESS?
M-MEGUMI ...!
NOO! DON'T COME NEAR ME!! IT'S DANGER-OUS!!
GO BACK TO WHERE YOU WERE, PLEASE!!
smack smack
smack smack
smack smack
blink

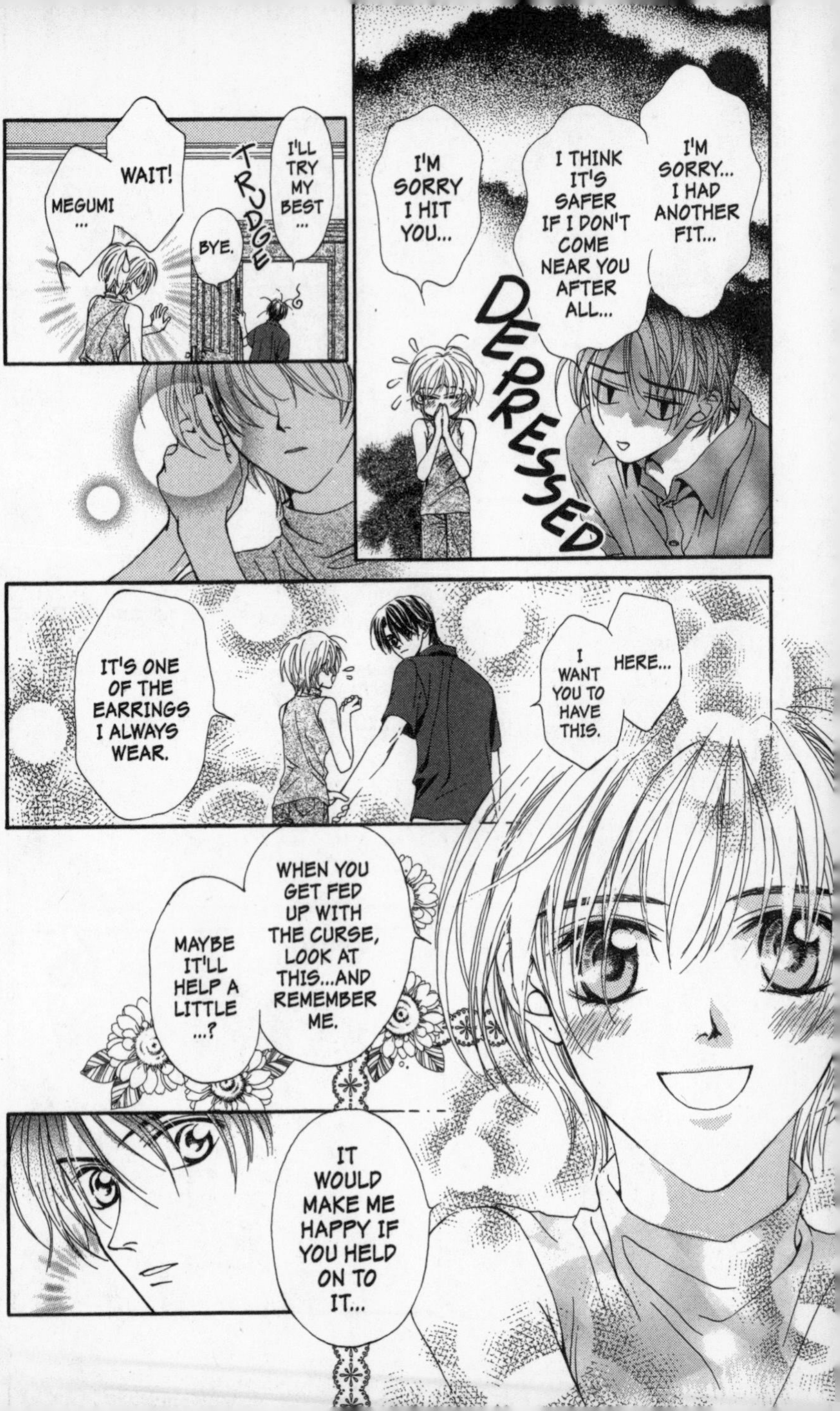

I'M SORRY... I HAD ANOTHER FIT...
I THINK IT'S SAFER IF I DON'T COME NEAR YOU AFTER ALL...
I'M SORRY I HIT YOU...
DEPRESSED
I'LL TRY MY BEST...
TRUDGE
BYE.
WAIT!
MEGUMI...
HERE...
I WANT YOU TO HAVE THIS.
IT'S ONE OF THE EARRINGS I ALWAYS WEAR.
WHEN YOU GET FED UP WITH THE CURSE, LOOK AT THIS...AND REMEMBER ME.
MAYBE IT'LL HELP A LITTLE...?
IT WOULD MAKE ME HAPPY IF YOU HELD ON TO IT...

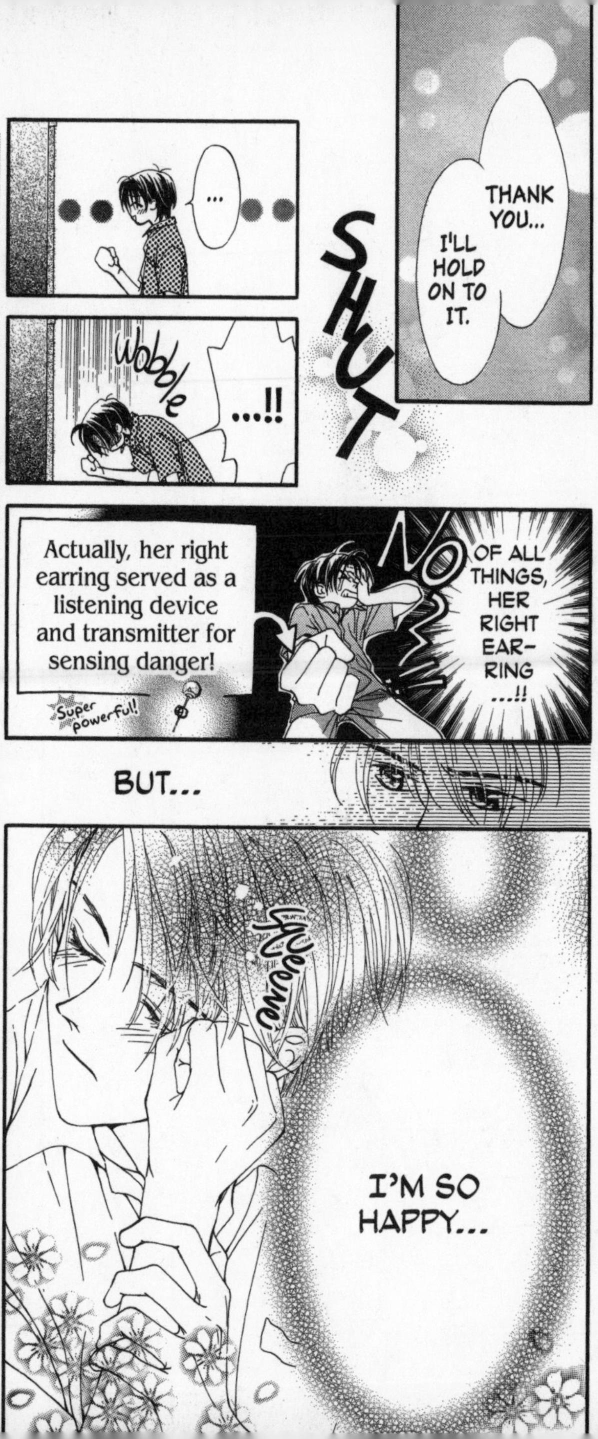
THANK YOU...
I'LL HOLD ON TO IT.
SHUT
...
Wobble
...!!
NO
OF ALL THINGS, HER RIGHT EAR-RING ...!!
Actually, her right earring served as a listening device and transmitter for sensing danger!
Super powerful!
BUT...
I'M SO HAPPY...

3

This is what one of my colleagues said two or three years ago...

(when I was only drawing manga on the side)

"Since I'm already going to read manga, I want it to be a story that could never happen in real life. A realistic manga? No, I'm tired of reality... Show me a fantasy!"

That was long.

I thought about that comment long and hard...

And what was born from that was...

...Captive Hearts.

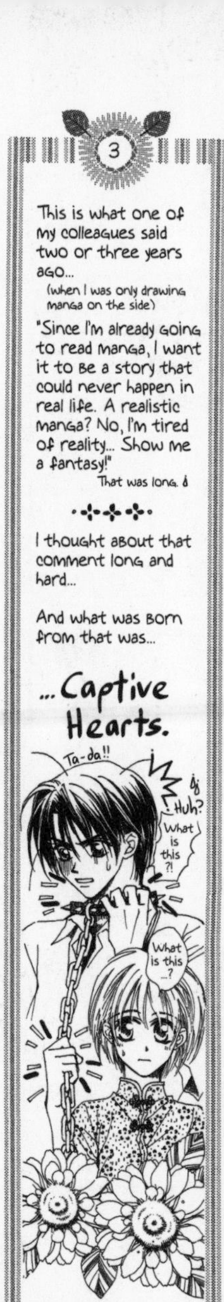
Ta-da!!
Huh?
What is this ?!
What is this ...?

Sorry this manga is so silly.

But it takes a lot of work to be this silly!

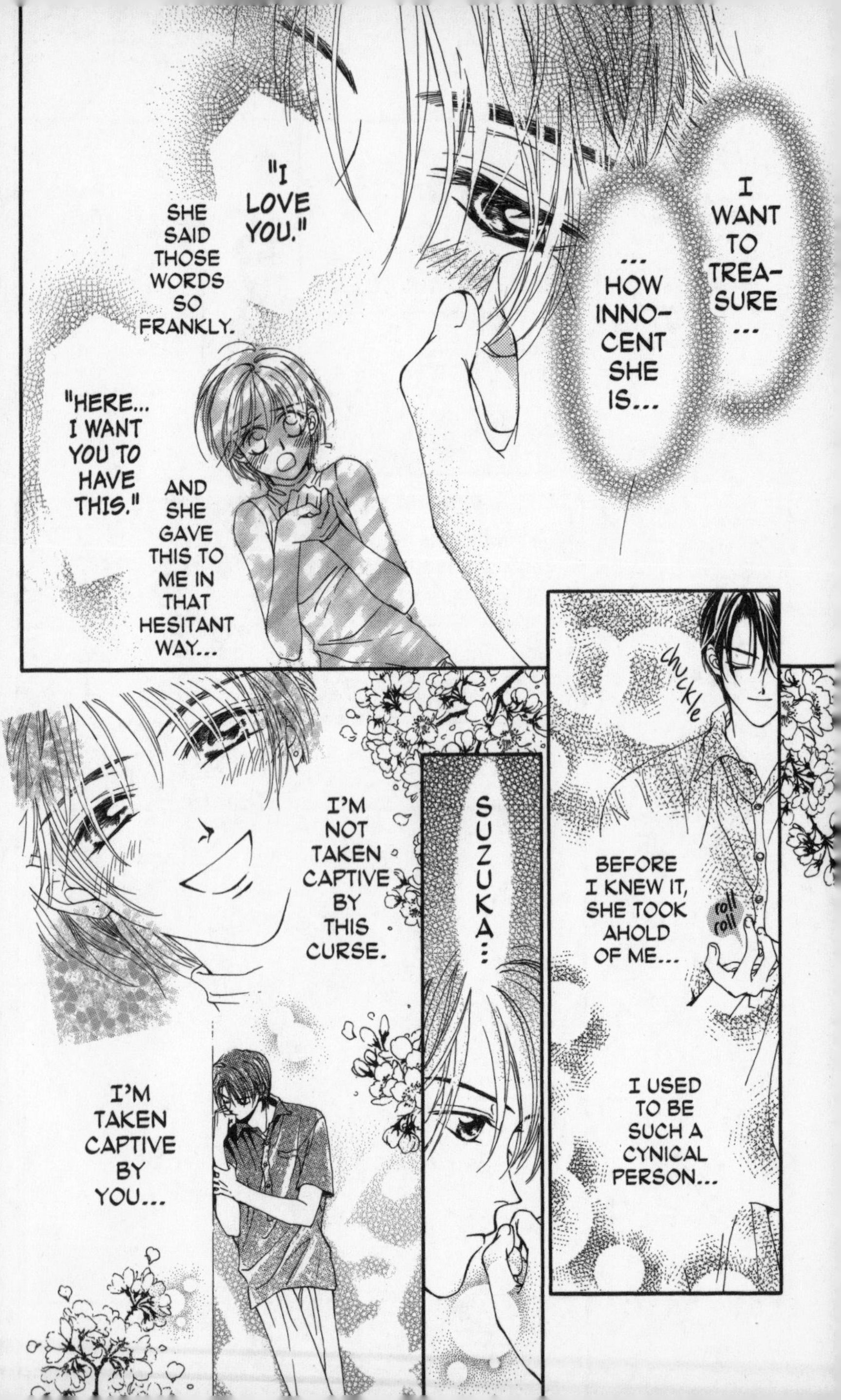
I WANT TO TREASURE...
...HOW INNOCENT SHE IS...
"I LOVE YOU."
SHE SAID THOSE WORDS SO FRANKLY.
"HERE... I WANT YOU TO HAVE THIS."
AND SHE GAVE THIS TO ME IN THAT HESITANT WAY...
chuckle
BEFORE I KNEW IT, SHE TOOK AHOLD OF ME...
roll roll
I USED TO BE SUCH A CYNICAL PERSON...
SUZUKA...
I'M NOT TAKEN CAPTIVE BY THIS CURSE.
I'M TAKEN CAPTIVE BY YOU...

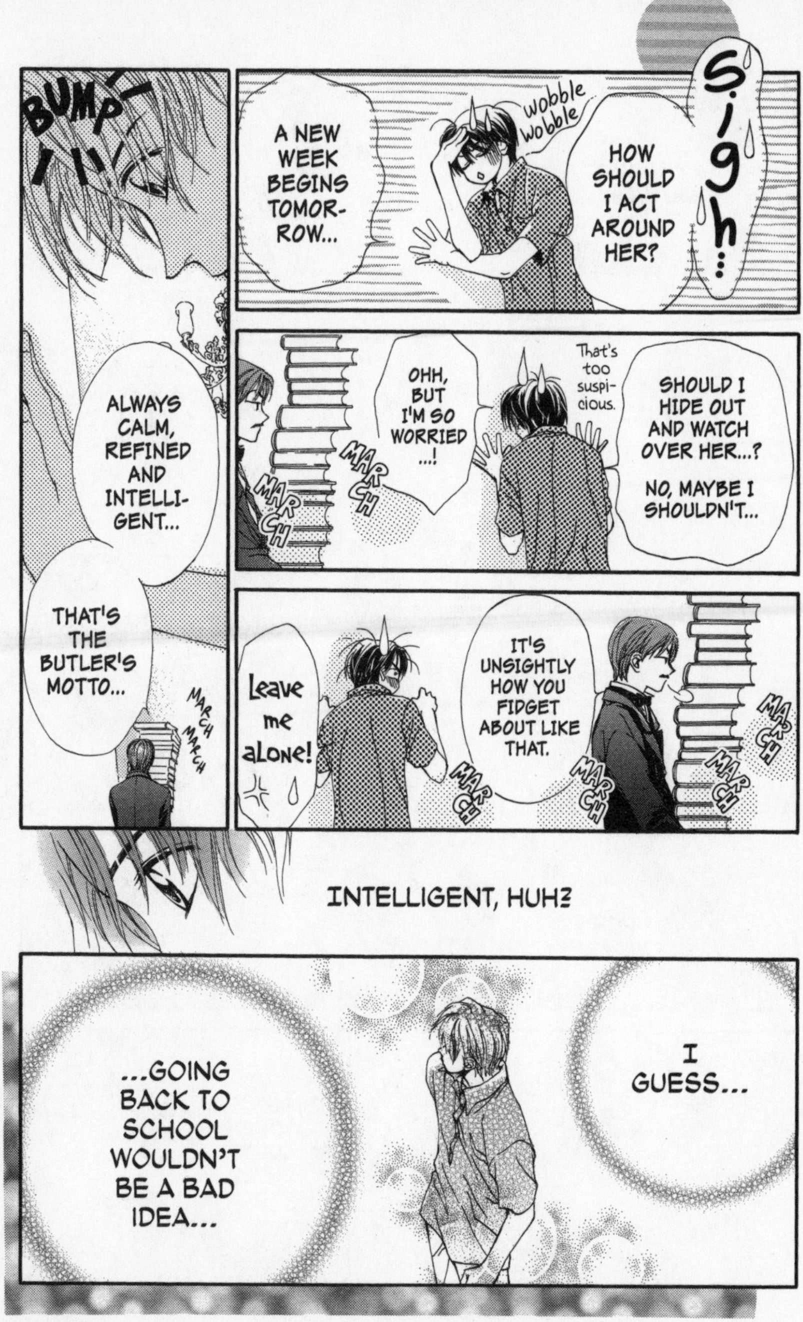
Sigh...
HOW SHOULD I ACT AROUND HER?
wobble wobble
A NEW WEEK BEGINS TOMORROW...
SHOULD I HIDE OUT AND WATCH OVER HER...?
NO, MAYBE I SHOULDN'T...
That's too suspicious.
OHH, BUT I'M SO WORRIED...!
MARCH
MARCH
MARCH
MARCH
IT'S UNSIGHTLY HOW YOU FIDGET ABOUT LIKE THAT.
MARCH
MARCH
Leave me alone!
BUMP
ALWAYS CALM, REFINED AND INTELLIGENT...
THAT'S THE BUTLER'S MOTTO...
MARCH MARCH
INTELLIGENT, HUH?
I GUESS...
...GOING BACK TO SCHOOL WOULDN'T BE A BAD IDEA...

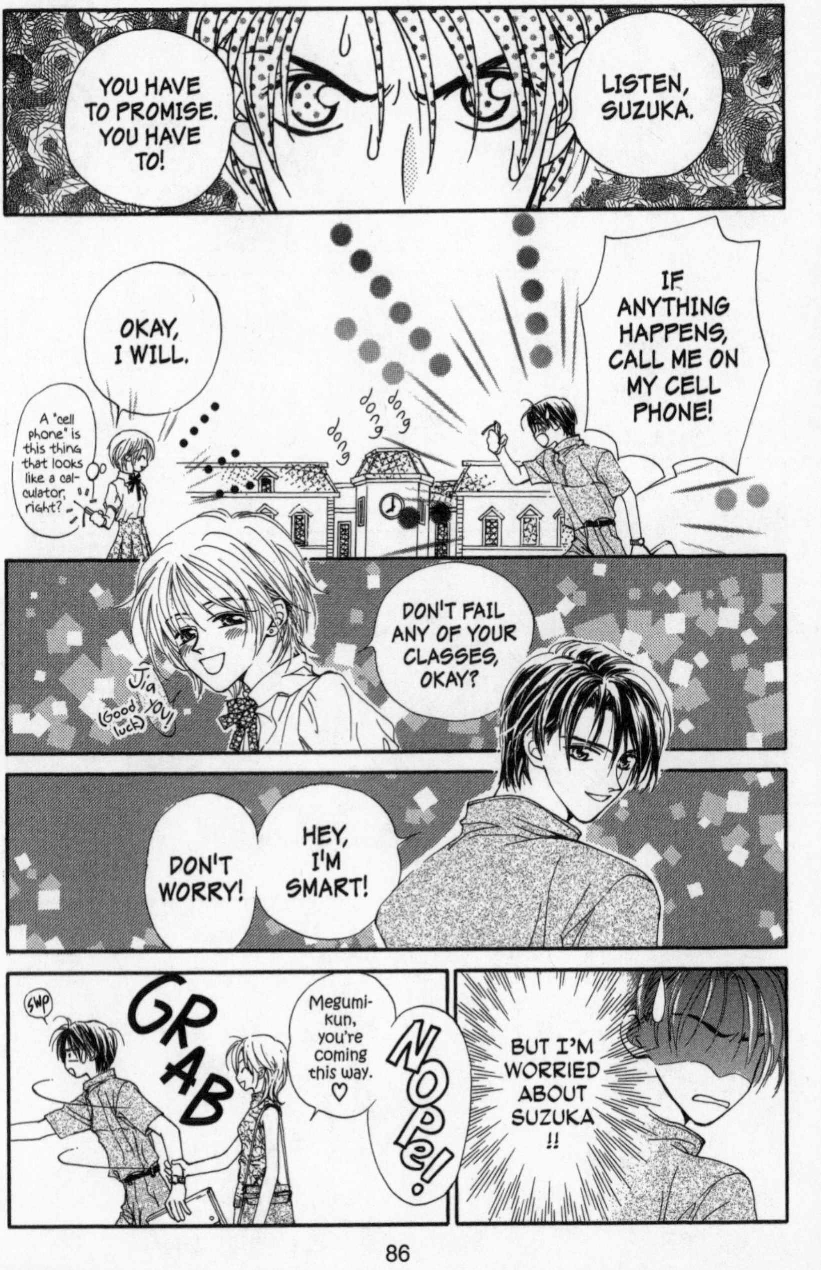
LISTEN, SUZUKA.
YOU HAVE TO PROMISE. YOU HAVE TO!
IF ANYTHING HAPPENS, CALL ME ON MY CELL PHONE!
dong dong dong
OKAY, I WILL.
A "cell phone" is this thing that looks like a calculator, right?
DON'T FAIL ANY OF YOUR CLASSES, OKAY?
Jia YOU! (Good luck)
HEY, I'M SMART!
DON'T WORRY!
BUT I'M WORRIED ABOUT SUZUKA !!
NOPE!
Megumi-kun, you're coming this way. ♡
GRAB
SWP

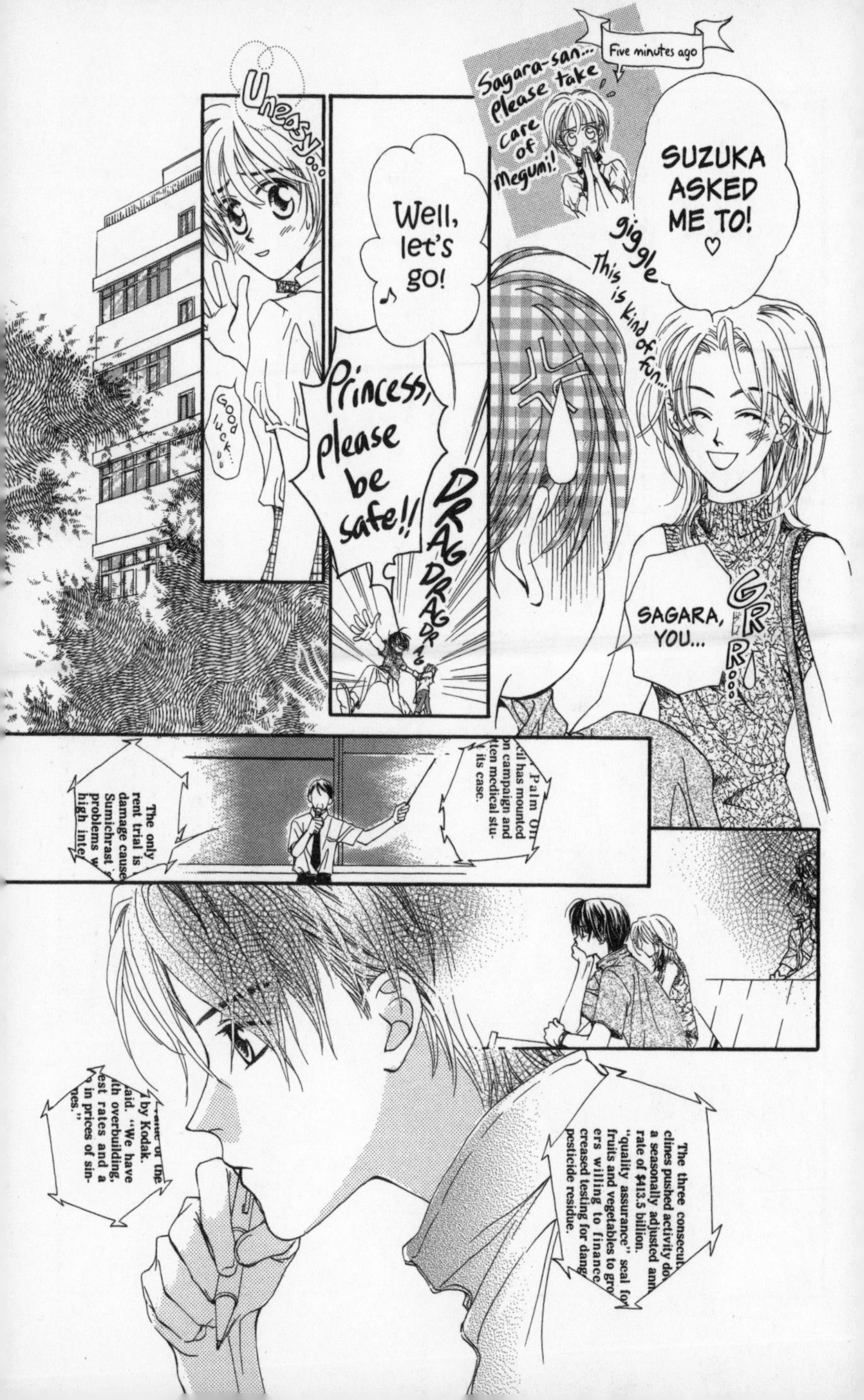

Five minutes ago
Sagara-san... please take care of Megumi!
SUZUKA ASKED ME TO! ♡
giggle
This is kind of fun...
SAGARA, YOU...
GRROOO
Well, let's go! ♪
Princess, please be safe!!
DRAG DRAG DRAG
Uneasy...
Good luck...

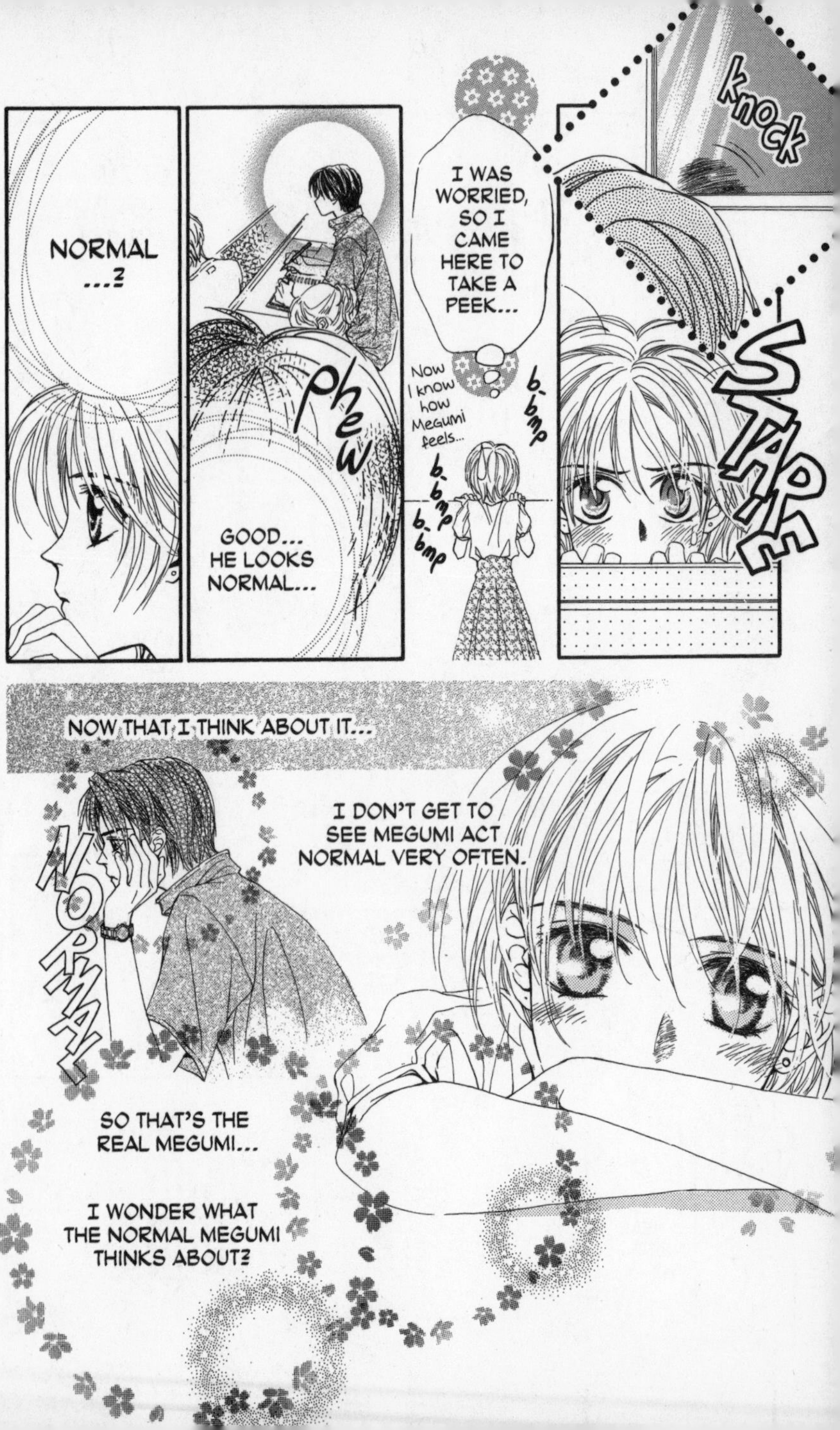
knock
STARE
I WAS WORRIED, SO I CAME HERE TO TAKE A PEEK...
Now I know how Megumi feels...
b-bmp
b-bmp
b-bmp
phew
GOOD... HE LOOKS NORMAL...
NORMAL...?
NOW THAT I THINK ABOUT IT...
I DON'T GET TO SEE MEGUMI ACT NORMAL VERY OFTEN.
NORMAL
SO THAT'S THE REAL MEGUMI...
I WONDER WHAT THE NORMAL MEGUMI THINKS ABOUT?

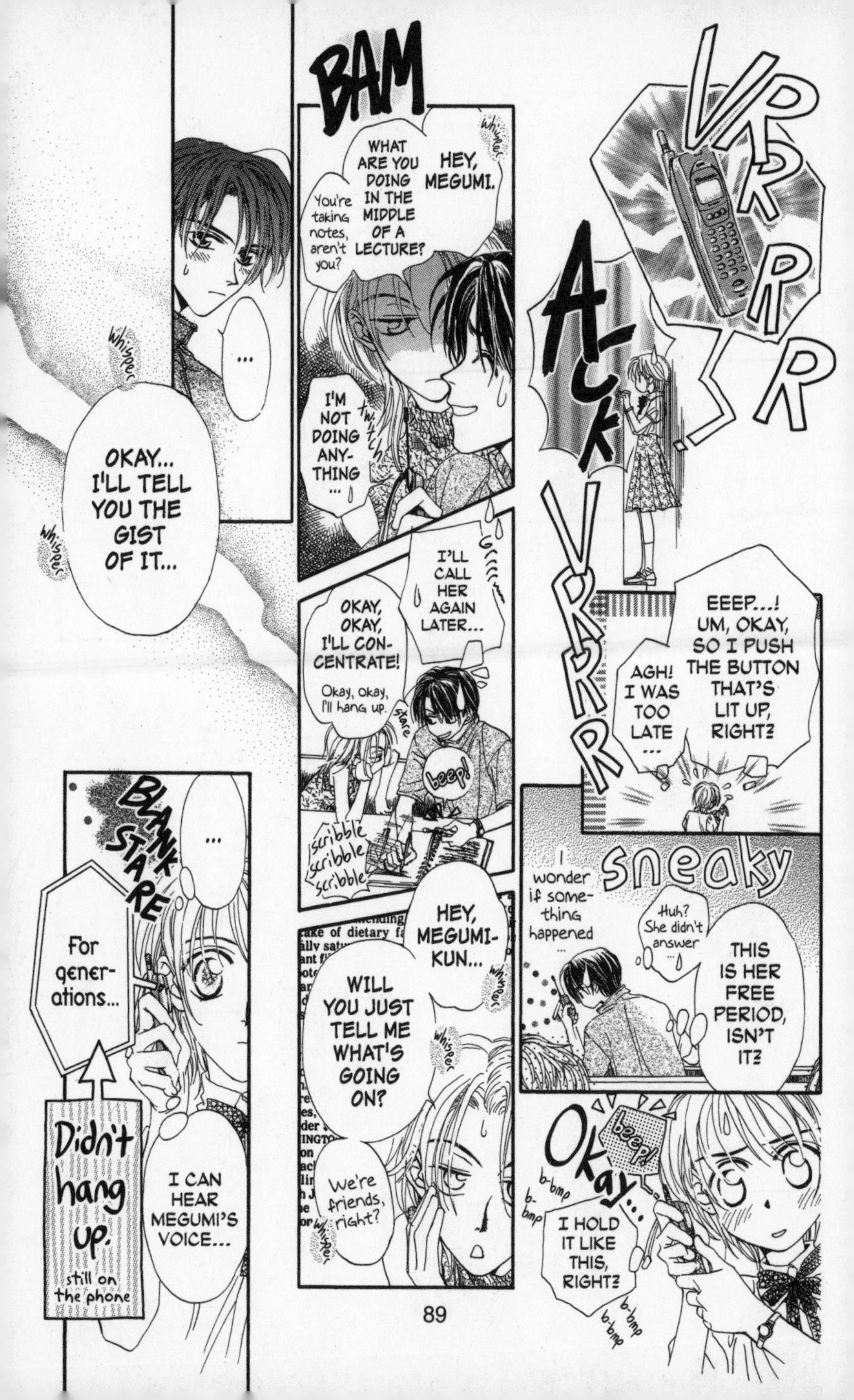
VRRRR
ACK
VRRRR
BAM
HEY, MEGUMI.
WHAT ARE YOU DOING IN THE MIDDLE OF A LECTURE?
whisper
You're taking notes, aren't you?
I'M NOT DOING ANYTHING...
twitch
I'LL CALL HER AGAIN LATER...
Grrr
OKAY, OKAY, I'LL CONCENTRATE!
Okay, okay, I'll hang up.
stare
beep!
scribble scribble scribble
EEEP...! UM, OKAY, SO I PUSH THE BUTTON THAT'S LIT UP, RIGHT?
AGH! I WAS TOO LATE...
sneaky
I wonder if something happened...
THIS IS HER FREE PERIOD, ISN'T IT?
Huh? She didn't answer...
Okay...
beep!
b-bmp b-bmp
I HOLD IT LIKE THIS, RIGHT?
b-bmp b-bmp
HEY, MEGUMI-KUN...
whisper
WILL YOU JUST TELL ME WHAT'S GOING ON?
whisper
We're friends, right?
whisper
...
whisper
OKAY... I'LL TELL YOU THE GIST OF IT...
whisper
BLANK STARE
...
For generations...
I CAN HEAR MEGUMI'S VOICE...
Didn't hang up.
still on the phone

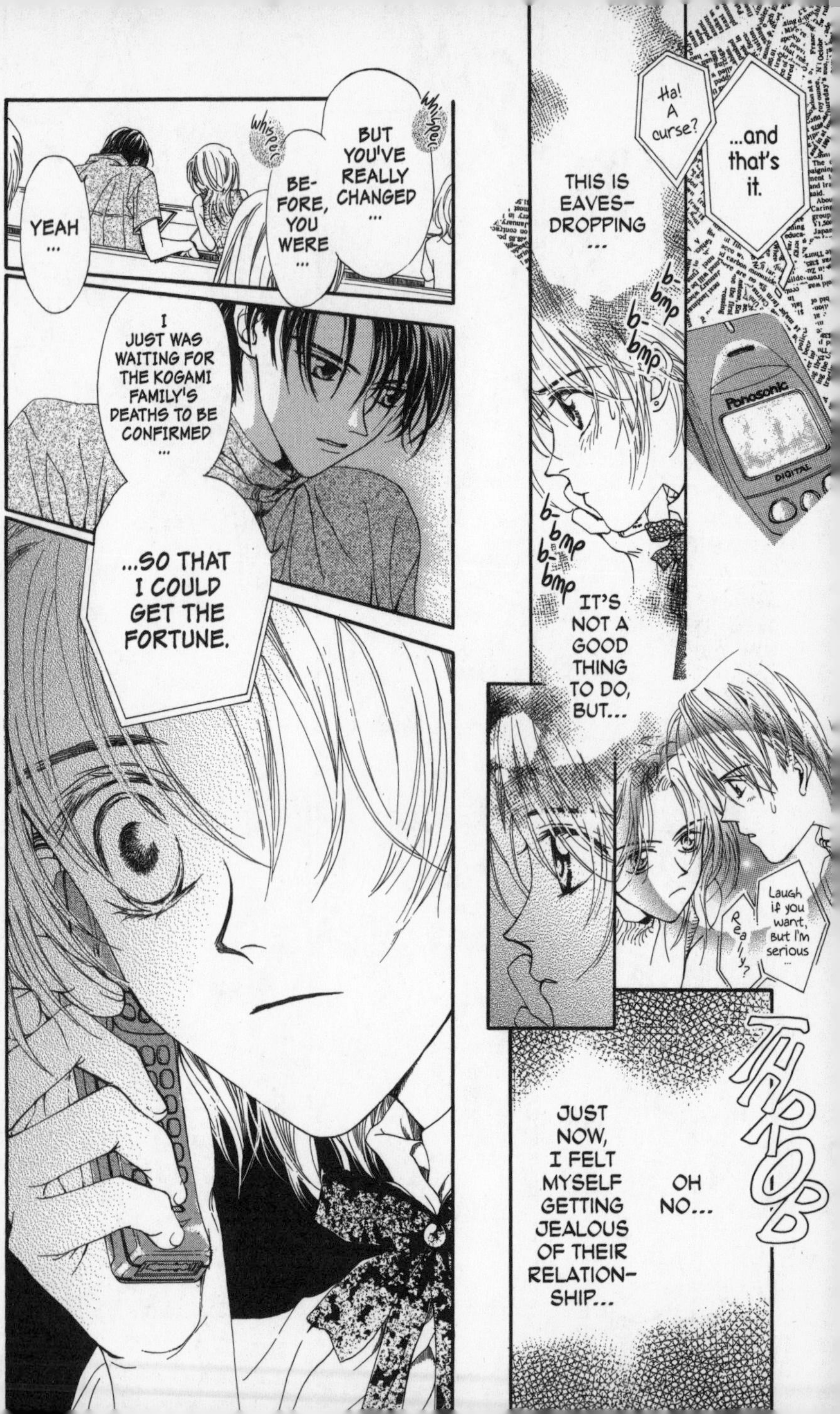
...and that's it.
Ha! A curse?
THIS IS EAVES-DROPPING...
b-bmp b-bmp
b-bmp b-bmp
IT'S NOT A GOOD THING TO DO, BUT...
Laugh if you want, but I'm serious...
Really?
THROB
OH NO...
JUST NOW, I FELT MYSELF GETTING JEALOUS OF THEIR RELATIONSHIP...
whisper
BUT YOU'VE REALLY CHANGED...
whisper
BEFORE, YOU WERE...
YEAH...
I JUST WAS WAITING FOR THE KOGAMI FAMILY'S DEATHS TO BE CONFIRMED...
...SO THAT I COULD GET THE FORTUNE.

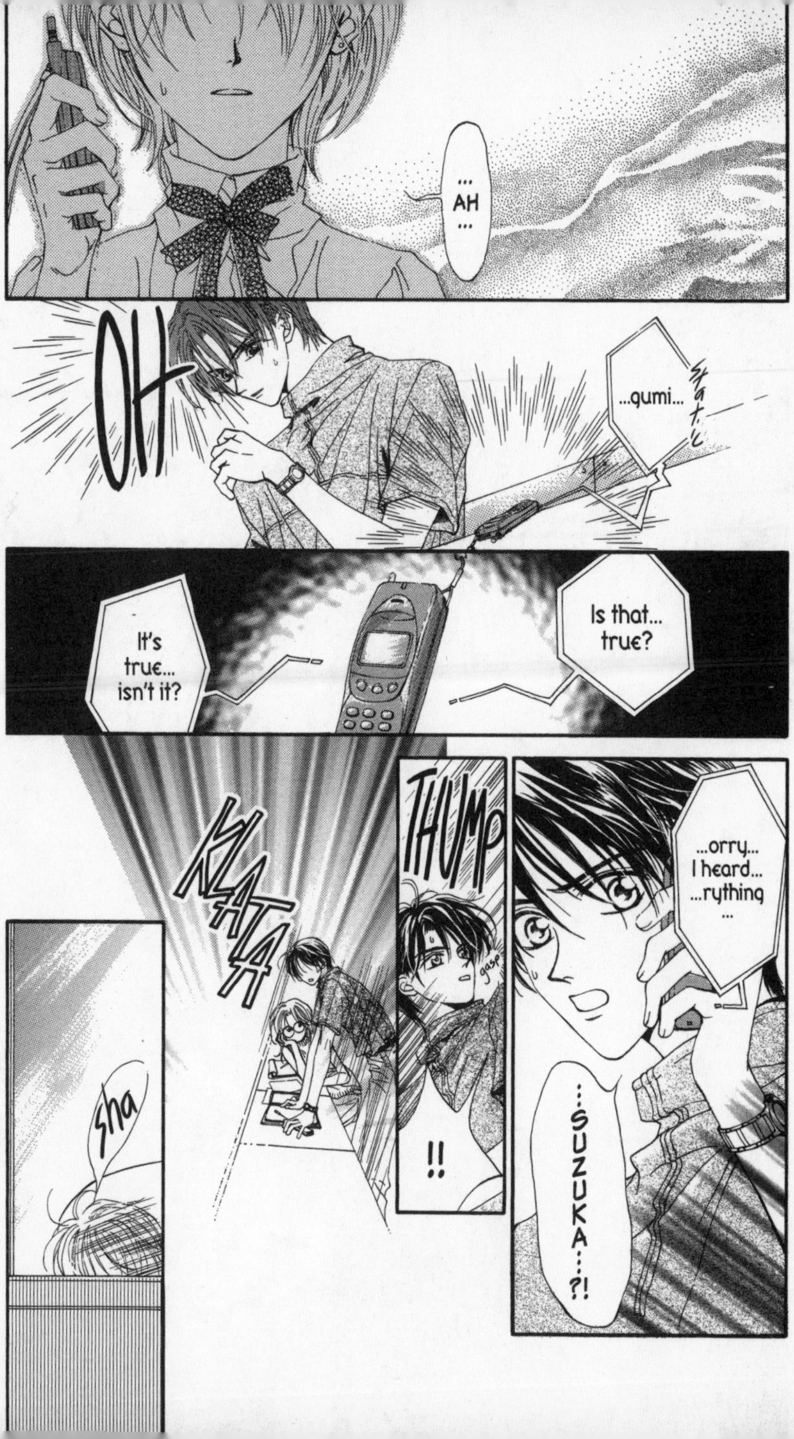
... AH ...
...gumi...
static
OH
Is that... true?
It's true... isn't it?
...orry... I heard... ...rything ...
...SUZUKA...?!
THUMP
gasp
!!
KLATATA
sha

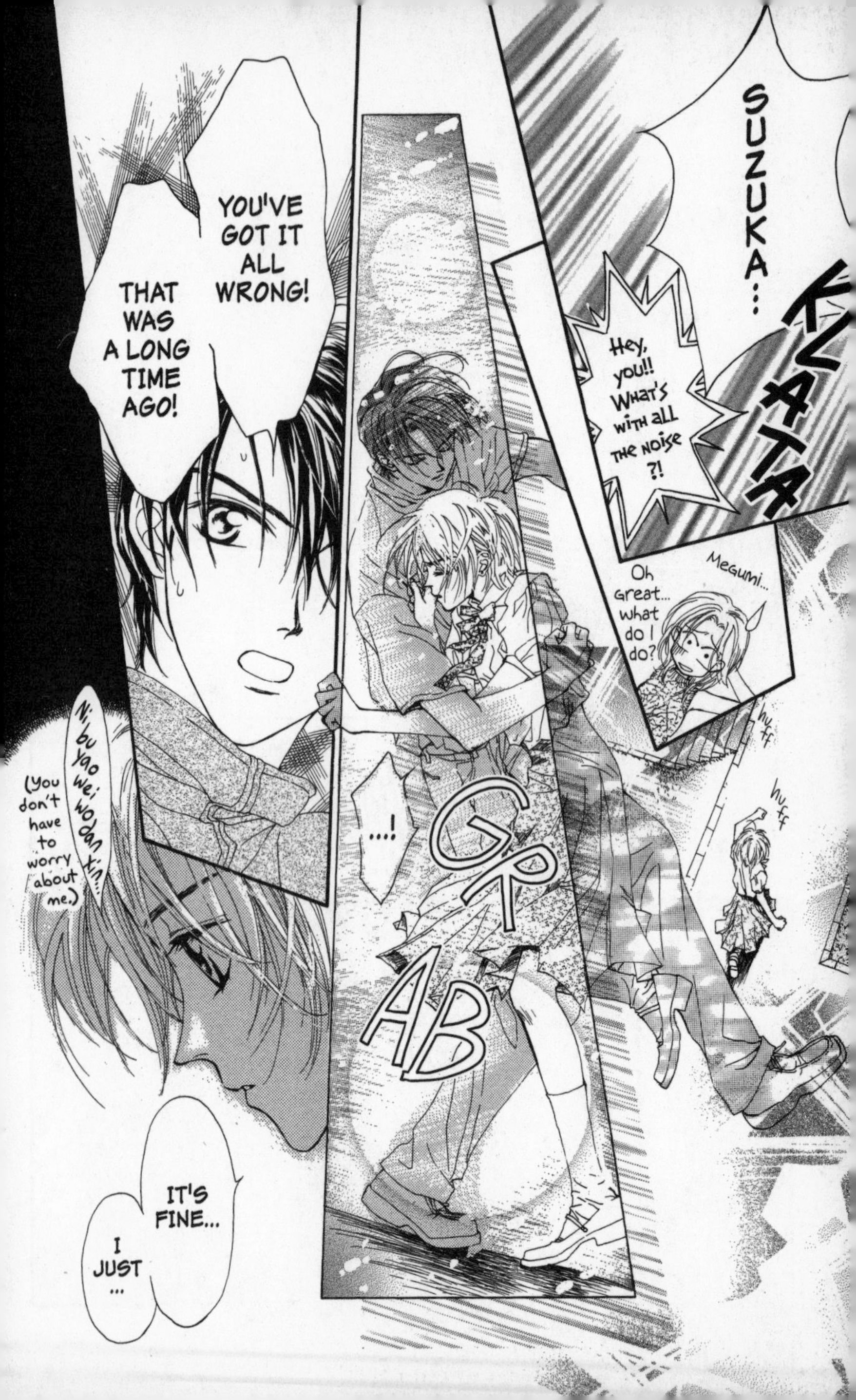
SUZUKA...
KLATA
Hey, you!! What's with all the noise ?!
Megumi...
Oh great... what do I do?
huff
huff
...!
GRAB
YOU'VE GOT IT ALL WRONG!
THAT WAS A LONG TIME AGO!
Ni bu yao wei wo dan xin...
(You don't have to worry about me.)
IT'S FINE...
I JUST...

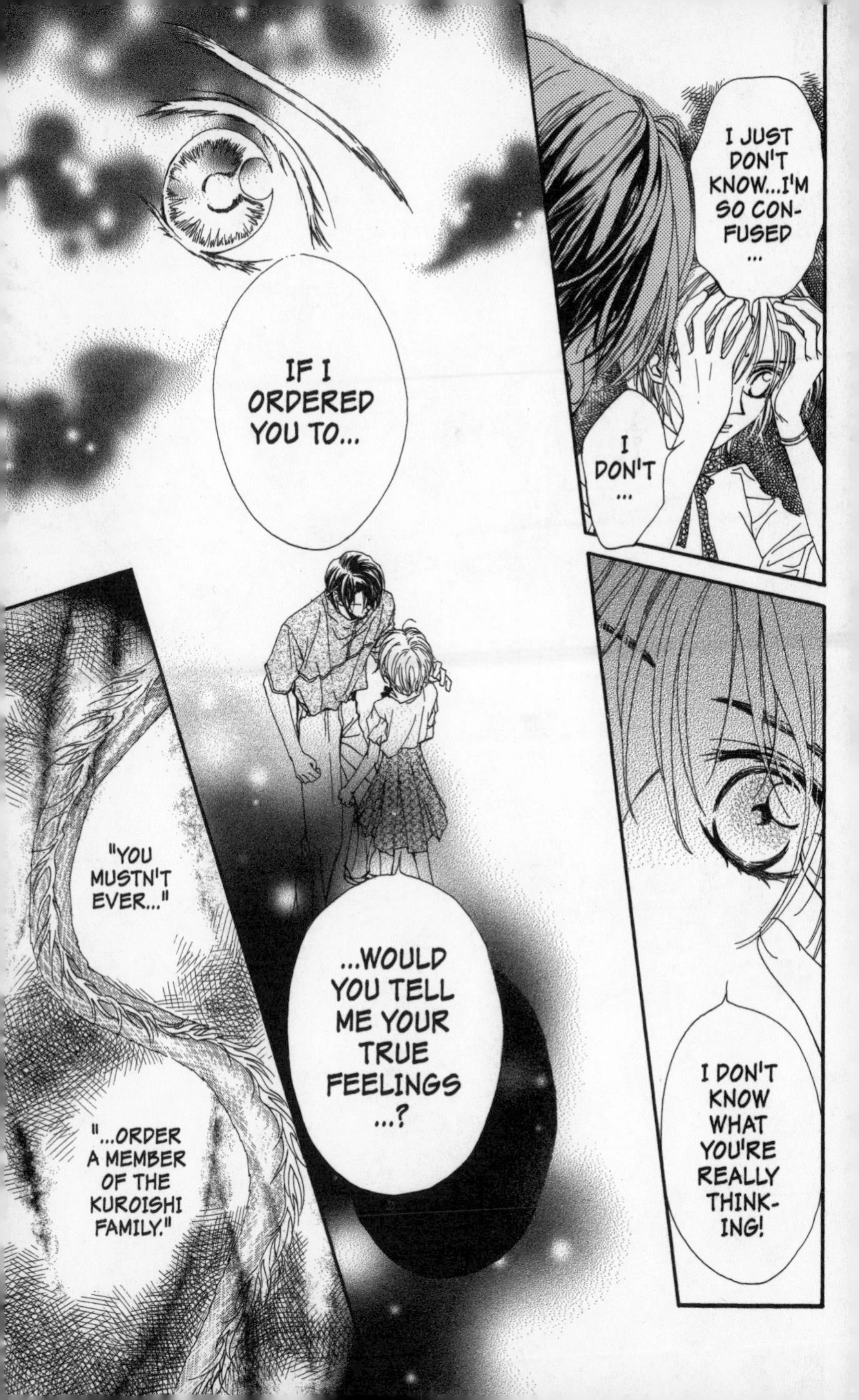
I JUST DON'T KNOW...I'M SO CONFUSED ...
I DON'T ...
I DON'T KNOW WHAT YOU'RE REALLY THINKING!
IF I ORDERED YOU TO...
...WOULD YOU TELL ME YOUR TRUE FEELINGS ...?
"YOU MUSTN'T EVER..."
"...ORDER A MEMBER OF THE KUROISHI FAMILY."

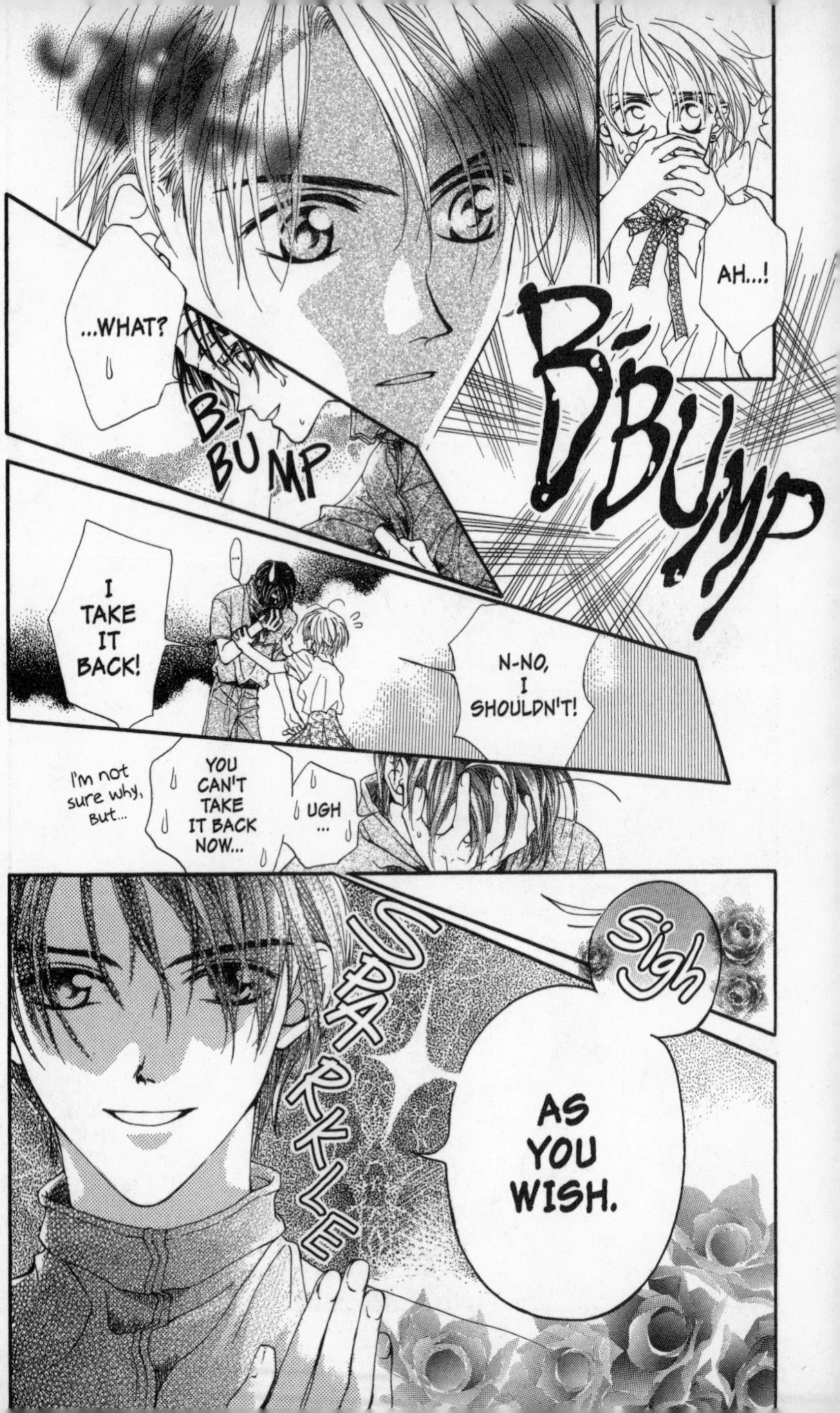
AH...!
B-BUMP
...WHAT?
B-BUMP
N-NO, I SHOULDN'T!
...
I TAKE IT BACK!
UGH ...
YOU CAN'T TAKE IT BACK NOW...
I'm not sure why, but...
Sigh
AS YOU WISH.
SPARKLE

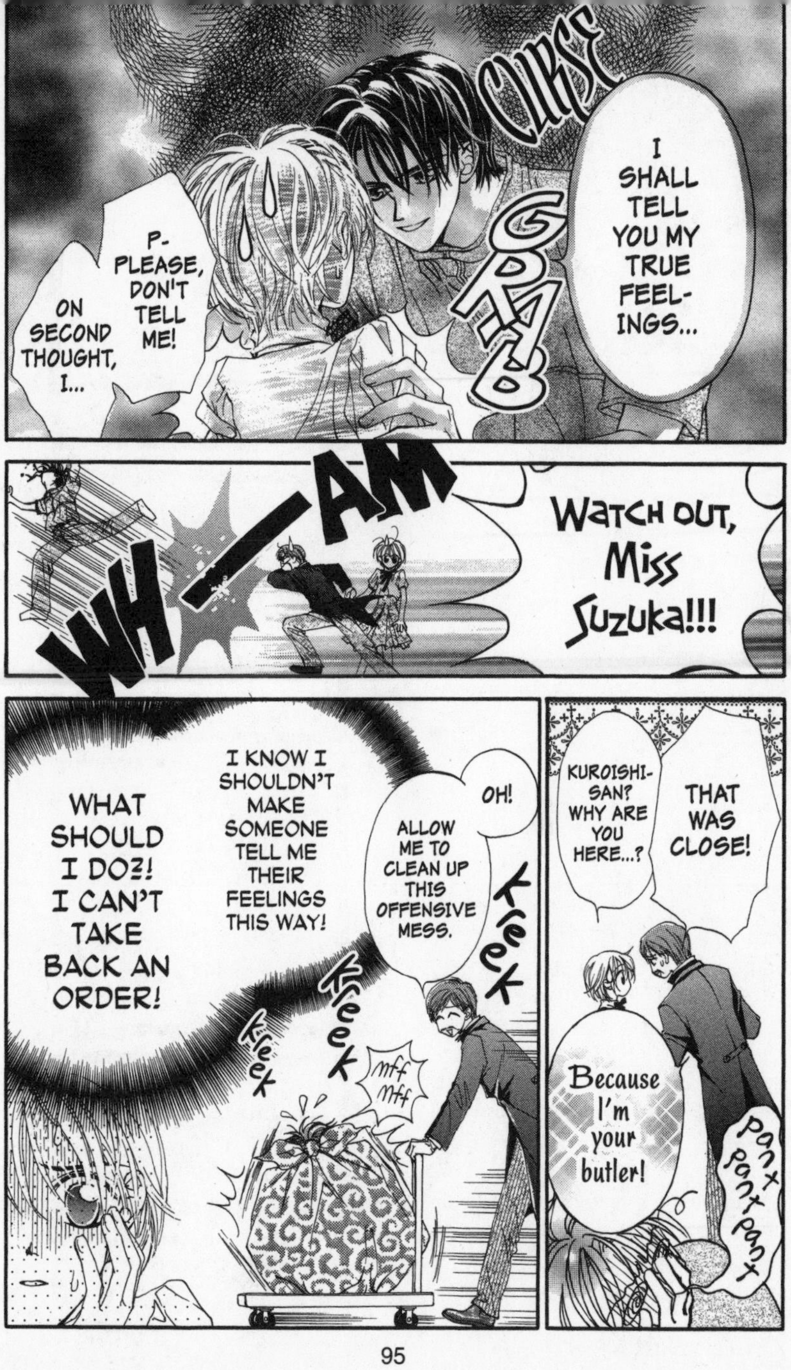
CURSE
I SHALL TELL YOU MY TRUE FEEL-INGS...
GRAB
P-PLEASE, DON'T TELL ME!
ON SECOND THOUGHT, I...
WATCH OUT, MISS SUZUKA!!!
WH—AM
THAT WAS CLOSE!
KUROISHI-SAN? WHY ARE YOU HERE...?
Because I'm your butler!
pant pant pant pant
OH!
kreek
ALLOW ME TO CLEAN UP THIS OFFENSIVE MESS.
I KNOW I SHOULDN'T MAKE SOMEONE TELL ME THEIR FEELINGS THIS WAY!
WHAT SHOULD I DO?! I CAN'T TAKE BACK AN ORDER!
kreek
kreek
mff mff

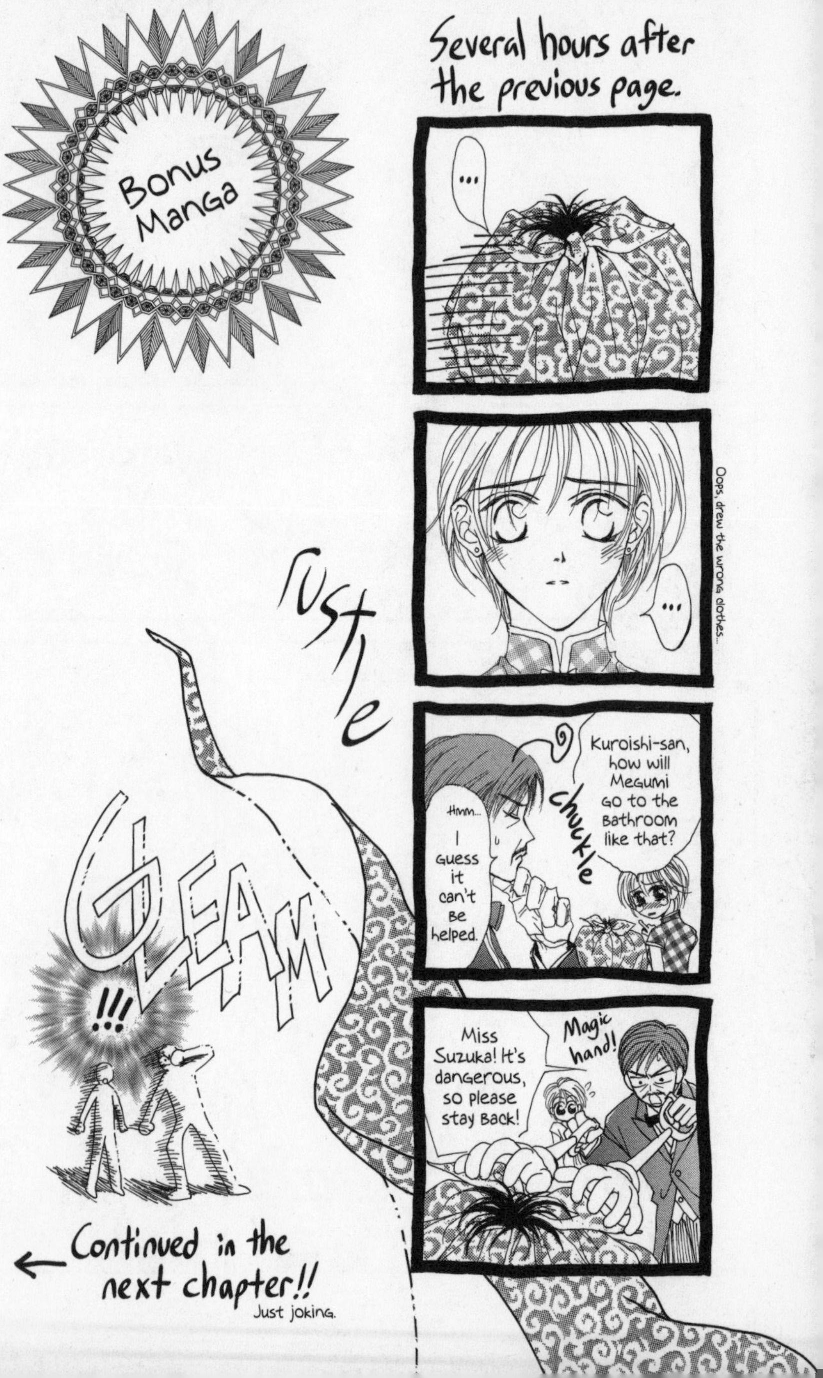
Bonus Manga
Several hours after the previous page.
...
...
Oops, drew the wrong clothes...
Kuroishi-san, how will Megumi go to the bathroom like that?
chuckle
Hmm... I guess it can't be helped.
Magic hand!
Miss Suzuka! It's dangerous, so please stay back!
rustle
GLEAM
!!!
← Continued in the next chapter!!
Just joking.

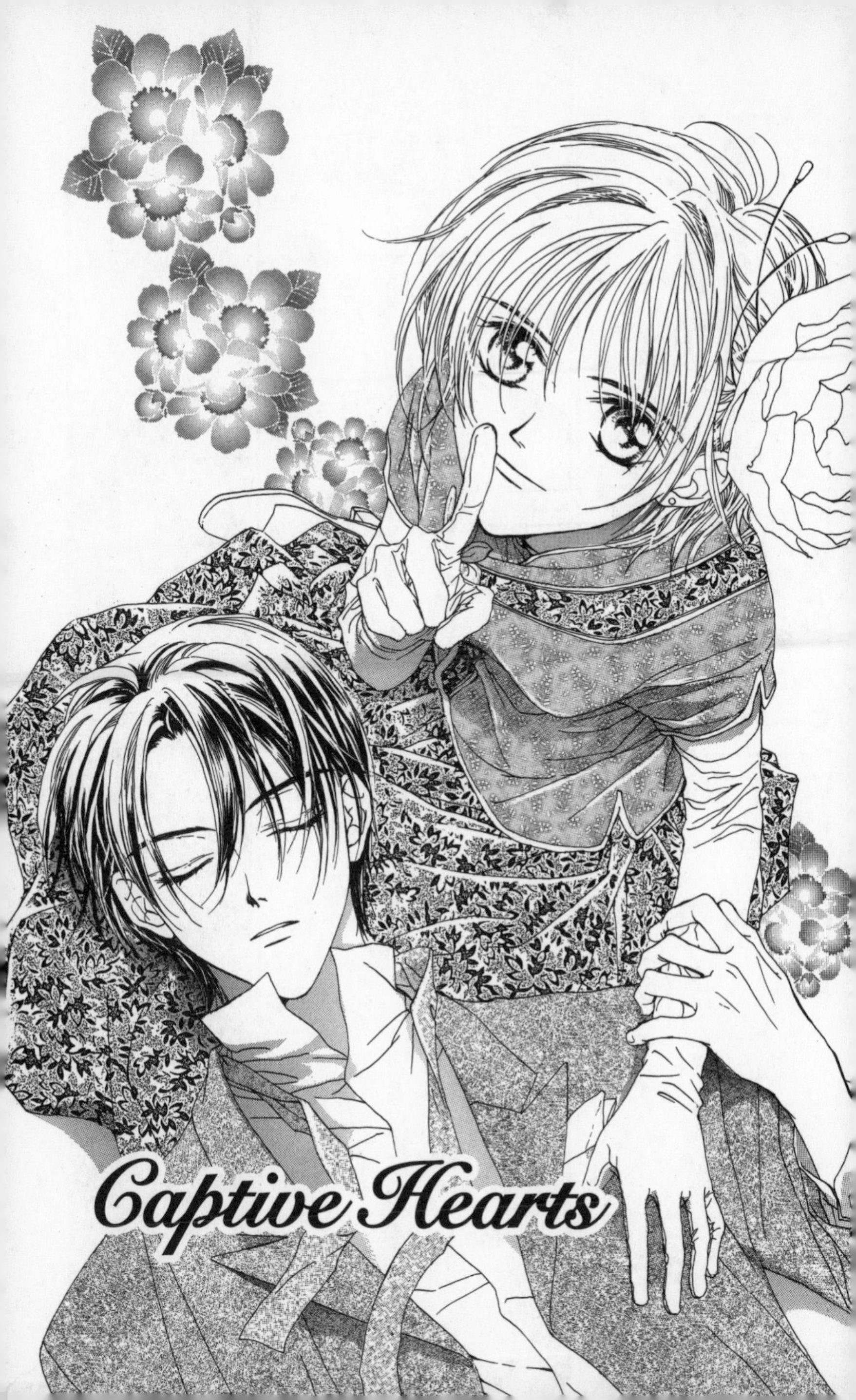
Captive Hearts

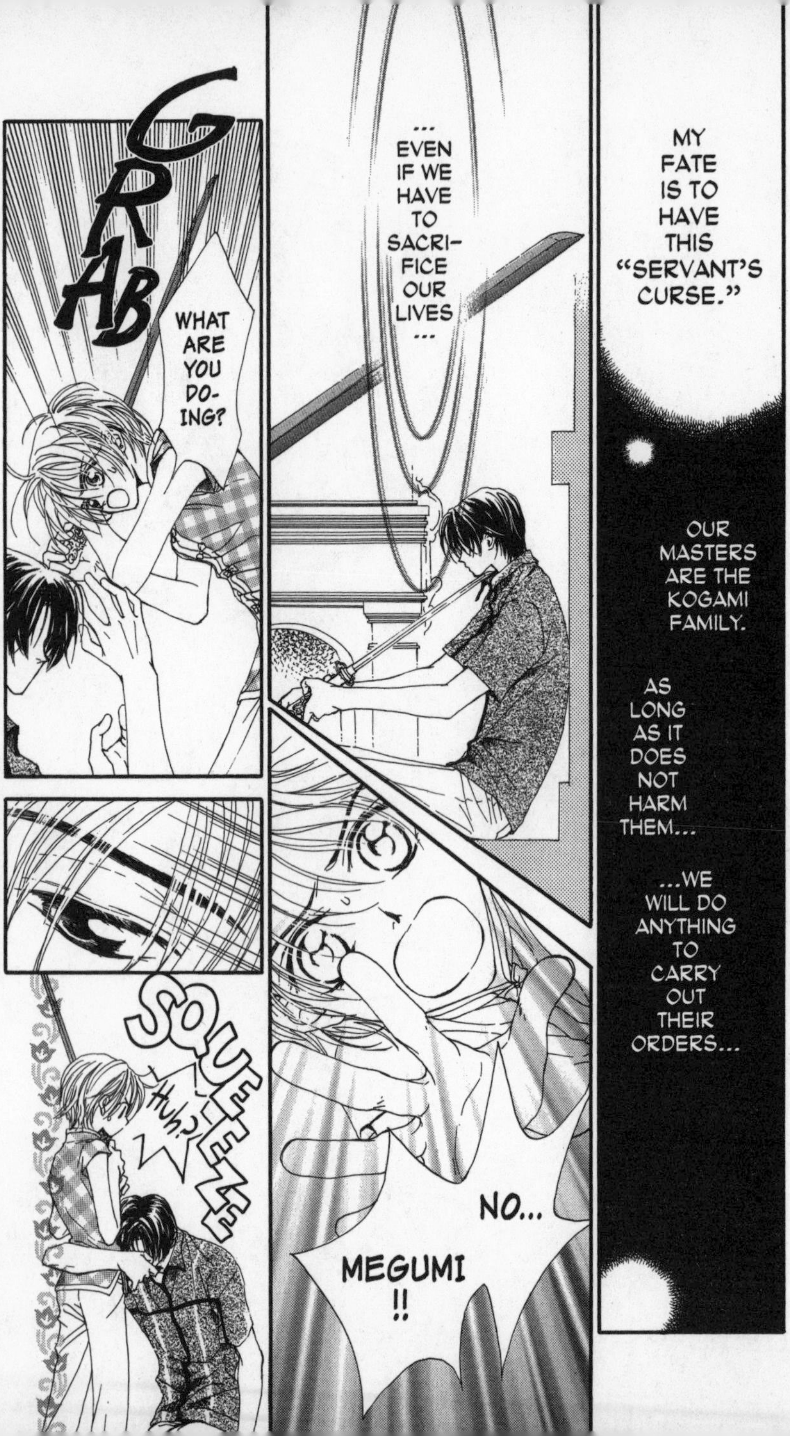
MY FATE IS TO HAVE THIS "SERVANT'S CURSE."
OUR MASTERS ARE THE KOGAMI FAMILY.
AS LONG AS IT DOES NOT HARM THEM...
...WE WILL DO ANYTHING TO CARRY OUT THEIR ORDERS...
...EVEN IF WE HAVE TO SACRIFICE OUR LIVES...
NO...
MEGUMI!!
GRAB
WHAT ARE YOU DOING?
SQUEEZE
Huh?!

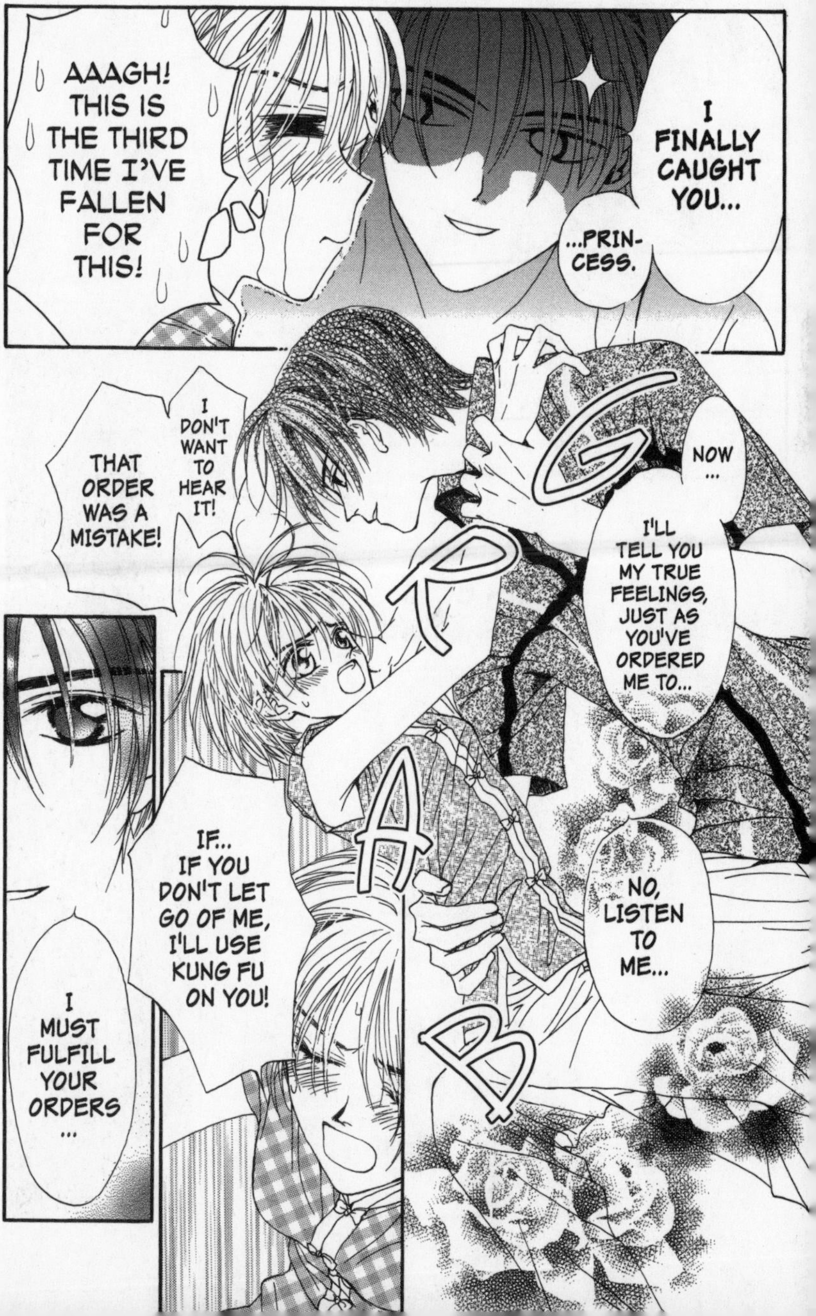
I FINALLY CAUGHT YOU...
...PRINCESS.
AAAGH! THIS IS THE THIRD TIME I'VE FALLEN FOR THIS!
GRAB
NOW...
I'LL TELL YOU MY TRUE FEELINGS, JUST AS YOU'VE ORDERED ME TO...
I DON'T WANT TO HEAR IT!
THAT ORDER WAS A MISTAKE!
NO, LISTEN TO ME...
IF... IF YOU DON'T LET GO OF ME, I'LL USE KUNG FU ON YOU!
I MUST FULFILL YOUR ORDERS...

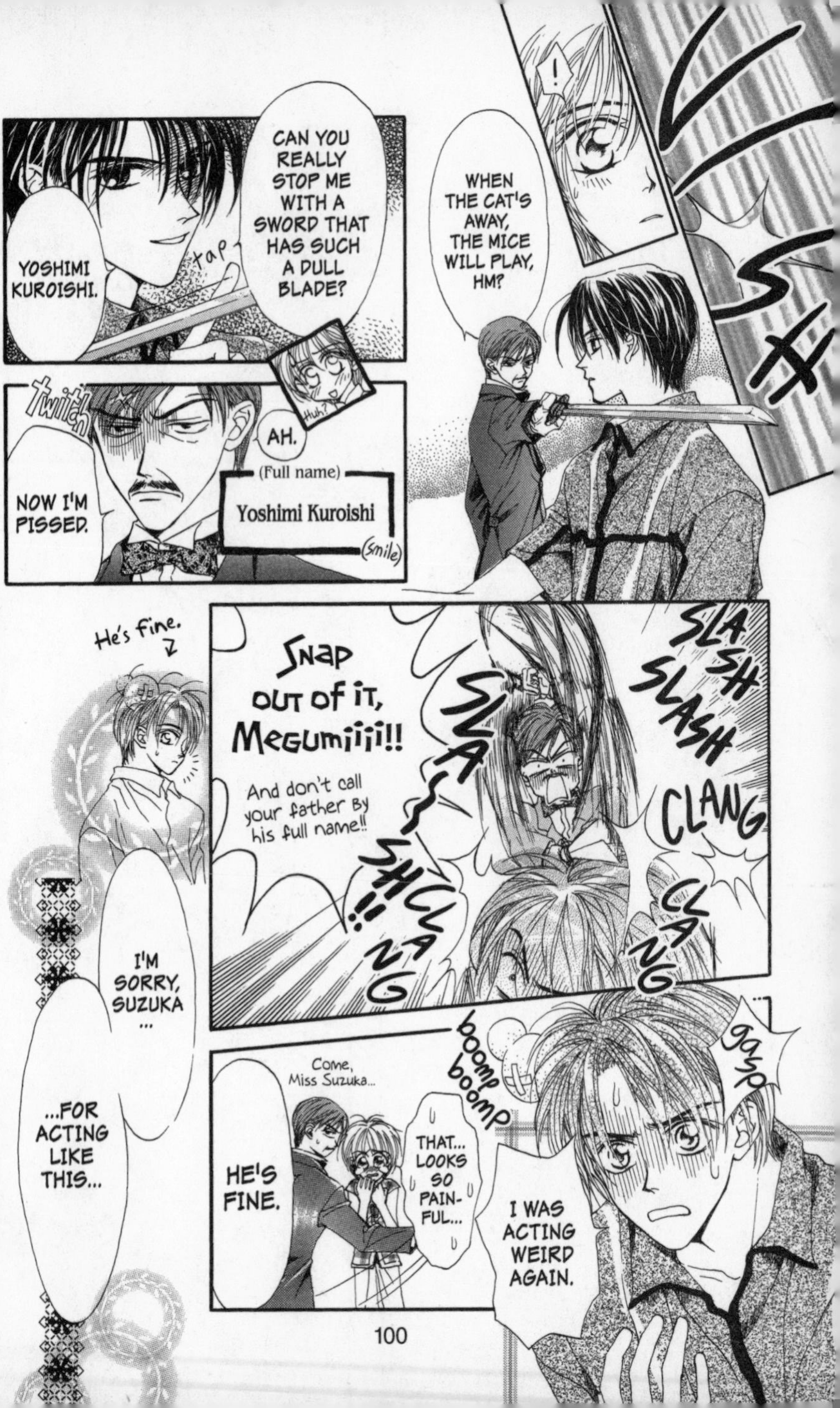
!
WHEN THE CAT'S AWAY, THE MICE WILL PLAY, HM?
CAN YOU REALLY STOP ME WITH A SWORD THAT HAS SUCH A DULL BLADE?
tap
YOSHIMI KUROISHI.
Huh?
AH.
(Full name)
Yoshimi Kuroishi
(smile)
twitch
NOW I'M PISSED.
SLASH
SLASH
CLANG
CLANG
CLANG
Snap out of it, Megumiiii!!
And don't call your father by his full name!!
SHCLANG!!
He's fine.
I'M SORRY, SUZUKA...
...FOR ACTING LIKE THIS...
...
gasp
boomp boomp
I WAS ACTING WEIRD AGAIN.
THAT... LOOKS SO PAIN-FUL...
Come, Miss Suzuka...
HE'S FINE.

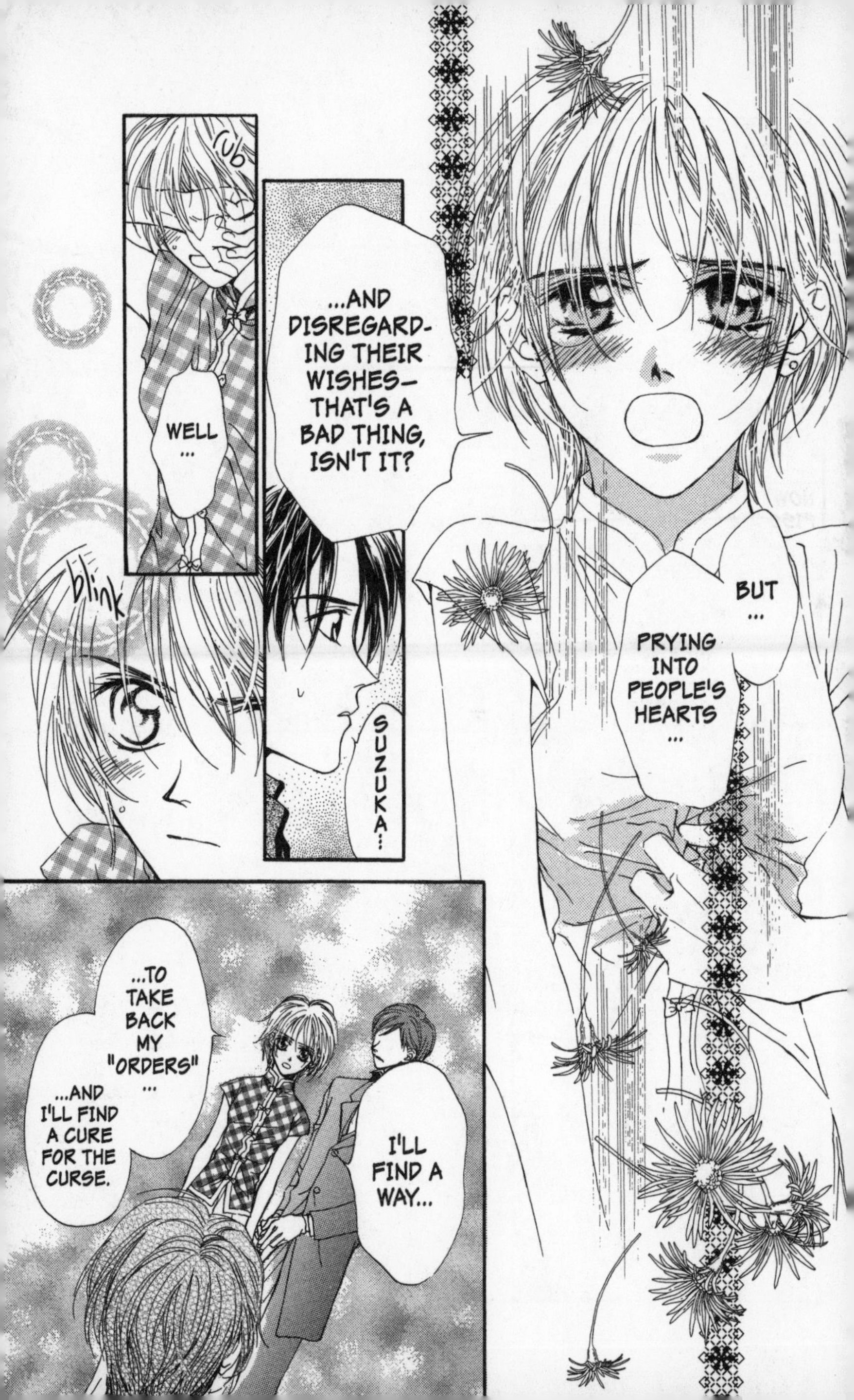
BUT ...
PRYING INTO PEOPLE'S HEARTS ...
...AND DISREGARDING THEIR WISHES—THAT'S A BAD THING, ISN'T IT?
SUZUKA...
rub
WELL ...
blink
I'LL FIND A WAY...
...TO TAKE BACK MY "ORDERS" ...
...AND I'LL FIND A CURE FOR THE CURSE.

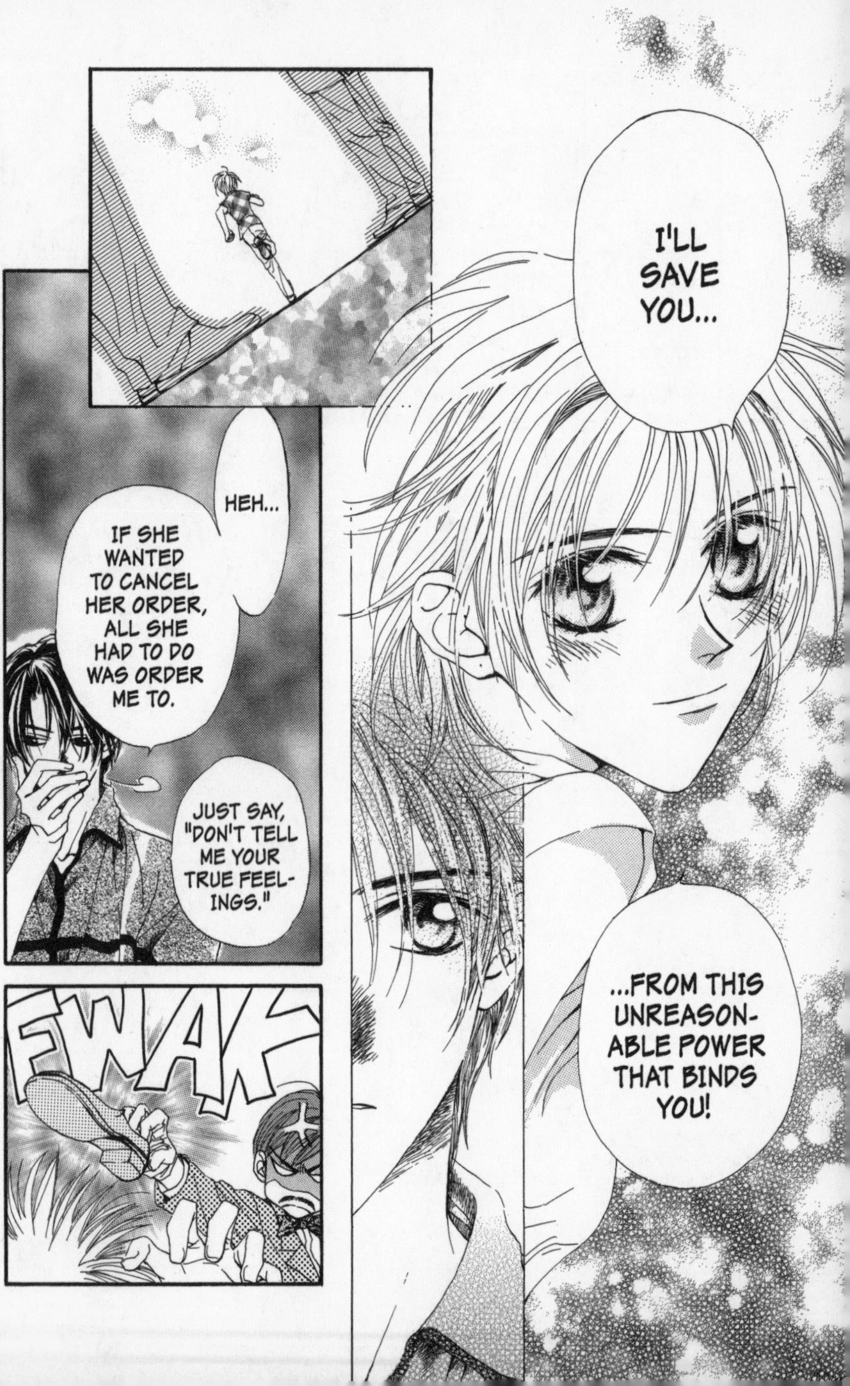
I'LL SAVE YOU...
...FROM THIS UNREASON-ABLE POWER THAT BINDS YOU!
HEH...
IF SHE WANTED TO CANCEL HER ORDER, ALL SHE HAD TO DO WAS ORDER ME TO.
JUST SAY, "DON'T TELL ME YOUR TRUE FEEL-INGS."
FWAK

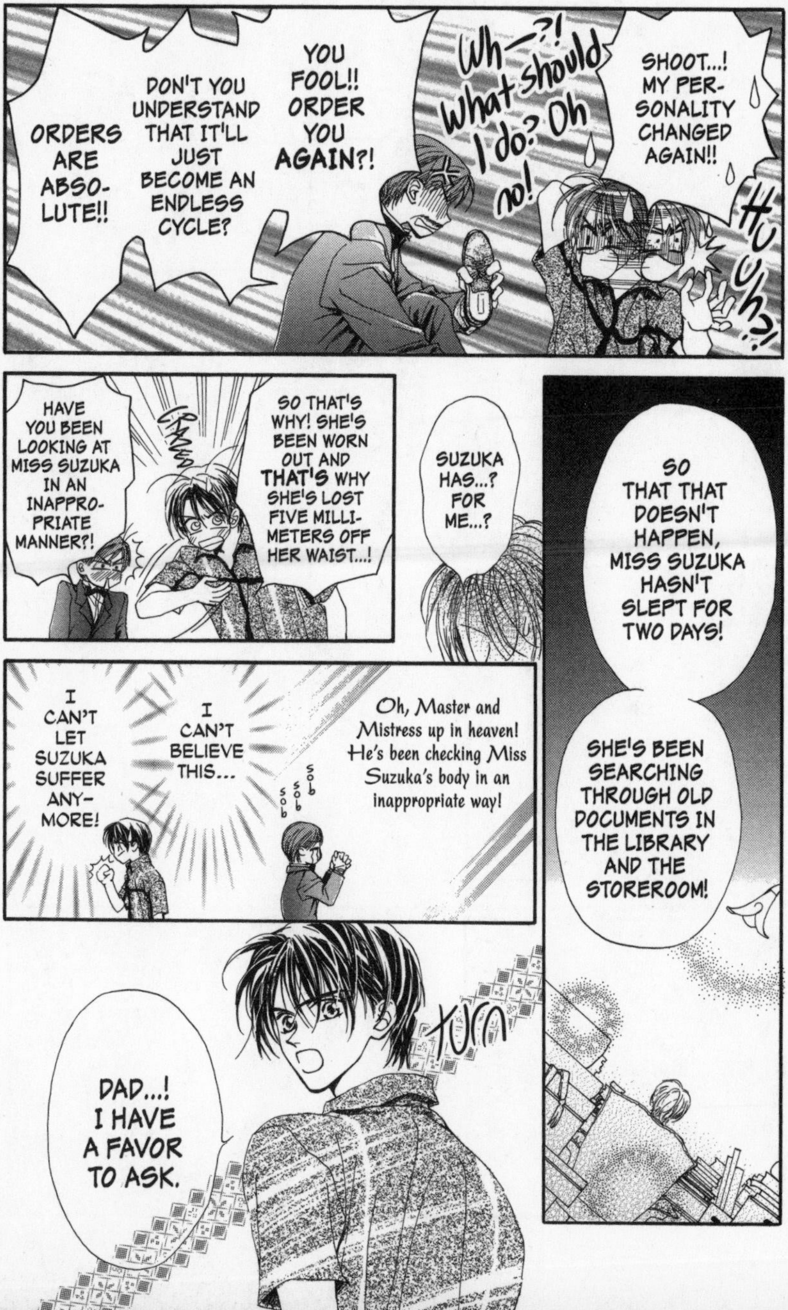
SHOOT...! MY PER-SONALITY CHANGED AGAIN!!
HUH?!
Wh—?! what should I do? Oh no!
YOU FOOL!! ORDER YOU AGAIN?!
DON'T YOU UNDERSTAND THAT IT'LL JUST BECOME AN ENDLESS CYCLE?
ORDERS ARE ABSO-LUTE!!
SO THAT THAT DOESN'T HAPPEN, MISS SUZUKA HASN'T SLEPT FOR TWO DAYS!
SHE'S BEEN SEARCHING THROUGH OLD DOCUMENTS IN THE LIBRARY AND THE STOREROOM!
SUZUKA HAS...? FOR ME...?
SO THAT'S WHY! SHE'S BEEN WORN OUT AND THAT'S WHY SHE'S LOST FIVE MILLI-METERS OFF HER WAIST...!
HAVE YOU BEEN LOOKING AT MISS SUZUKA IN AN INAPPRO-PRIATE MANNER?!
Oh, Master and Mistress up in heaven! He's been checking Miss Suzuka's body in an inappropriate way!
sob sob sob
I CAN'T BELIEVE THIS...
I CAN'T LET SUZUKA SUFFER ANY-MORE!
turn
DAD...! I HAVE A FAVOR TO ASK.

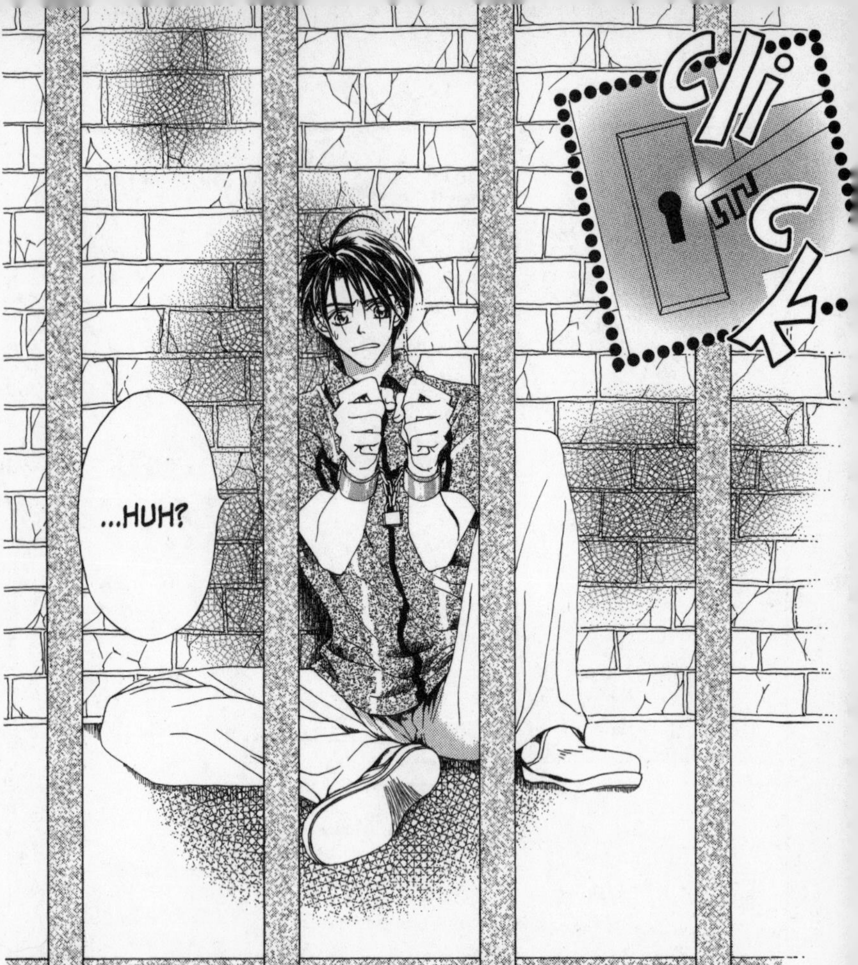
CLICK...
...HUH?

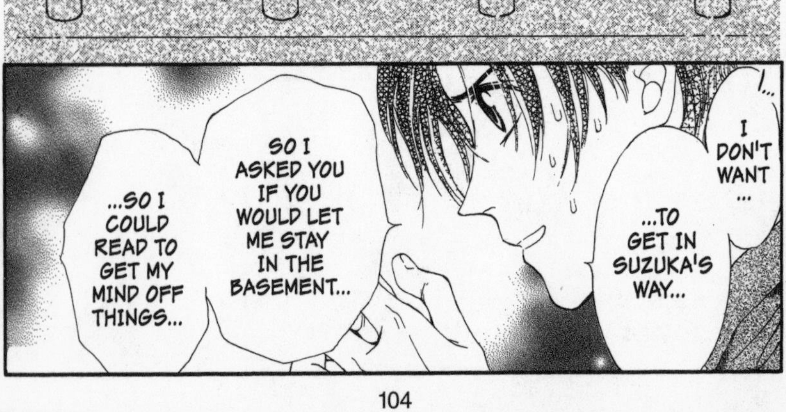
I...
I DON'T WANT...
...TO GET IN SUZUKA'S WAY...
SO I ASKED YOU IF YOU WOULD LET ME STAY IN THE BASEMENT...
...SO I COULD READ TO GET MY MIND OFF THINGS...

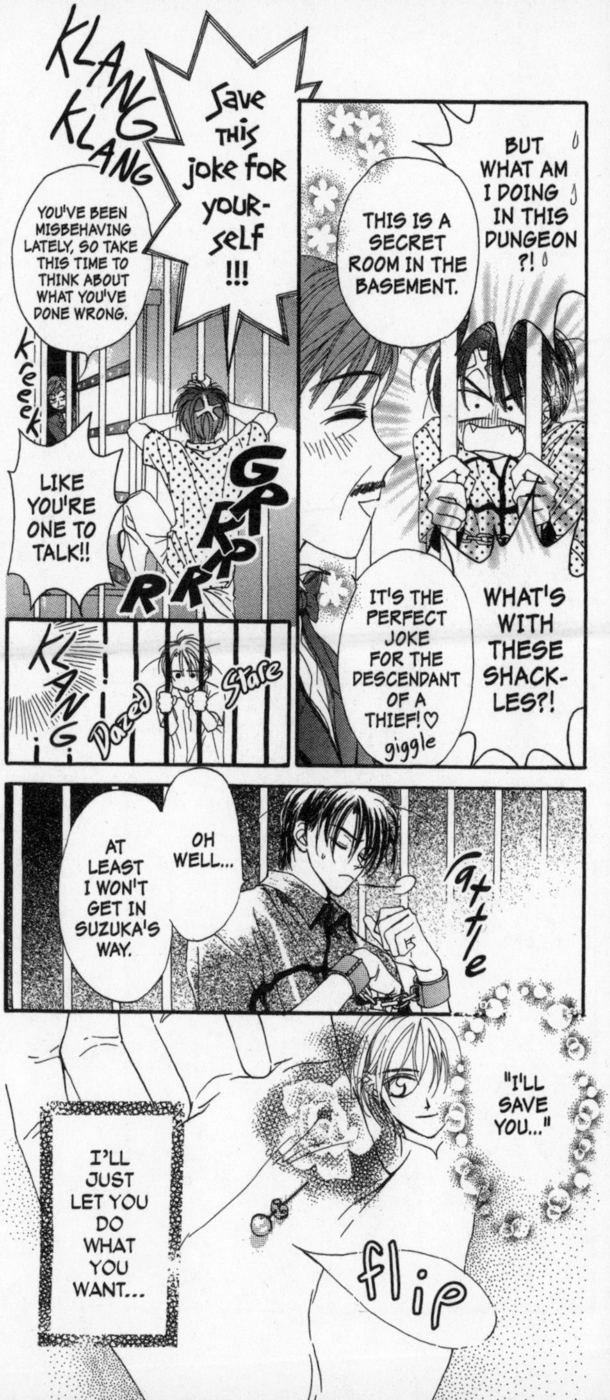
BUT WHAT AM I DOING IN THIS DUNGEON?!
THIS IS A SECRET ROOM IN THE BASEMENT.
WHAT'S WITH THESE SHACKLES?!
IT'S THE PERFECT JOKE FOR THE DESCENDANT OF A THIEF! ♡ giggle
Save this joke for yourself!!!
KLANG KLANG
YOU'VE BEEN MISBEHAVING LATELY, SO TAKE THIS TIME TO THINK ABOUT WHAT YOU'VE DONE WRONG.
kreeek
GRRRR
LIKE YOU'RE ONE TO TALK!!
Stare
Dazed
KLANG
OH WELL...
AT LEAST I WON'T GET IN SUZUKA'S WAY.
rattle
"I'LL SAVE YOU..."
I'LL JUST LET YOU DO WHAT YOU WANT...
flip

4

I've Been taken captive By Captive Hearts.

This is... my very first **SERIALIZED MANGA!!**

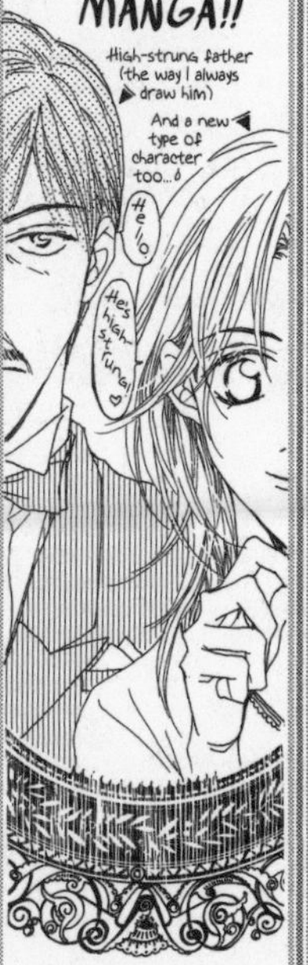
High-strung father (the way I always draw him)
And a new type of character too...
Hello
He's high-strung! ♡

When I was drawing my first story, I never imagined this would ever happen.

I never thought I would get something serialized!

And I get to continue this story!

It's all Because of you. I'm so happy!

I better work harder!

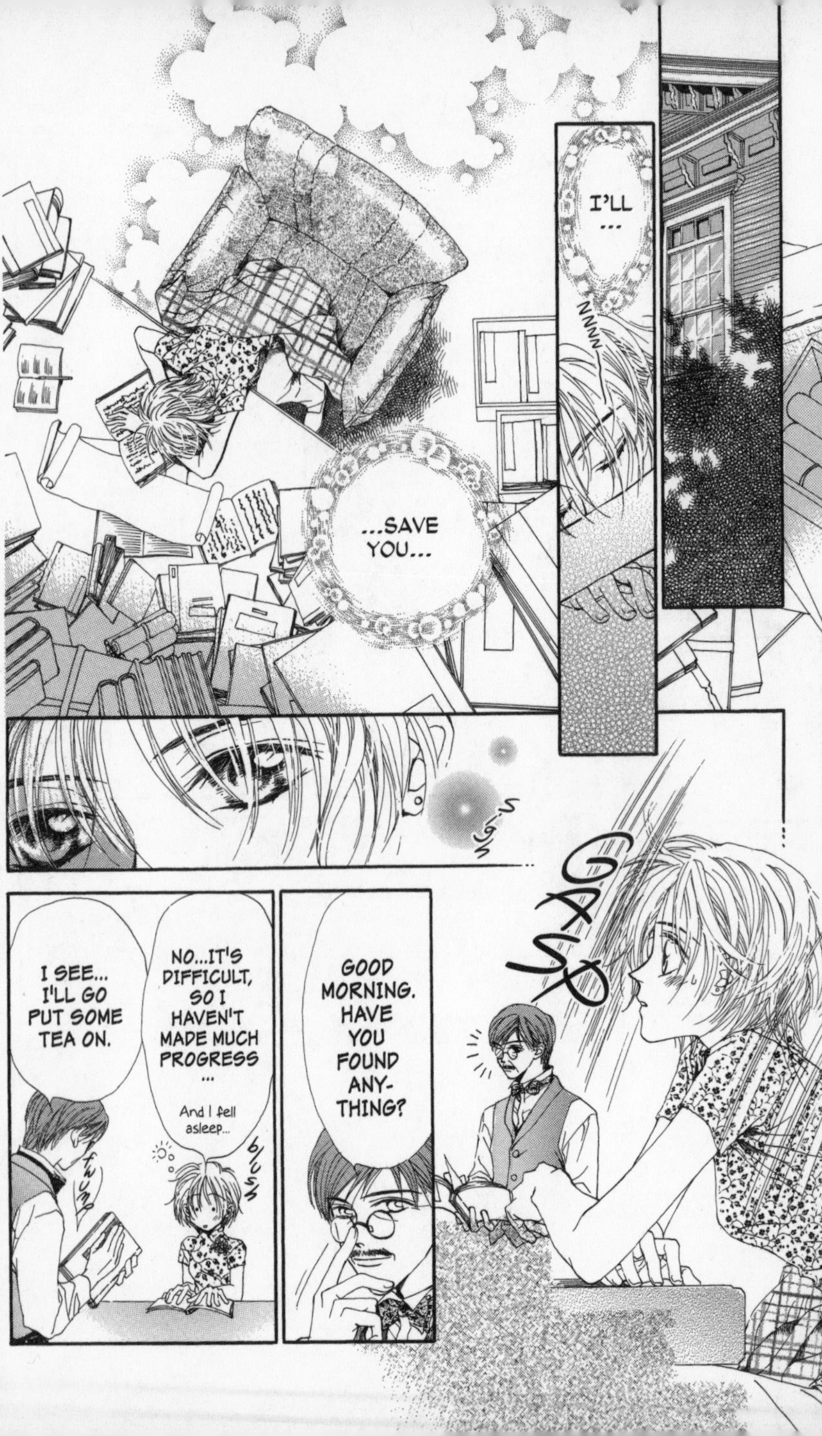
I'LL...
NNNN
...SAVE YOU...
sigh
GASP
GOOD MORNING. HAVE YOU FOUND ANYTHING?
NO...IT'S DIFFICULT, SO I HAVEN'T MADE MUCH PROGRESS...
And I fell asleep...
blush
I SEE... I'LL GO PUT SOME TEA ON.
fwump

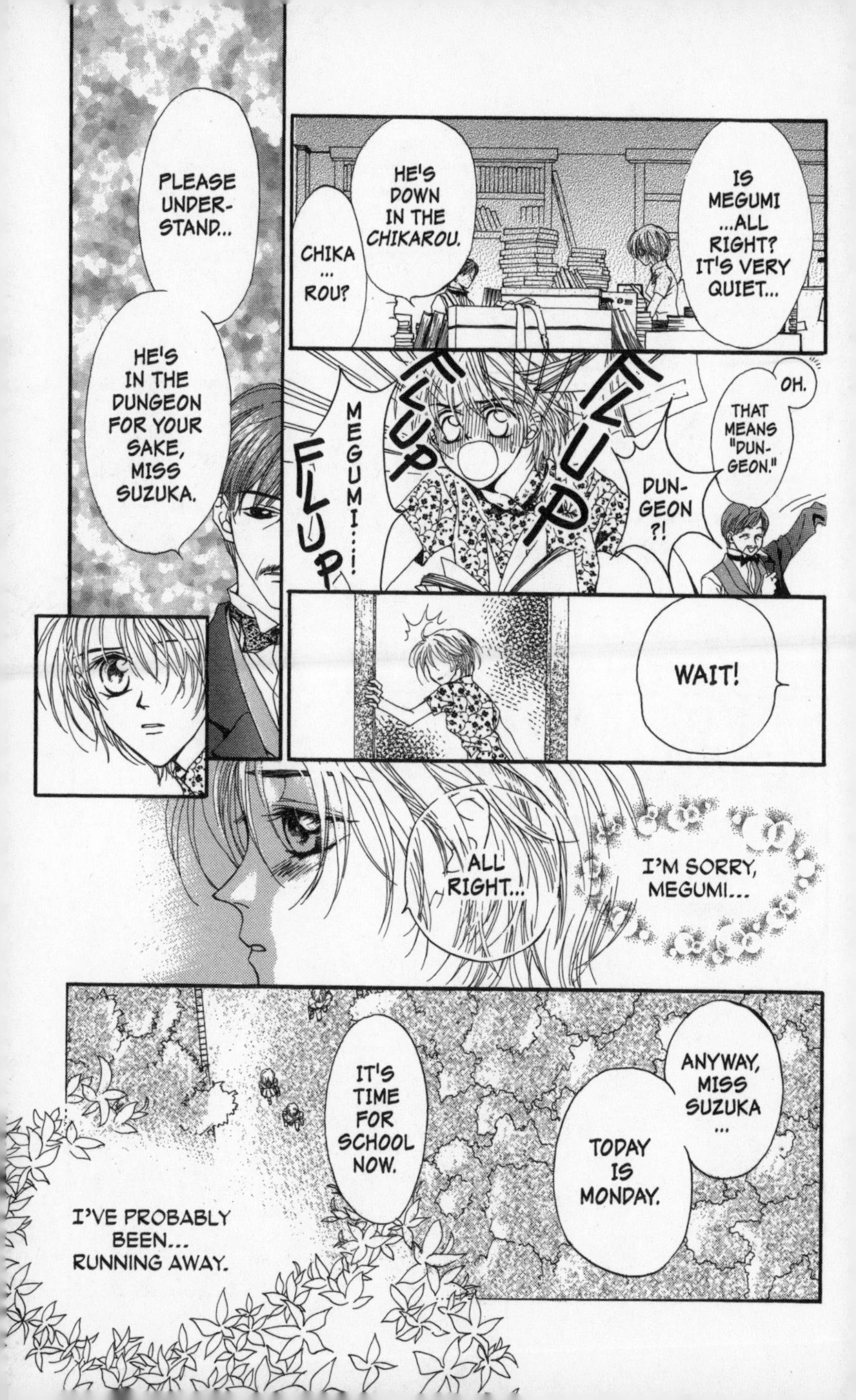
IS MEGUMI ...ALL RIGHT? IT'S VERY QUIET...
HE'S DOWN IN THE CHIKAROU.
CHIKA ... ROU?
OH.
THAT MEANS "DUN-GEON."
DUN-GEON ?!
FLUP
FLUP
FLUP
MEGUMI...!
WAIT!
PLEASE UNDER-STAND...
HE'S IN THE DUNGEON FOR YOUR SAKE, MISS SUZUKA.
I'M SORRY, MEGUMI...
ALL RIGHT...
ANYWAY, MISS SUZUKA ...
TODAY IS MONDAY.
IT'S TIME FOR SCHOOL NOW.
I'VE PROBABLY BEEN... RUNNING AWAY.

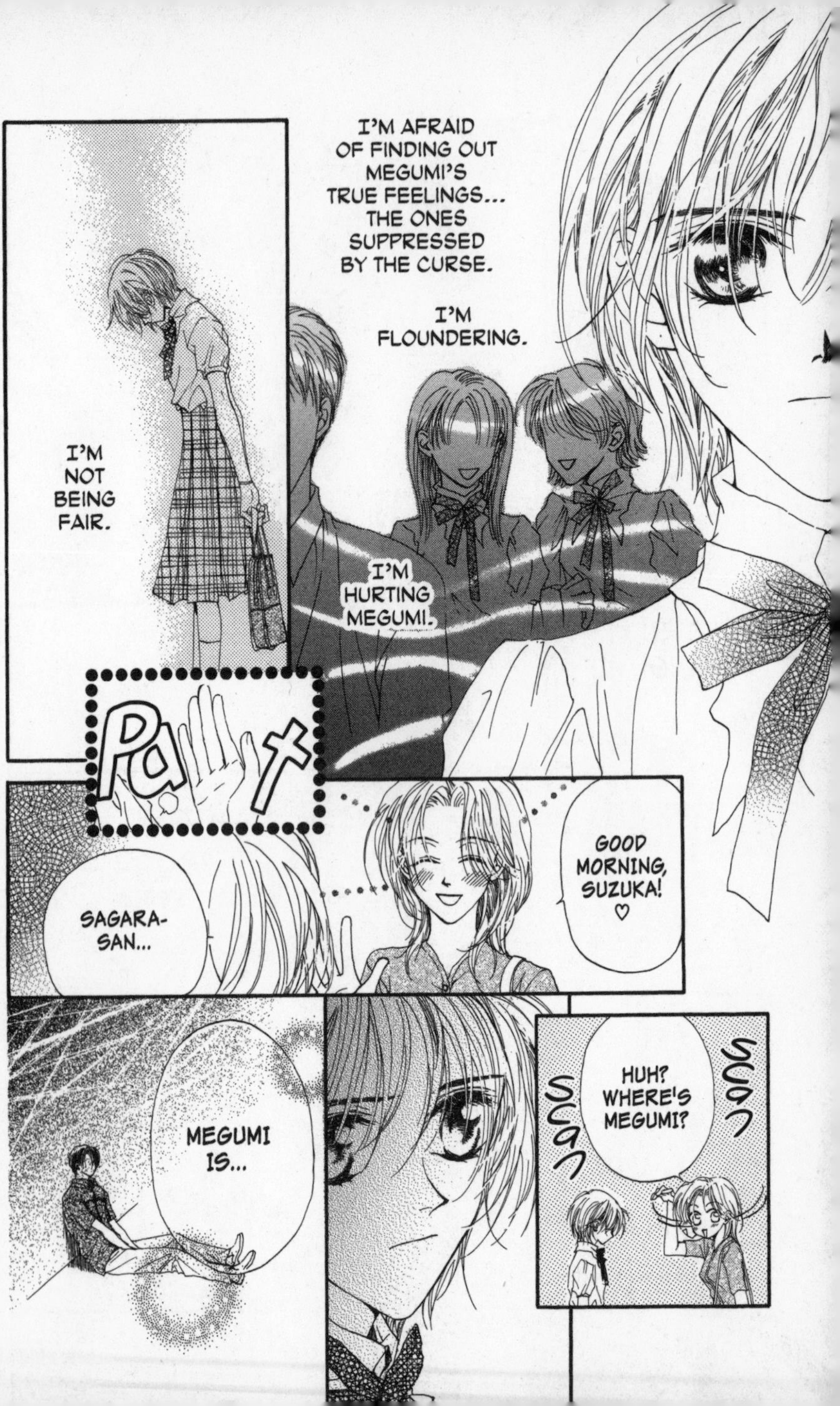
I'M AFRAID OF FINDING OUT MEGUMI'S TRUE FEELINGS... THE ONES SUPPRESSED BY THE CURSE.
I'M FLOUNDERING.
I'M HURTING MEGUMI.
I'M NOT BEING FAIR.
Pat
GOOD MORNING, SUZUKA! ♡
SAGARA-SAN...
SCAN
HUH? WHERE'S MEGUMI?
SCAN
MEGUMI IS...

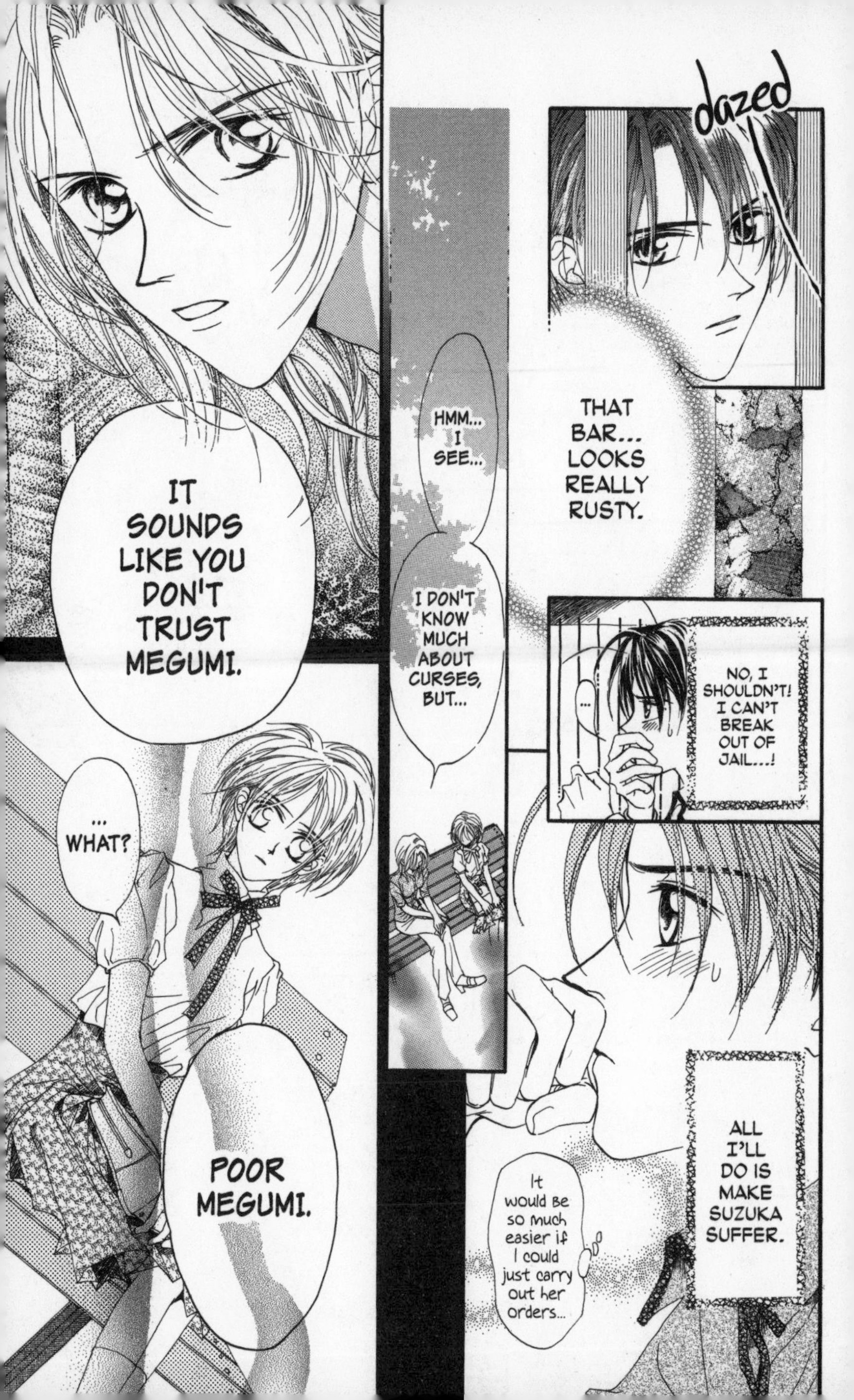
dazed
THAT BAR... LOOKS REALLY RUSTY.
...
NO, I SHOULDN'T! I CAN'T BREAK OUT OF JAIL...!
ALL I'LL DO IS MAKE SUZUKA SUFFER.
It would be so much easier if I could just carry out her orders...
HMM... I SEE...
I DON'T KNOW MUCH ABOUT CURSES, BUT...
IT SOUNDS LIKE YOU DON'T TRUST MEGUMI.
... WHAT?
POOR MEGUMI.

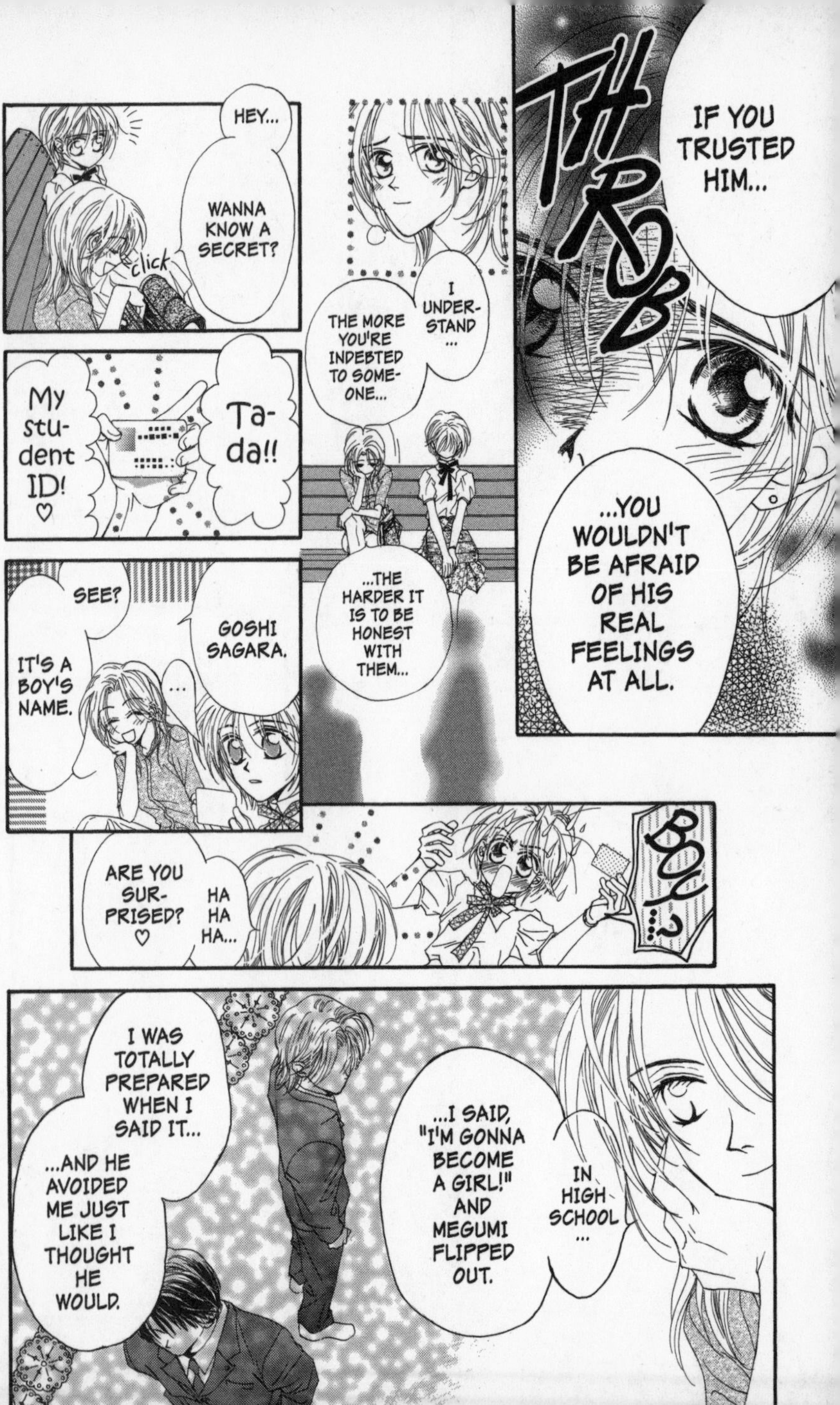
THROB
IF YOU TRUSTED HIM...
...YOU WOULDN'T BE AFRAID OF HIS REAL FEELINGS AT ALL.
I UNDERSTAND...
THE MORE YOU'RE INDEBTED TO SOMEONE...
...THE HARDER IT IS TO BE HONEST WITH THEM...
HEY...
WANNA KNOW A SECRET?
click
Ta-da!!
My student ID! ♡
GOSHI SAGARA.
SEE?
IT'S A BOY'S NAME.
...
BOY...?
...
HA HA HA...
ARE YOU SURPRISED? ♡
IN HIGH SCHOOL...
...I SAID, "I'M GONNA BECOME A GIRL!" AND MEGUMI FLIPPED OUT.
I WAS TOTALLY PREPARED WHEN I SAID IT...
...AND HE AVOIDED ME JUST LIKE I THOUGHT HE WOULD.

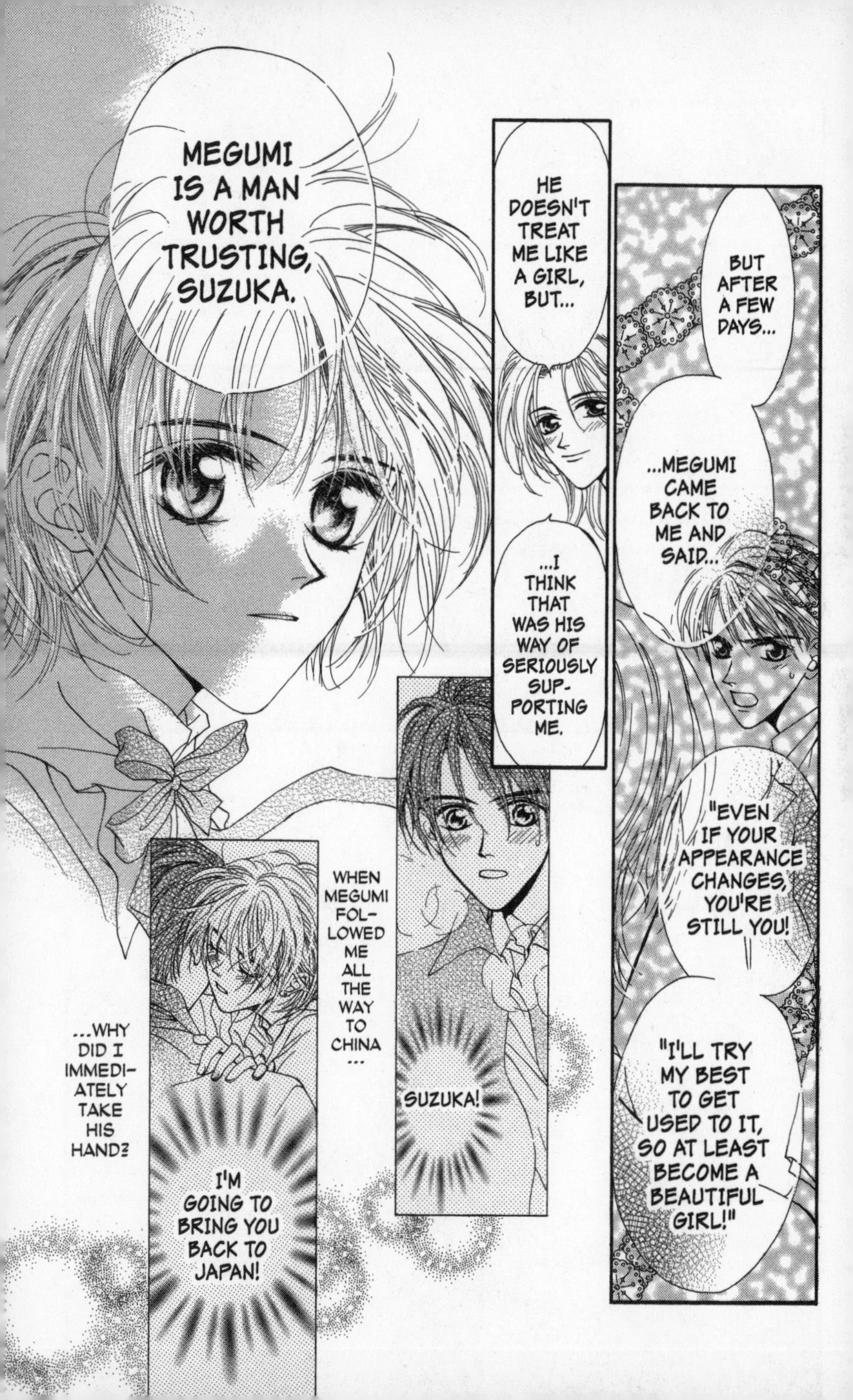
BUT AFTER A FEW DAYS...
...MEGUMI CAME BACK TO ME AND SAID...
"EVEN IF YOUR APPEARANCE CHANGES, YOU'RE STILL YOU!
"I'LL TRY MY BEST TO GET USED TO IT, SO AT LEAST BECOME A BEAUTIFUL GIRL!"
HE DOESN'T TREAT ME LIKE A GIRL, BUT...
...I THINK THAT WAS HIS WAY OF SERIOUSLY SUP-PORTING ME.
MEGUMI IS A MAN WORTH TRUSTING, SUZUKA.
SUZUKA!
WHEN MEGUMI FOL-LOWED ME ALL THE WAY TO CHINA ...
I'M GOING TO BRING YOU BACK TO JAPAN!
...WHY DID I IMMEDI-ATELY TAKE HIS HAND?

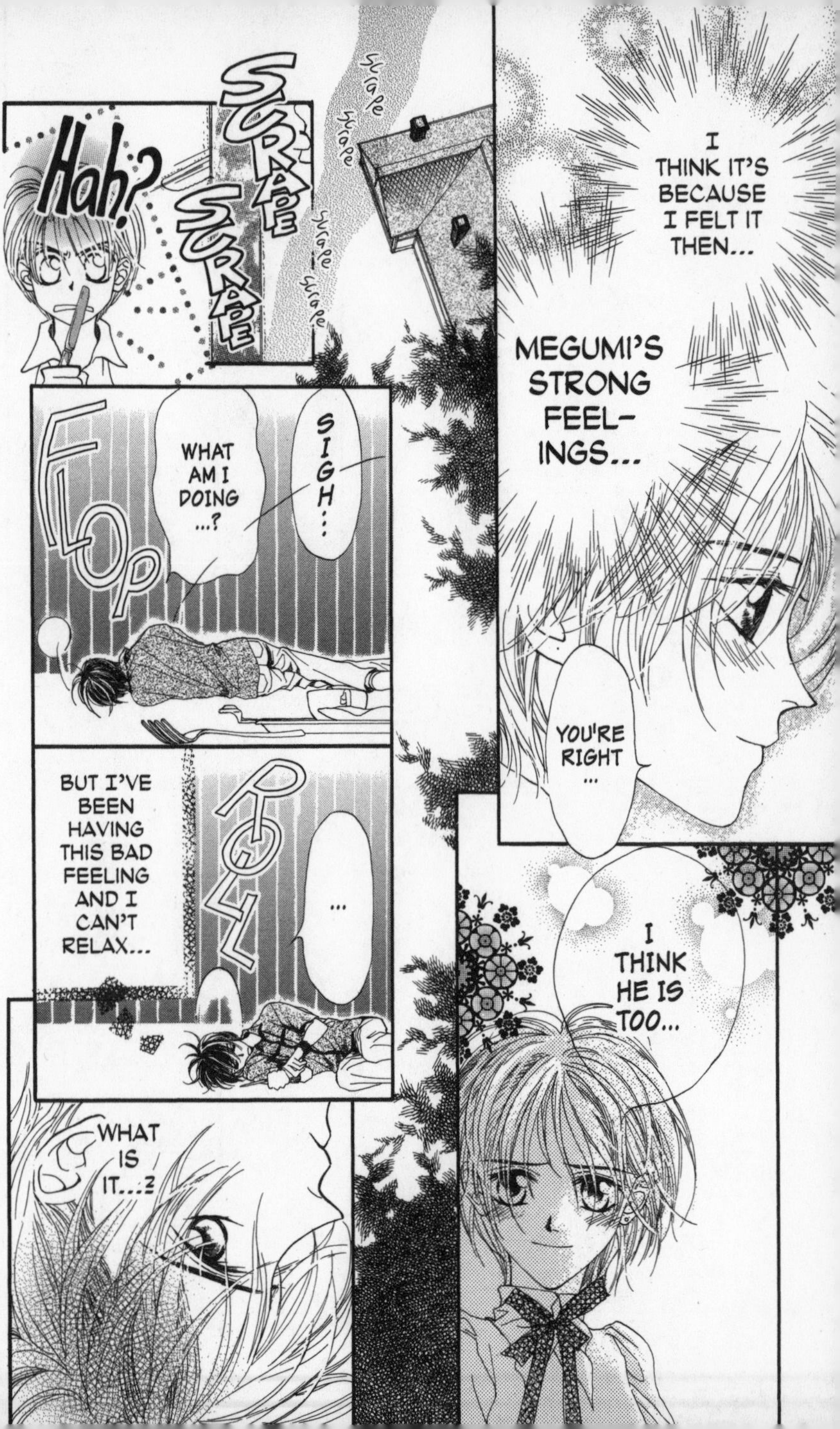
I THINK IT'S BECAUSE I FELT IT THEN...
MEGUMI'S STRONG FEEL-INGS...
YOU'RE RIGHT ...
Hah?
SCRAPE SCRAPE
scrape scrape scrape scrape
SIGH...
WHAT AM I DOING ...?
FLOP
ROLL
...
BUT I'VE BEEN HAVING THIS BAD FEELING AND I CAN'T RELAX...
I THINK HE IS TOO...
WHAT IS IT...?

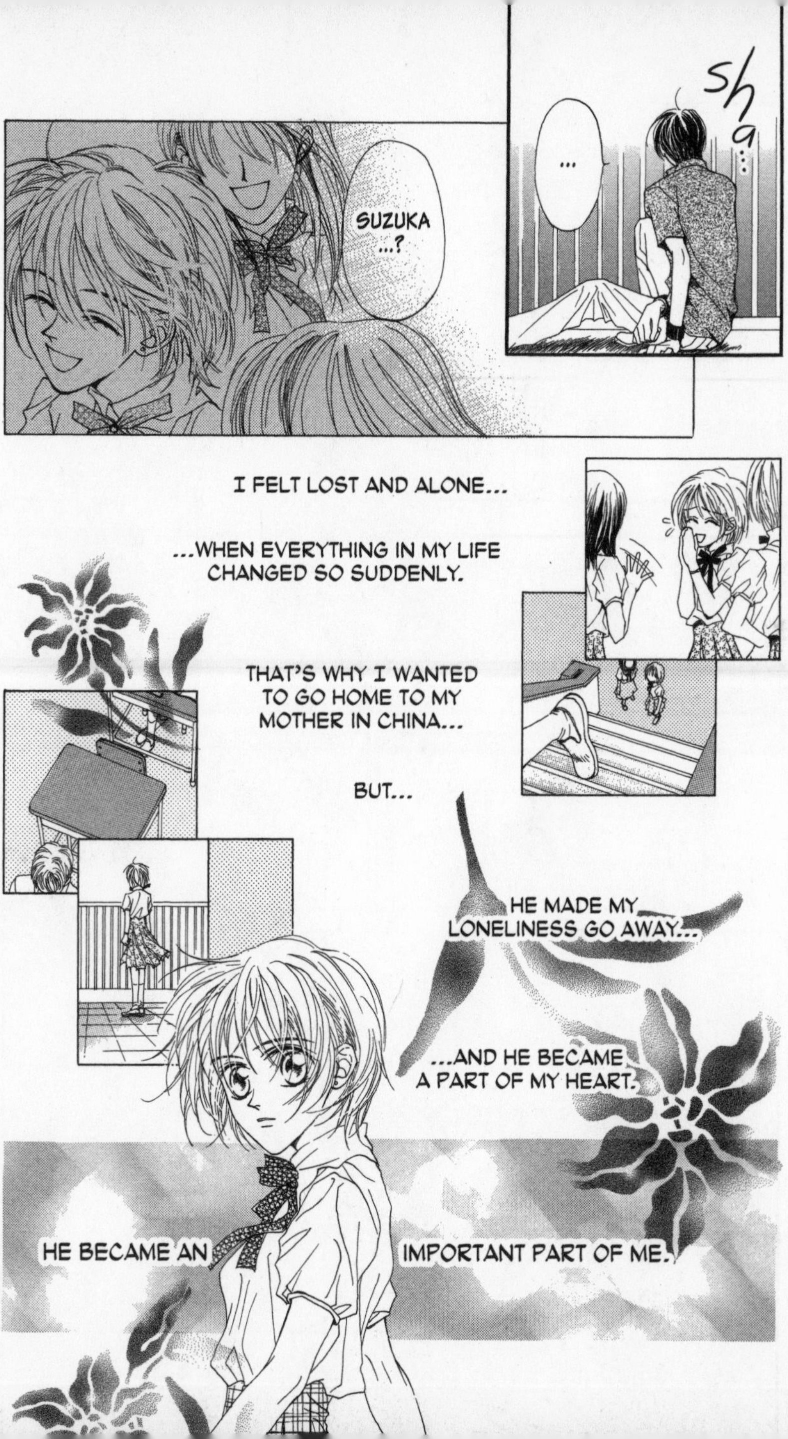

Sha...
...
SUZUKA ...?
I FELT LOST AND ALONE...
...WHEN EVERYTHING IN MY LIFE CHANGED SO SUDDENLY.
THAT'S WHY I WANTED TO GO HOME TO MY MOTHER IN CHINA...
BUT...
HE MADE MY LONELINESS GO AWAY...
...AND HE BECAME A PART OF MY HEART.
HE BECAME AN IMPORTANT PART OF ME.

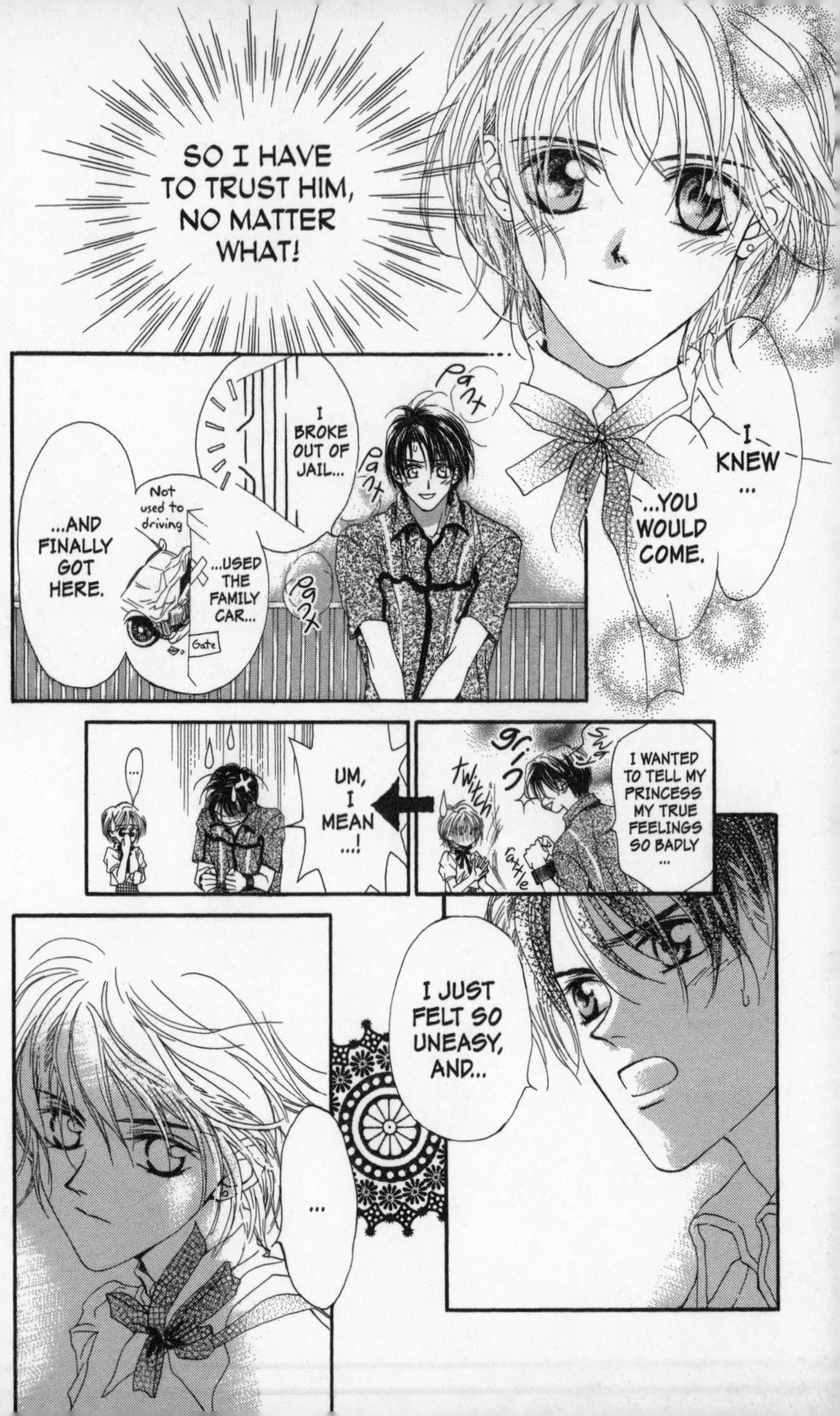
SO I HAVE TO TRUST HIM, NO MATTER WHAT!
I KNEW ...
...YOU WOULD COME.
pant
I BROKE OUT OF JAIL...
pant
pant
...USED THE FAMILY CAR...
Not used to driving
Gate
...AND FINALLY GOT HERE.
I WANTED TO TELL MY PRINCESS MY TRUE FEELINGS SO BADLY ...
grin
twitch
rattle
UM, I MEAN ...!
...
I JUST FELT SO UNEASY, AND...
...

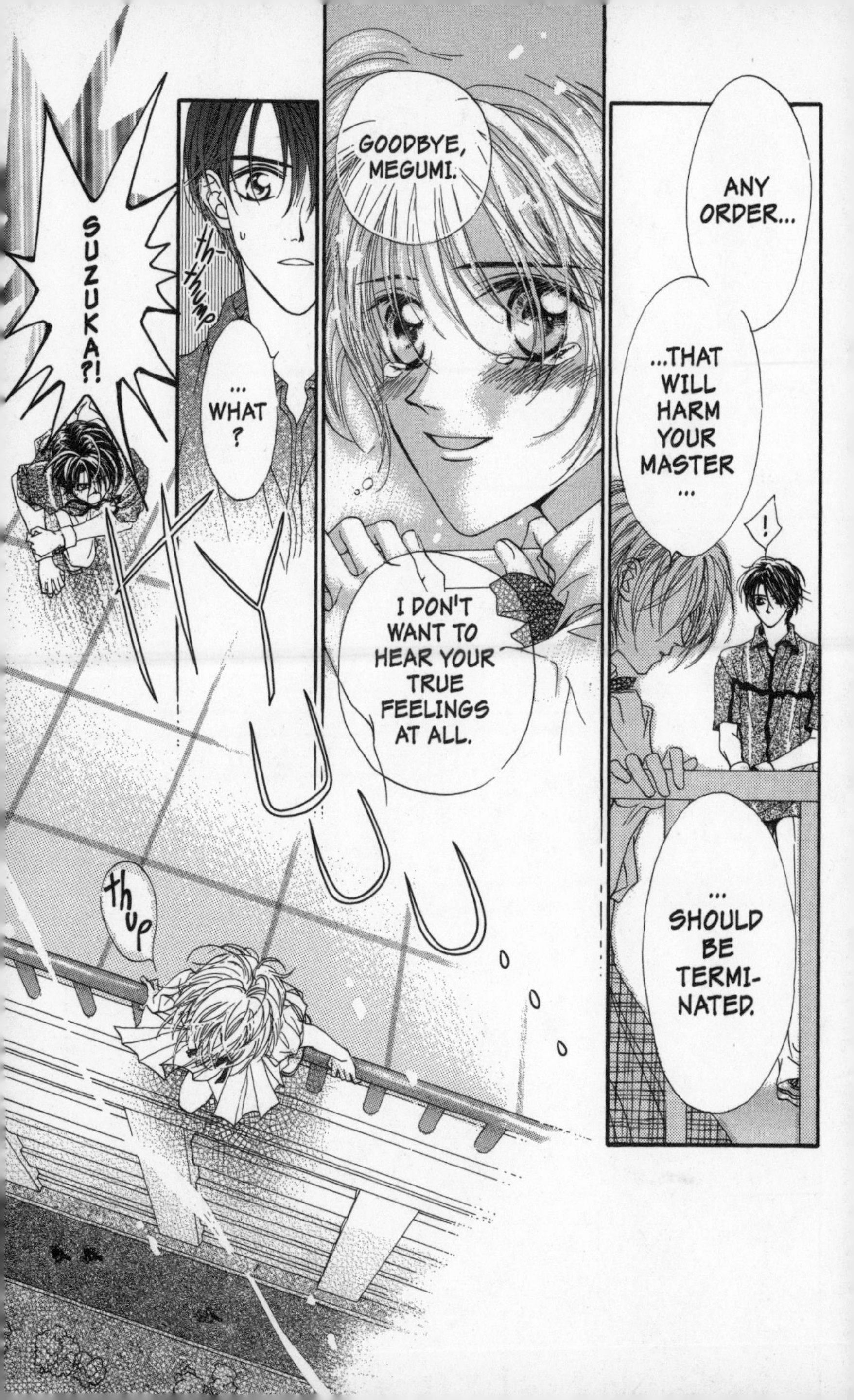
ANY ORDER...
...THAT WILL HARM YOUR MASTER...
!
...SHOULD BE TERMINATED.
GOODBYE, MEGUMI.
I DON'T WANT TO HEAR YOUR TRUE FEELINGS AT ALL.
th-thump
...WHAT?
SUZUKA?!
HYUUU
thup

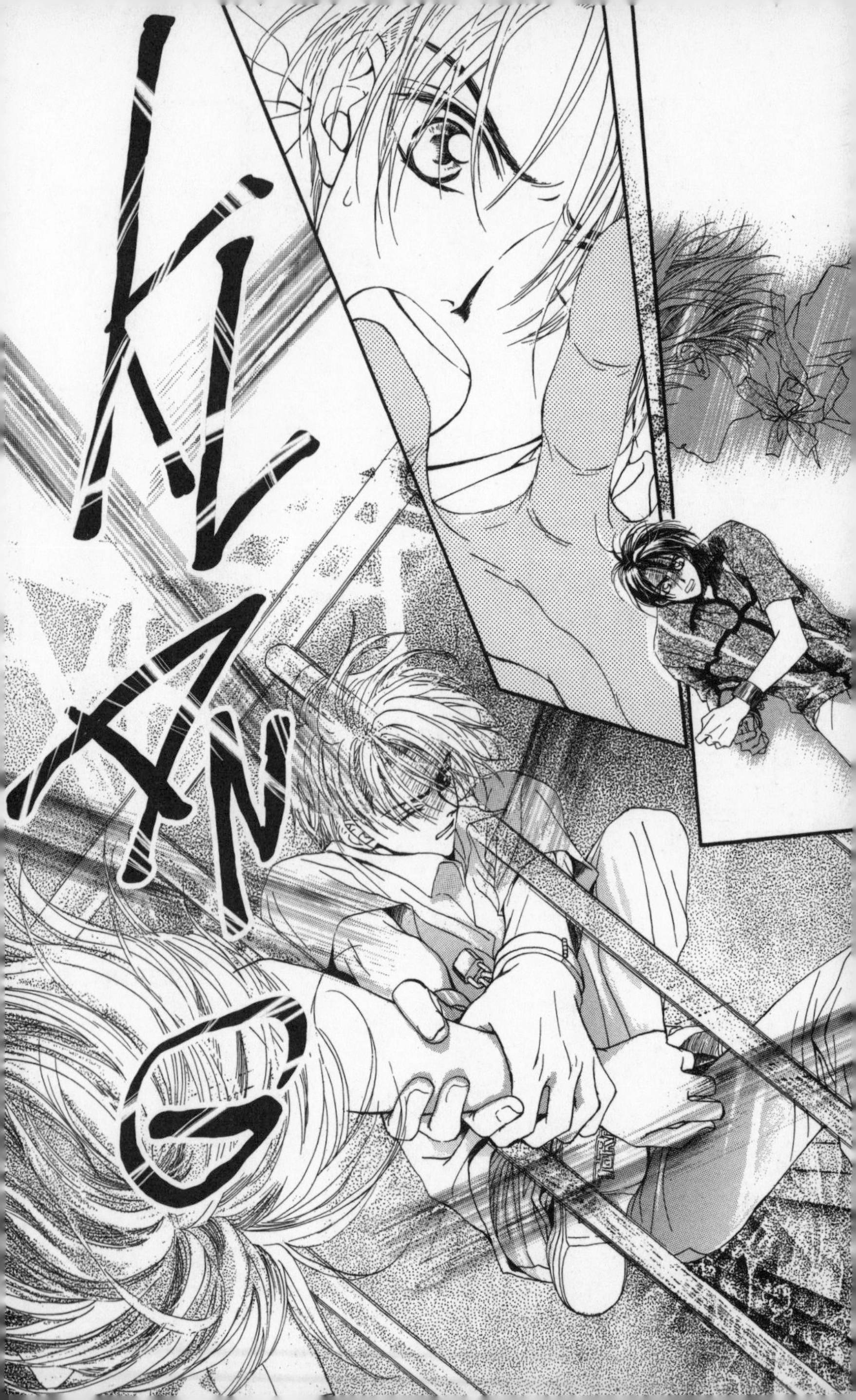
KLANG

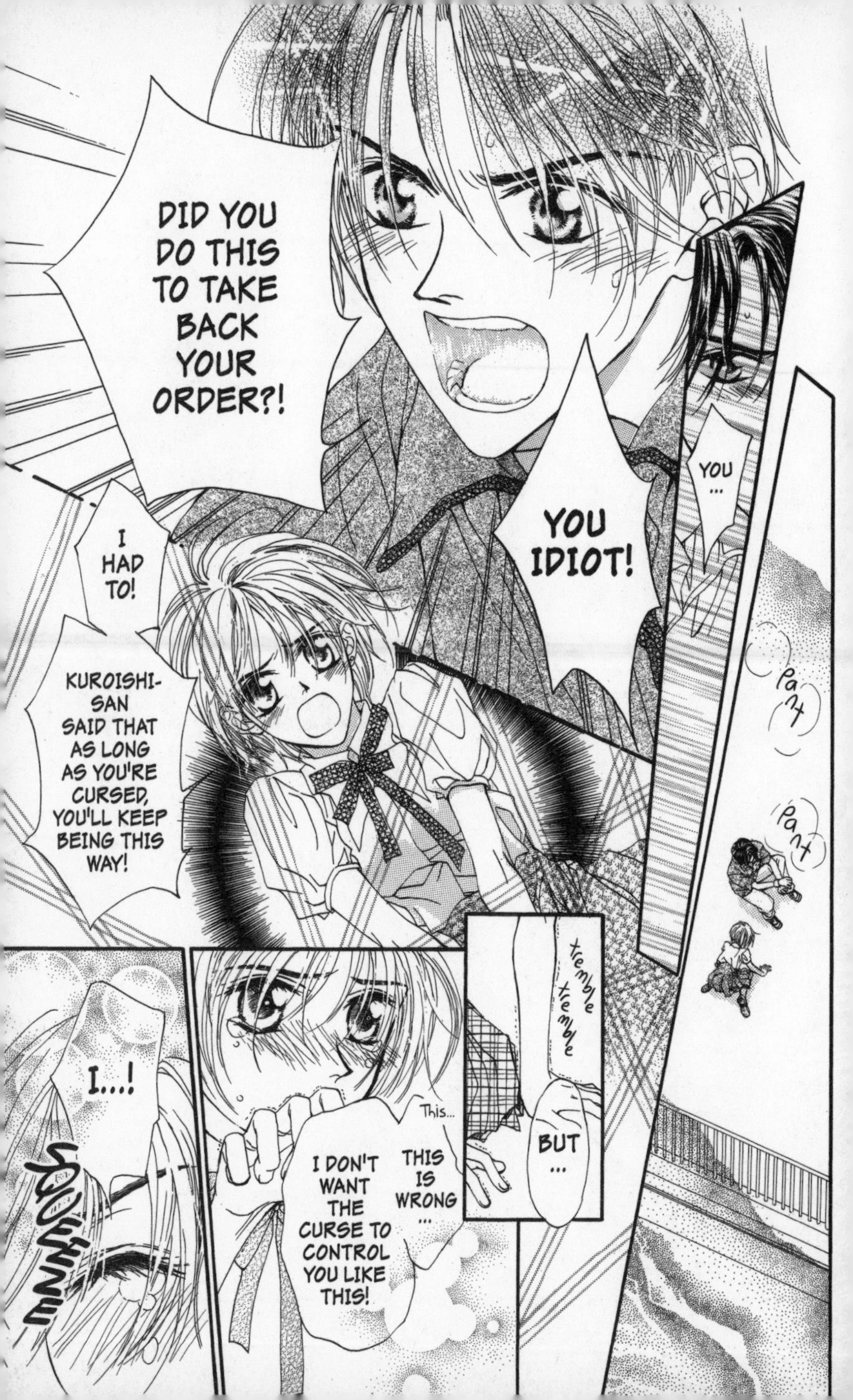
YOU ...
Pant
Pant
DID YOU DO THIS TO TAKE BACK YOUR ORDER?!
YOU IDIOT!
I HAD TO!
KUROISHI-SAN SAID THAT AS LONG AS YOU'RE CURSED, YOU'LL KEEP BEING THIS WAY!
tremble tremble
BUT ...
This...
THIS IS WRONG ...
I DON'T WANT THE CURSE TO CONTROL YOU LIKE THIS!
I...!
SQUEEZE

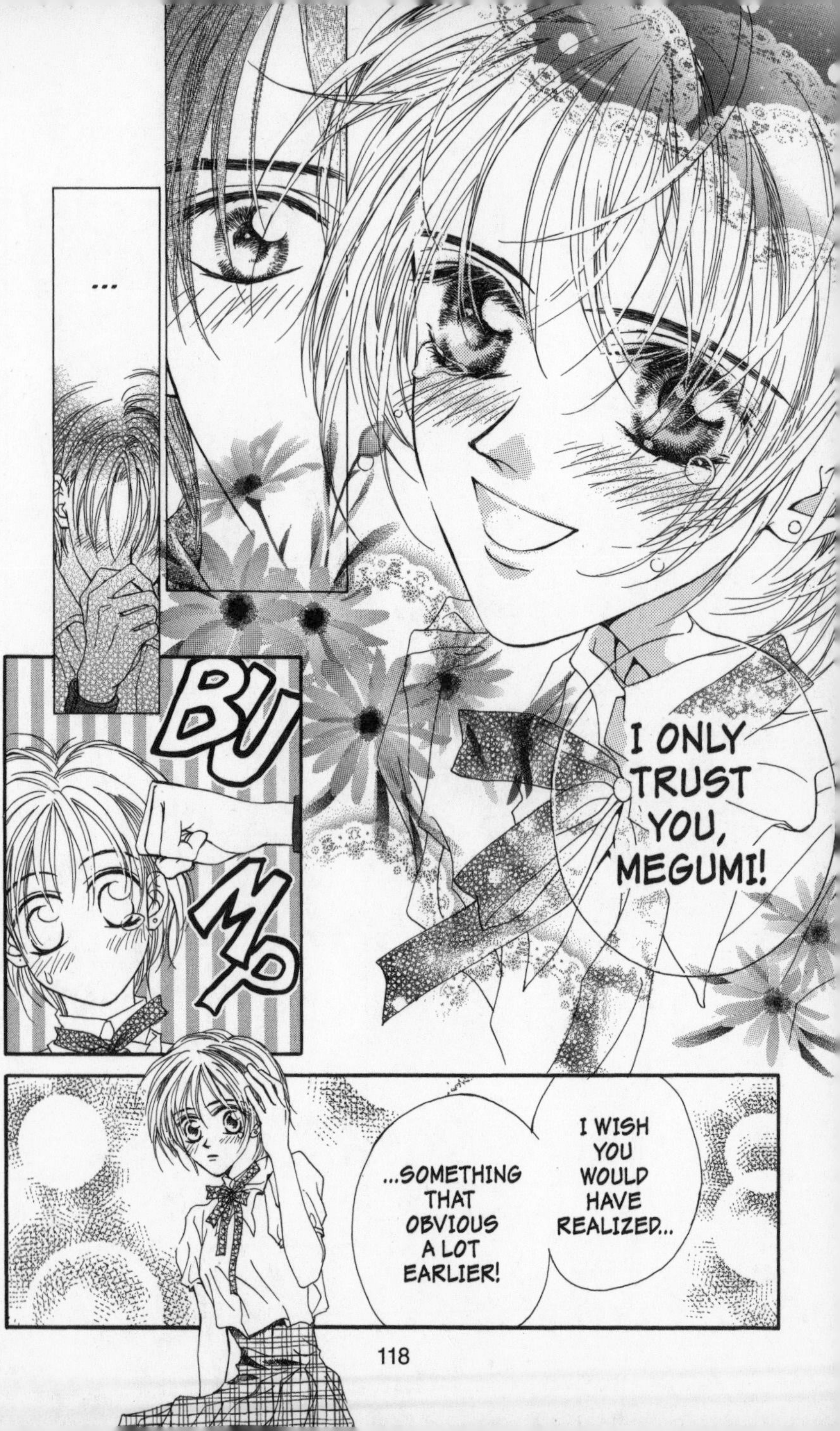
I ONLY TRUST YOU, MEGUMI!
...
BUMP
I WISH YOU WOULD HAVE REALIZED...
...SOMETHING THAT OBVIOUS A LOT EARLIER!

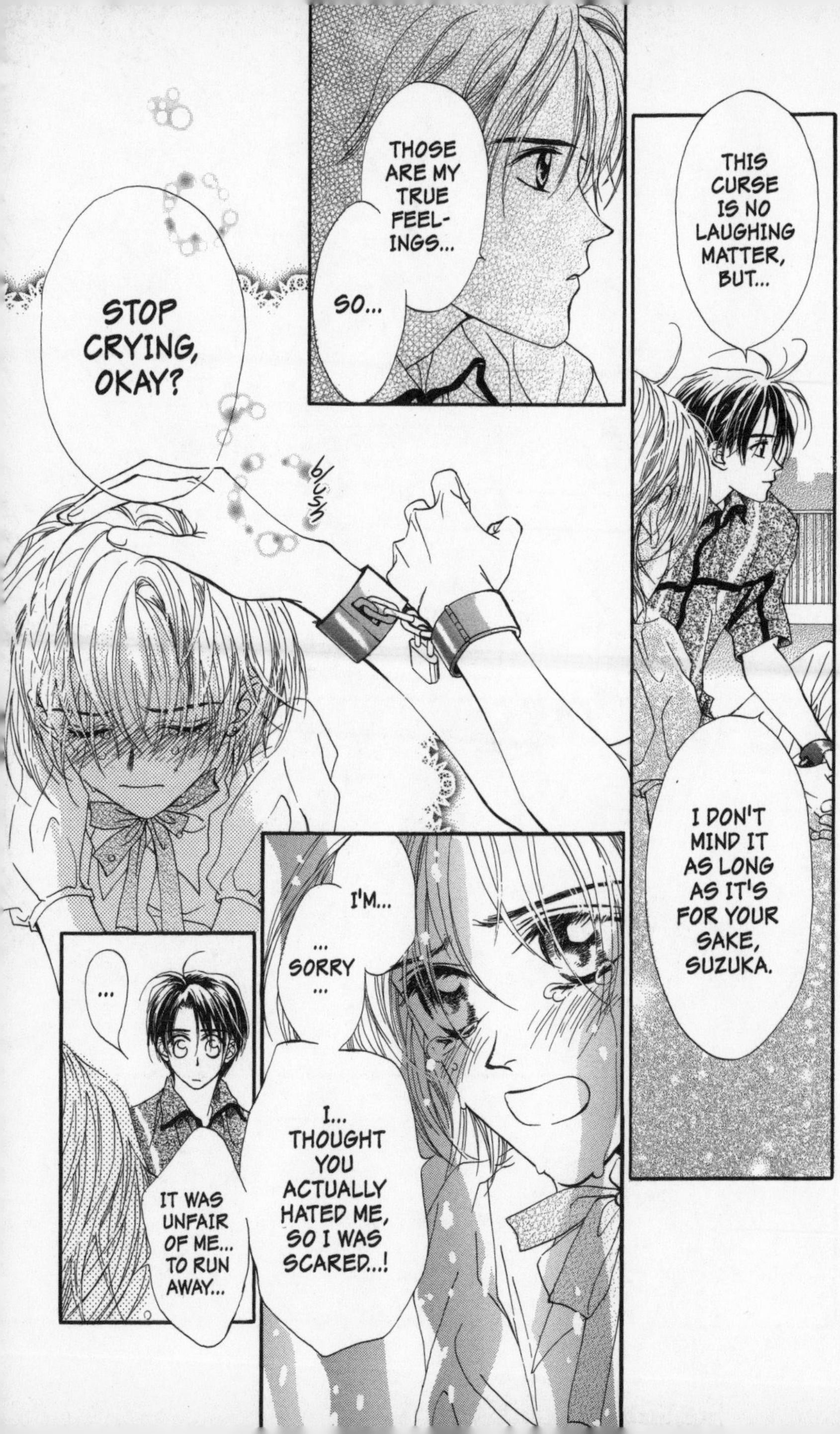
THIS CURSE IS NO LAUGHING MATTER, BUT...
I DON'T MIND IT AS LONG AS IT'S FOR YOUR SAKE, SUZUKA.
THOSE ARE MY TRUE FEEL-INGS...
SO...
STOP CRYING, OKAY?
blush
I'M...
... SORRY ...
I... THOUGHT YOU ACTUALLY HATED ME, SO I WAS SCARED...!
...
IT WAS UNFAIR OF ME... TO RUN AWAY...

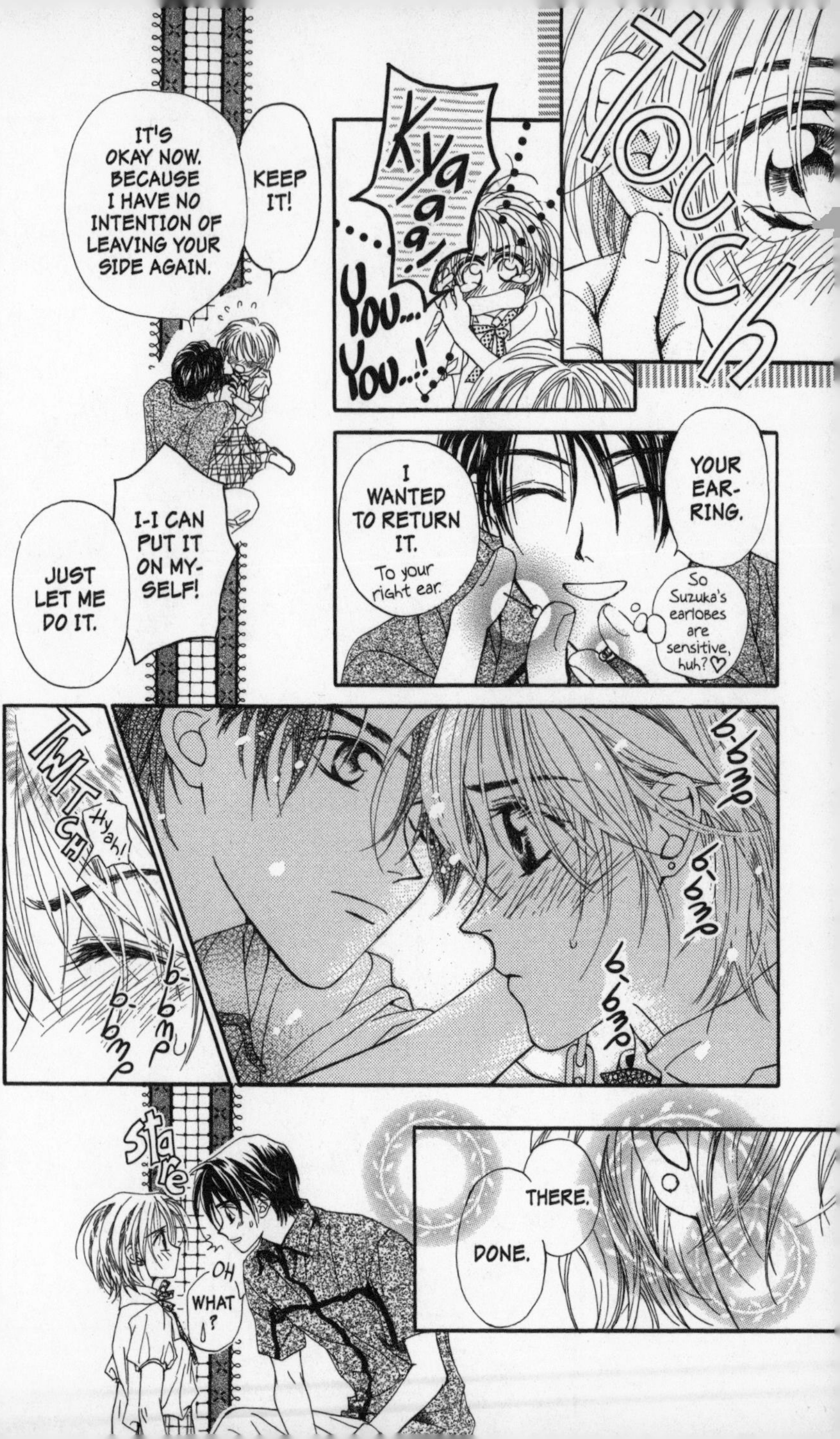
TOUCH
KYAA!
YOU... YOU...!
YOUR EAR-RING.
I WANTED TO RETURN IT.
To your right ear.
So Suzuka's earlobes are sensitive, huh?♡
KEEP IT!
IT'S OKAY NOW. BECAUSE I HAVE NO INTENTION OF LEAVING YOUR SIDE AGAIN.
I-I CAN PUT IT ON MY-SELF!
JUST LET ME DO IT.
b-bmp b-bmp
b-bmp
TWITCH
Hyah!
b-bmp b-bmp
THERE.
DONE.
stare
OH
WHAT?

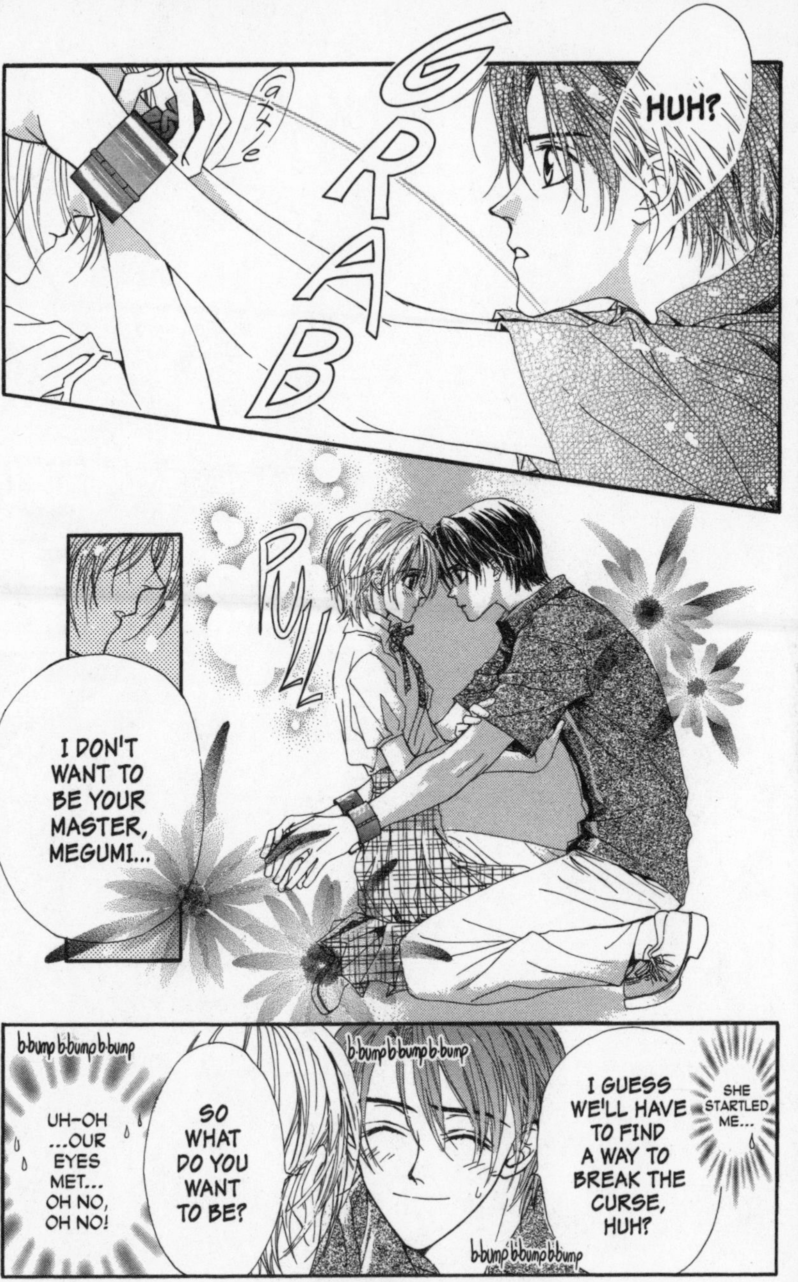
HUH?
GRAB
PULL
I DON'T WANT TO BE YOUR MASTER, MEGUMI...
SHE STARTLED ME...
I GUESS WE'LL HAVE TO FIND A WAY TO BREAK THE CURSE, HUH?
b-bump b-bump b-bump
b-bump b-bump b-bump
SO WHAT DO YOU WANT TO BE?
UH-OH ...OUR EYES MET... OH NO, OH NO!
b-bump b-bump b-bump

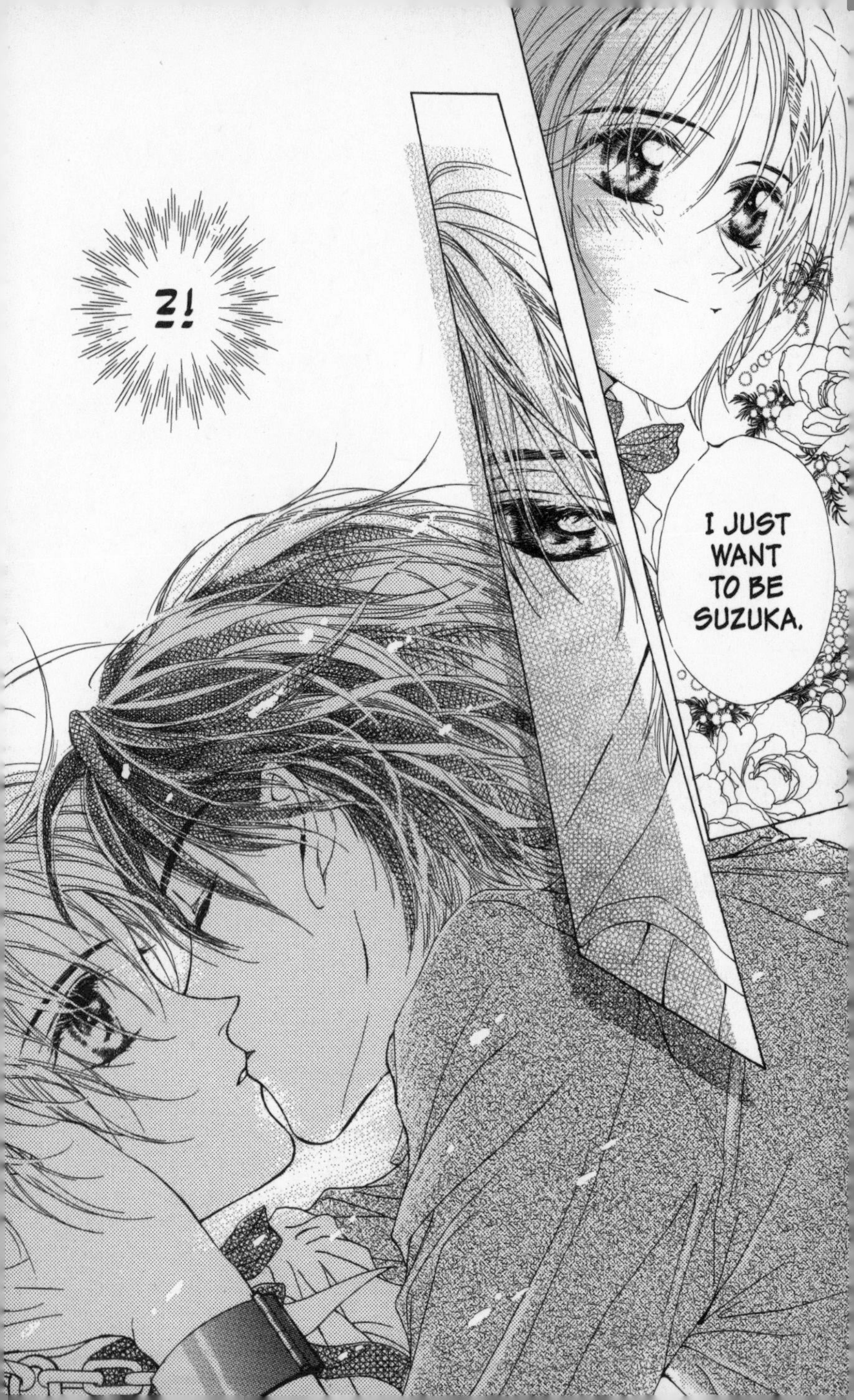
I JUST WANT TO BE SUZUKA.
!?

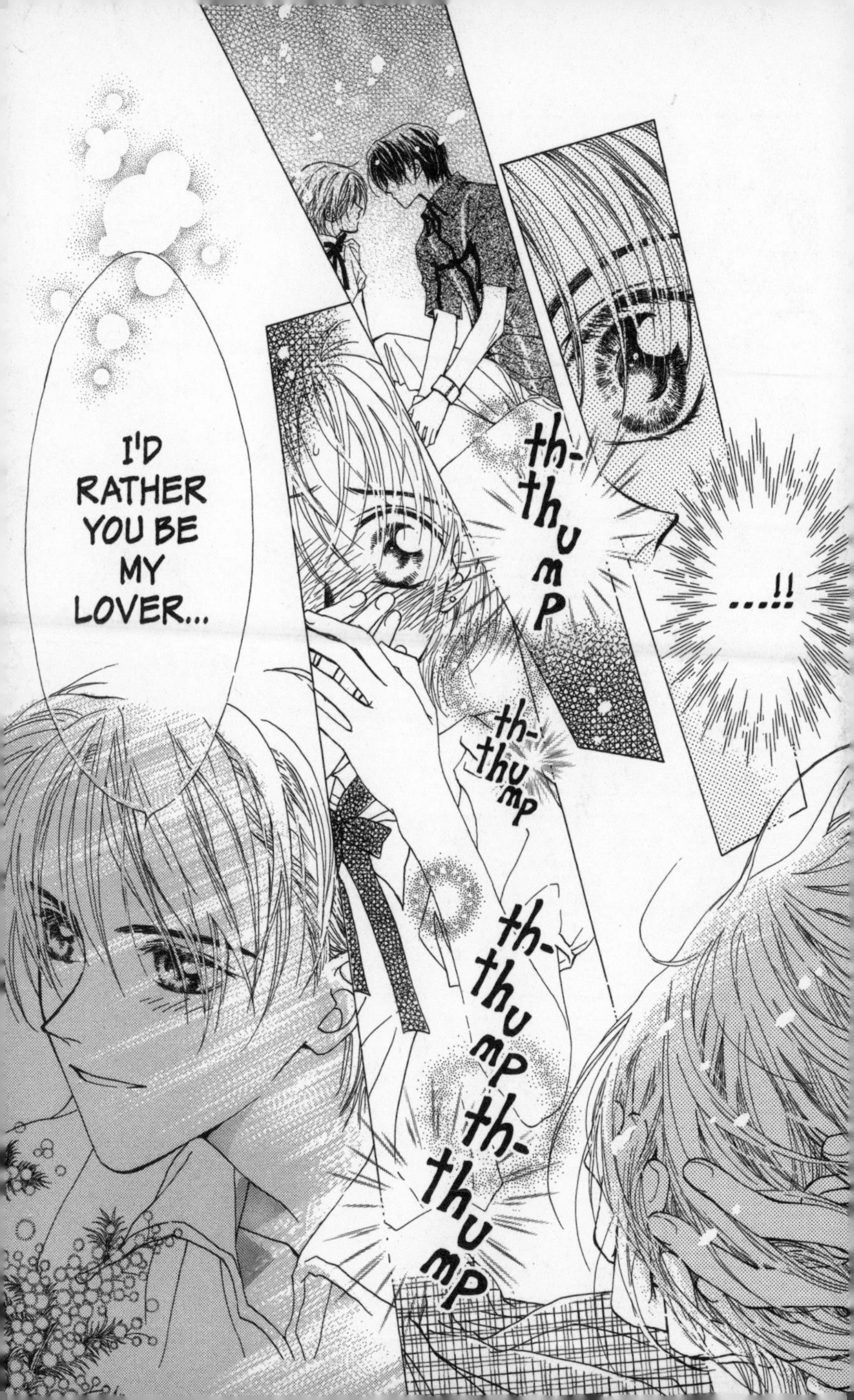
th-thump
...!!
I'D RATHER YOU BE MY LOVER...
th-thump
th-thump th-thump

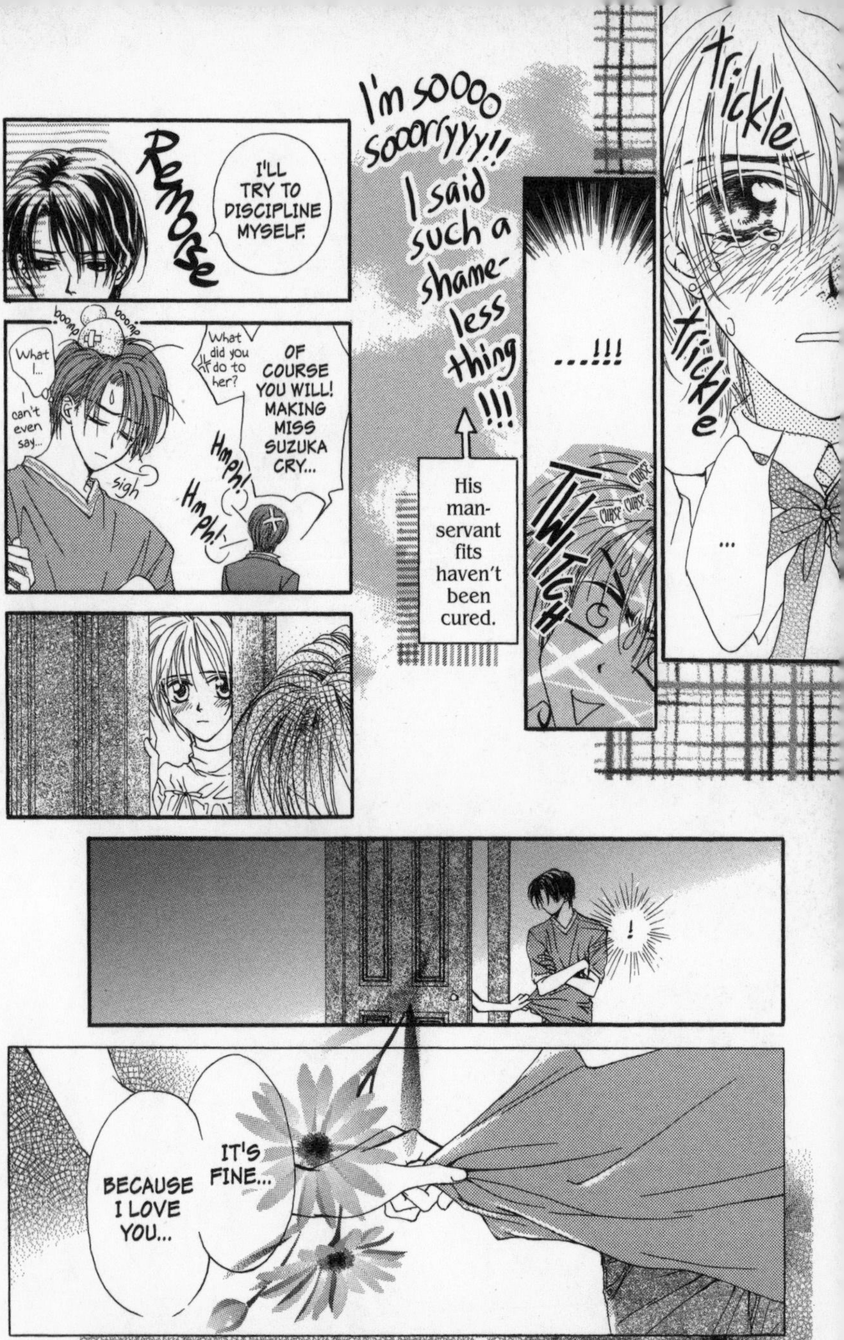
trickle
trickle
...
...!!!
TWITCH
CURSE CURSE CURSE
I'm soooo sooorryyy!! I said such a shameless thing!!!
His manservant fits haven't been cured.
Remorse
I'LL TRY TO DISCIPLINE MYSELF.
boomp boomp
OF COURSE YOU WILL! MAKING MISS SUZUKA CRY...
What did you do to her?
Hmph! Hmph!
What I... I can't even say...
sigh
!
IT'S FINE...
BECAUSE I LOVE YOU...

Captive Hearts 1 / The End

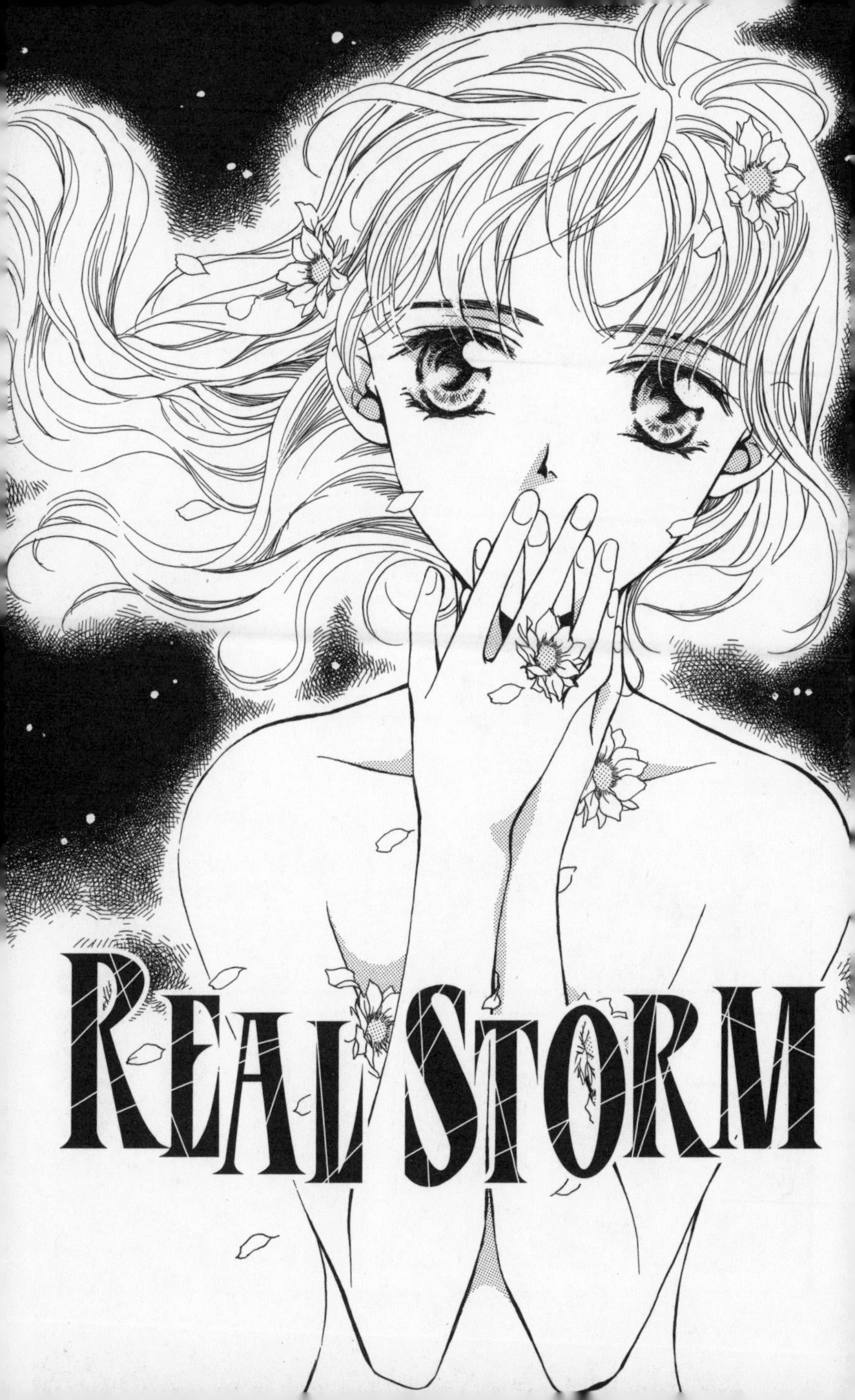
REAL STORM

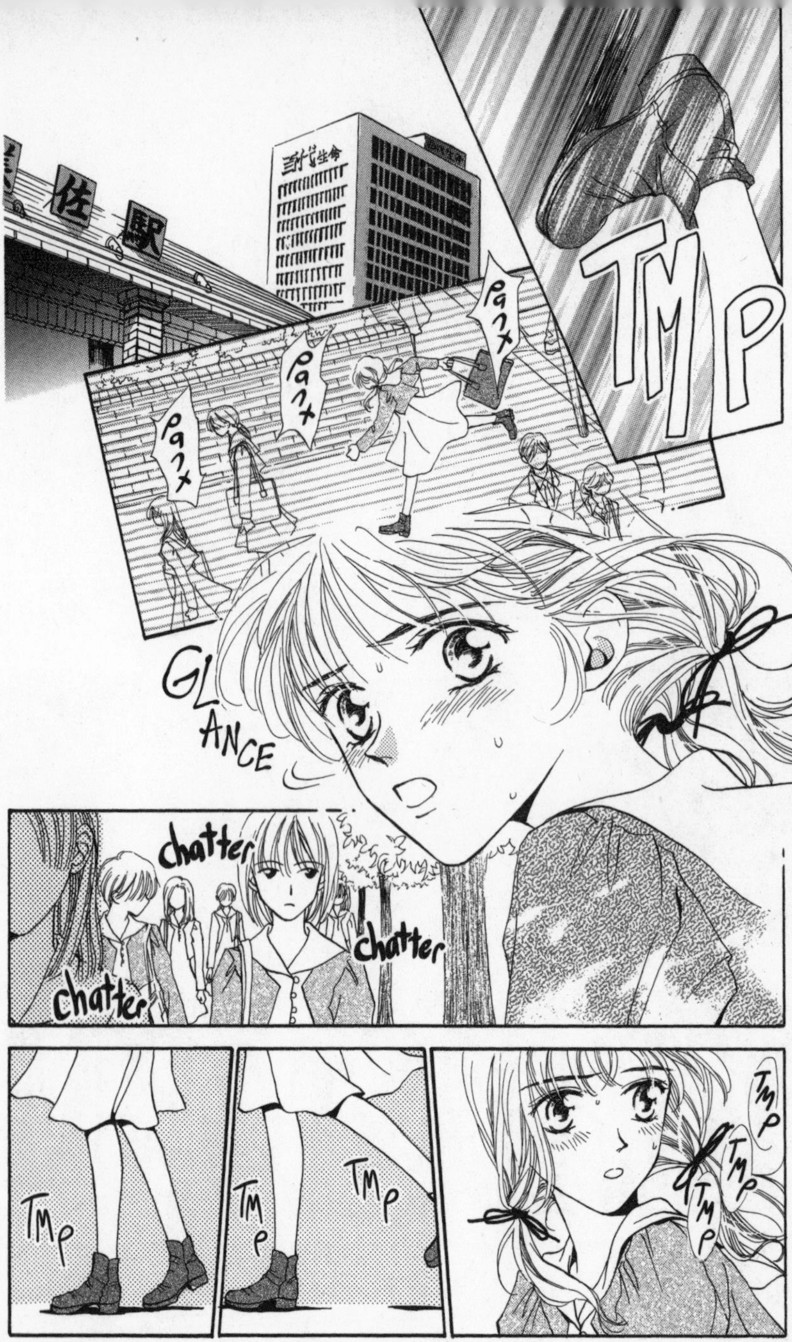
TMP
GLANCE
chatter
chatter
chatter
TMP
TMP
TMP
TMP
TMP
TMP

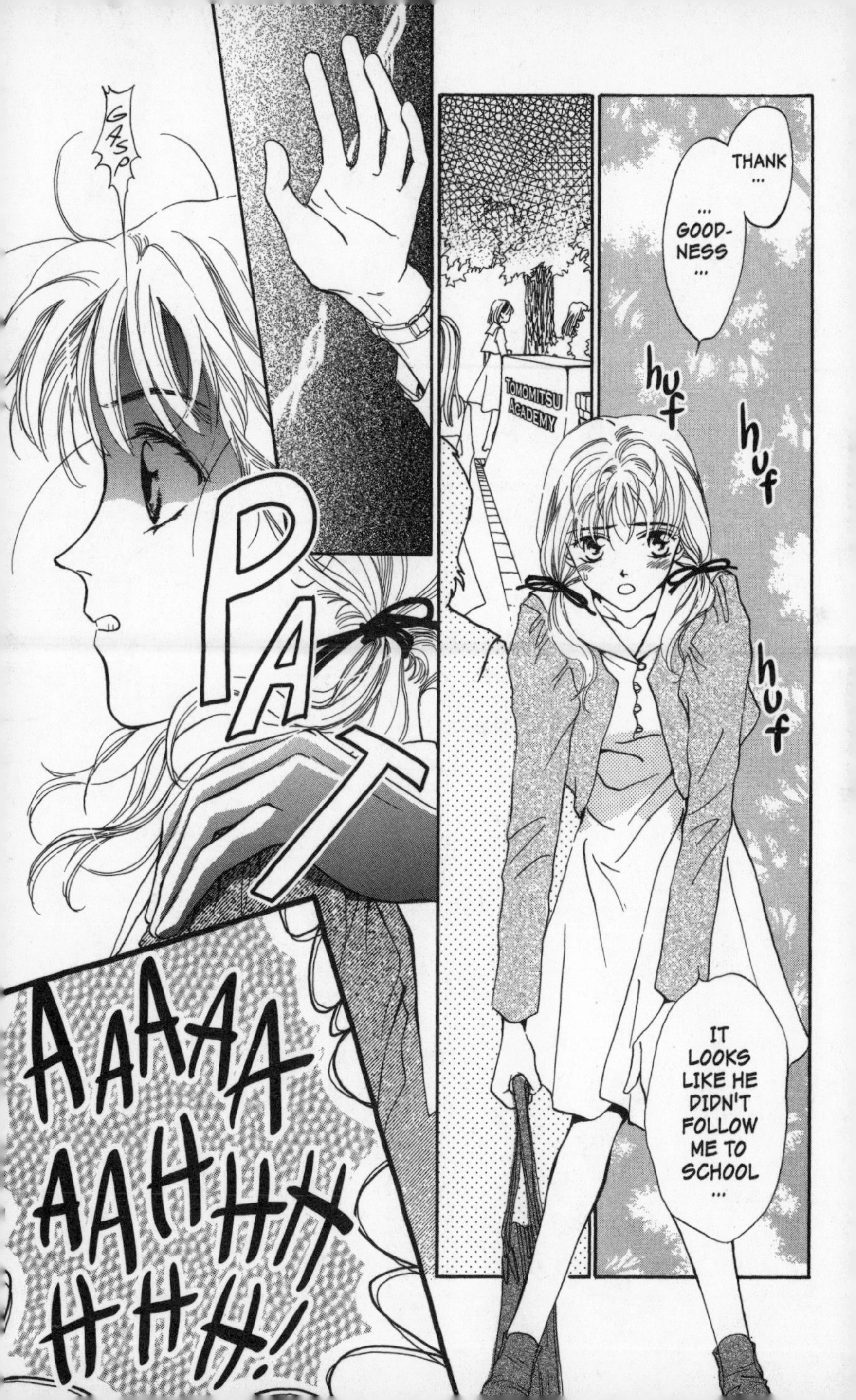

TOMOMITSU ACADEMY
THANK... ...GOODNESS...
huf huf huf
IT LOOKS LIKE HE DIDN'T FOLLOW ME TO SCHOOL...
GASP
PAT
AAAAAAHHHHHH!

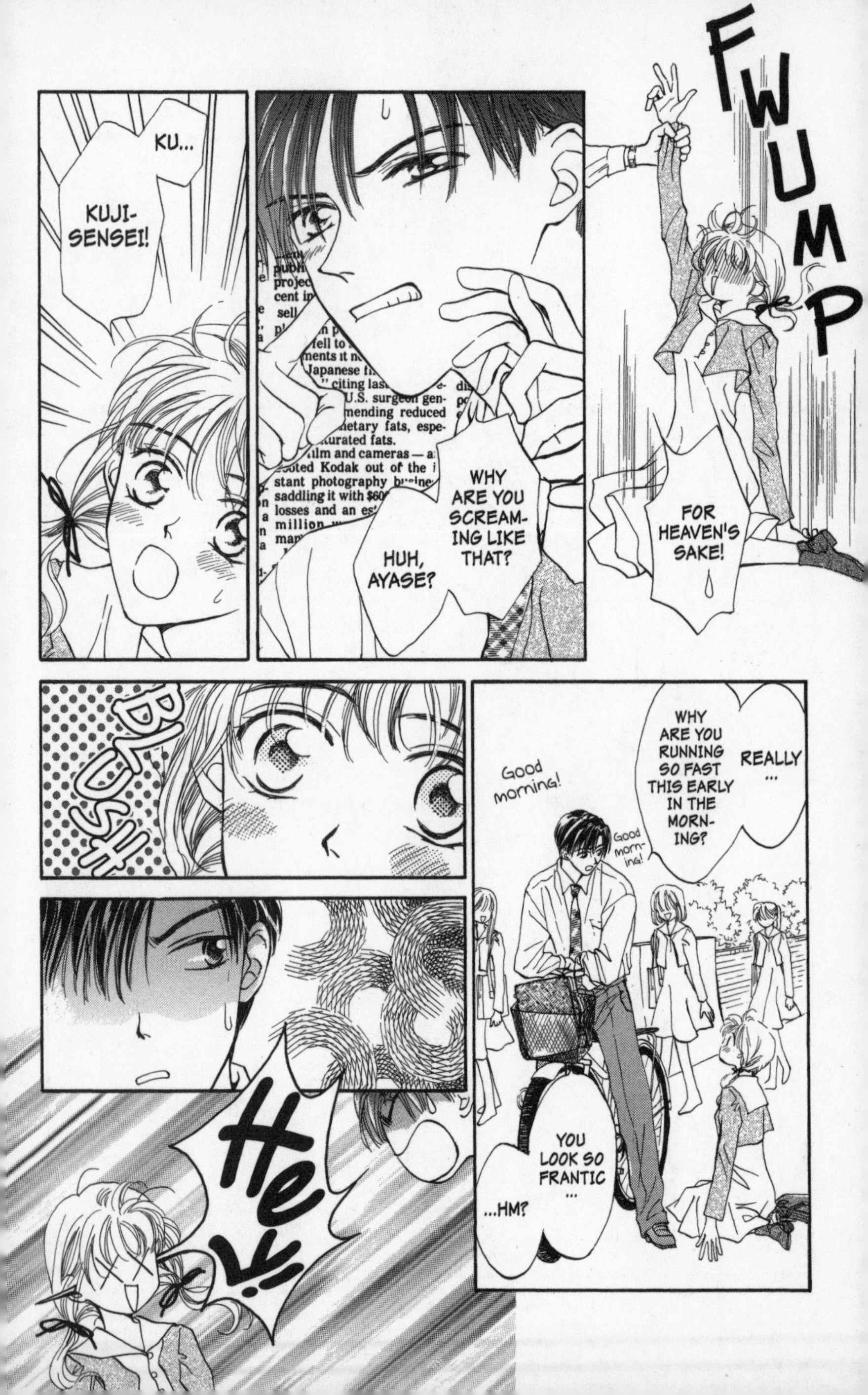
FWUMP
FOR HEAVEN'S SAKE!
WHY ARE YOU SCREAMING LIKE THAT?
HUH, AYASE?
KU...
KUJI-SENSEI!
REALLY...
WHY ARE YOU RUNNING SO FAST THIS EARLY IN THE MORNING?
Good morning!
Good morning!
YOU LOOK SO FRANTIC...
...HM?
BLUSH
HEY!

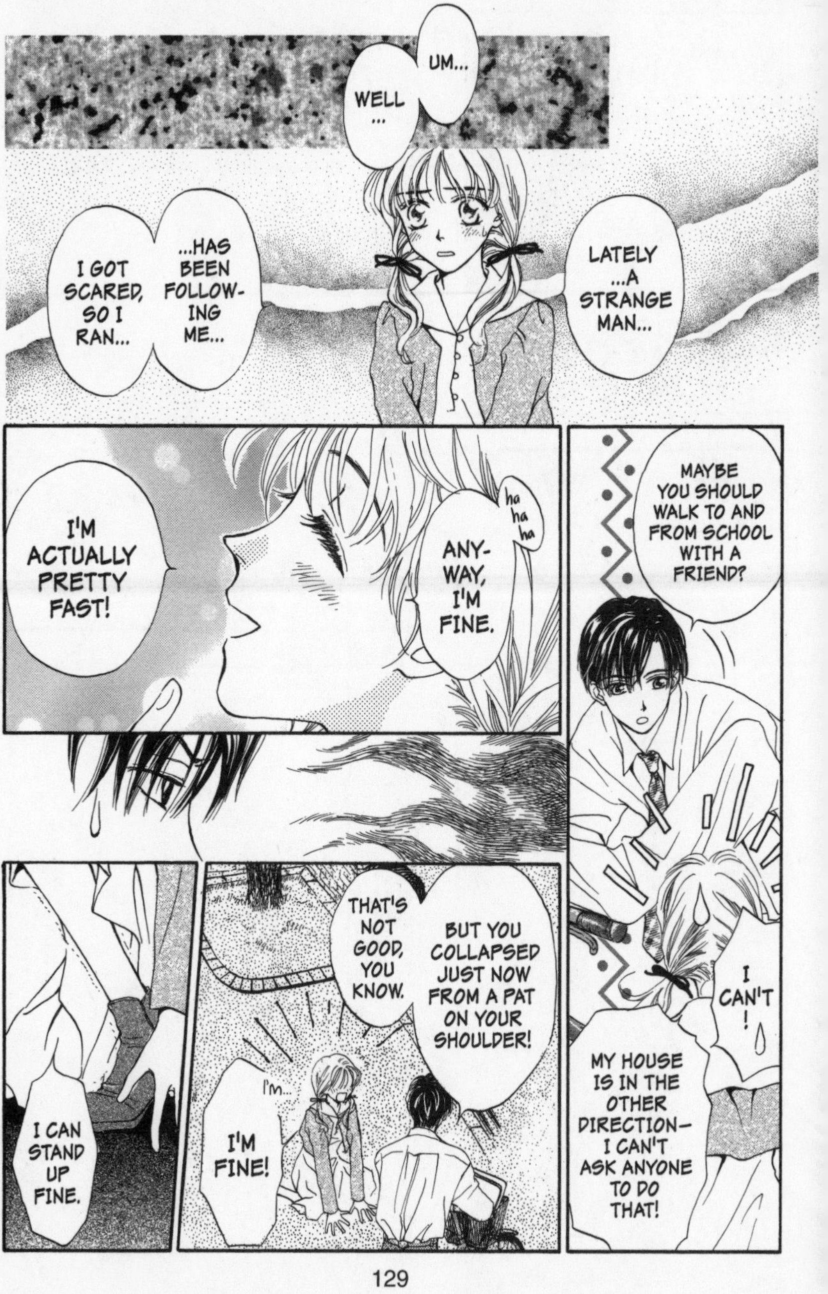
UM...
WELL ...
LATELY ...A STRANGE MAN...
...HAS BEEN FOLLOWING ME...
I GOT SCARED, SO I RAN...
MAYBE YOU SHOULD WALK TO AND FROM SCHOOL WITH A FRIEND?
I CAN'T!
MY HOUSE IS IN THE OTHER DIRECTION— I CAN'T ASK ANYONE TO DO THAT!
ha ha ha
ANY-WAY, I'M FINE.
I'M ACTUALLY PRETTY FAST!
THAT'S NOT GOOD, YOU KNOW.
BUT YOU COLLAPSED JUST NOW FROM A PAT ON YOUR SHOULDER!
I'm...
I'M FINE!
I CAN STAND UP FINE.

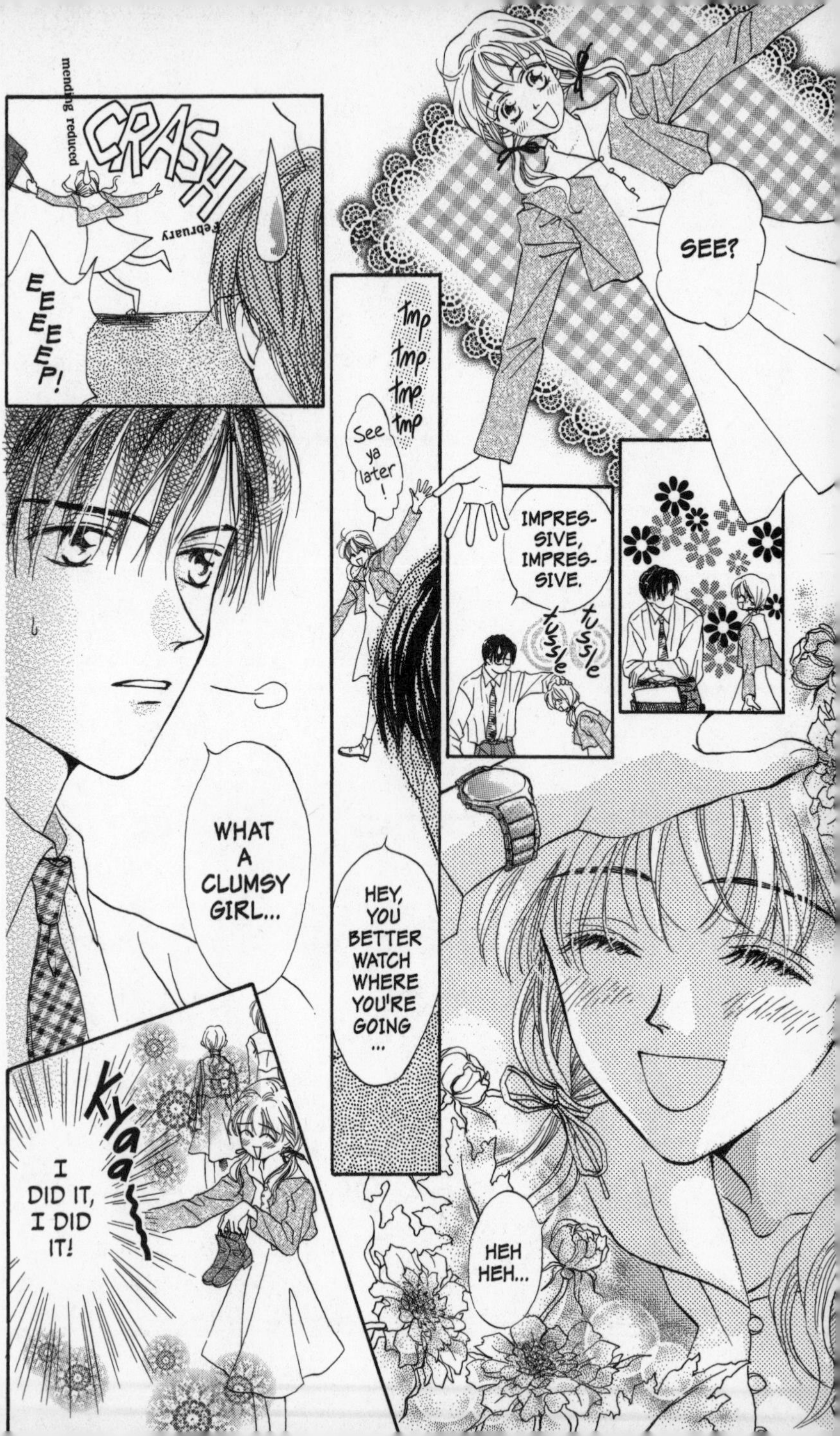
SEE?
IMPRESSIVE, IMPRESSIVE.
tussle tussle
HEH HEH...
tmp tmp tmp tmp
See ya later!
HEY, YOU BETTER WATCH WHERE YOU'RE GOING...
CRASH
EEEEEP!
mending reduced
February
WHAT A CLUMSY GIRL...
KYAA~
I DID IT, I DID IT!

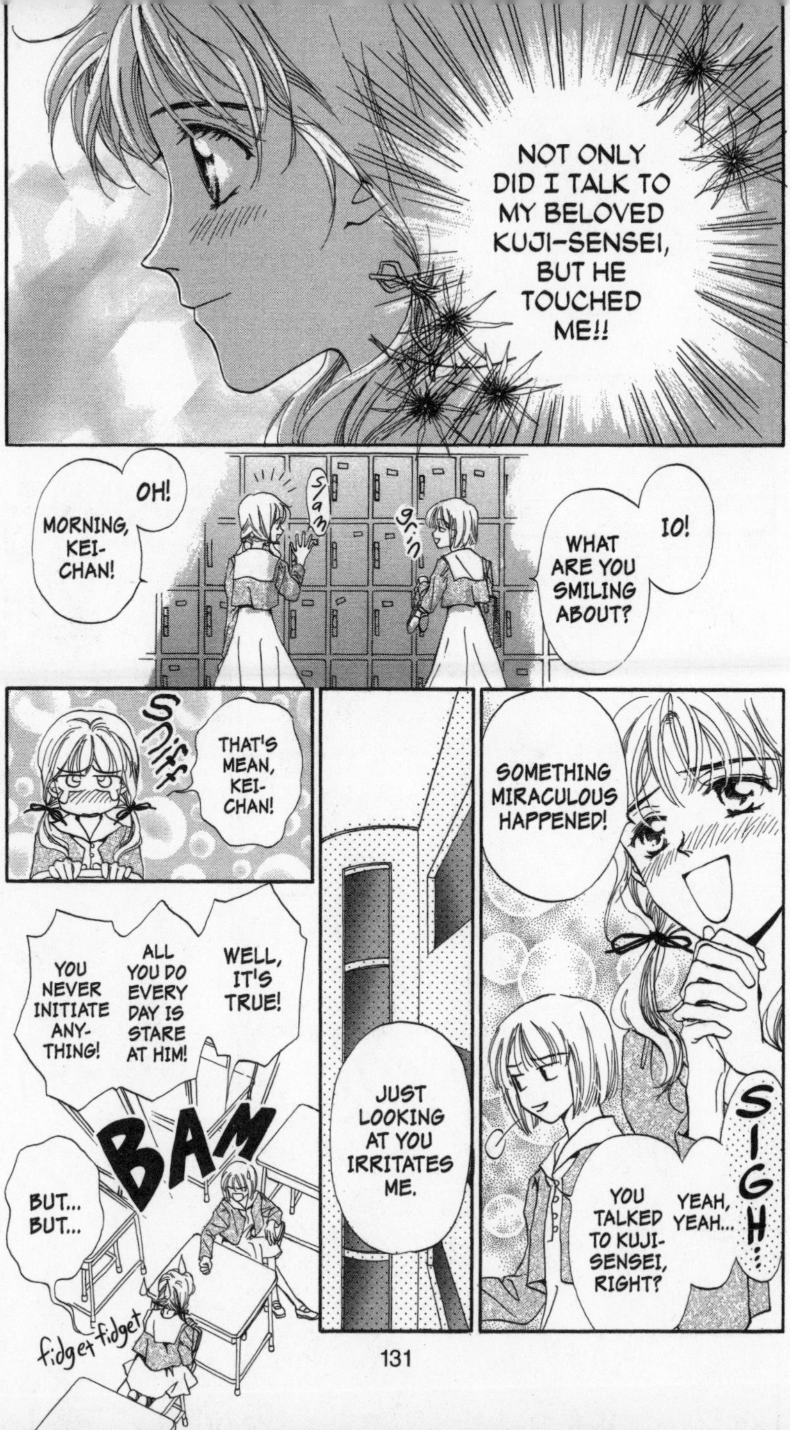
NOT ONLY DID I TALK TO MY BELOVED KUJI-SENSEI, BUT HE TOUCHED ME!!
IO!
WHAT ARE YOU SMILING ABOUT?
grin
slam
OH!
MORNING, KEI-CHAN!
SOMETHING MIRACULOUS HAPPENED!
YEAH, YEAH...
YOU TALKED TO KUJI-SENSEI, RIGHT?
SIGH...
JUST LOOKING AT YOU IRRITATES ME.
THAT'S MEAN, KEI-CHAN!
SNIFF
WELL, IT'S TRUE!
ALL YOU DO EVERY DAY IS STARE AT HIM!
YOU NEVER INITIATE ANY-THING!
BAM
BUT... BUT...
fidget fidget

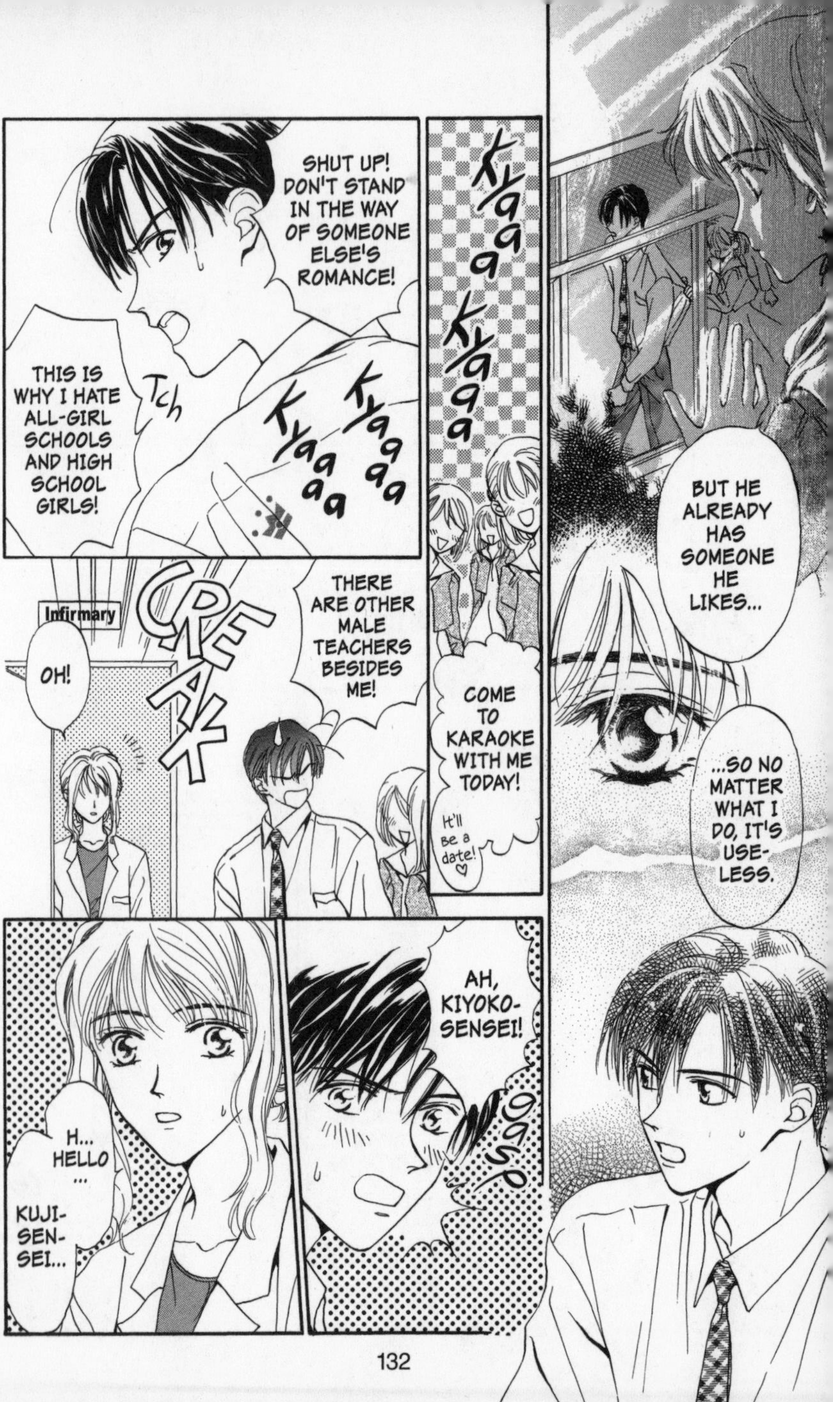

BUT HE ALREADY HAS SOMEONE HE LIKES...
...SO NO MATTER WHAT I DO, IT'S USELESS.
Kyaaa Kyaaa
COME TO KARAOKE WITH ME TODAY!
It'll be a date! ♡
SHUT UP! DON'T STAND IN THE WAY OF SOMEONE ELSE'S ROMANCE!
Kyaaa Kyaaa
Tch
THIS IS WHY I HATE ALL-GIRL SCHOOLS AND HIGH SCHOOL GIRLS!
THERE ARE OTHER MALE TEACHERS BESIDES ME!
CREAK
Infirmary
OH!
AH, KIYOKO-SENSEI!
gasp
H... HELLO ... KUJI-SENSEI...

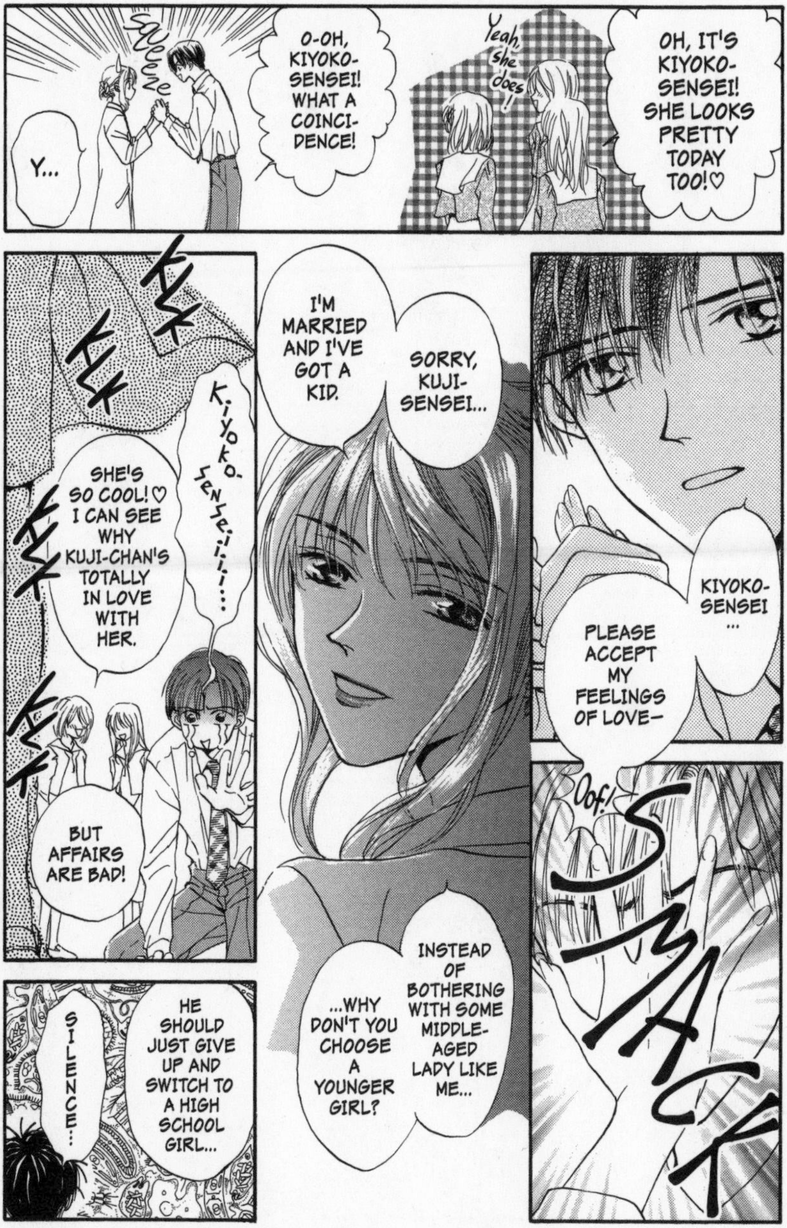
OH, IT'S KIYOKO-SENSEI! SHE LOOKS PRETTY TODAY TOO!♡
Yeah, she does!
O-OH, KIYOKO-SENSEI! WHAT A COINCIDENCE!
SQUEEZE
Y...
KIYOKO-SENSEI...
PLEASE ACCEPT MY FEELINGS OF LOVE—
Oof!
SMACK
SORRY, KUJI-SENSEI...
I'M MARRIED AND I'VE GOT A KID.
INSTEAD OF BOTHERING WITH SOME MIDDLE-AGED LADY LIKE ME...
...WHY DON'T YOU CHOOSE A YOUNGER GIRL?
KLK KLK KLK KLK KLK
Kiyoko-Sensei-i-i-i...
SHE'S SO COOL!♡ I CAN SEE WHY KUJI-CHAN'S TOTALLY IN LOVE WITH HER.
BUT AFFAIRS ARE BAD!
HE SHOULD JUST GIVE UP AND SWITCH TO A HIGH SCHOOL GIRL...
SILENCE...

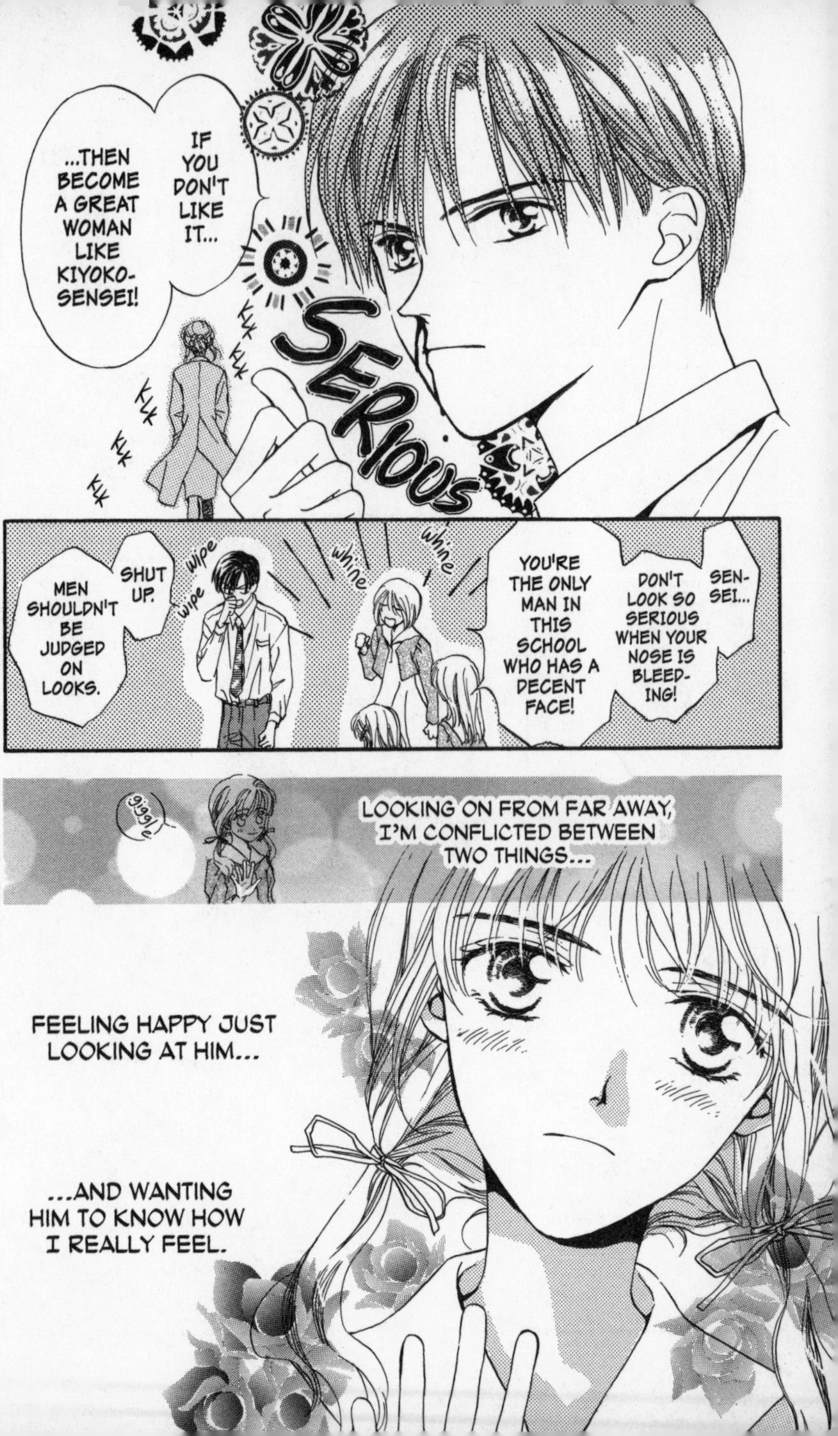
IF YOU DON'T LIKE IT...
...THEN BECOME A GREAT WOMAN LIKE KIYOKO-SENSEI!
SERIOUS
KLK KLK
KLK KLK KLK
SEN-SEI...
DON'T LOOK SO SERIOUS WHEN YOUR NOSE IS BLEED-ING!
YOU'RE THE ONLY MAN IN THIS SCHOOL WHO HAS A DECENT FACE!
whine whine
wipe wipe
SHUT UP.
MEN SHOULDN'T BE JUDGED ON LOOKS.
LOOKING ON FROM FAR AWAY, I'M CONFLICTED BETWEEN TWO THINGS...
giggle
FEELING HAPPY JUST LOOKING AT HIM...
...AND WANTING HIM TO KNOW HOW I REALLY FEEL.

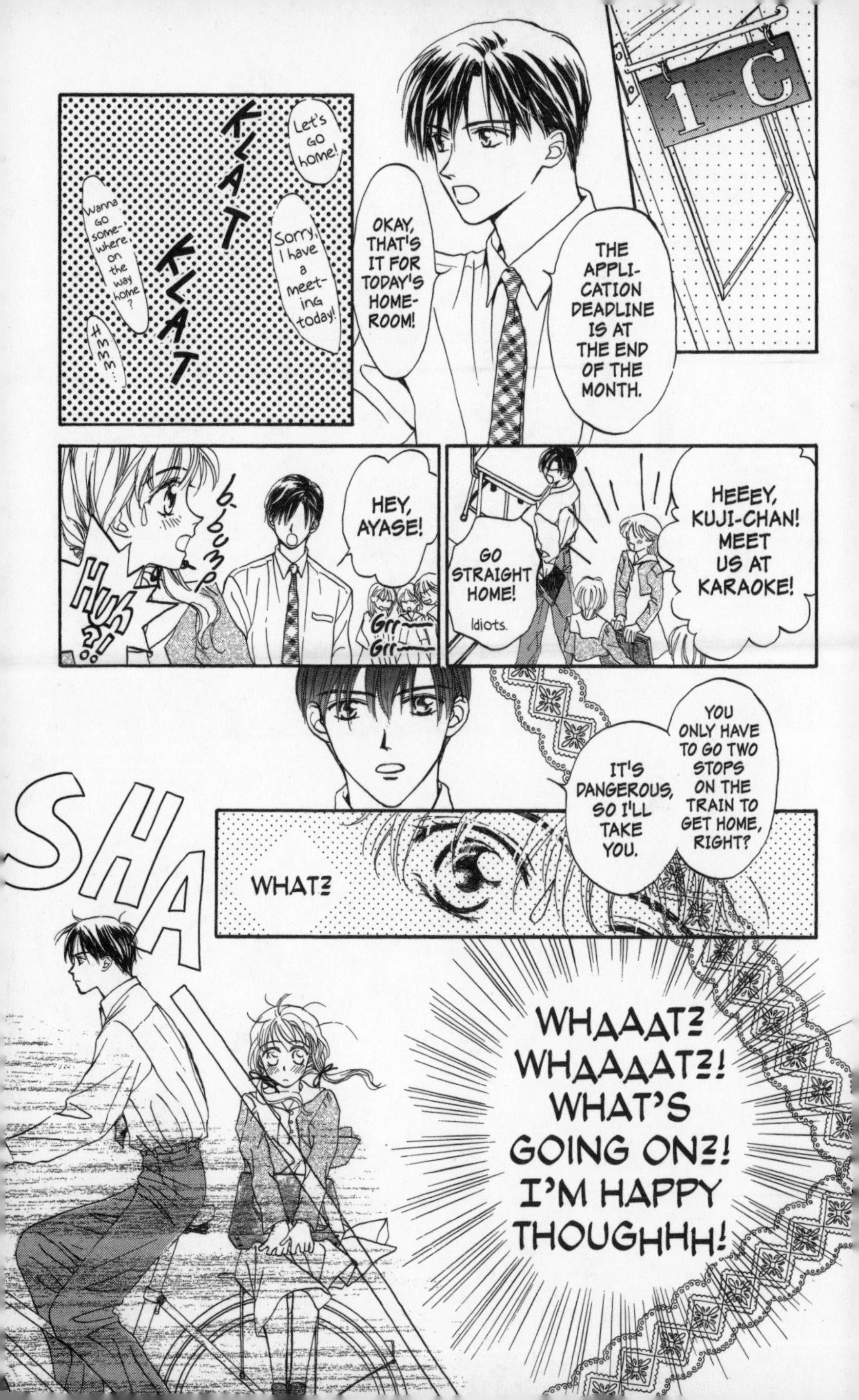
1-C
THE APPLICATION DEADLINE IS AT THE END OF THE MONTH.
OKAY, THAT'S IT FOR TODAY'S HOMEROOM!
KLAT KLAT
Let's go home!
Sorry, I have a meeting today!
Wanna go somewhere on the way home?
Hmm...
HEEEY, KUJI-CHAN! MEET US AT KARAOKE!
GO STRAIGHT HOME!
Idiots.
HEY, AYASE!
b-bump
Huh?!
Grr— Grr—
YOU ONLY HAVE TO GO TWO STOPS ON THE TRAIN TO GET HOME, RIGHT?
IT'S DANGEROUS, SO I'LL TAKE YOU.
WHAT?
SHA
WHAAAT? WHAAAAT?! WHAT'S GOING ON?! I'M HAPPY THOUGHHH!

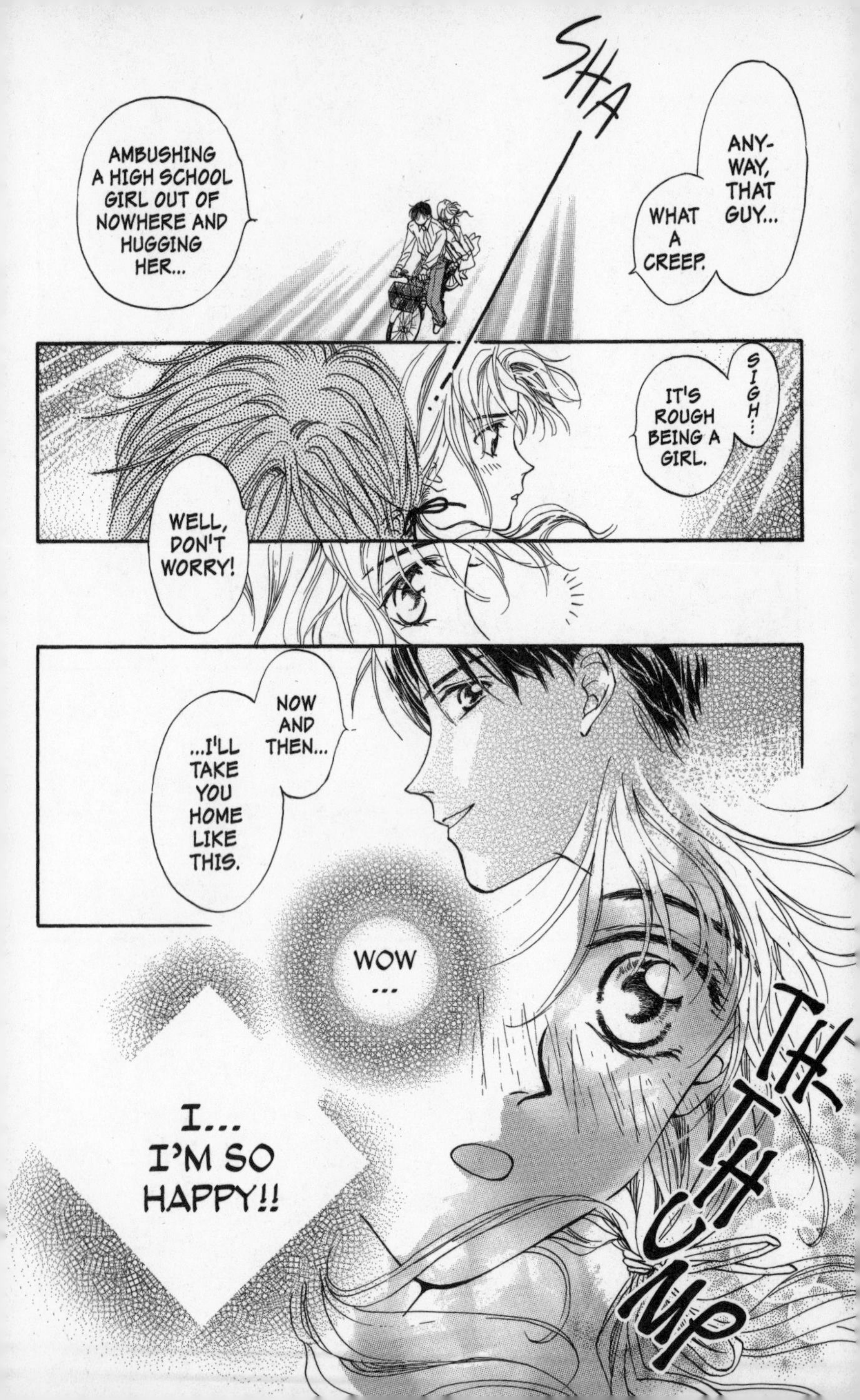
SHA
ANYWAY, THAT GUY... WHAT A CREEP.
AMBUSHING A HIGH SCHOOL GIRL OUT OF NOWHERE AND HUGGING HER...
SIGH...
IT'S ROUGH BEING A GIRL.
WELL, DON'T WORRY!
NOW AND THEN... ...I'LL TAKE YOU HOME LIKE THIS.
THTHUMP
WOW...
I... I'M SO HAPPY!!

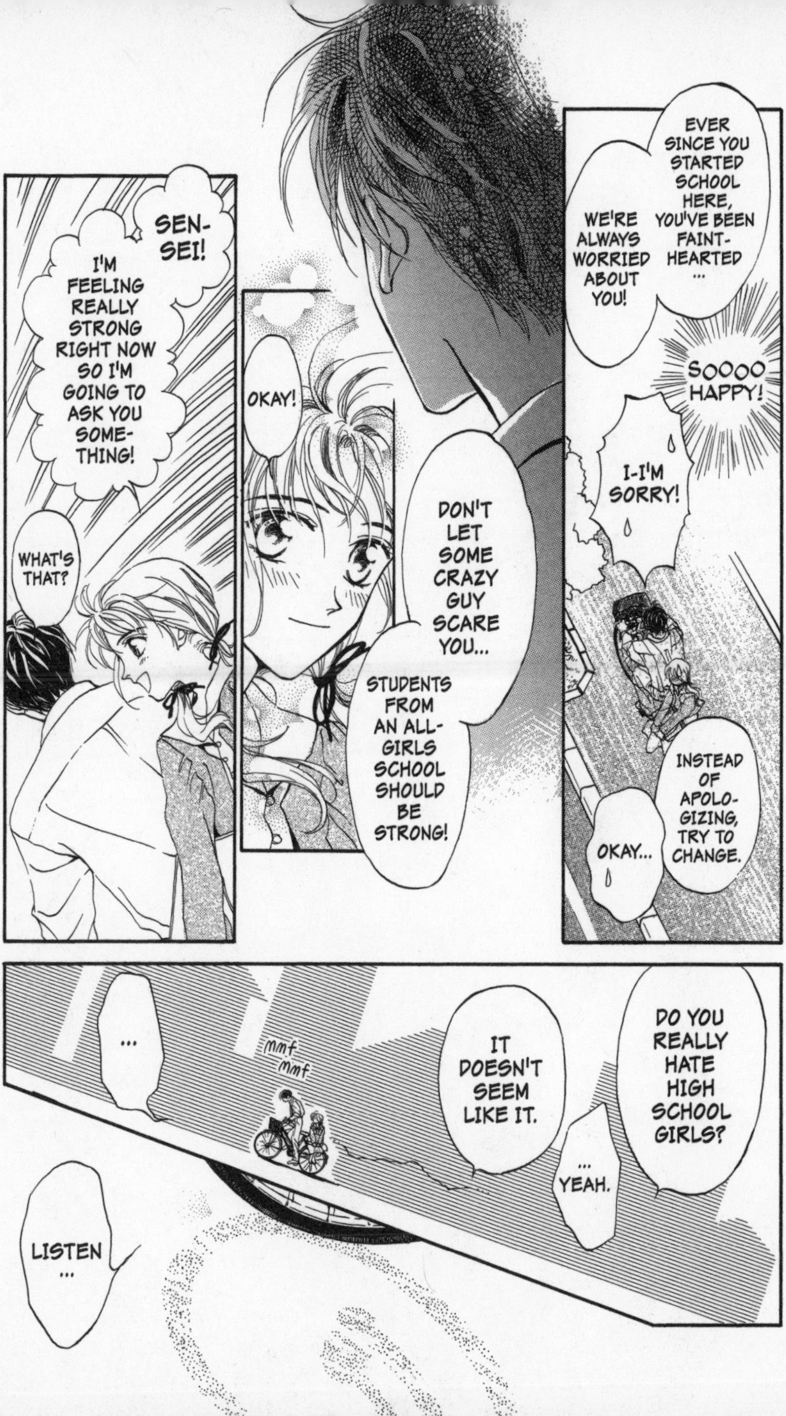
EVER SINCE YOU STARTED SCHOOL HERE, YOU'VE BEEN FAINT-HEARTED...
WE'RE ALWAYS WORRIED ABOUT YOU!
SOOOO HAPPY!
I-I'M SORRY!
INSTEAD OF APOLOGIZING, TRY TO CHANGE.
OKAY...
DON'T LET SOME CRAZY GUY SCARE YOU...
STUDENTS FROM AN ALL-GIRLS SCHOOL SHOULD BE STRONG!
OKAY!
SEN-SEI!
I'M FEELING REALLY STRONG RIGHT NOW SO I'M GOING TO ASK YOU SOMETHING!
WHAT'S THAT?
DO YOU REALLY HATE HIGH SCHOOL GIRLS?
... YEAH.
IT DOESN'T SEEM LIKE IT.
mmf mmf
...
LISTEN...

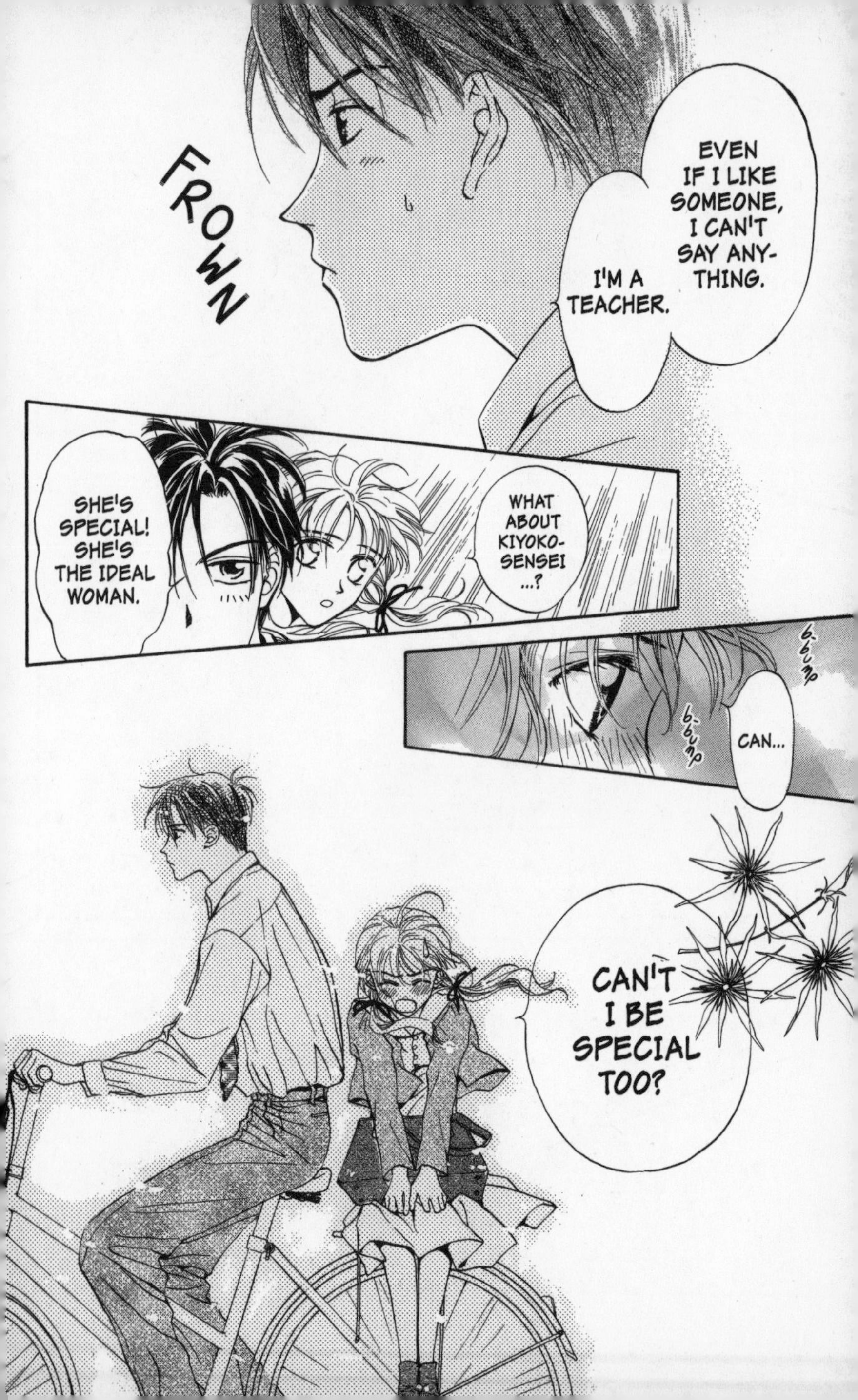
EVEN IF I LIKE SOMEONE, I CAN'T SAY ANYTHING.
I'M A TEACHER.
FROWN
WHAT ABOUT KIYOKO-SENSEI ...?
SHE'S SPECIAL! SHE'S THE IDEAL WOMAN.
B-BUMP
B-BUMP
CAN...
CAN'T I BE SPECIAL TOO?

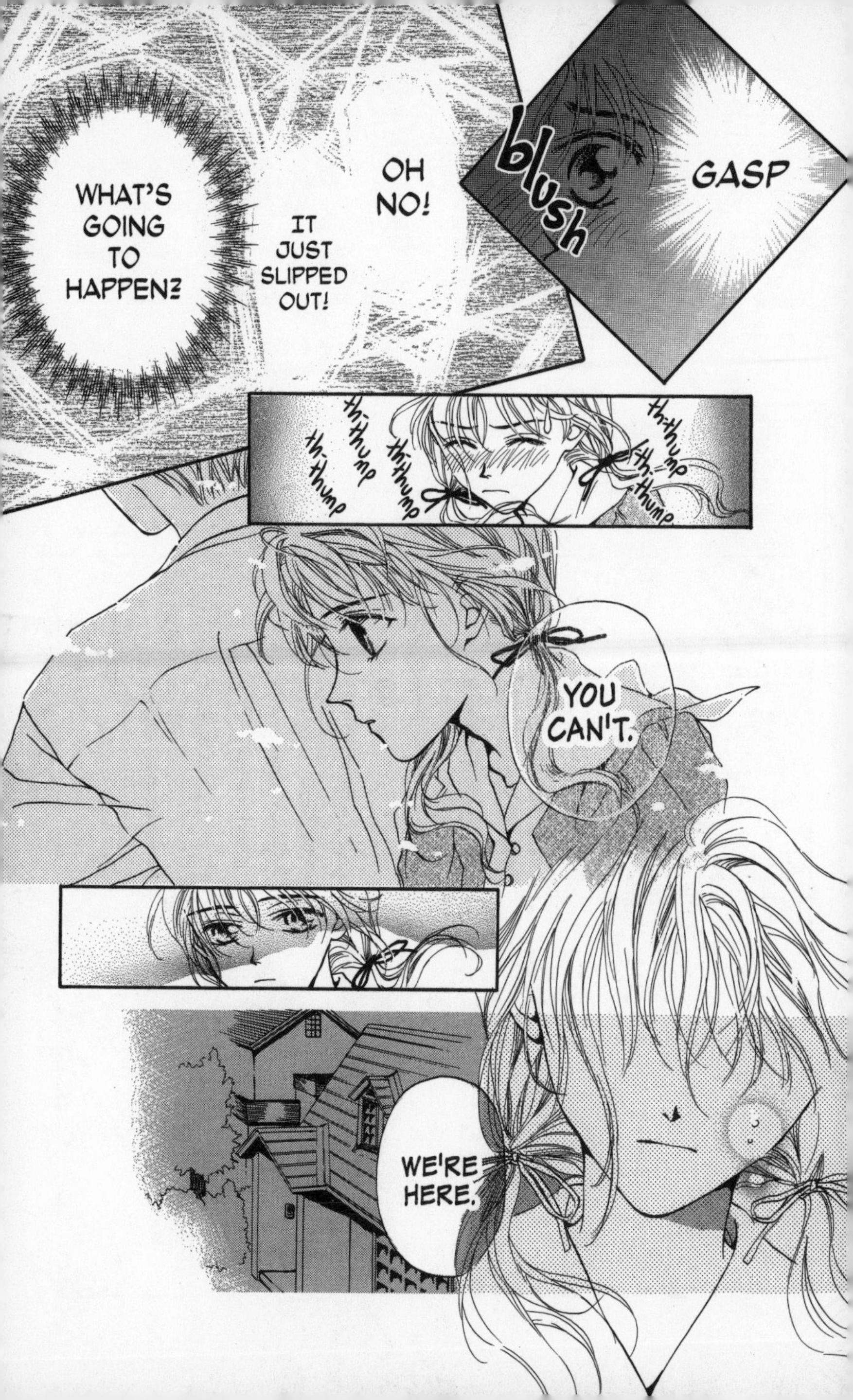
blush
GASP
OH NO!
IT JUST SLIPPED OUT!
WHAT'S GOING TO HAPPEN?
th-thump
th-thump
th-thump
th-thump
th-thump
YOU CAN'T.
WE'RE HERE.

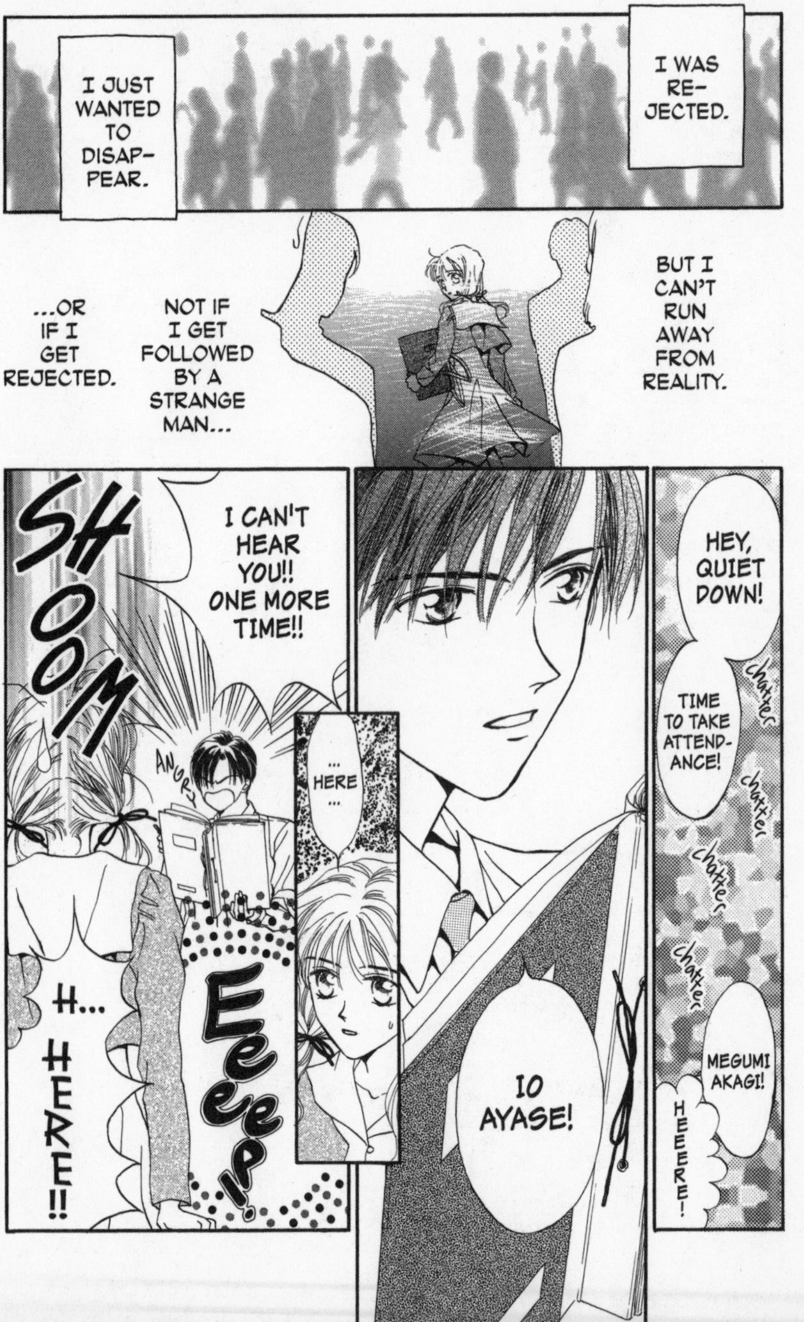
I WAS RE-JECTED.
I JUST WANTED TO DISAP-PEAR.
BUT I CAN'T RUN AWAY FROM REALITY.
NOT IF I GET FOLLOWED BY A STRANGE MAN...
...OR IF I GET REJECTED.
HEY, QUIET DOWN!
TIME TO TAKE ATTEND-ANCE!
chatter
chatter
chatter
chatter
MEGUMI AKAGI!
HEEERE!
IO AYASE!
... HERE ...
I CAN'T HEAR YOU!! ONE MORE TIME!!
SHOOM
ANGRY
Eeeep!
H... HERE!!

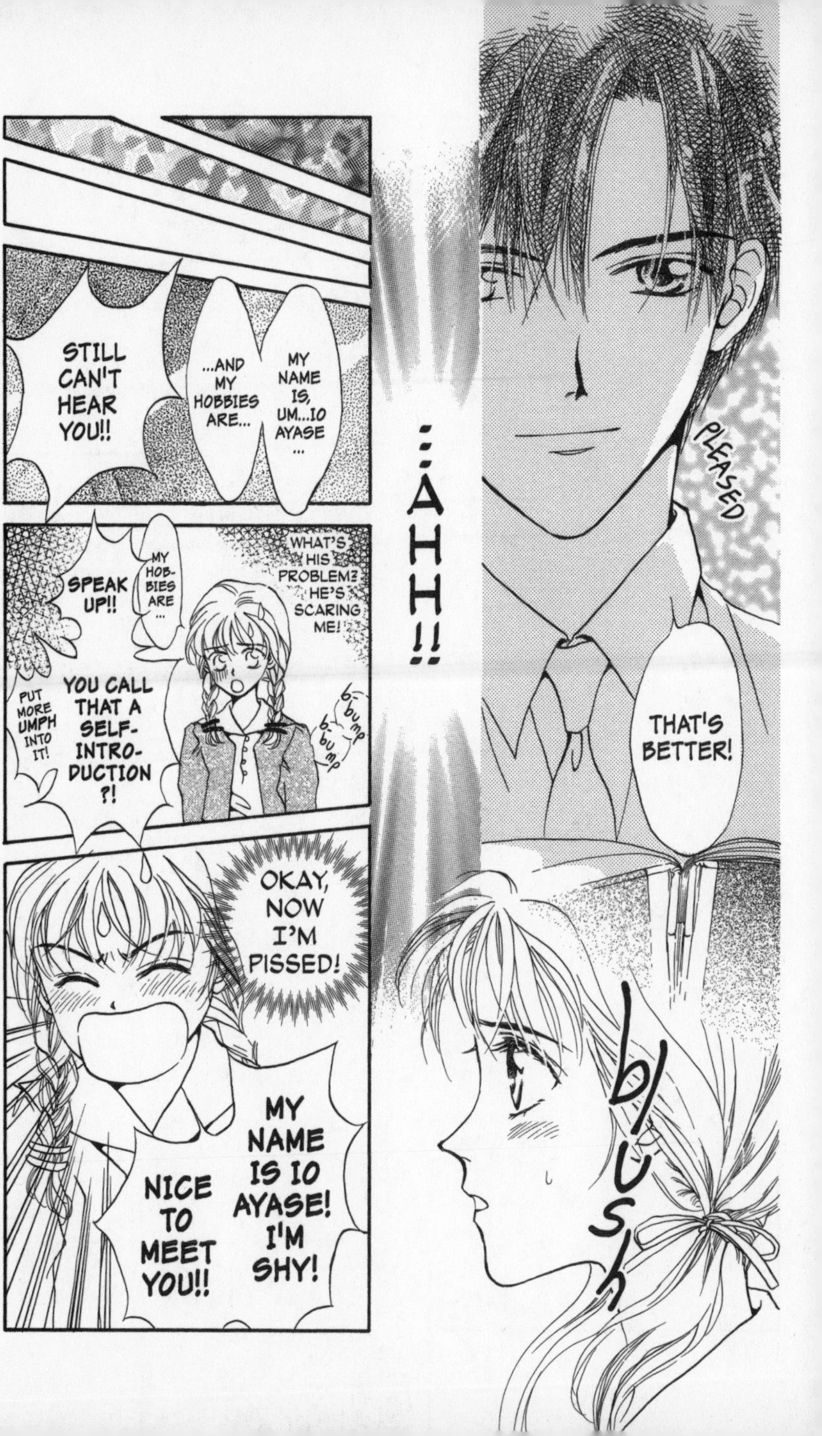
PLEASED
THAT'S BETTER!
AHH!!
blush
MY NAME IS, UM...IO AYASE ...
...AND MY HOBBIES ARE...
STILL CAN'T HEAR YOU!!
WHAT'S HIS PROBLEM? HE'S SCARING ME!
MY HOB-BIES ARE ...
SPEAK UP!!
b-bump b-bump
YOU CALL THAT A SELF-INTRO-DUCTION ?!
PUT MORE UMPH INTO IT!
OKAY, NOW I'M PISSED!
MY NAME IS IO AYASE! I'M SHY!
NICE TO MEET YOU!!

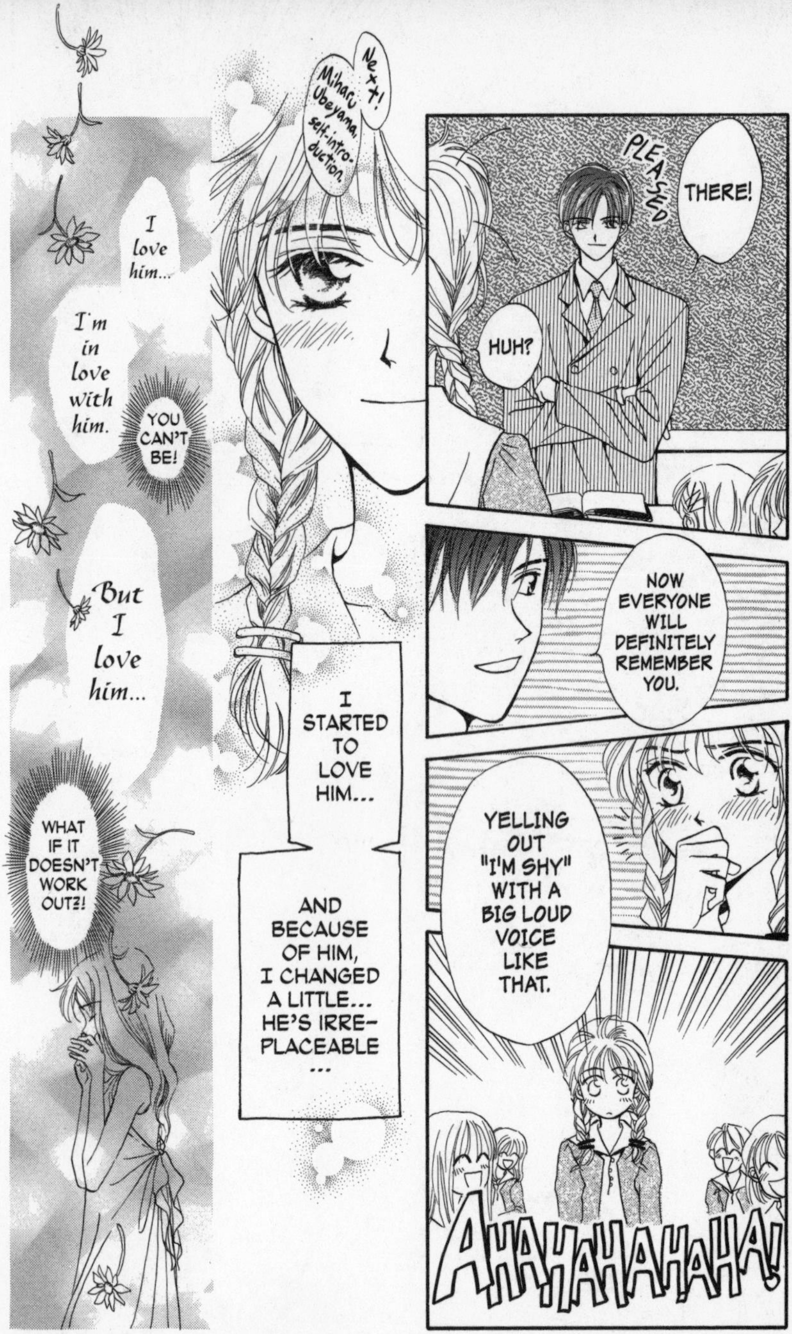
PLEASED
THERE!
HUH?
NOW EVERYONE WILL DEFINITELY REMEMBER YOU.
YELLING OUT "I'M SHY" WITH A BIG LOUD VOICE LIKE THAT.
AHAHAHAHAHA!
Next! Miharu Ubeyama, self-introduction.
I STARTED TO LOVE HIM...
AND BECAUSE OF HIM, I CHANGED A LITTLE... HE'S IRRE-PLACEABLE...
I love him...
I'm in love with him.
YOU CAN'T BE!
But I love him...
WHAT IF IT DOESN'T WORK OUT?!

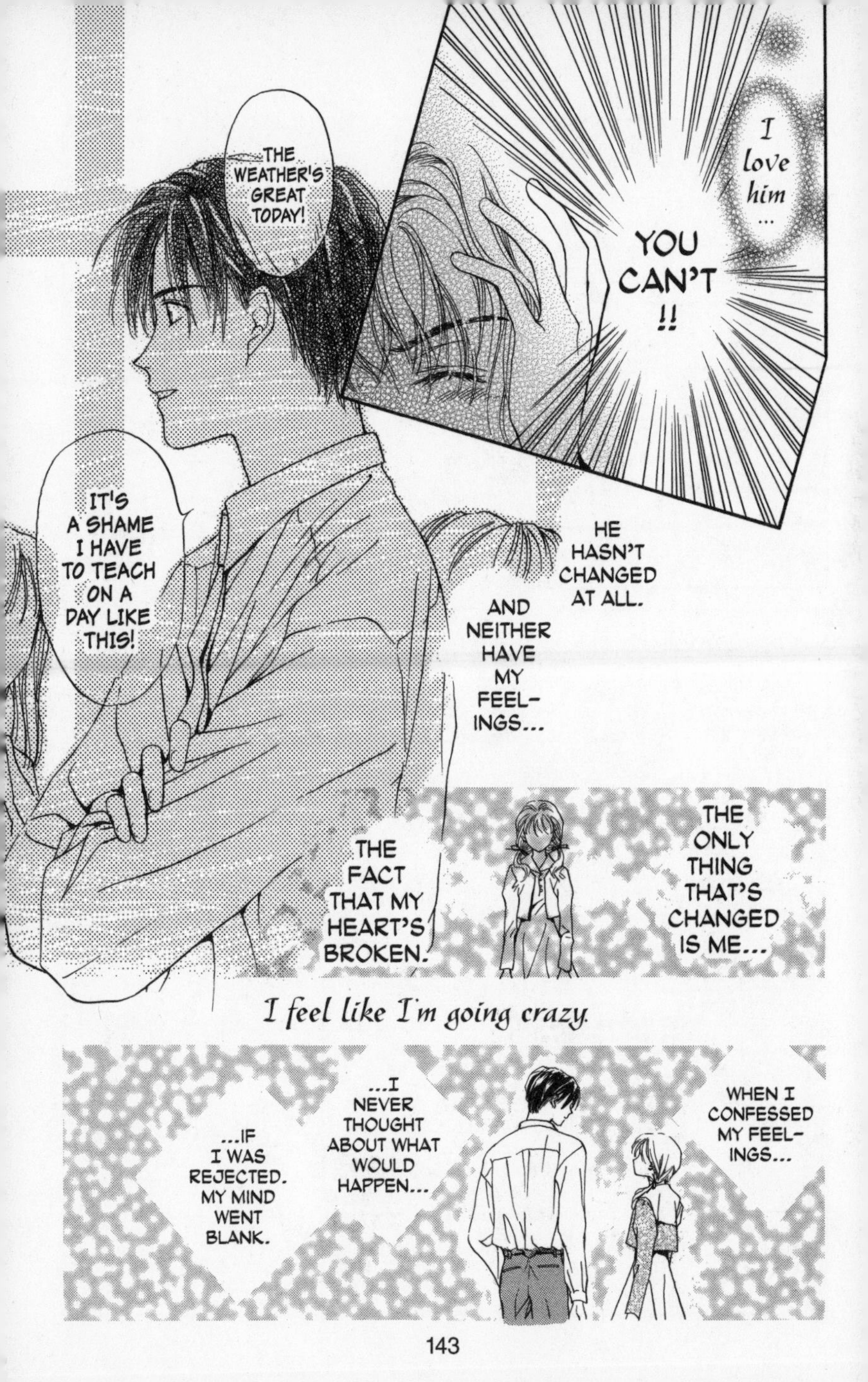
I love him ...
YOU CAN'T !!
THE WEATHER'S GREAT TODAY!
IT'S A SHAME I HAVE TO TEACH ON A DAY LIKE THIS!
HE HASN'T CHANGED AT ALL.
AND NEITHER HAVE MY FEEL-INGS...
THE ONLY THING THAT'S CHANGED IS ME...
THE FACT THAT MY HEART'S BROKEN.
I feel like I'm going crazy.
WHEN I CONFESSED MY FEEL-INGS...
...I NEVER THOUGHT ABOUT WHAT WOULD HAPPEN...
...IF I WAS REJECTED. MY MIND WENT BLANK.

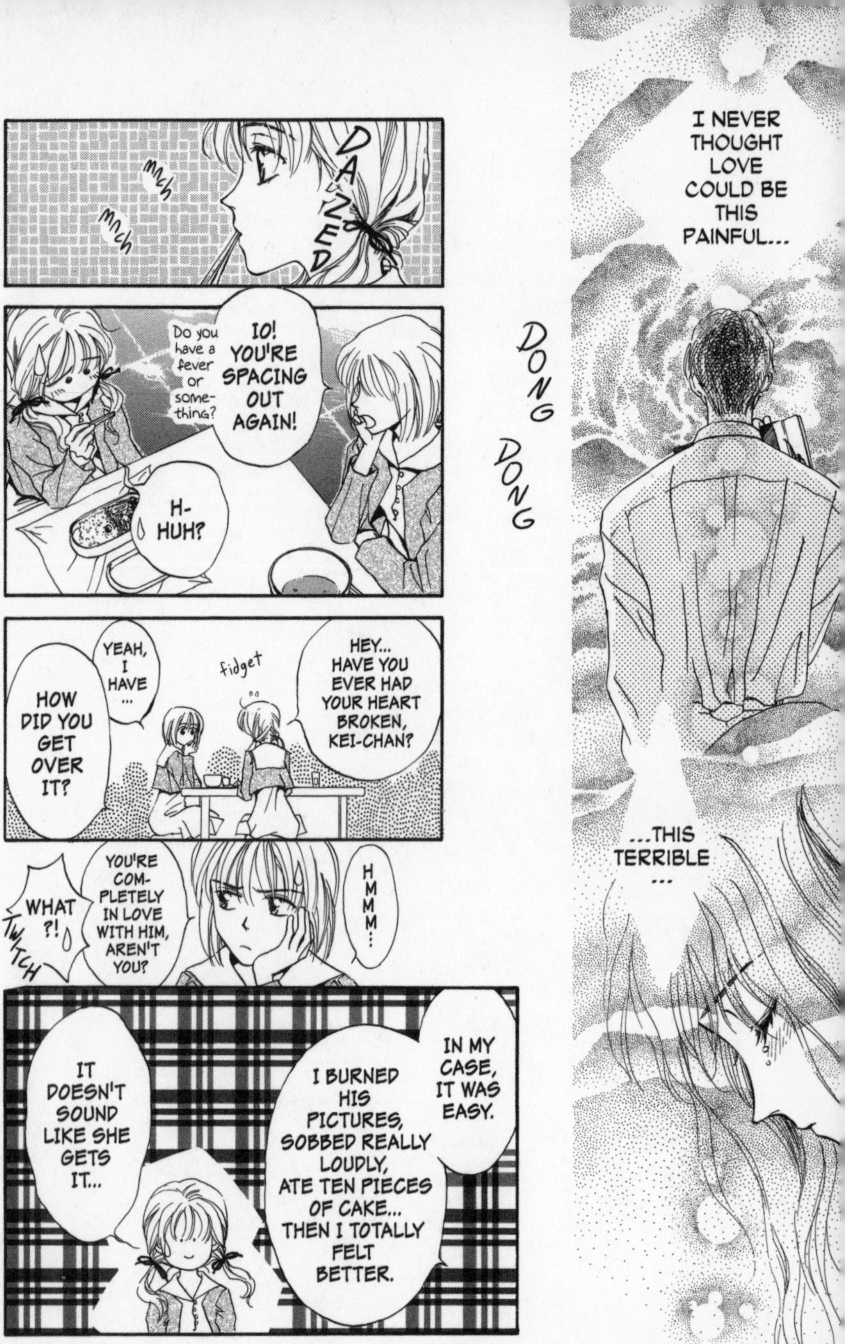
I NEVER THOUGHT LOVE COULD BE THIS PAINFUL...
DONG
DONG
...THIS TERRIBLE...
DAZED
mnch
mnch
IO! YOU'RE SPACING OUT AGAIN!
Do you have a fever or something?
H-HUH?
HEY... HAVE YOU EVER HAD YOUR HEART BROKEN, KEI-CHAN?
fidget
YEAH, I HAVE...
HOW DID YOU GET OVER IT?
HMMM...
YOU'RE COMPLETELY IN LOVE WITH HIM, AREN'T YOU?
WHAT?!
TWITCH
IN MY CASE, IT WAS EASY.
I BURNED HIS PICTURES, SOBBED REALLY LOUDLY, ATE TEN PIECES OF CAKE... THEN I TOTALLY FELT BETTER.
IT DOESN'T SOUND LIKE SHE GETS IT...

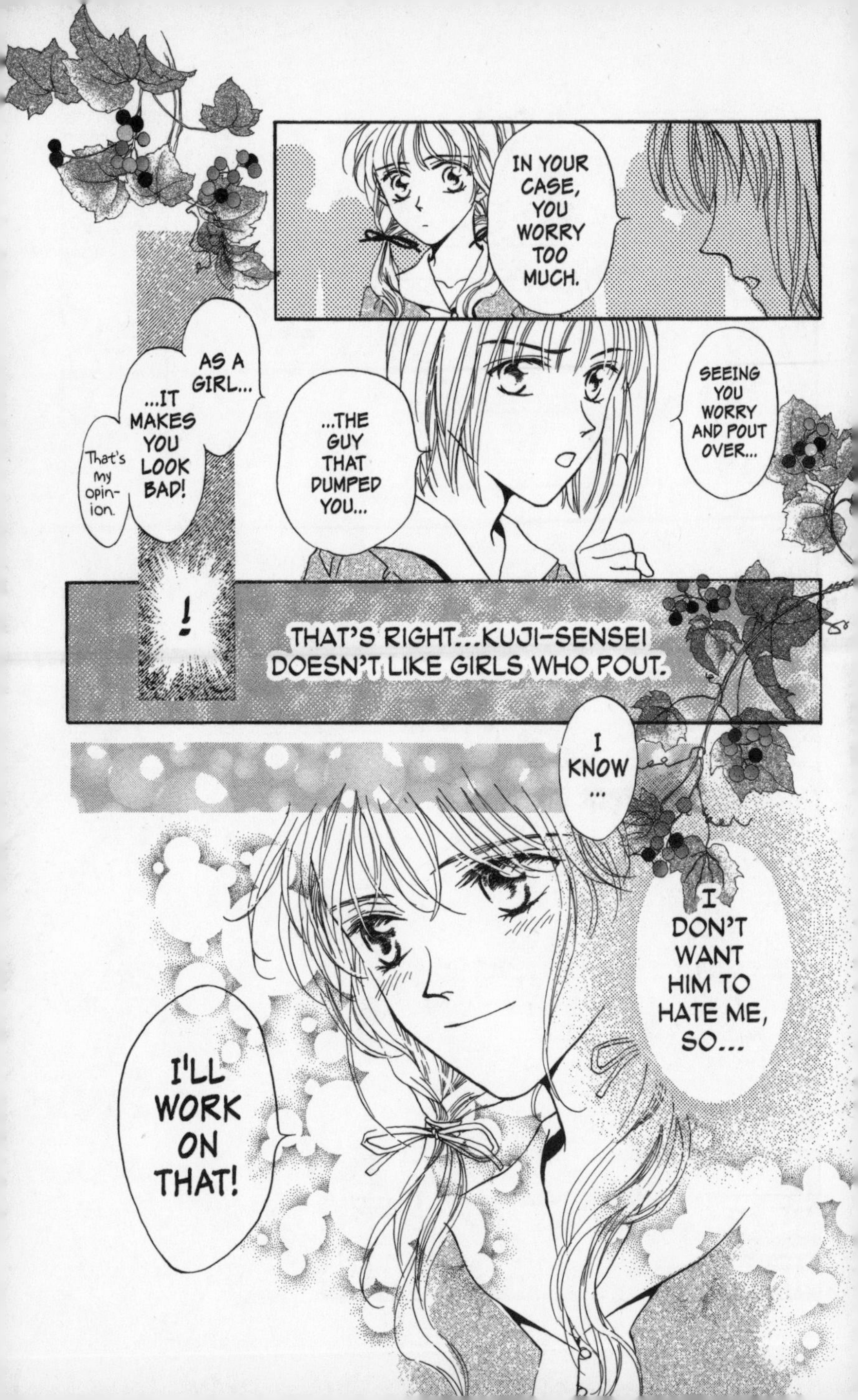
IN YOUR CASE, YOU WORRY TOO MUCH.
SEEING YOU WORRY AND POUT OVER...
...THE GUY THAT DUMPED YOU...
AS A GIRL...
...IT MAKES YOU LOOK BAD!
That's my opin-ion.
!
THAT'S RIGHT...KUJI-SENSEI DOESN'T LIKE GIRLS WHO POUT.
I KNOW...
I DON'T WANT HIM TO HATE ME, SO...
I'LL WORK ON THAT!

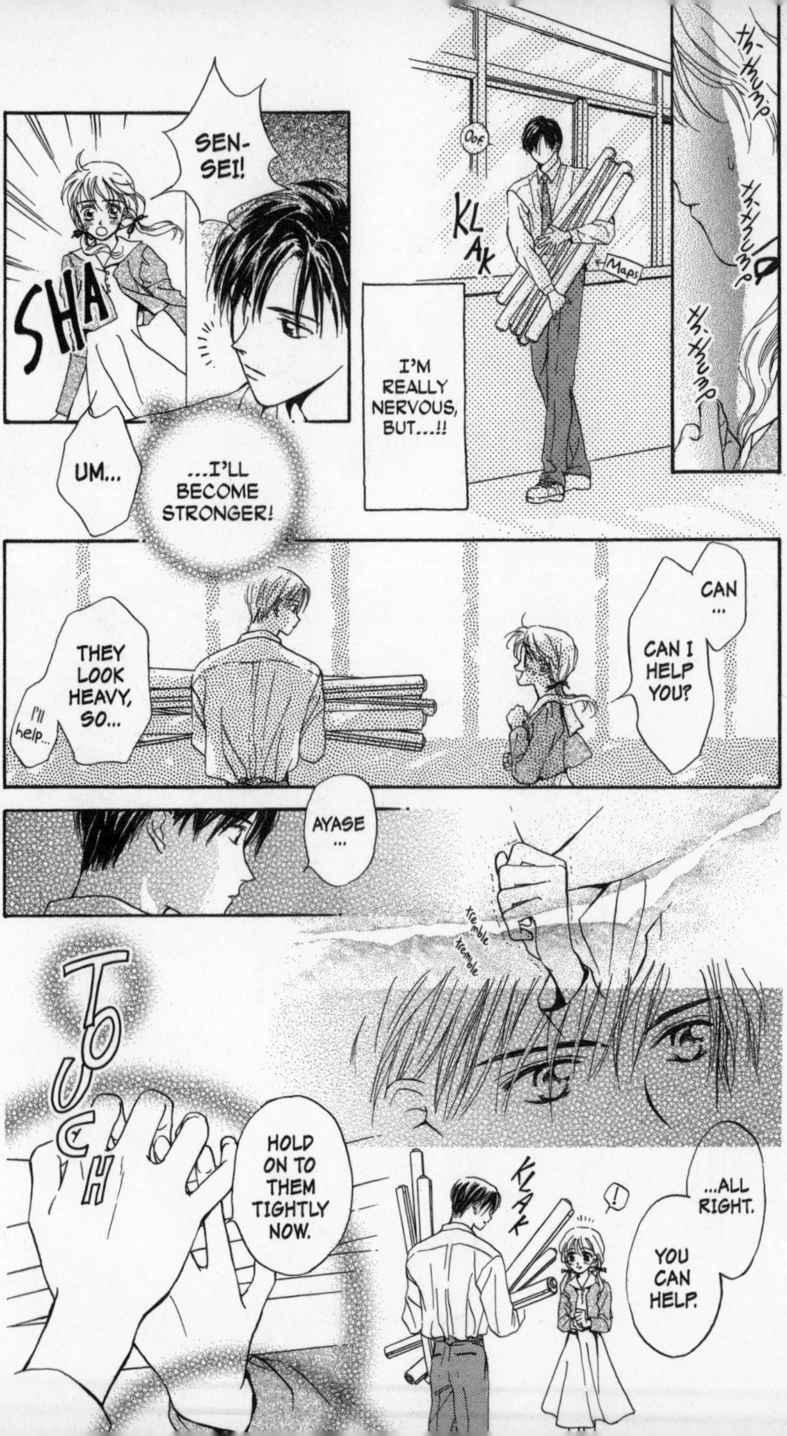
th-thump
th-thump
th-thump
Oof
KLAK
Maps
I'M REALLY NERVOUS, BUT...!!
SEN-SEI!
SHA
UM...
...I'LL BECOME STRONGER!
CAN... CAN I HELP YOU?
THEY LOOK HEAVY, SO...
I'll help...
tremble tremble
AYASE...
...ALL RIGHT.
YOU CAN HELP.
!
KLAK
HOLD ON TO THEM TIGHTLY NOW.
TOUCH

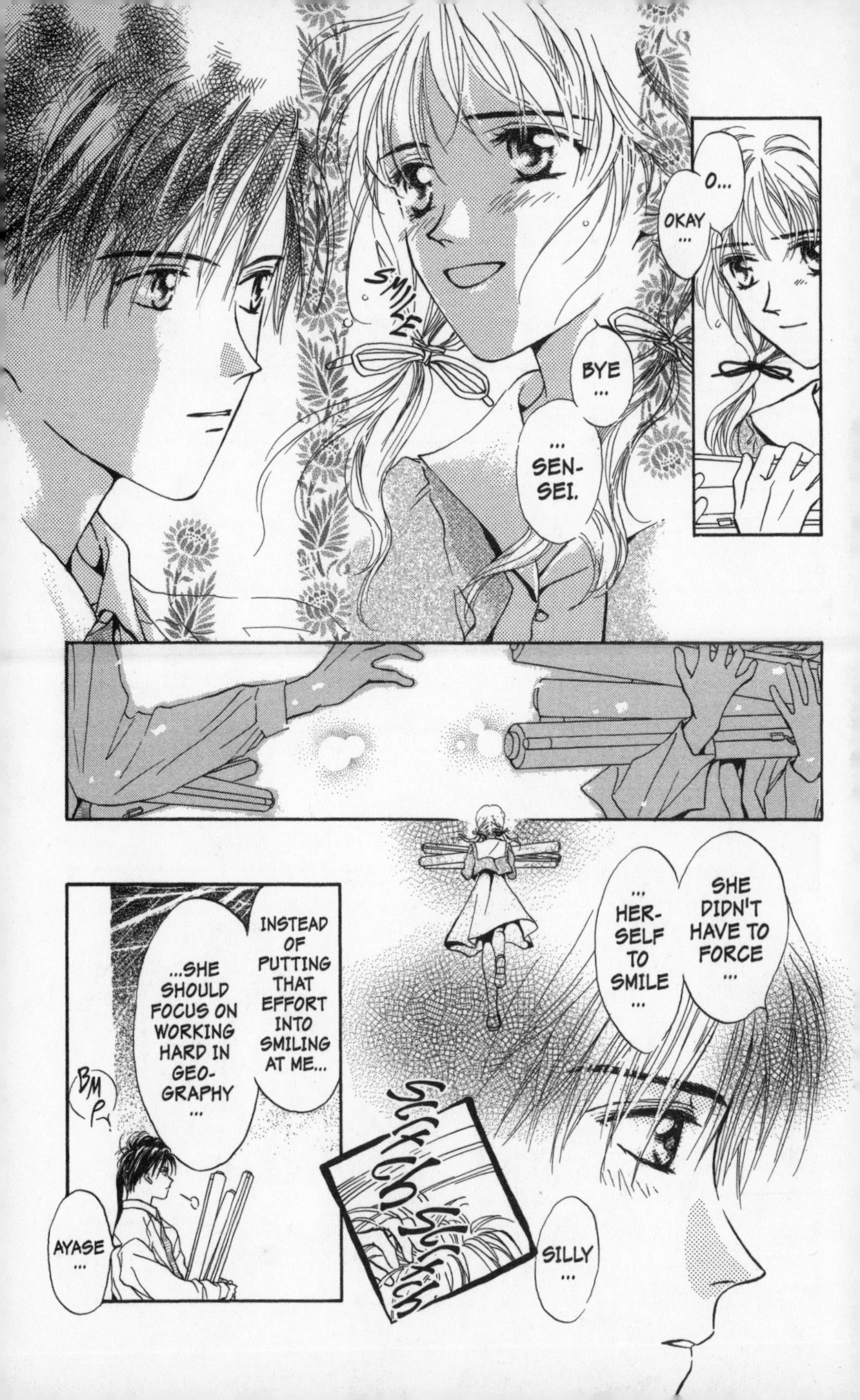
O... OKAY...
SMILE
BYE...
...SEN-SEI.
SHE DIDN'T HAVE TO FORCE...
...HER-SELF TO SMILE...
SILLY...
INSTEAD OF PUTTING THAT EFFORT INTO SMILING AT ME...
...SHE SHOULD FOCUS ON WORKING HARD IN GEO-GRAPHY...
BMP
AYASE...

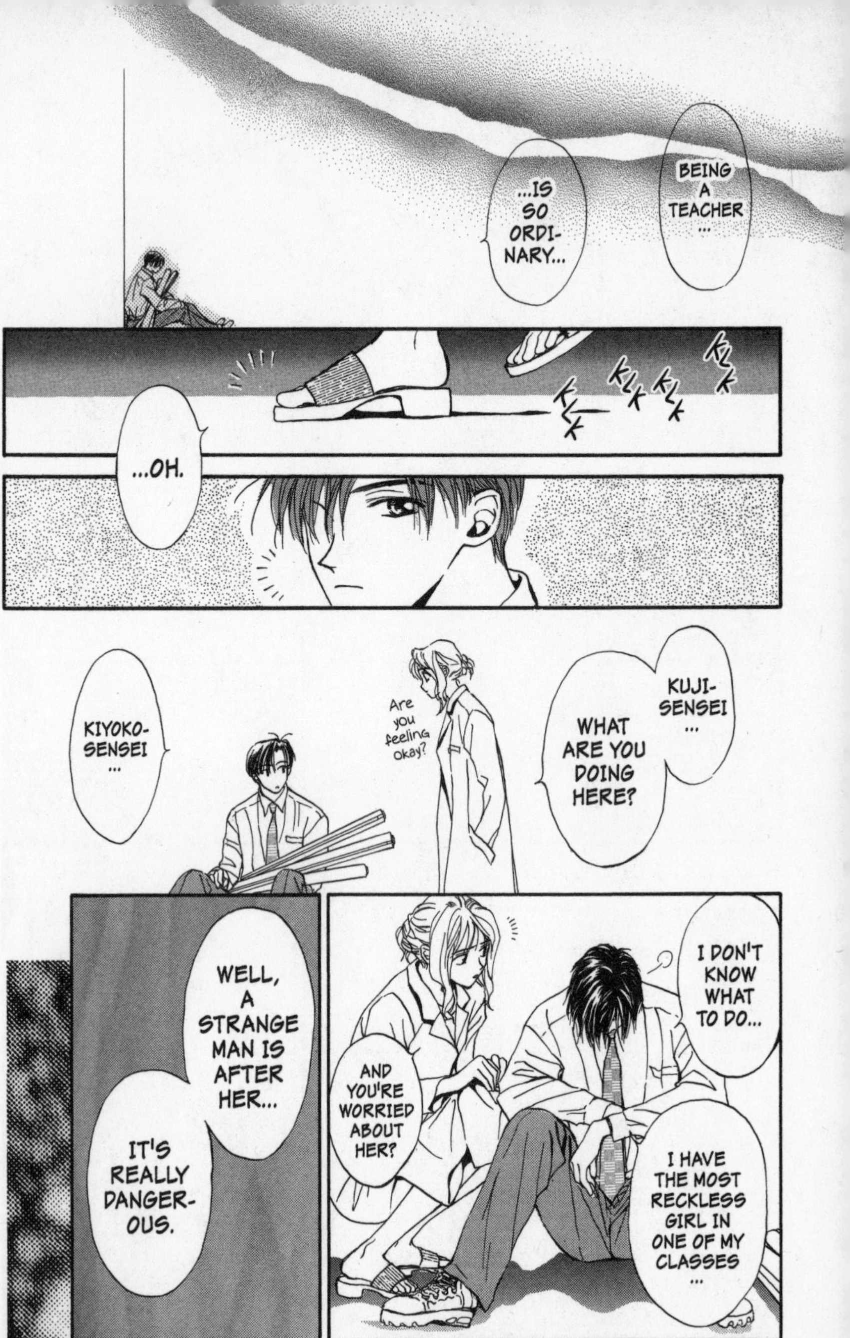
BEING A TEACHER ...
...IS SO ORDINARY...
KLK KLK KLK KLK
...OH.
KUJI-SENSEI ...
WHAT ARE YOU DOING HERE?
Are you feeling okay?
KIYOKO-SENSEI ...
I DON'T KNOW WHAT TO DO...
I HAVE THE MOST RECKLESS GIRL IN ONE OF MY CLASSES ...
AND YOU'RE WORRIED ABOUT HER?
WELL, A STRANGE MAN IS AFTER HER...
IT'S REALLY DANGER-OUS.

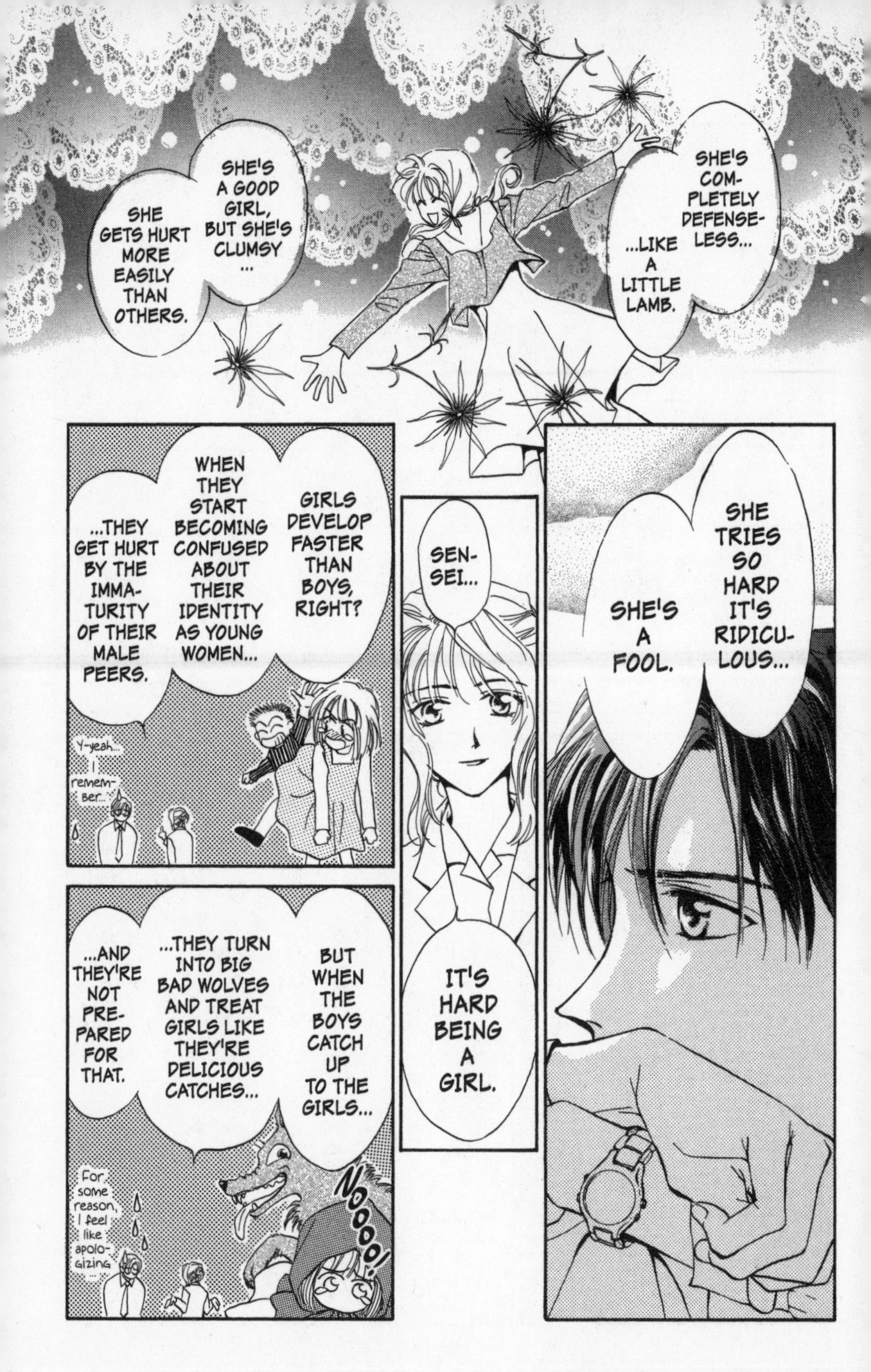
SHE'S COMPLETELY DEFENSELESS...
...LIKE A LITTLE LAMB.
SHE'S A GOOD GIRL, BUT SHE'S CLUMSY...
SHE GETS HURT MORE EASILY THAN OTHERS.
SHE TRIES SO HARD IT'S RIDICULOUS...
SHE'S A FOOL.
SENSEI...
IT'S HARD BEING A GIRL.
GIRLS DEVELOP FASTER THAN BOYS, RIGHT?
WHEN THEY START BECOMING CONFUSED ABOUT THEIR IDENTITY AS YOUNG WOMEN...
...THEY GET HURT BY THE IMMATURITY OF THEIR MALE PEERS.
Y-yeah... I remember...
BUT WHEN THE BOYS CATCH UP TO THE GIRLS...
...THEY TURN INTO BIG BAD WOLVES AND TREAT GIRLS LIKE THEY'RE DELICIOUS CATCHES...
...AND THEY'RE NOT PREPARED FOR THAT.
NOOOO!
For some reason, I feel like apologizing...

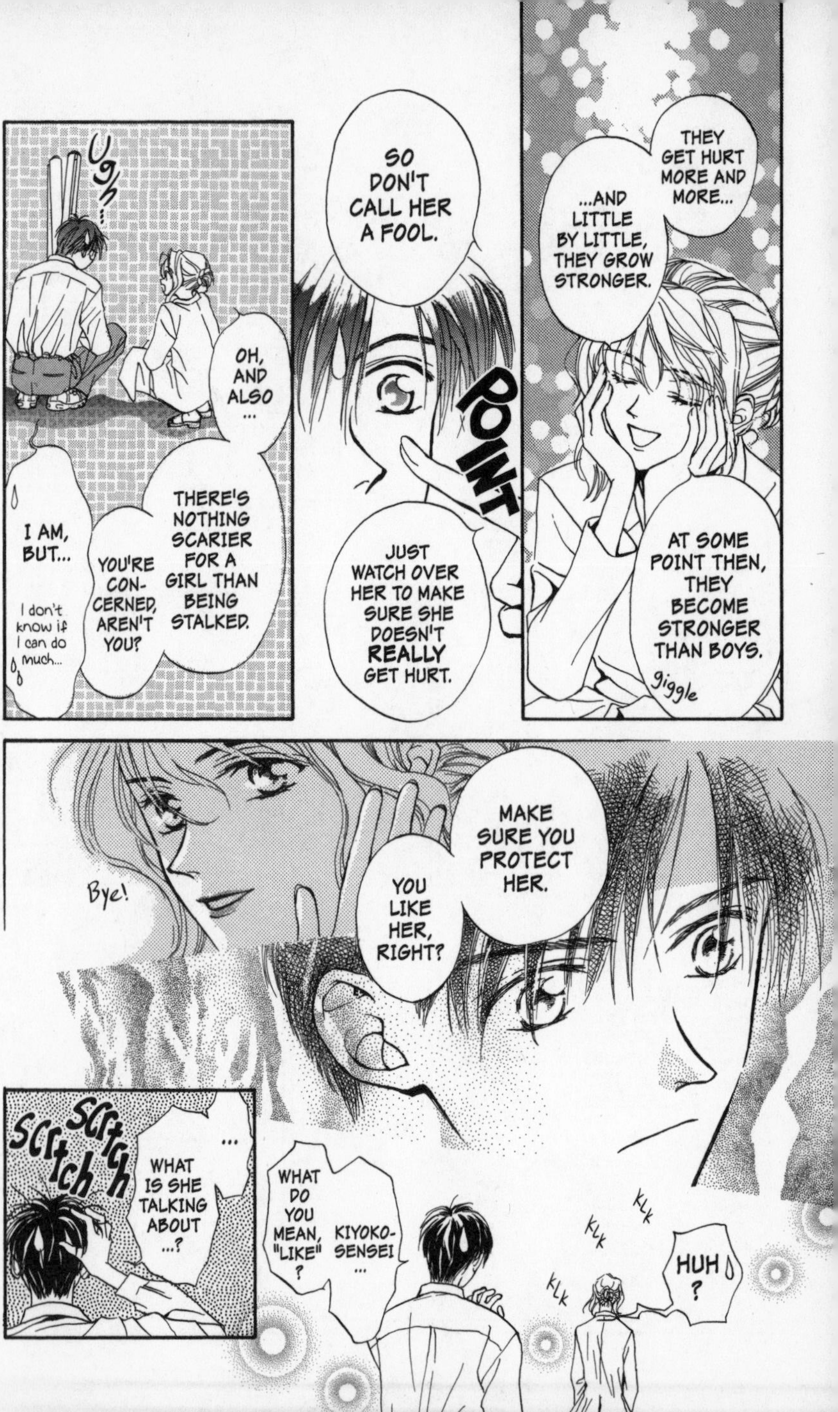
THEY GET HURT MORE AND MORE...
...AND LITTLE BY LITTLE, THEY GROW STRONGER.
AT SOME POINT THEN, THEY BECOME STRONGER THAN BOYS.
giggle
SO DON'T CALL HER A FOOL.
POINT
JUST WATCH OVER HER TO MAKE SURE SHE DOESN'T REALLY GET HURT.
Ugh...
OH, AND ALSO ...
THERE'S NOTHING SCARIER FOR A GIRL THAN BEING STALKED.
YOU'RE CON- CERNED, AREN'T YOU?
I AM, BUT...
I don't know if I can do much...
MAKE SURE YOU PROTECT HER.
YOU LIKE HER, RIGHT?
Bye!
KLK
KLK
KLK
HUH ?
KIYOKO-SENSEI ...
WHAT DO YOU MEAN, "LIKE" ?
...
WHAT IS SHE TALKING ABOUT ...?
SCRTCH
SCRTCH

5

I'm sure boys have their problems too, but...

I just want to say that girls go through a lot!

(This pattern is wrong here...)

That's why I thought of writing *Real Storm*.

It's gotten good reviews, so I'm happy. Did my message come through?
(As much as it can, anyway...)

The meaning of the story is up to the readers' interpretation.

But I just want to say that forgetting about your dreams and losing to reality is too sad.

Heh heh. ♡ Sorry if I sound self-important.
(That comes across sometimes in *Captive Hearts*...)

Actually, I'm just saying that to remind myself!
Giggle...

(By the way, the characters in *Real Storm* are modified characters from *Captive Hearts*!
Can you believe it...?)

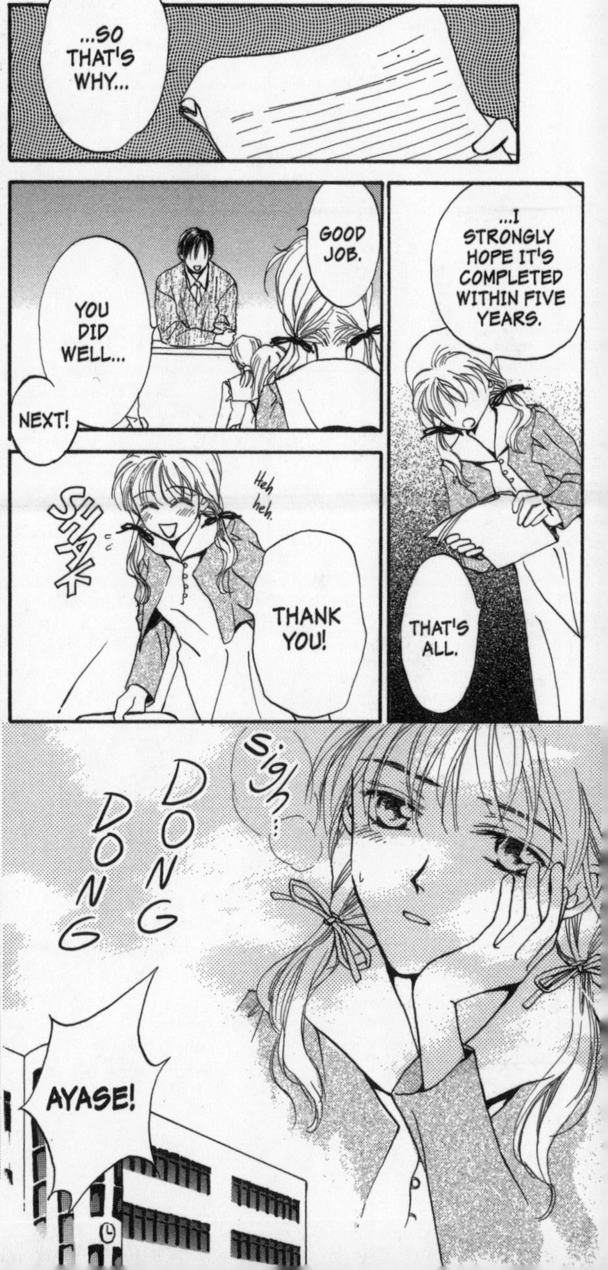
...SO THAT'S WHY...
...I STRONGLY HOPE IT'S COMPLETED WITHIN FIVE YEARS.
THAT'S ALL.
GOOD JOB.
YOU DID WELL...
NEXT!
Heh heh.
THANK YOU!
SHAK
Sigh...
DONG
DONG
AYASE!

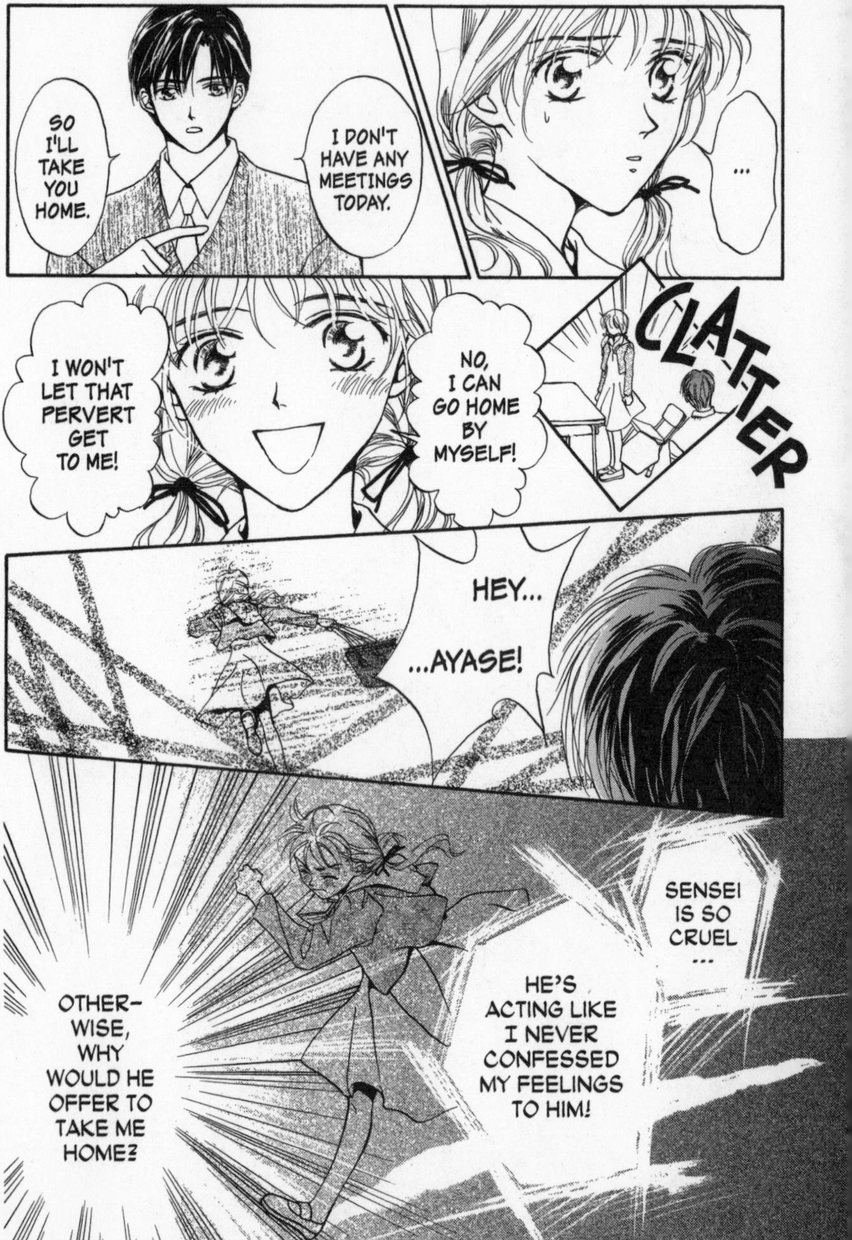
...
I DON'T HAVE ANY MEETINGS TODAY.
SO I'LL TAKE YOU HOME.
CLATTER
NO, I CAN GO HOME BY MYSELF!
I WON'T LET THAT PERVERT GET TO ME!
HEY...
...AYASE!
SENSEI IS SO CRUEL...
HE'S ACTING LIKE I NEVER CONFESSED MY FEELINGS TO HIM!
OTHER-WISE, WHY WOULD HE OFFER TO TAKE ME HOME?

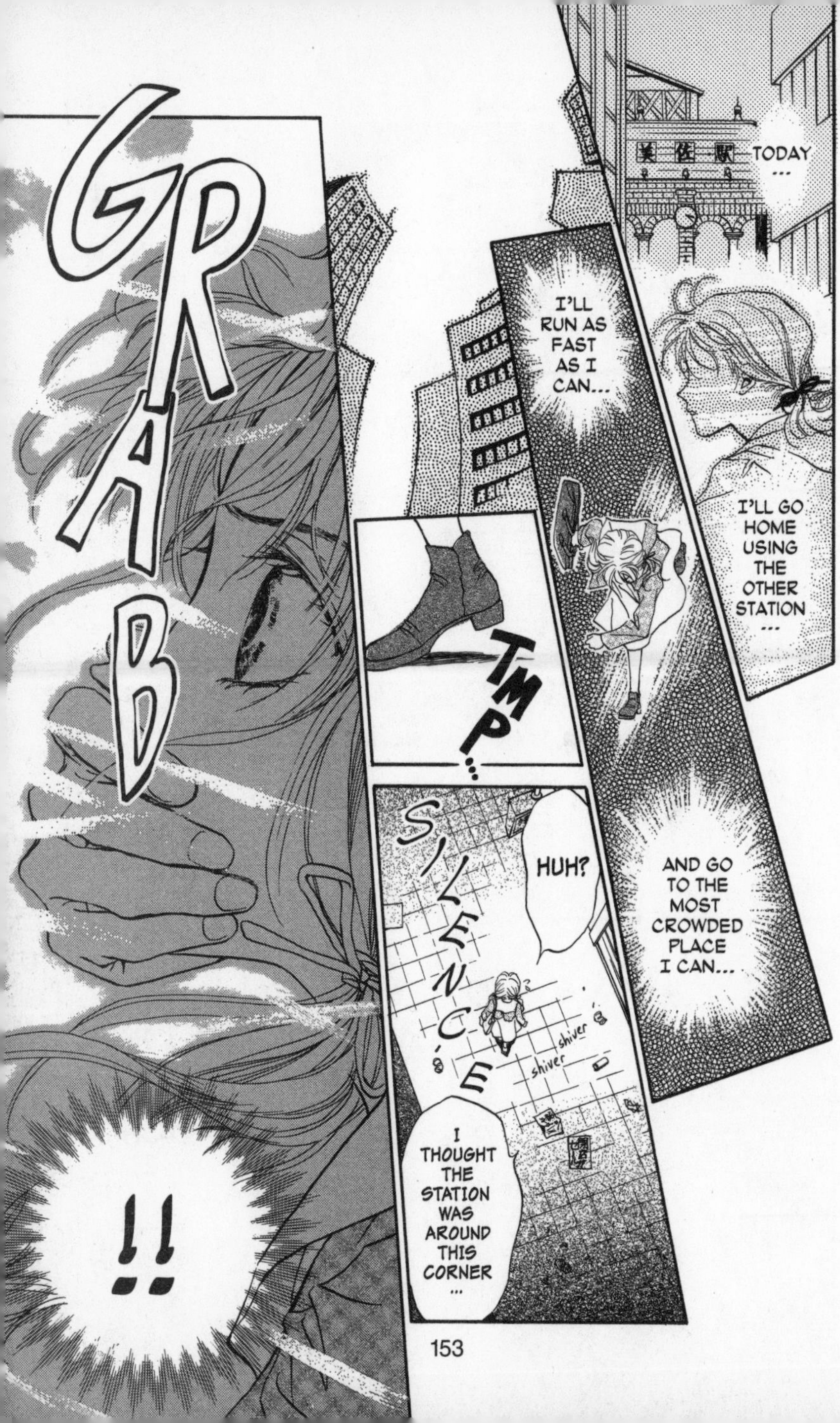

美佐駅
TODAY ...
I'LL GO HOME USING THE OTHER STATION ...
I'LL RUN AS FAST AS I CAN...
AND GO TO THE MOST CROWDED PLACE I CAN...
TMP...
HUH?
SILENCE
shiver shiver
I THOUGHT THE STATION WAS AROUND THIS CORNER ...
GRAB
!!

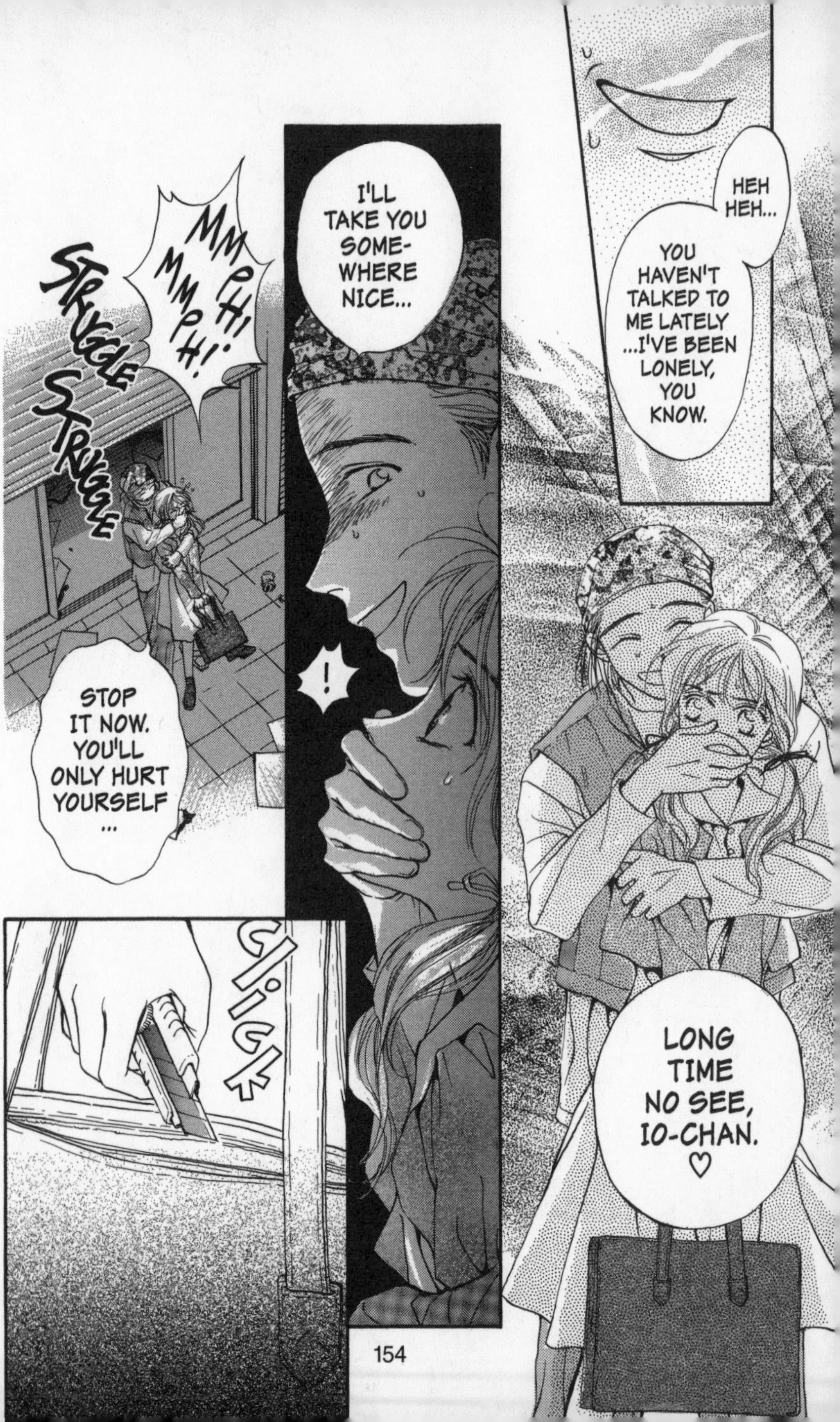
HEH HEH...
YOU HAVEN'T TALKED TO ME LATELY ...I'VE BEEN LONELY, YOU KNOW.
LONG TIME NO SEE, IO-CHAN. ♡
I'LL TAKE YOU SOME-WHERE NICE...
!
MMPH! MMPH!
STRUGGLE STRUGGLE
STOP IT NOW. YOU'LL ONLY HURT YOURSELF ...
CLICK

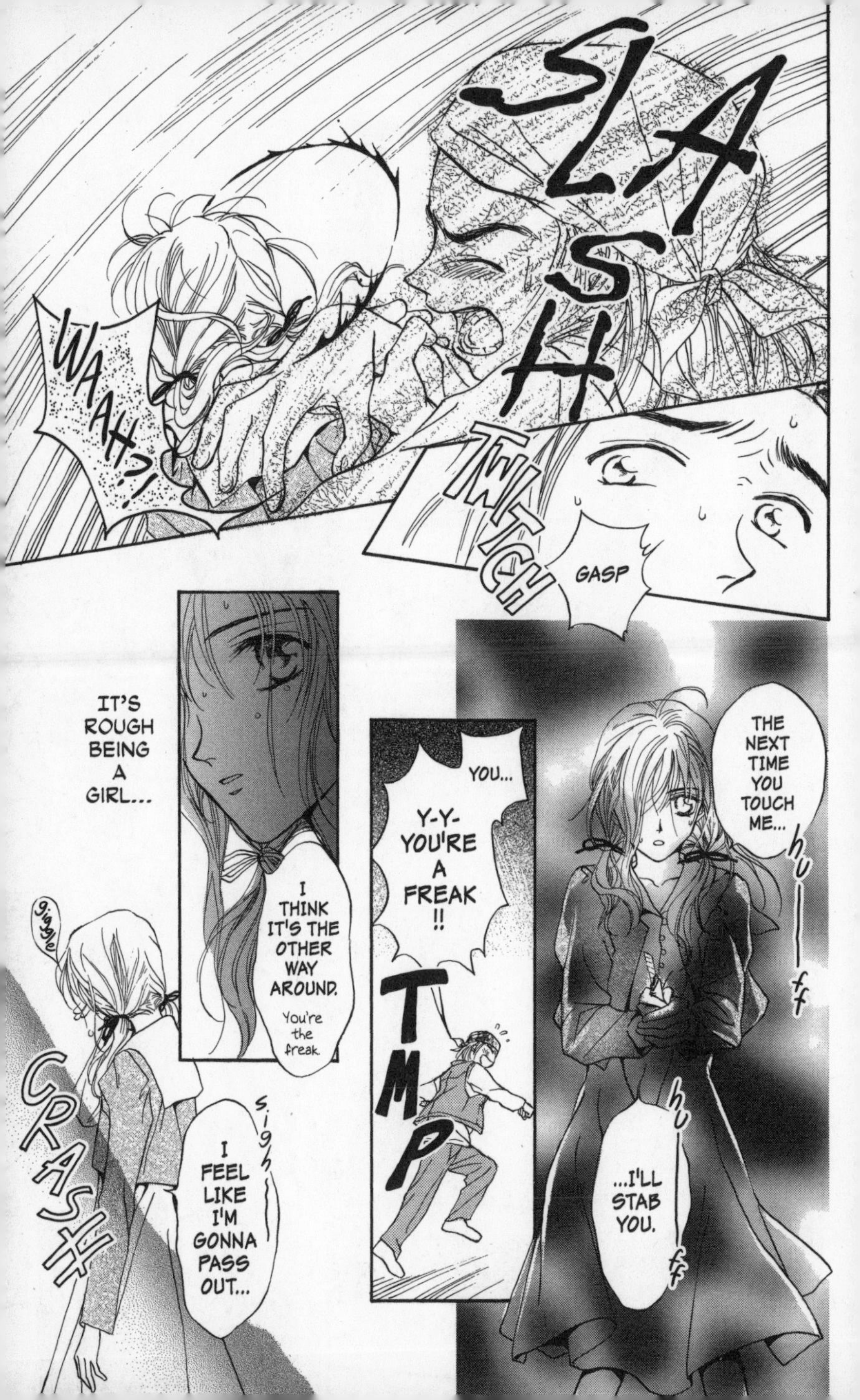
SLASH
WAAH?!
TWITCH
GASP
THE NEXT TIME YOU TOUCH ME...
hu—ff
...I'LL STAB YOU.
hu—ff
YOU...
Y-Y-YOU'RE A FREAK!!
TMP
I THINK IT'S THE OTHER WAY AROUND.
You're the freak.
IT'S ROUGH BEING A GIRL...
giggle
CRASH
sigh
I FEEL LIKE I'M GONNA PASS OUT...

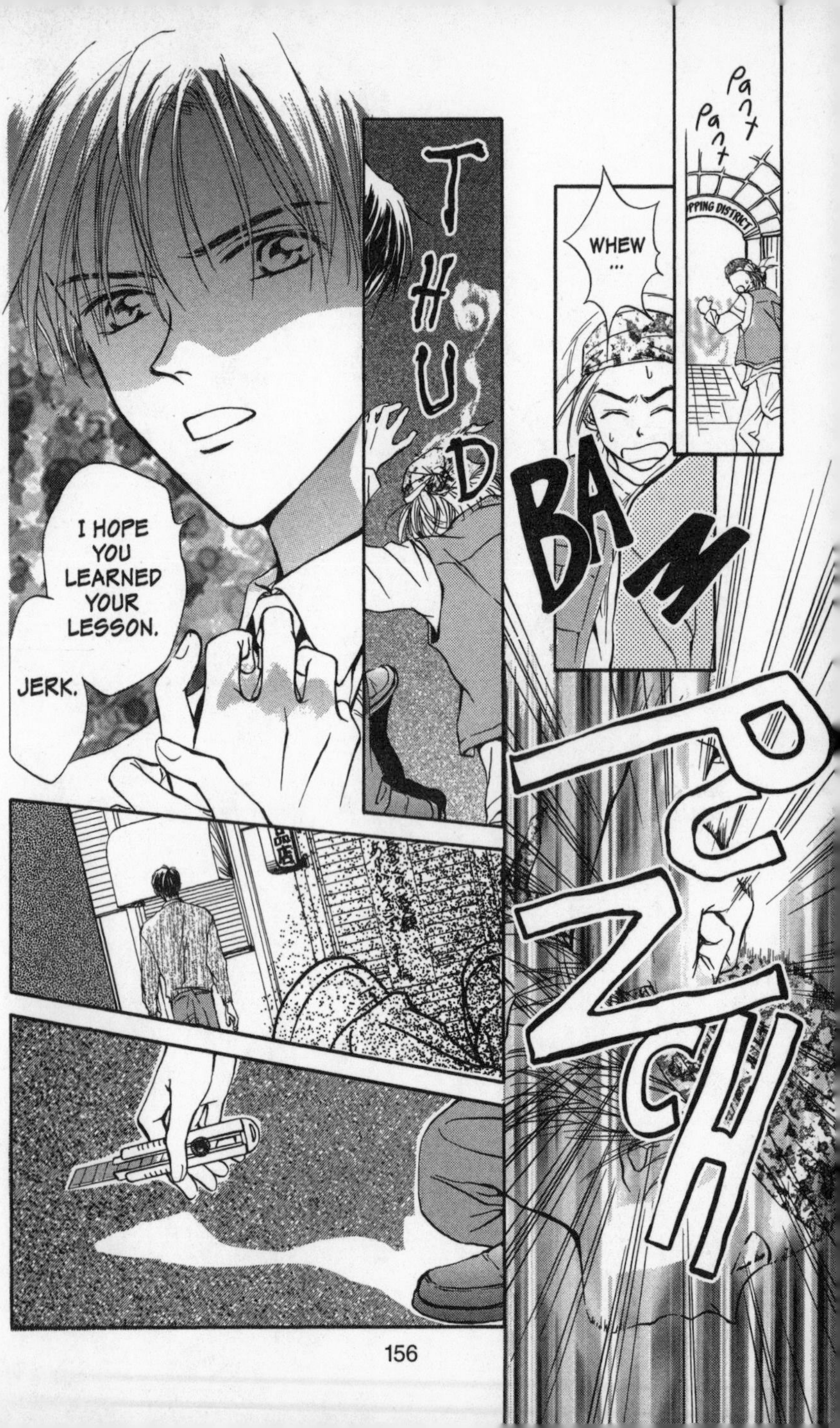
Pant
Pant
PPING DISTRICT
WHEW ...
BAM
PUNCH
THUD
I HOPE YOU LEARNED YOUR LESSON.
JERK.

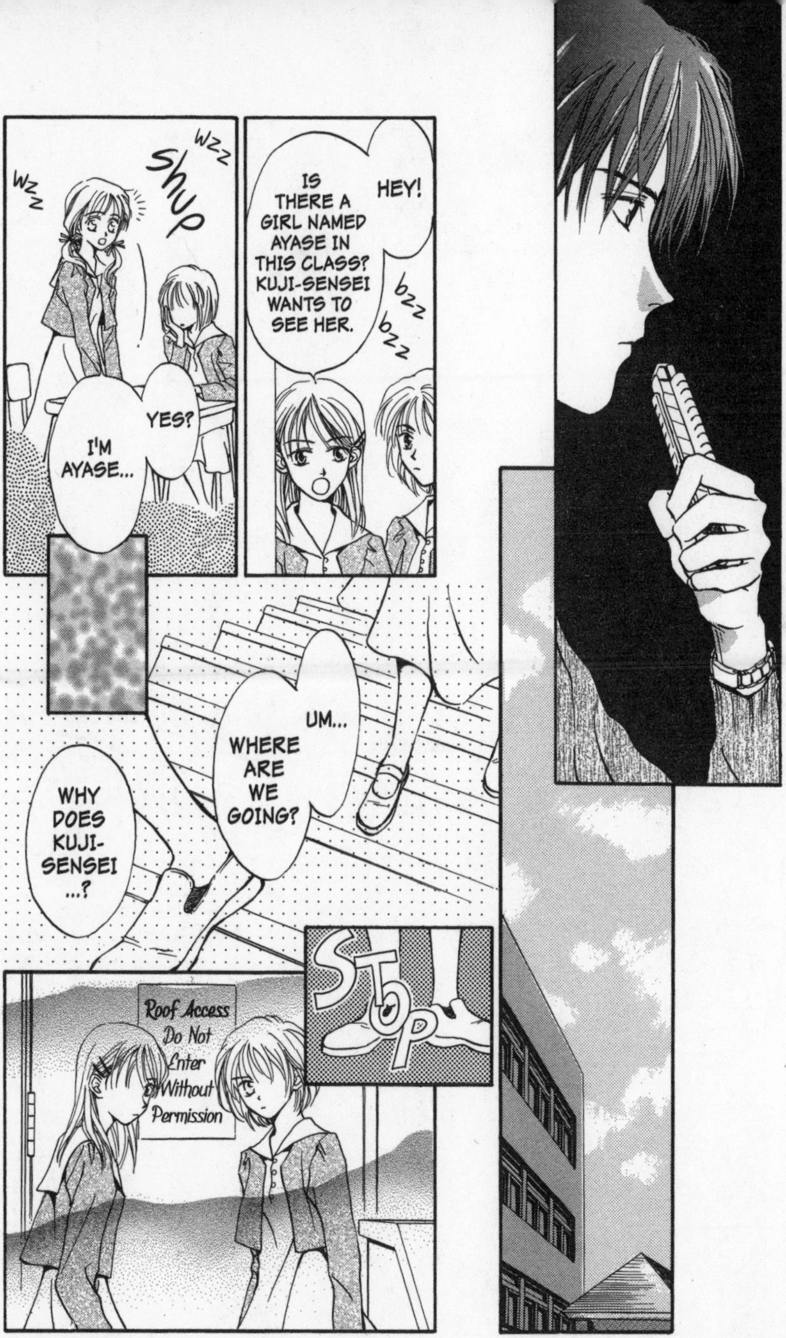
HEY!
IS THERE A GIRL NAMED AYASE IN THIS CLASS? KUJI-SENSEI WANTS TO SEE HER.
bzz bzz
wzz
SHUP
wzz
YES?
I'M AYASE...
UM... WHERE ARE WE GOING?
WHY DOES KUJI-SENSEI ...?
STOP
Roof Access Do Not Enter Without Permission

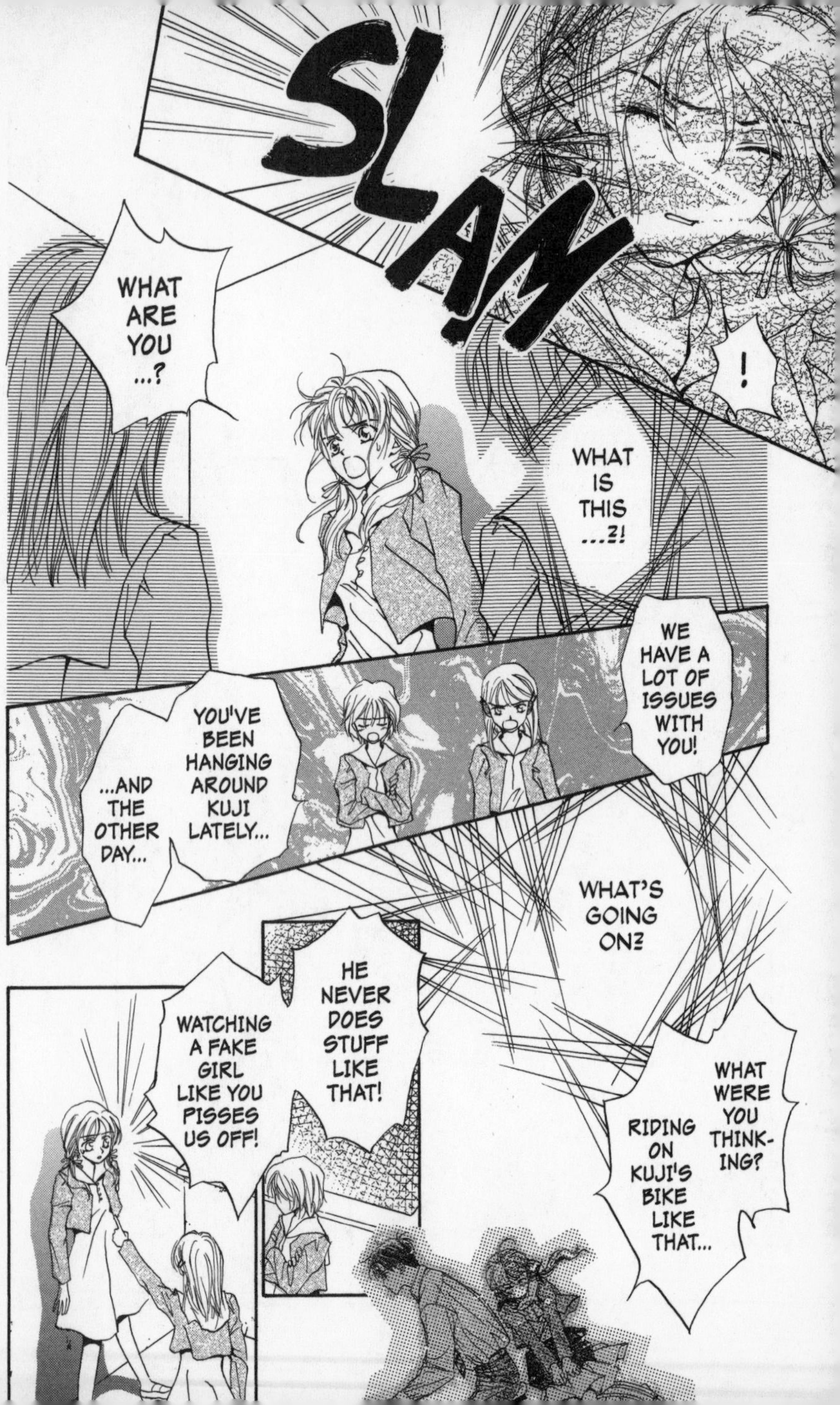
SLAM
!
WHAT IS THIS ...?!
WHAT ARE YOU ...?
WE HAVE A LOT OF ISSUES WITH YOU!
YOU'VE BEEN HANGING AROUND KUJI LATELY...
...AND THE OTHER DAY...
WHAT'S GOING ON?
WHAT WERE YOU THINKING?
RIDING ON KUJI'S BIKE LIKE THAT...
HE NEVER DOES STUFF LIKE THAT!
WATCHING A FAKE GIRL LIKE YOU PISSES US OFF!

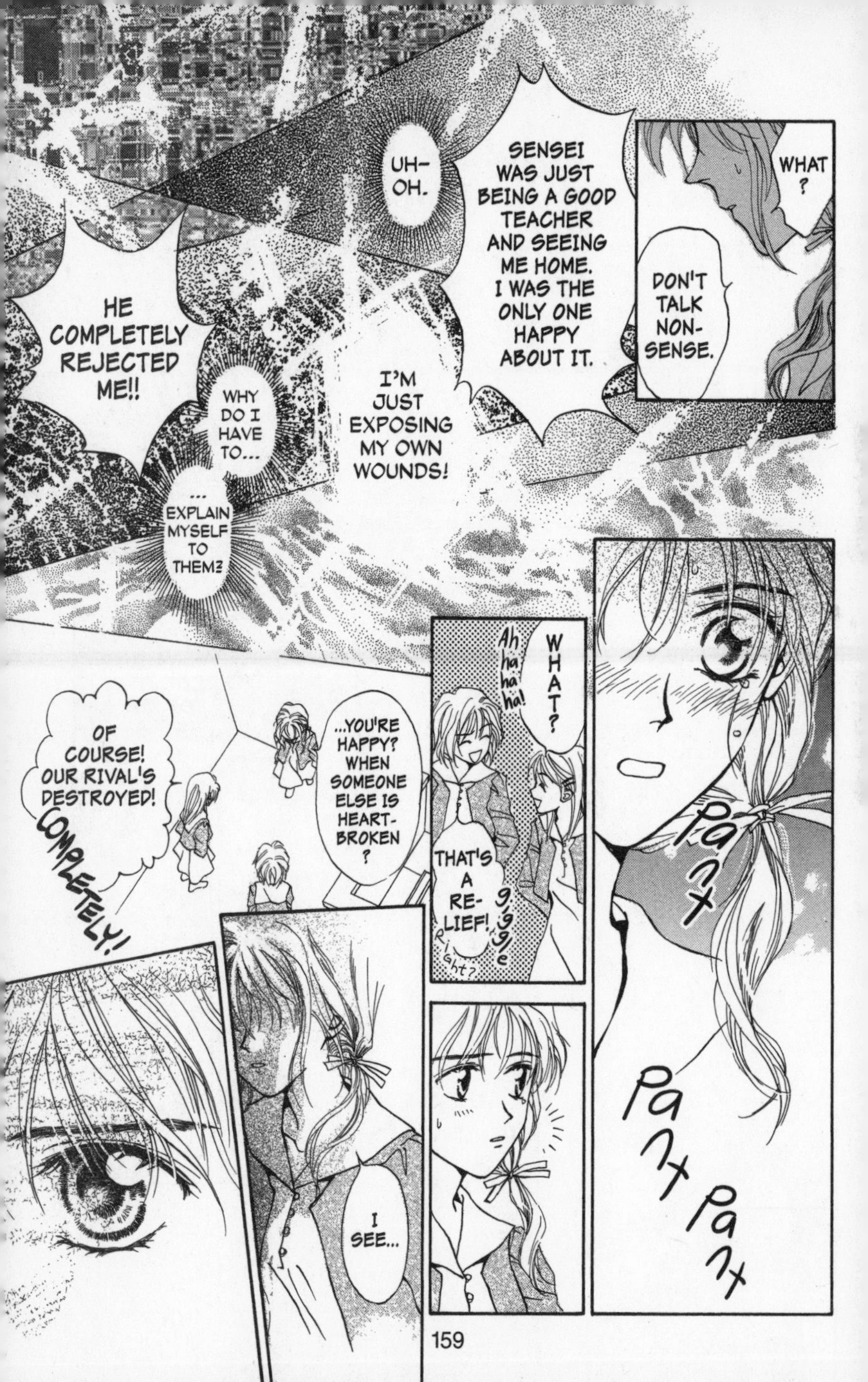
WHAT?
DON'T TALK NONSENSE.
SENSEI WAS JUST BEING A GOOD TEACHER AND SEEING ME HOME. I WAS THE ONLY ONE HAPPY ABOUT IT.
UH-OH.
I'M JUST EXPOSING MY OWN WOUNDS!
HE COMPLETELY REJECTED ME!!
WHY DO I HAVE TO...
...EXPLAIN MYSELF TO THEM?
Pant
Pant Pant Pant
WHAT?
Ah ha ha ha!
THAT'S A RELIEF!
giggle
Right?
...YOU'RE HAPPY? WHEN SOMEONE ELSE IS HEARTBROKEN?
OF COURSE! OUR RIVAL'S DESTROYED!
COMPLETELY!
I SEE...

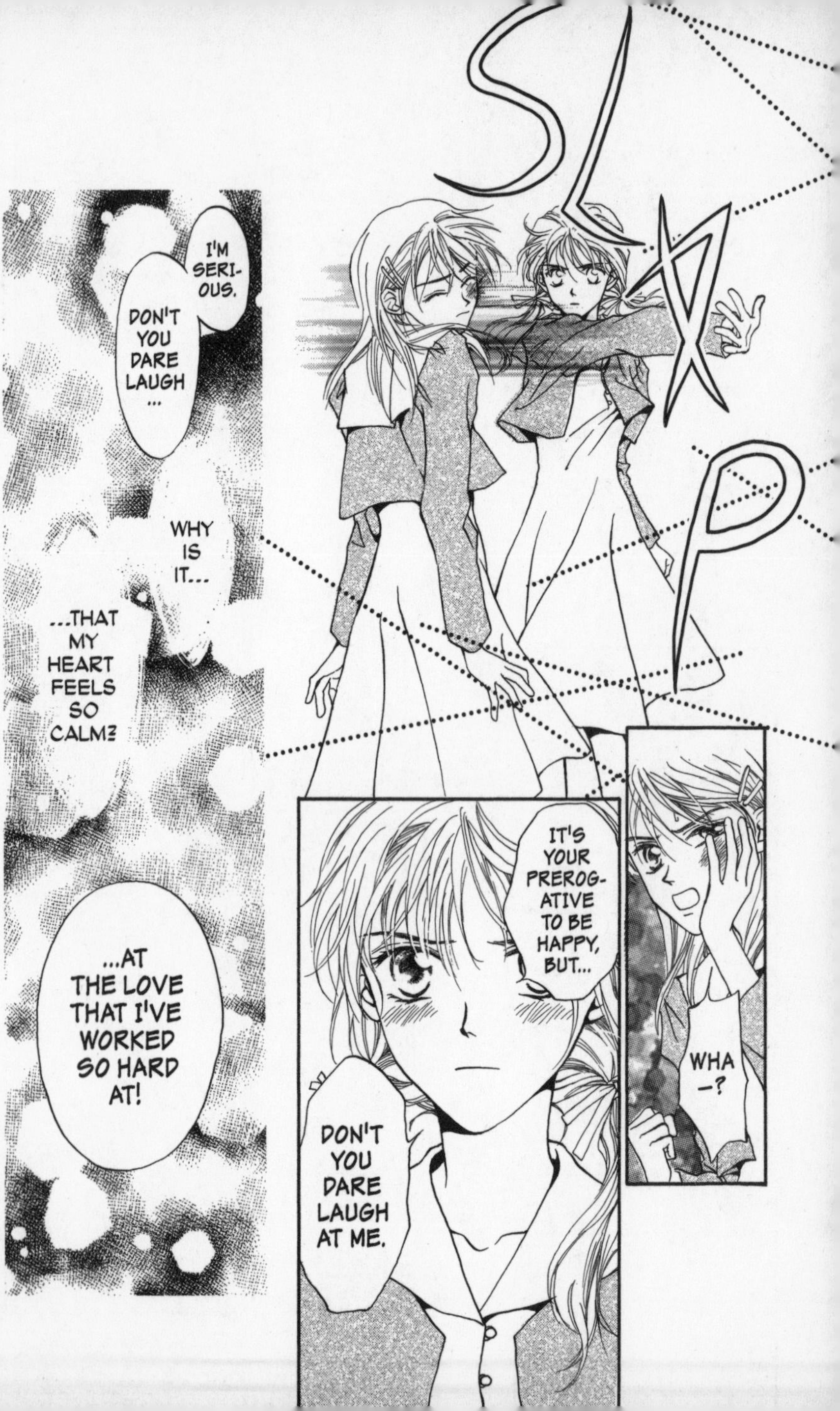
SLAP
WHA—?
IT'S YOUR PREROGATIVE TO BE HAPPY, BUT...
DON'T YOU DARE LAUGH AT ME.
I'M SERIOUS.
DON'T YOU DARE LAUGH...
WHY IS IT...
...THAT MY HEART FEELS SO CALM?
...AT THE LOVE THAT I'VE WORKED SO HARD AT!

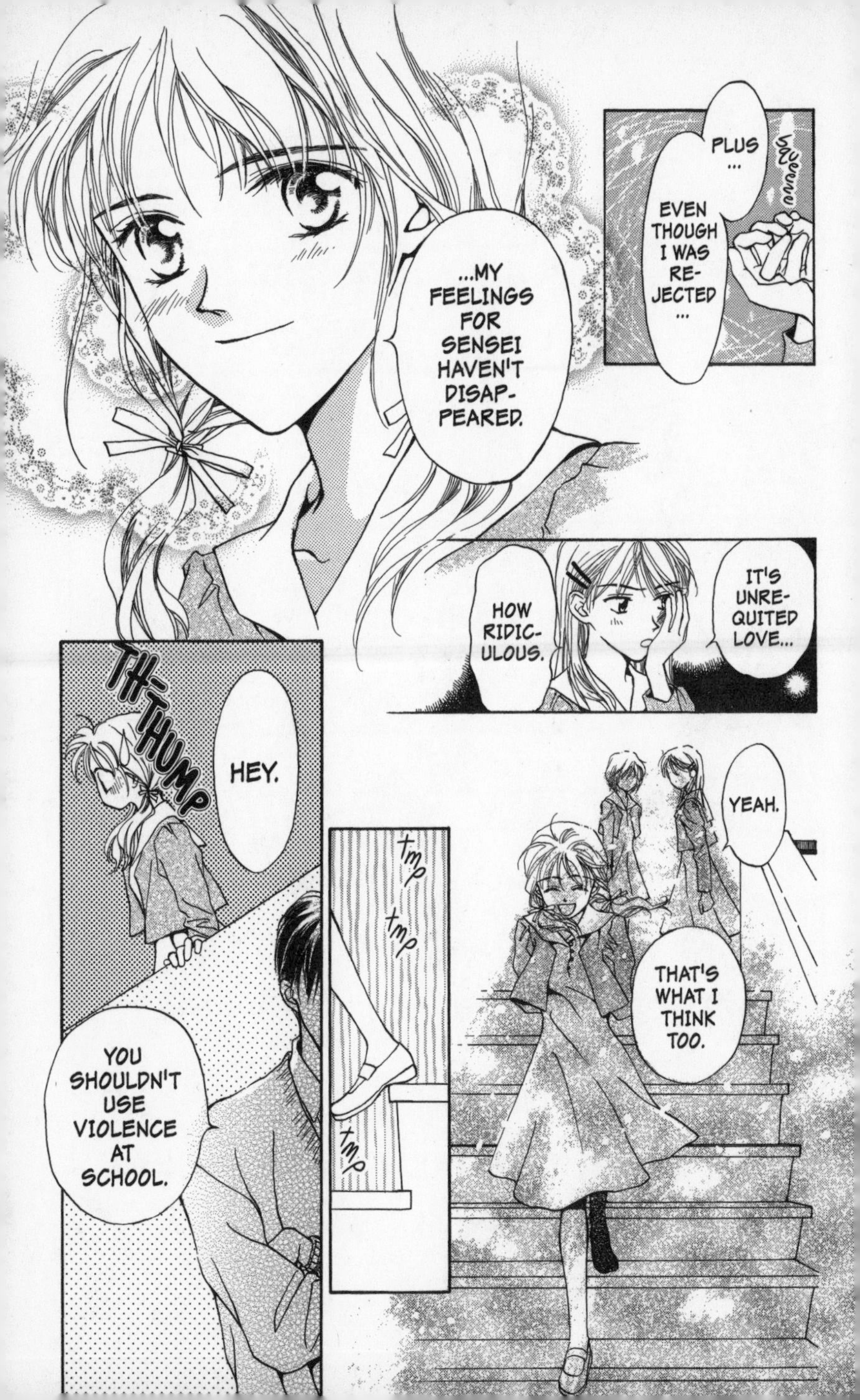
PLUS ...
squeeeze
EVEN THOUGH I WAS RE-JECTED ...
...MY FEELINGS FOR SENSEI HAVEN'T DISAP-PEARED.
IT'S UNRE-QUITED LOVE...
HOW RIDIC-ULOUS.
YEAH.
THAT'S WHAT I THINK TOO.
tmp
tmp
tmp
TH-THUMP
HEY.
YOU SHOULDN'T USE VIOLENCE AT SCHOOL.

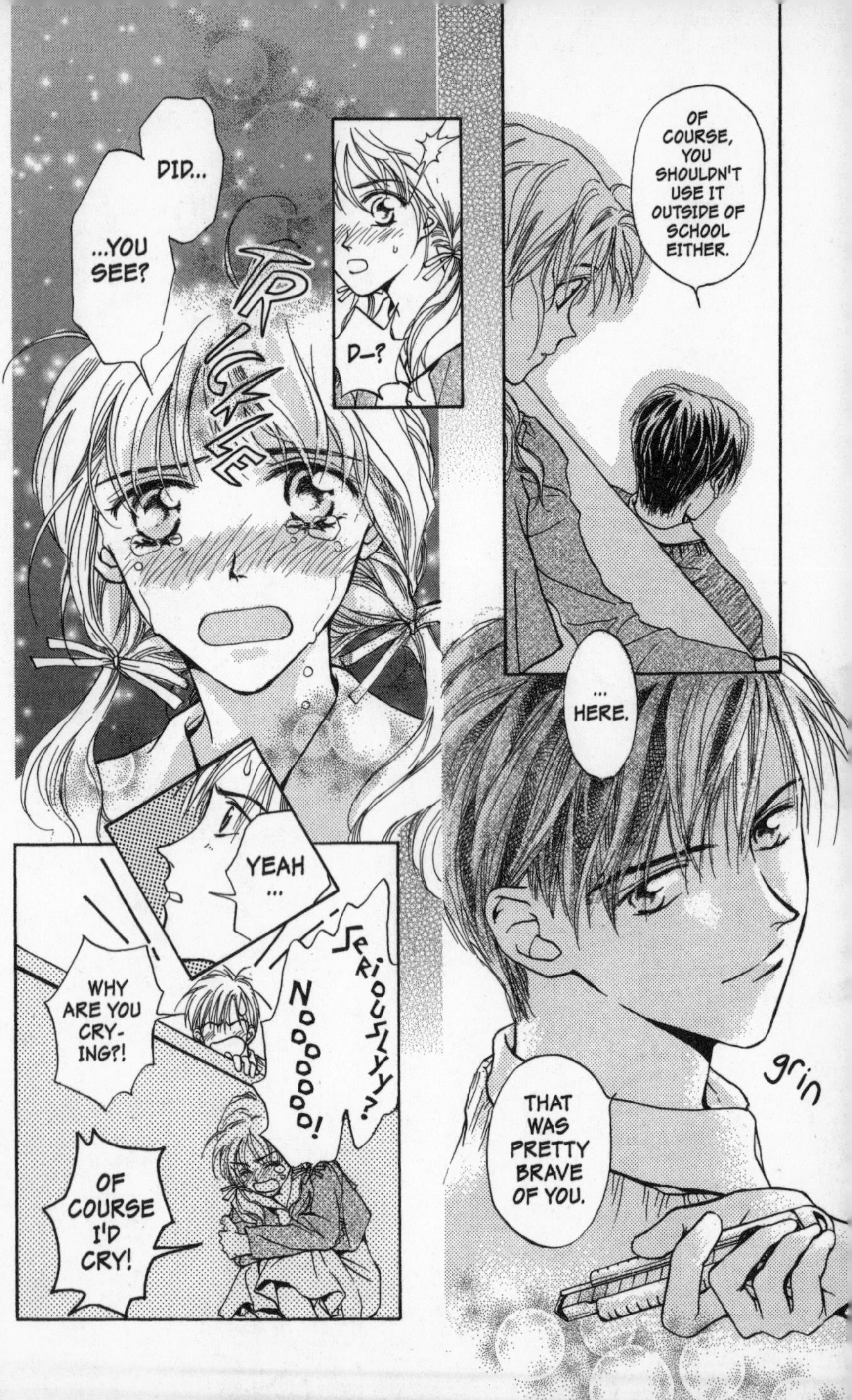
OF COURSE, YOU SHOULDN'T USE IT OUTSIDE OF SCHOOL EITHER.
... HERE.
THAT WAS PRETTY BRAVE OF YOU.
grin
D–?
DID...
...YOU SEE?
TRICKLE
YEAH ...
WHY ARE YOU CRY-ING?!
SERIOUSLYYY?
NOOOOOOO!
OF COURSE I'D CRY!

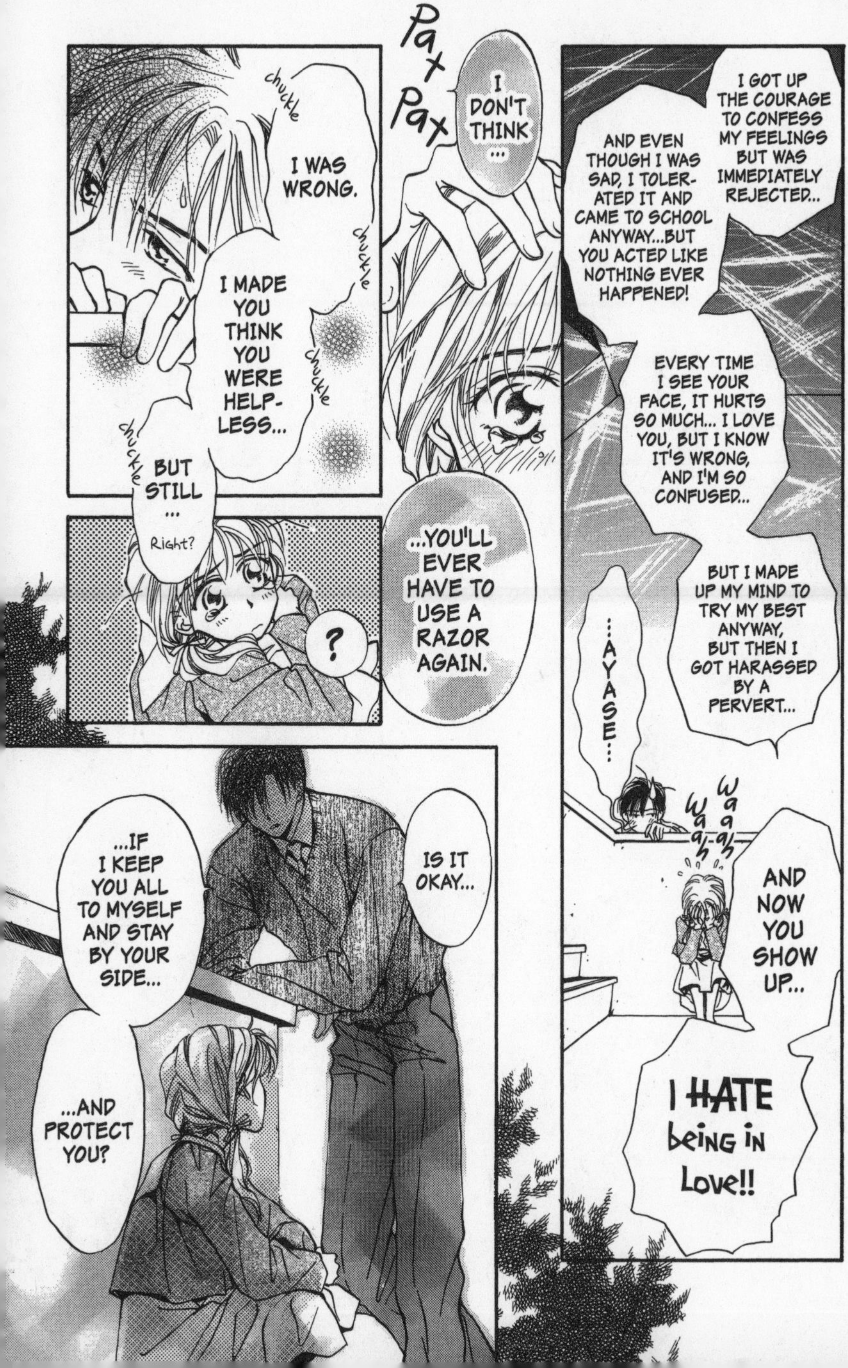
I GOT UP THE COURAGE TO CONFESS MY FEELINGS BUT WAS IMMEDIATELY REJECTED...
AND EVEN THOUGH I WAS SAD, I TOLER-ATED IT AND CAME TO SCHOOL ANYWAY...BUT YOU ACTED LIKE NOTHING EVER HAPPENED!
EVERY TIME I SEE YOUR FACE, IT HURTS SO MUCH... I LOVE YOU, BUT I KNOW IT'S WRONG, AND I'M SO CONFUSED...
BUT I MADE UP MY MIND TO TRY MY BEST ANYWAY, BUT THEN I GOT HARASSED BY A PERVERT...
...AYASE...
Waaah
Waaah
AND NOW YOU SHOW UP...
I HATE being in Love!!
chuckle
I WAS WRONG.
chuckle
I MADE YOU THINK YOU WERE HELP-LESS...
chuckle
chuckle
BUT STILL...
Pat Pat
I DON'T THINK...
...YOU'LL EVER HAVE TO USE A RAZOR AGAIN.
Right?
?
IS IT OKAY...
...IF I KEEP YOU ALL TO MYSELF AND STAY BY YOUR SIDE...
...AND PROTECT YOU?

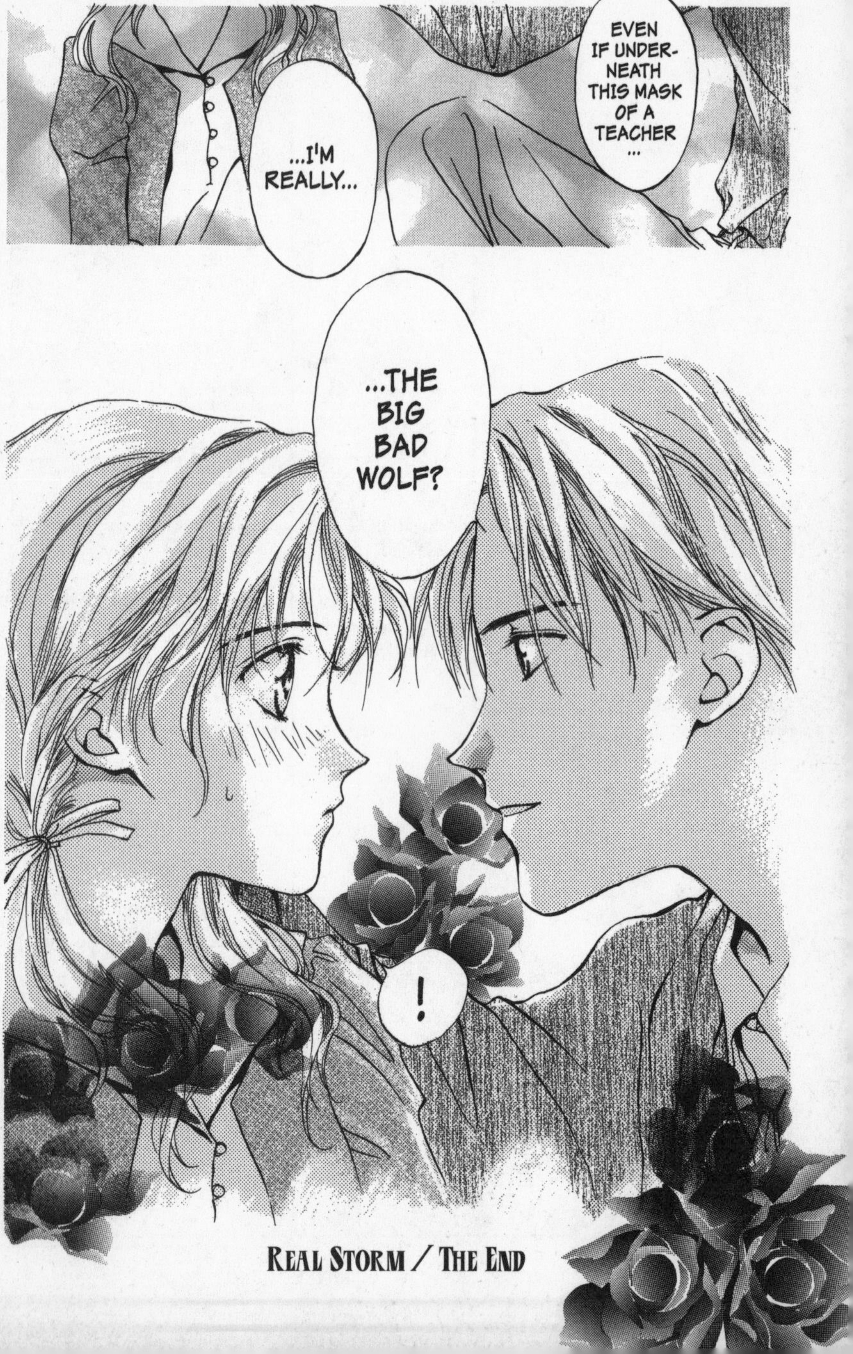
EVEN IF UNDER-NEATH THIS MASK OF A TEACHER ...
...I'M REALLY...
...THE BIG BAD WOLF?
!
REAL STORM / THE END

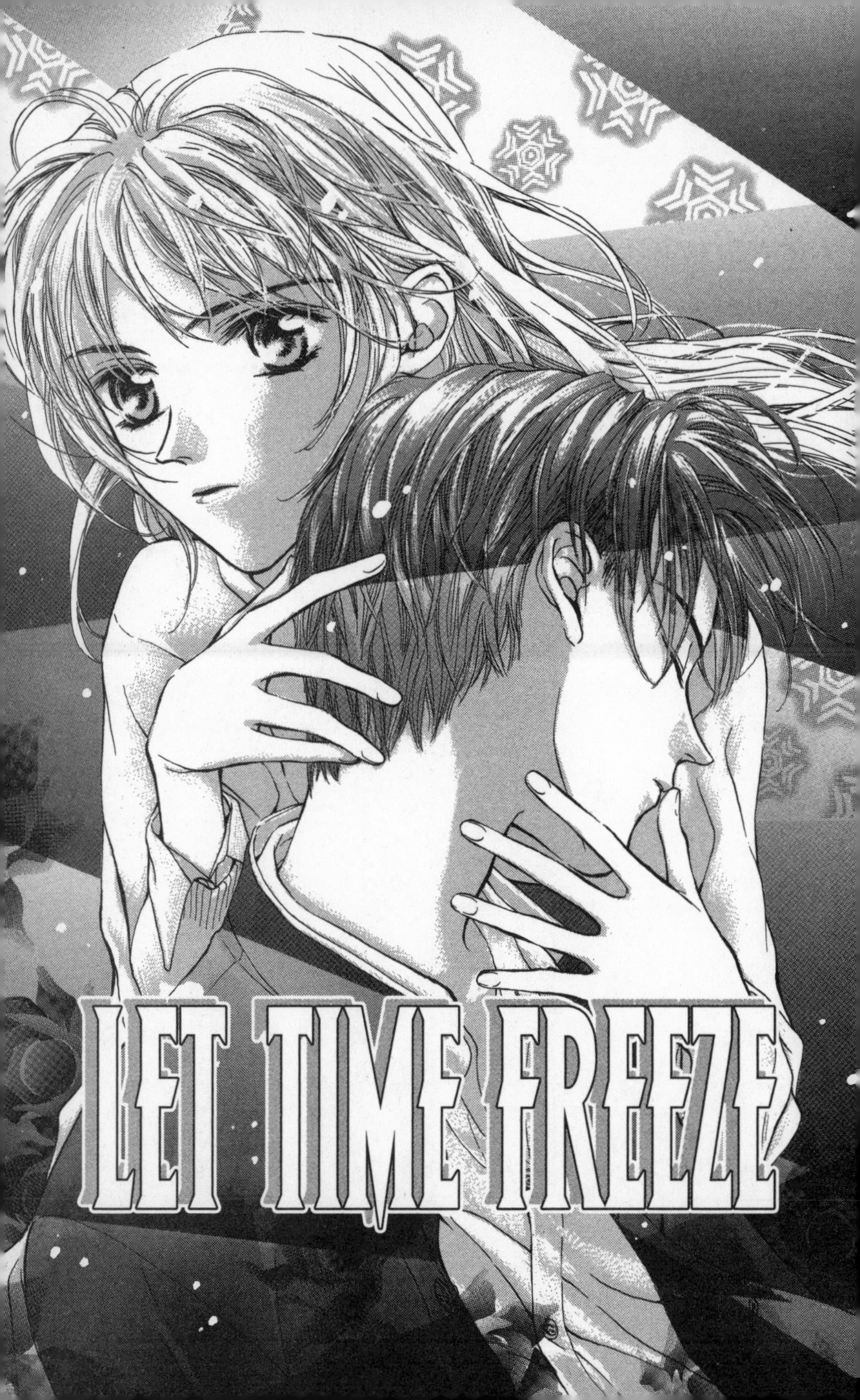
LET TIME FREEZE

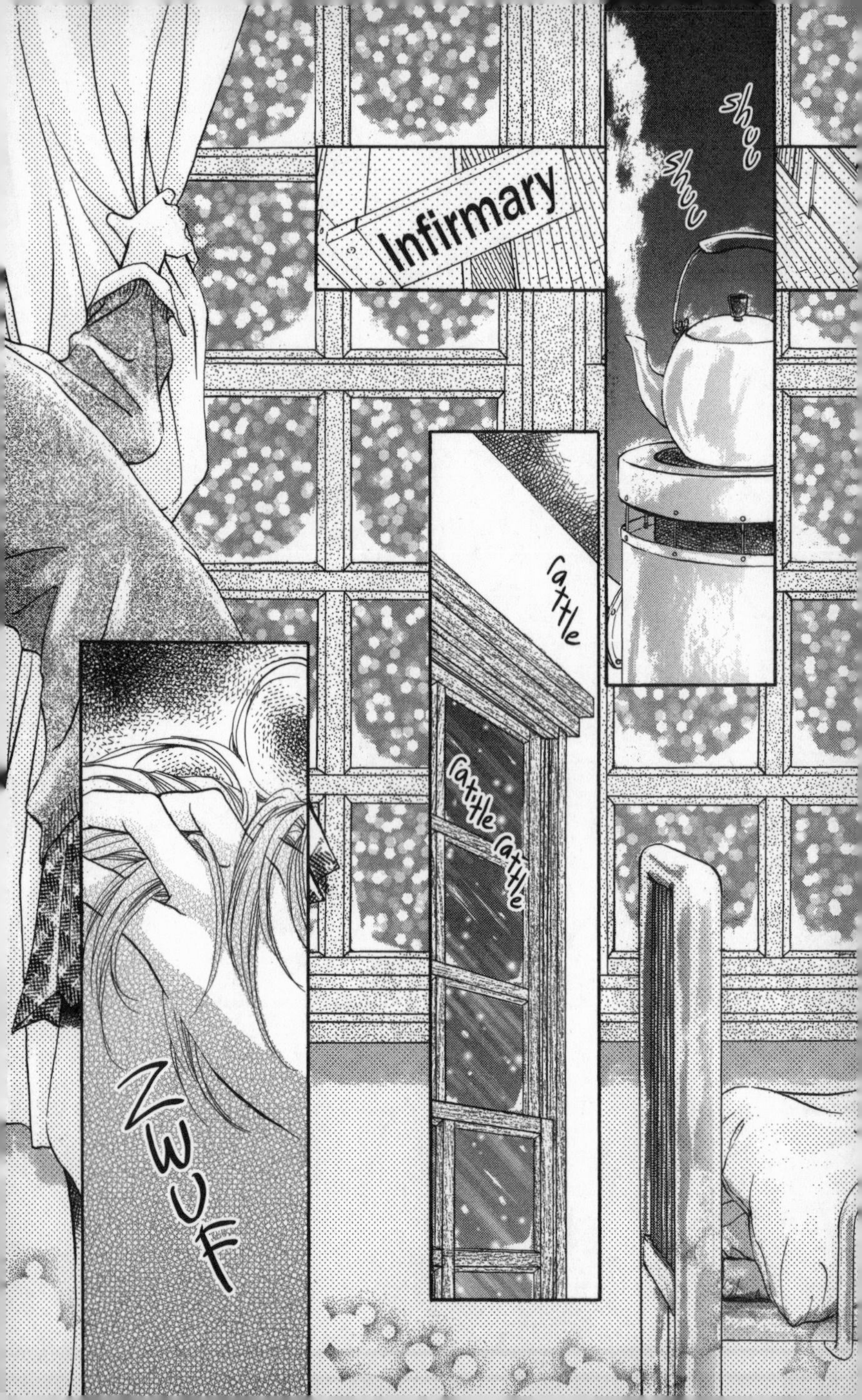
shuu
shuu
Infirmary
rattle
rattle rattle rattle
ZWUF

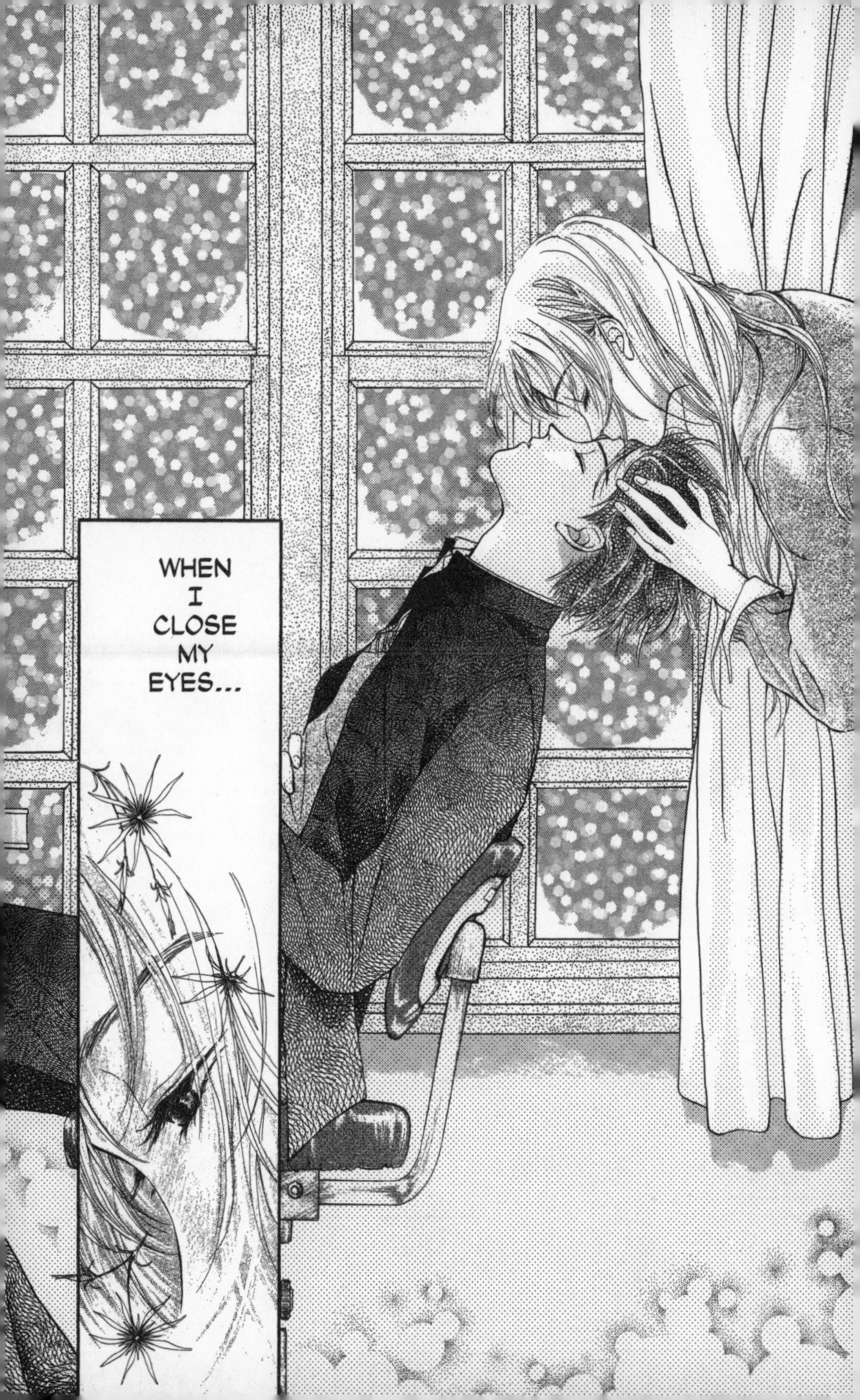
WHEN I CLOSE MY EYES...

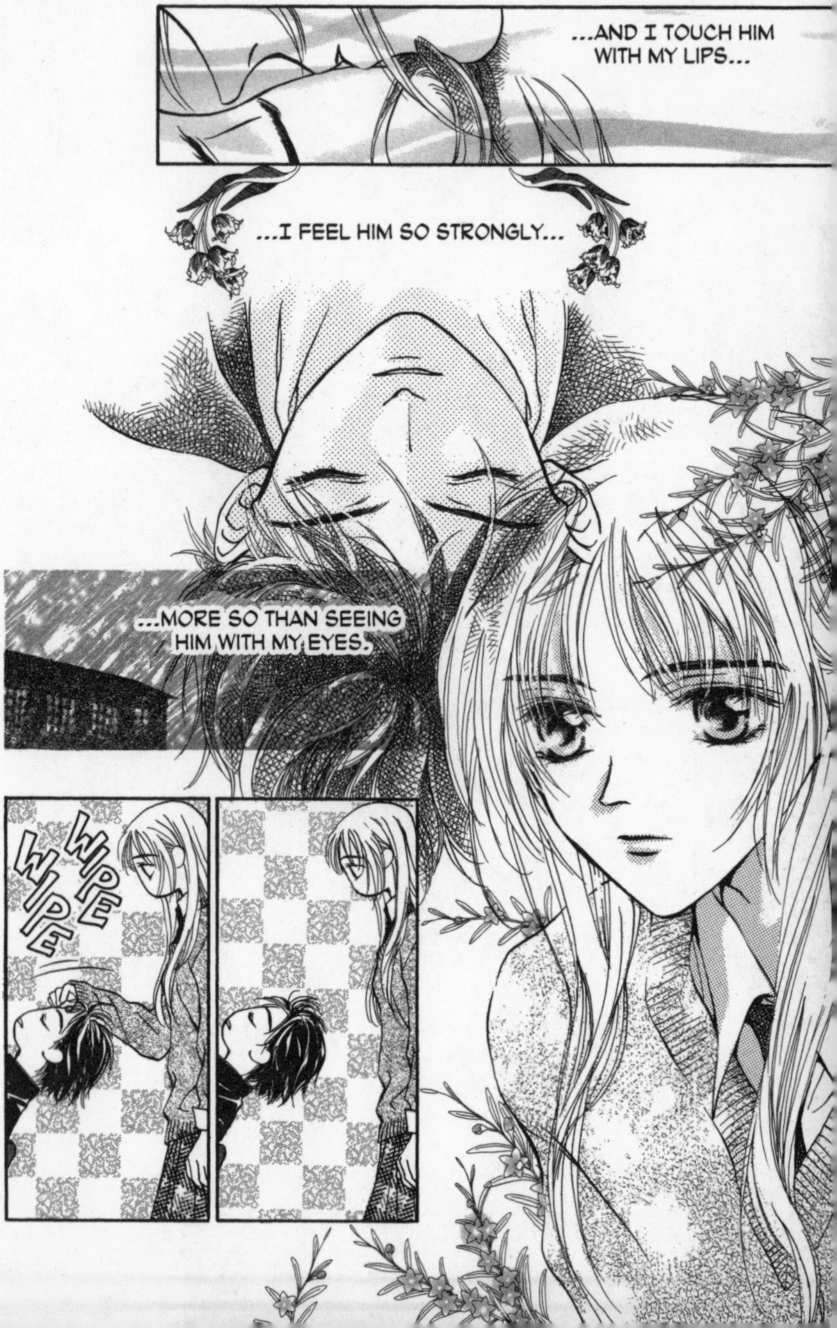
...AND I TOUCH HIM WITH MY LIPS...
...I FEEL HIM SO STRONGLY...
...MORE SO THAN SEEING HIM WITH MY EYES.
WIPE WIPE

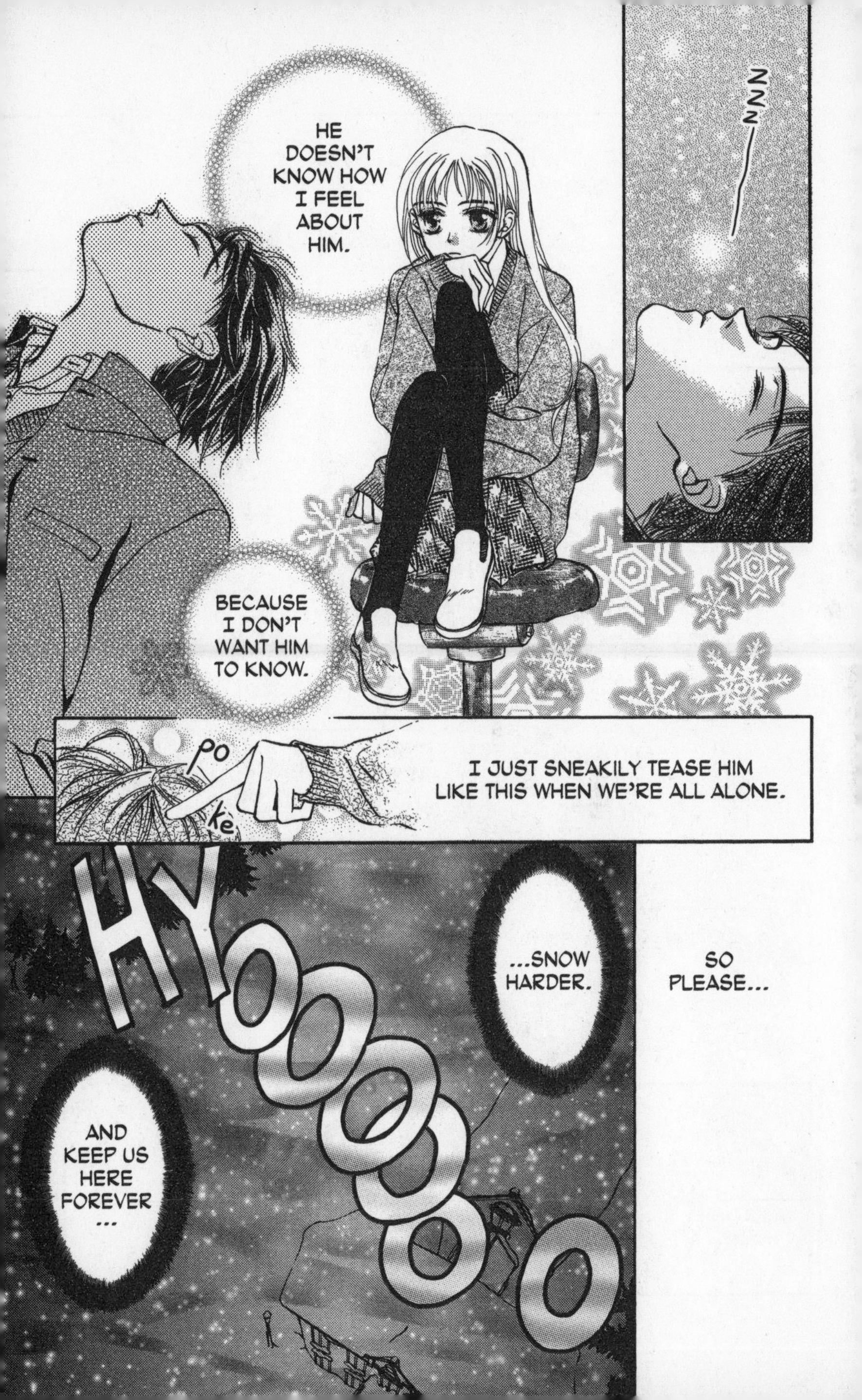
ZZZ—
HE DOESN'T KNOW HOW I FEEL ABOUT HIM.
BECAUSE I DON'T WANT HIM TO KNOW.
I JUST SNEAKILY TEASE HIM LIKE THIS WHEN WE'RE ALL ALONE.
PO
KE
SO PLEASE...
...SNOW HARDER.
HYOOOOOOOOO
AND KEEP US HERE FOREVER ...

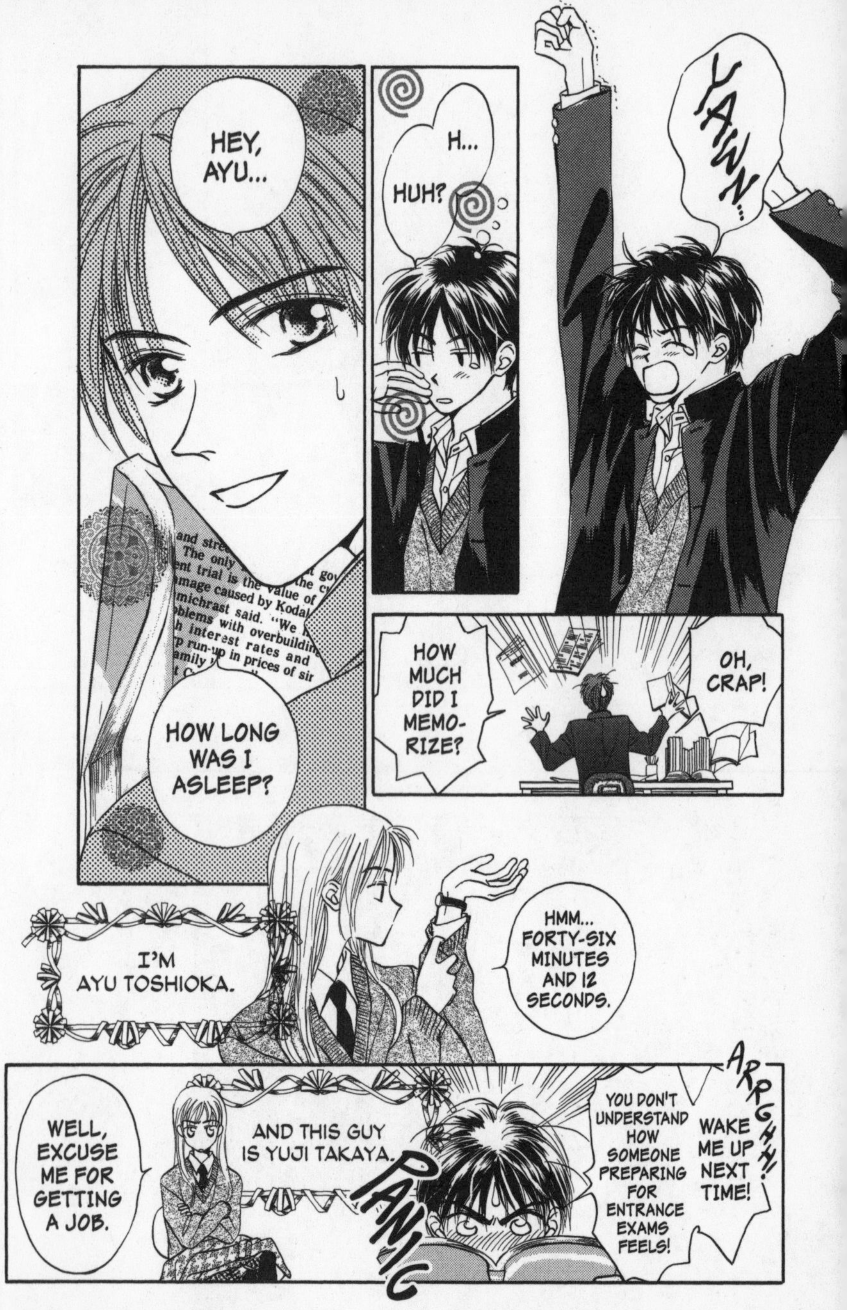
YAWN...
H...
HUH?
OH, CRAP!
HOW MUCH DID I MEMORIZE?
HEY, AYU...
HOW LONG WAS I ASLEEP?
HMM... FORTY-SIX MINUTES AND 12 SECONDS.
I'M AYU TOSHIOKA.
ARRGHH!
WAKE ME UP NEXT TIME!
YOU DON'T UNDERSTAND HOW SOMEONE PREPARING FOR ENTRANCE EXAMS FEELS!
PANIC
AND THIS GUY IS YUJI TAKAYA.
WELL, EXCUSE ME FOR GETTING A JOB.

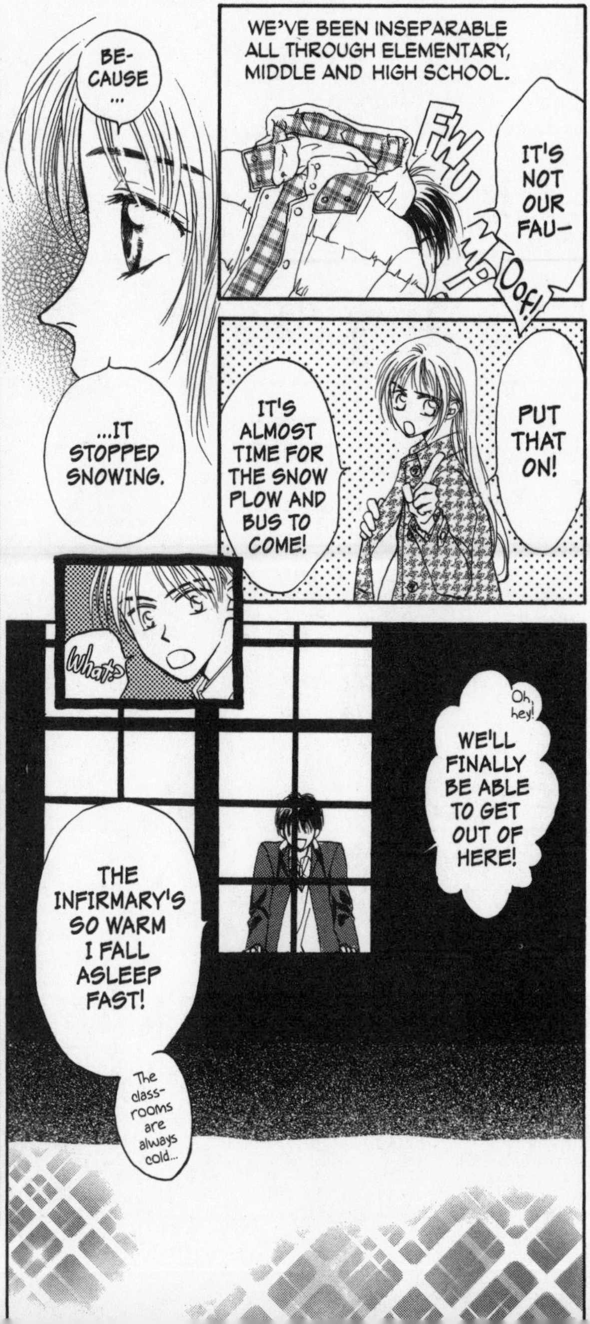
WE'VE BEEN INSEPARABLE ALL THROUGH ELEMENTARY, MIDDLE AND HIGH SCHOOL.
IT'S NOT OUR FAU—
FWUMP
OOF!
PUT THAT ON!
IT'S ALMOST TIME FOR THE SNOW PLOW AND BUS TO COME!
BE-CAUSE...
...IT STOPPED SNOWING.
What?
Oh, hey!
WE'LL FINALLY BE ABLE TO GET OUT OF HERE!
THE INFIRMARY'S SO WARM I FALL ASLEEP FAST!
The class-rooms are always cold...

6

I wanted to convey the romanticism of a snow country.

But it's not that good.

Let Time Freeze is set in my stomping grounds, Hokkaido!

Also, the Kogami mansion from Captive Hearts is modeled after an old building in Sapporo.

I love refreshing places in Hokkaido.

The end

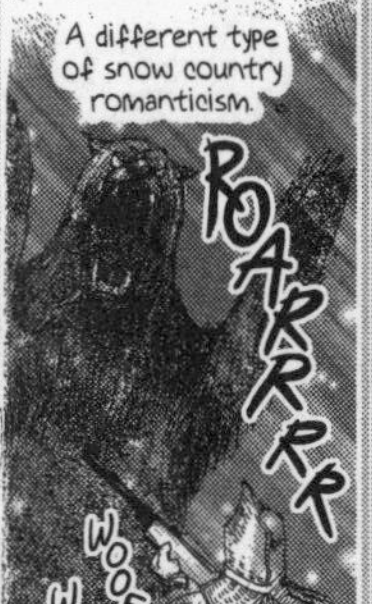
A different type of snow country romanticism.
ROARRRR
WOOF
WOOF
WOOF
Brown bear vs. Matagi

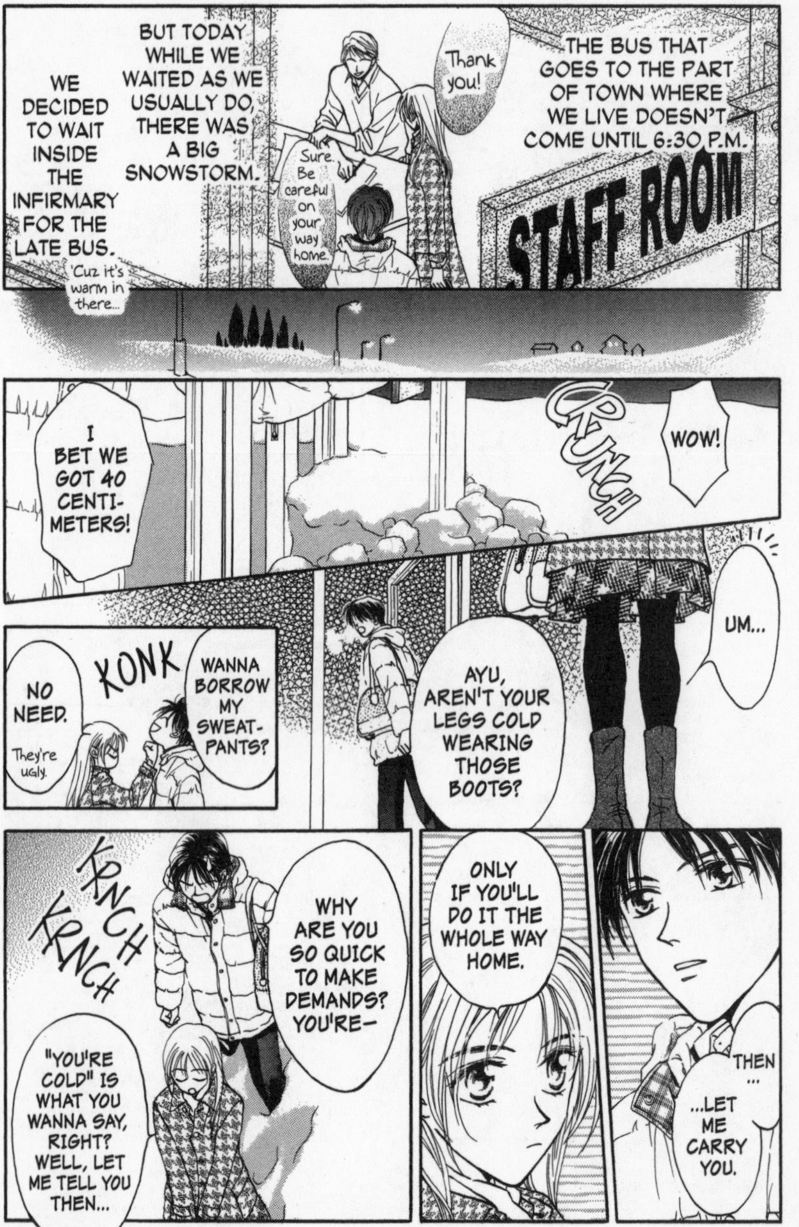
THE BUS THAT GOES TO THE PART OF TOWN WHERE WE LIVE DOESN'T COME UNTIL 6:30 P.M.
STAFF ROOM
Thank you!
Sure. Be careful on your way home.
BUT TODAY WHILE WE WAITED AS WE USUALLY DO, THERE WAS A BIG SNOWSTORM.
WE DECIDED TO WAIT INSIDE THE INFIRMARY FOR THE LATE BUS.
'Cuz it's warm in there...
WOW!
CRUNCH
I BET WE GOT 40 CENTIMETERS!
UM...
AYU, AREN'T YOUR LEGS COLD WEARING THOSE BOOTS?
WANNA BORROW MY SWEATPANTS?
KONK
NO NEED.
They're ugly.
THEN ...
...LET ME CARRY YOU.
ONLY IF YOU'LL DO IT THE WHOLE WAY HOME.
WHY ARE YOU SO QUICK TO MAKE DEMANDS? YOU'RE–
KRNCH KRNCH
"YOU'RE COLD" IS WHAT YOU WANNA SAY, RIGHT? WELL, LET ME TELL YOU THEN...

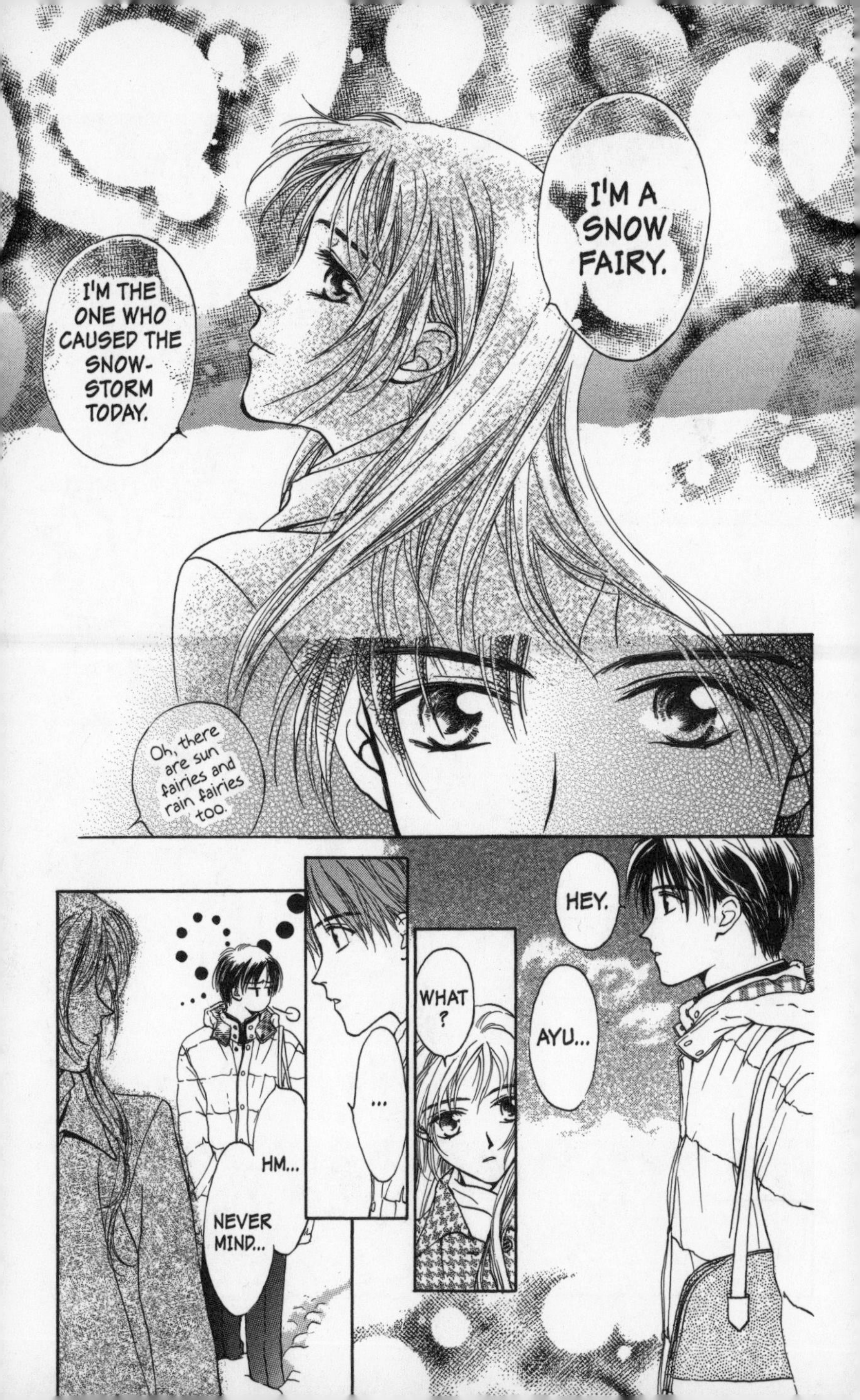
I'M A SNOW FAIRY.
I'M THE ONE WHO CAUSED THE SNOW-STORM TODAY.
Oh, there are sun fairies and rain fairies too.
HEY.
AYU...
WHAT?
...
HM...
NEVER MIND...

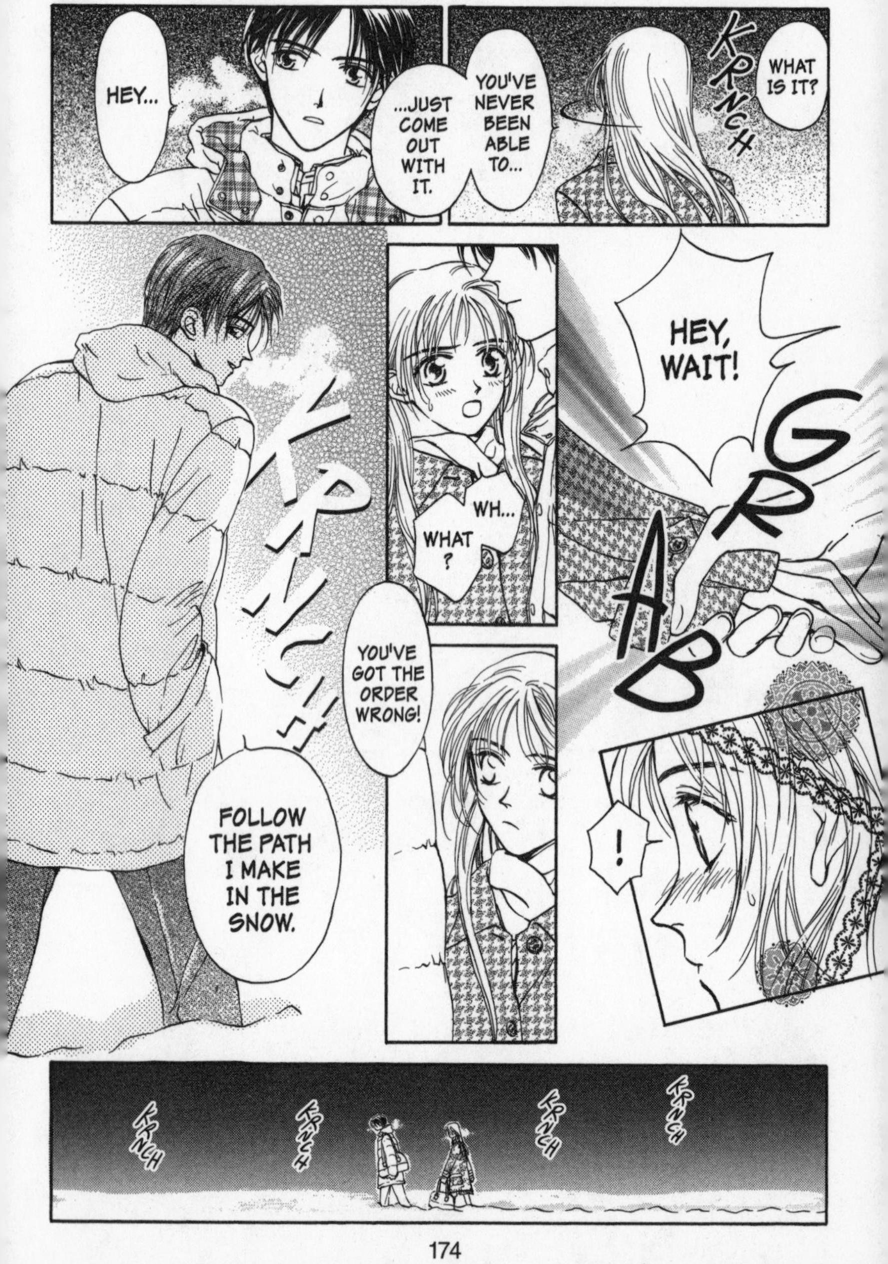
KRNCH
WHAT IS IT?
YOU'VE NEVER BEEN ABLE TO...
...JUST COME OUT WITH IT.
HEY...
HEY, WAIT!
GRAB
WH... WHAT?
!
YOU'VE GOT THE ORDER WRONG!
KRNCH
FOLLOW THE PATH I MAKE IN THE SNOW.
KRNCH
KRNCH
KRNCH
KRNCH

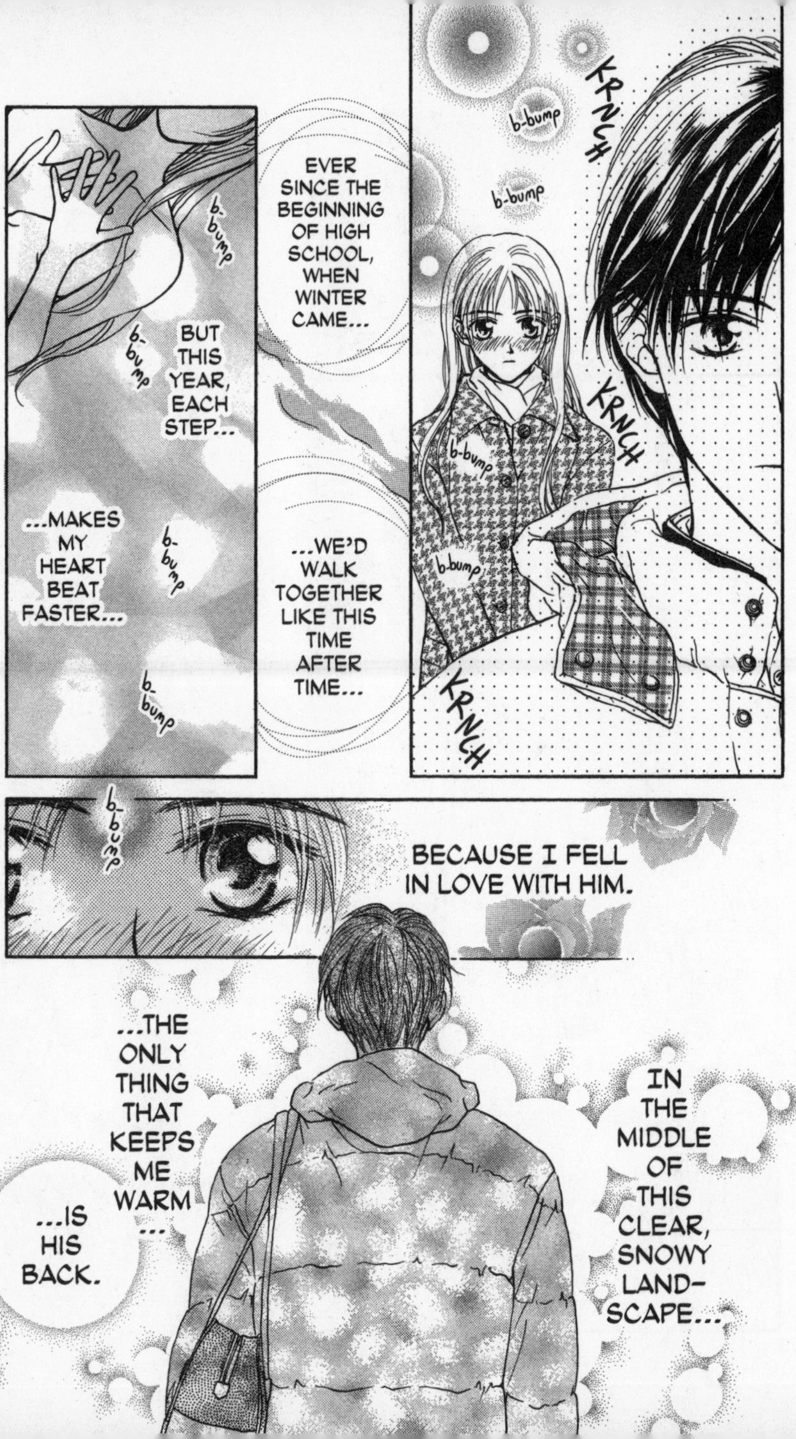

KRNCH
b-bump
b-bump
KRNCH
b-bump
b-bump
KRNCH
EVER SINCE THE BEGINNING OF HIGH SCHOOL, WHEN WINTER CAME...
...WE'D WALK TOGETHER LIKE THIS TIME AFTER TIME...
b-bump
b-bump
BUT THIS YEAR, EACH STEP...
b-bump
...MAKES MY HEART BEAT FASTER...
b-bump
BECAUSE I FELL IN LOVE WITH HIM.
b-bump
IN THE MIDDLE OF THIS CLEAR, SNOWY LANDSCAPE...
...THE ONLY THING THAT KEEPS ME WARM...
...IS HIS BACK.

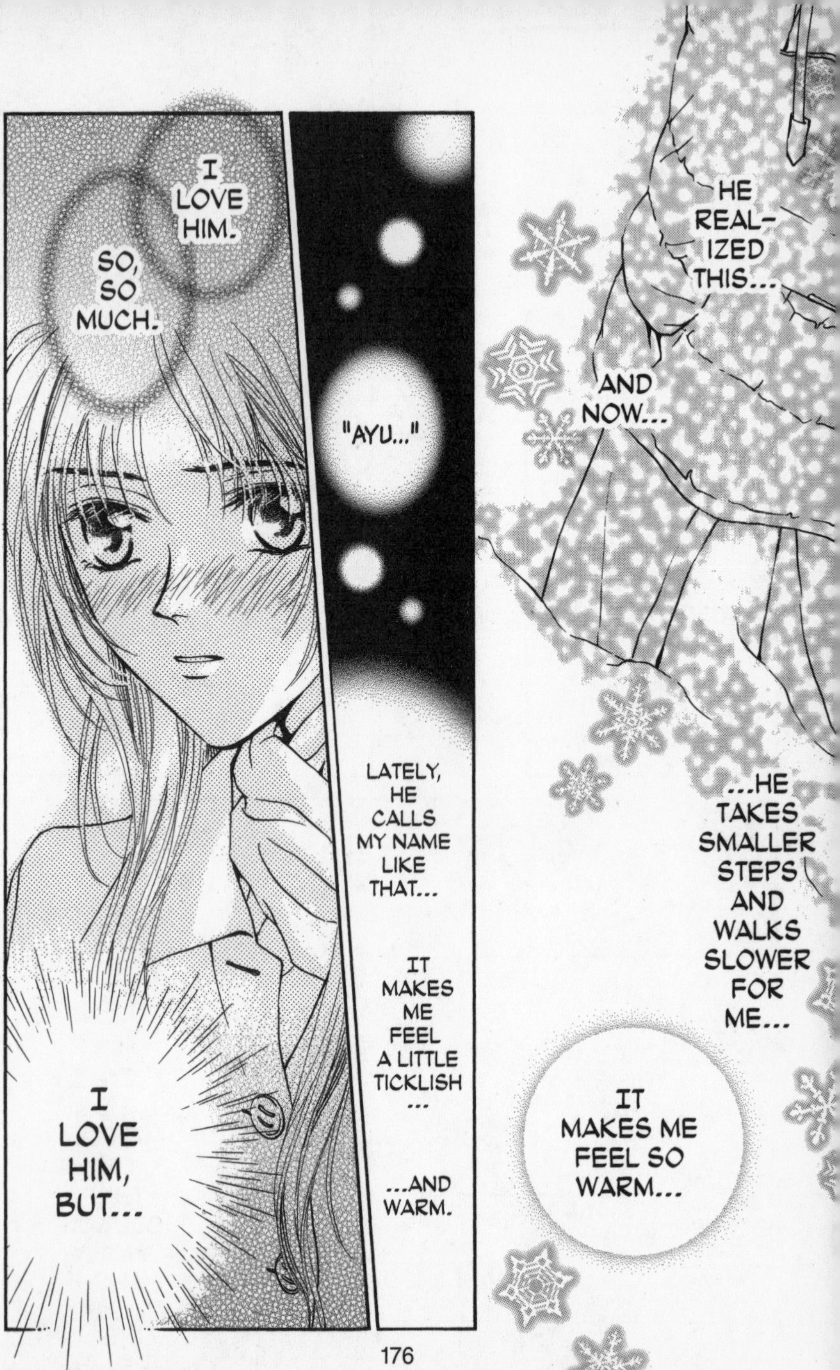
HE REALIZED THIS...
AND NOW...
...HE TAKES SMALLER STEPS AND WALKS SLOWER FOR ME...
IT MAKES ME FEEL SO WARM...
"AYU..."
LATELY, HE CALLS MY NAME LIKE THAT...
IT MAKES ME FEEL A LITTLE TICKLISH...
...AND WARM.
I LOVE HIM.
SO, SO MUCH.
I LOVE HIM, BUT...

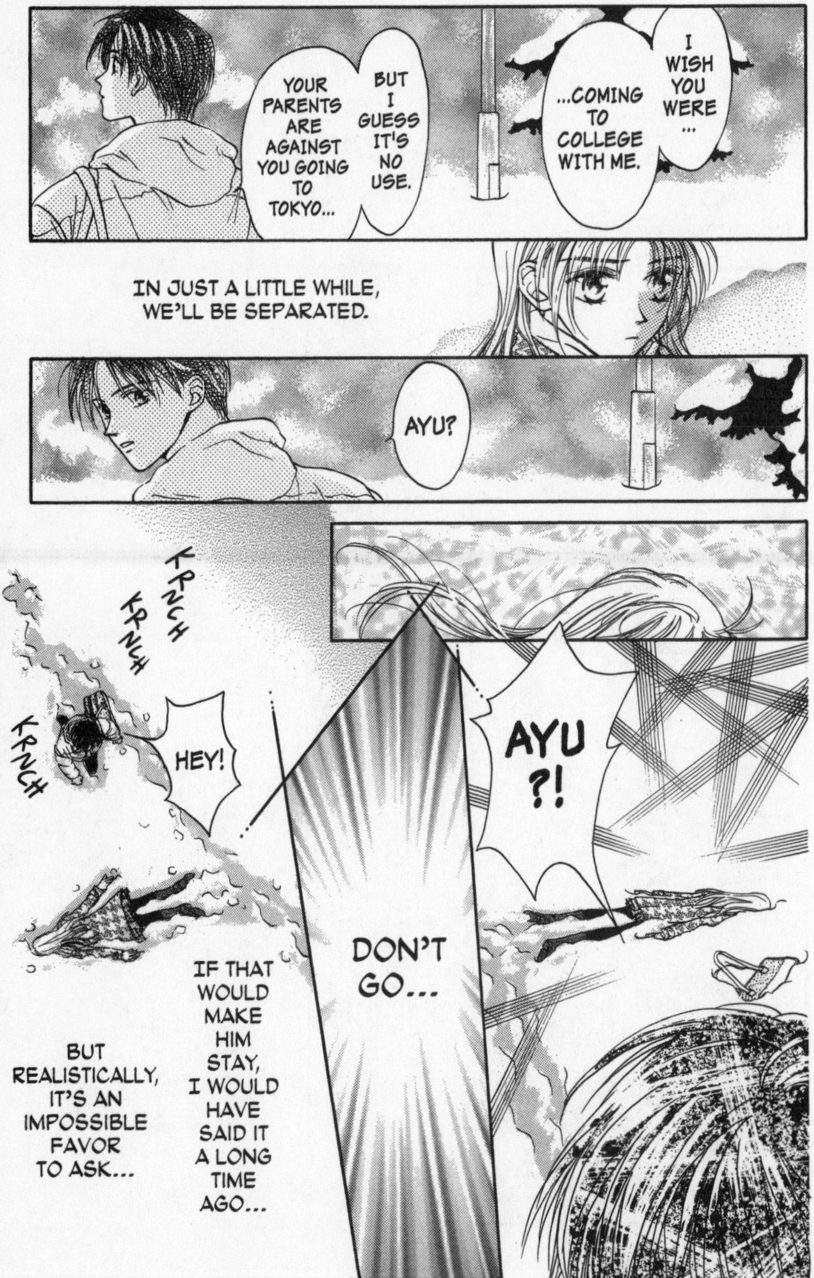
I WISH YOU WERE...
...COMING TO COLLEGE WITH ME.
BUT I GUESS IT'S NO USE.
YOUR PARENTS ARE AGAINST YOU GOING TO TOKYO...
IN JUST A LITTLE WHILE, WE'LL BE SEPARATED.
AYU?
AYU ?!
DON'T GO...
HEY!
KRNCH KRNCH
KRNCH
IF THAT WOULD MAKE HIM STAY, I WOULD HAVE SAID IT A LONG TIME AGO...
BUT REALISTICALLY, IT'S AN IMPOSSIBLE FAVOR TO ASK...

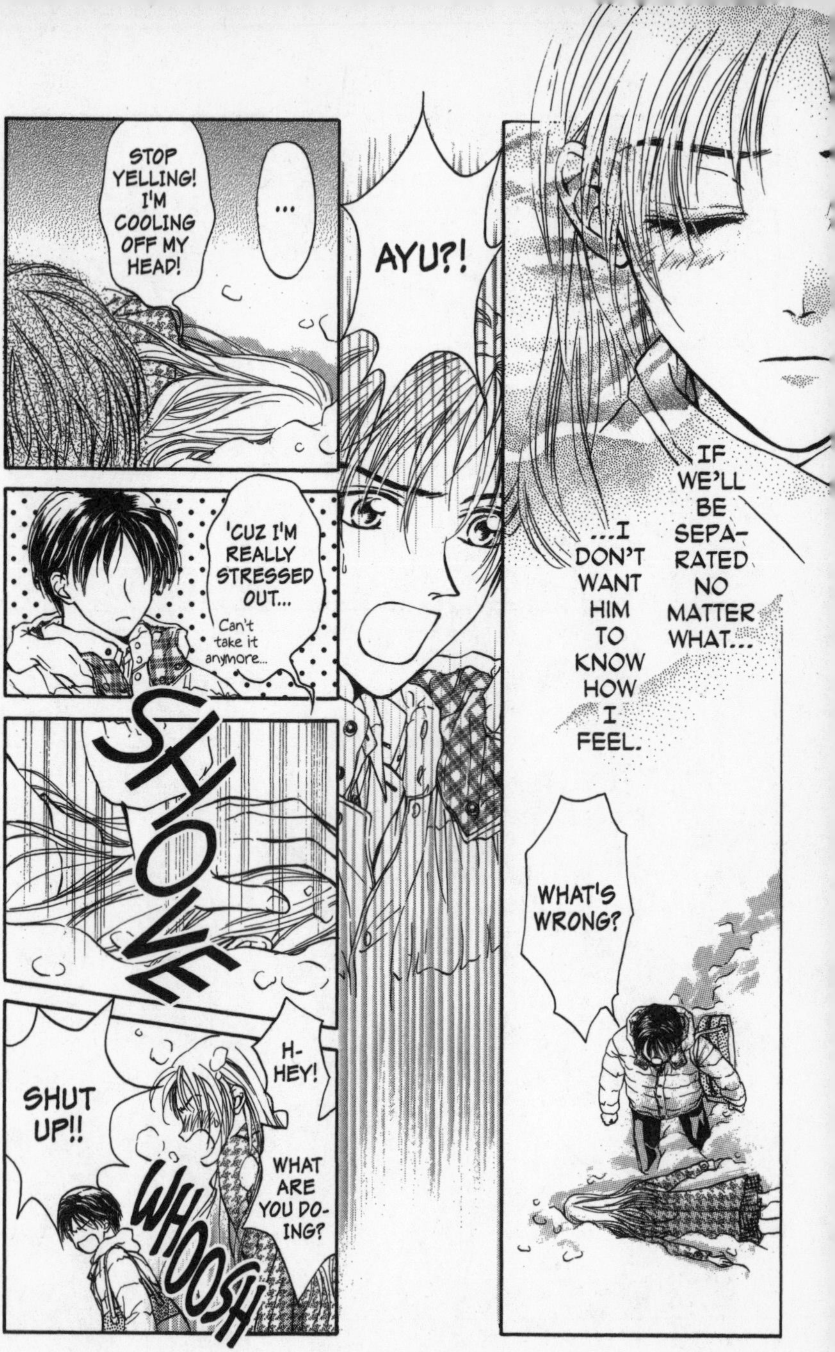
IF WE'LL BE SEPARATED NO MATTER WHAT...
...I DON'T WANT HIM TO KNOW HOW I FEEL.
WHAT'S WRONG?
AYU?!
...
STOP YELLING! I'M COOLING OFF MY HEAD!
'CUZ I'M REALLY STRESSED OUT...
Can't take it anymore...
SHOVE
H-HEY!
WHAT ARE YOU DOING?
WHOOSH
SHUT UP!!

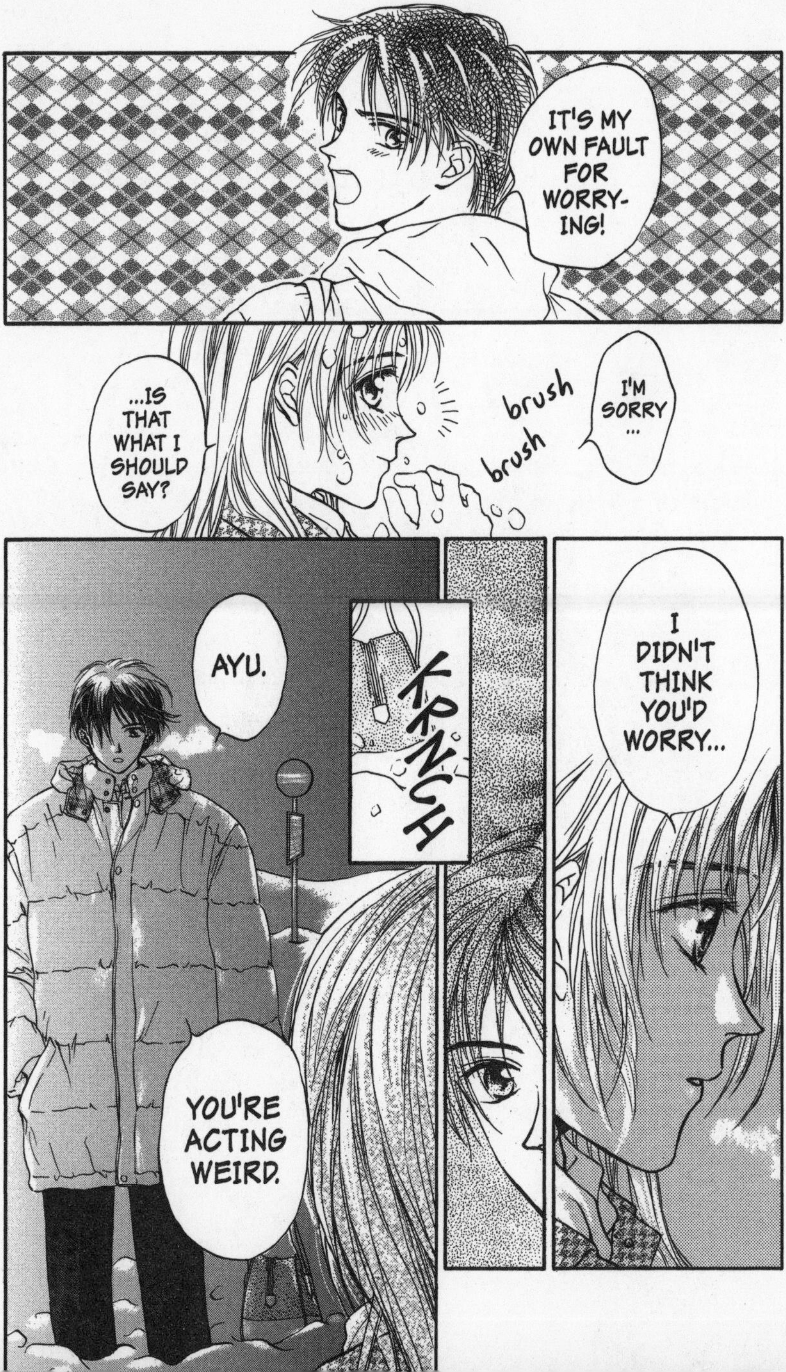
IT'S MY OWN FAULT FOR WORRY-ING!
I'M SORRY ...
brush brush
...IS THAT WHAT I SHOULD SAY?
I DIDN'T THINK YOU'D WORRY...
KRNCH
AYU.
YOU'RE ACTING WEIRD.

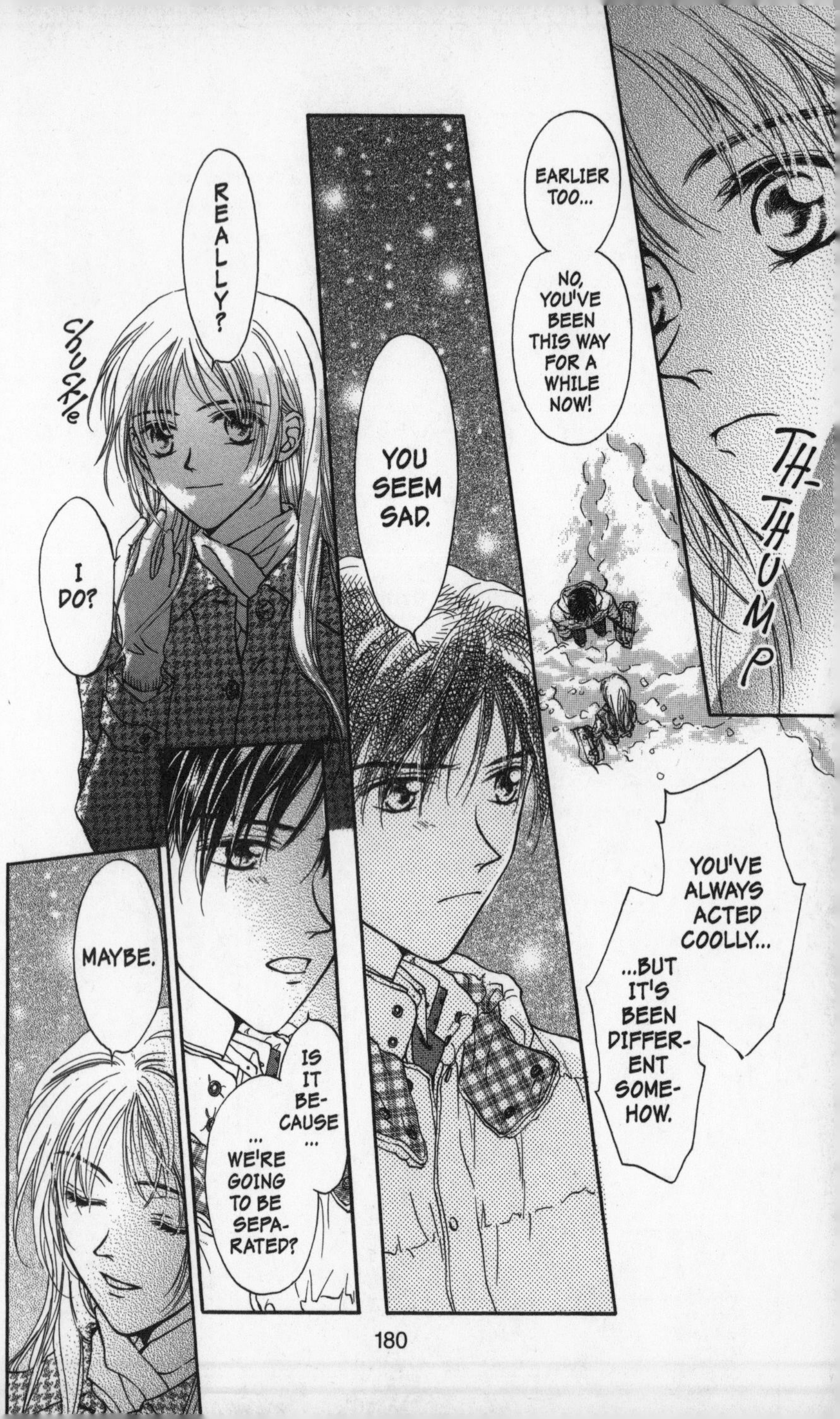
EARLIER TOO...
NO, YOU'VE BEEN THIS WAY FOR A WHILE NOW!
TH-THUMP
YOU'VE ALWAYS ACTED COOLLY...
...BUT IT'S BEEN DIFFER-ENT SOME-HOW.
YOU SEEM SAD.
REALLY?
chuckle
I DO?
IS IT BE-CAUSE... ...WE'RE GOING TO BE SEPA-RATED?
MAYBE.

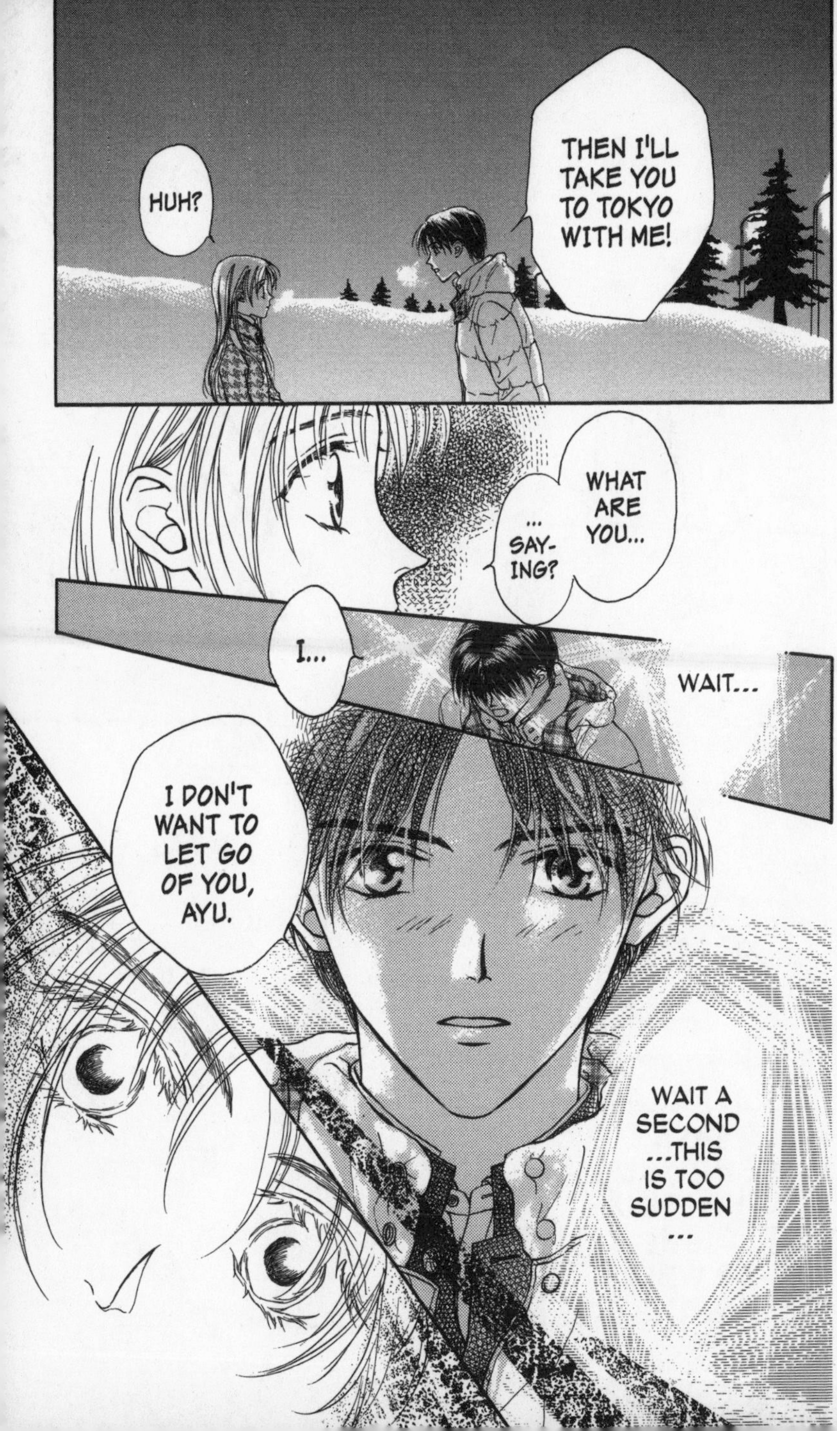
THEN I'LL TAKE YOU TO TOKYO WITH ME!
HUH?
WHAT ARE YOU...
...SAYING?
WAIT...
I...
I DON'T WANT TO LET GO OF YOU, AYU.
WAIT A SECOND ...THIS IS TOO SUDDEN ...

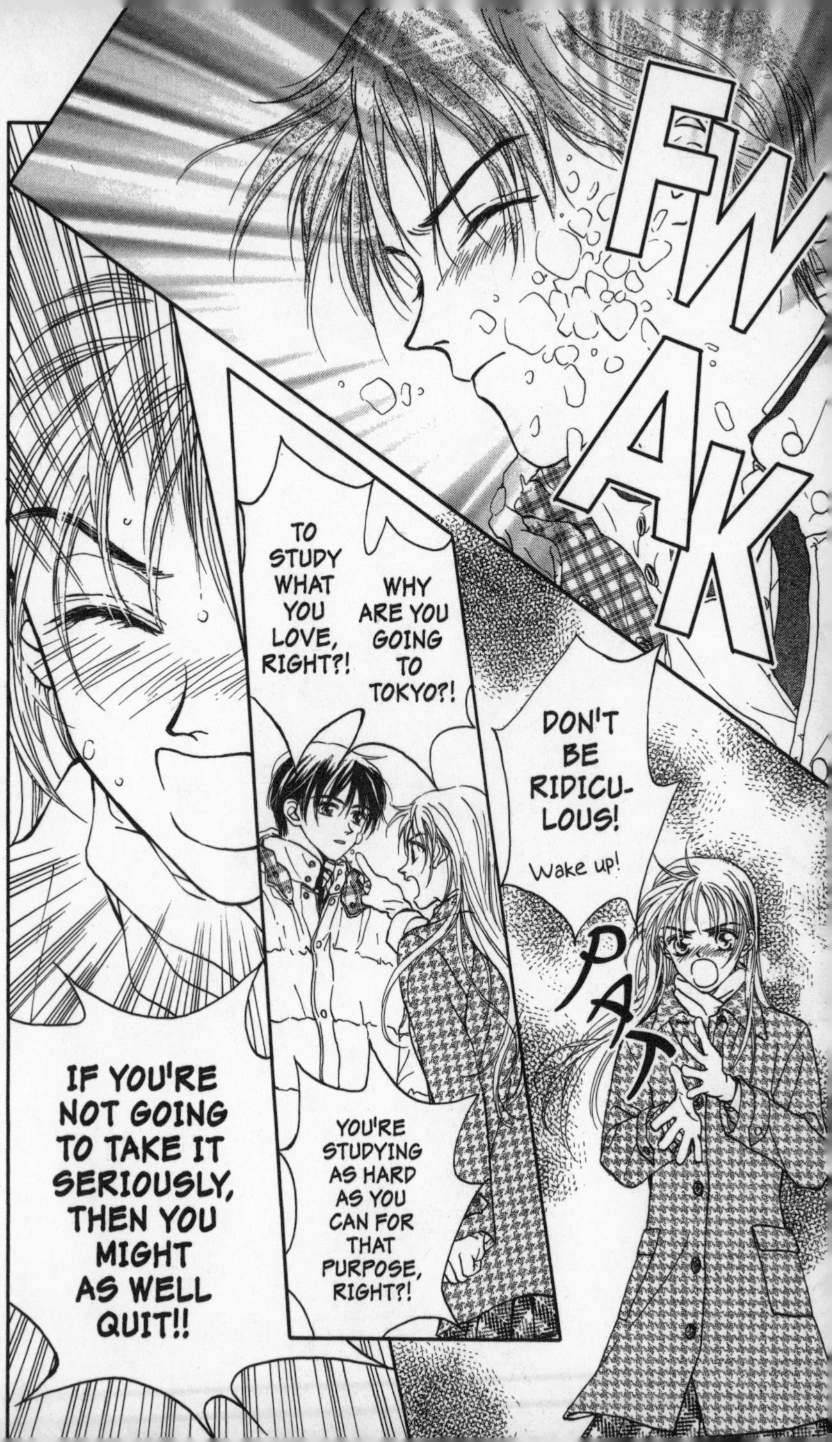
FWAK
DON'T BE RIDICULOUS!
Wake up!
PAT
WHY ARE YOU GOING TO TOKYO?!
TO STUDY WHAT YOU LOVE, RIGHT?!
YOU'RE STUDYING AS HARD AS YOU CAN FOR THAT PURPOSE, RIGHT?!
IF YOU'RE NOT GOING TO TAKE IT SERIOUSLY, THEN YOU MIGHT AS WELL QUIT!!

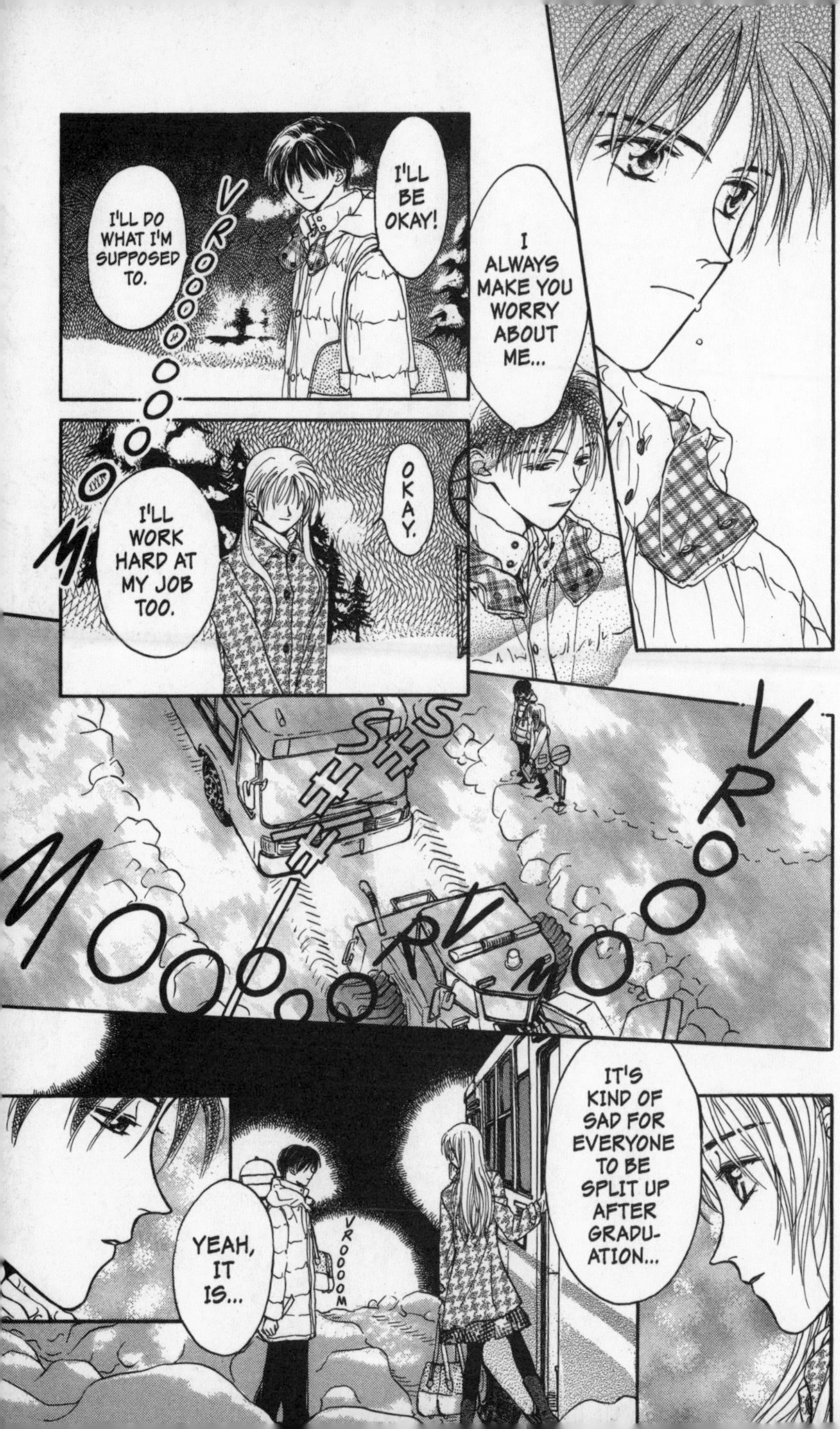
I ALWAYS MAKE YOU WORRY ABOUT ME...
I'LL BE OKAY!
I'LL DO WHAT I'M SUPPOSED TO.
VROOOOOOOOOM
OKAY.
I'LL WORK HARD AT MY JOB TOO.
VROOOOOOM
SHHH
IT'S KIND OF SAD FOR EVERYONE TO BE SPLIT UP AFTER GRADUATION...
VROOOOOM
YEAH, IT IS...

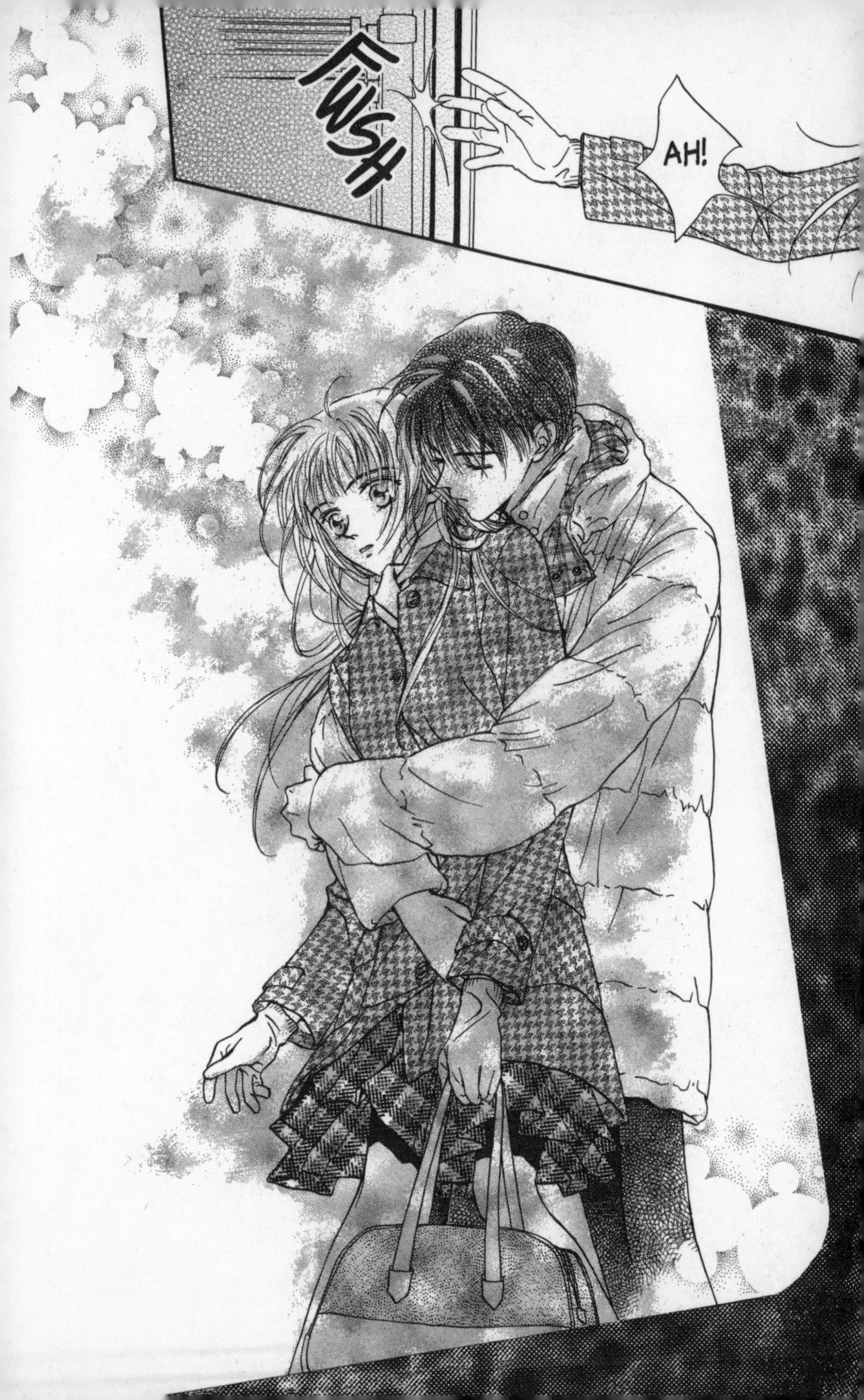
AH!
FWSH

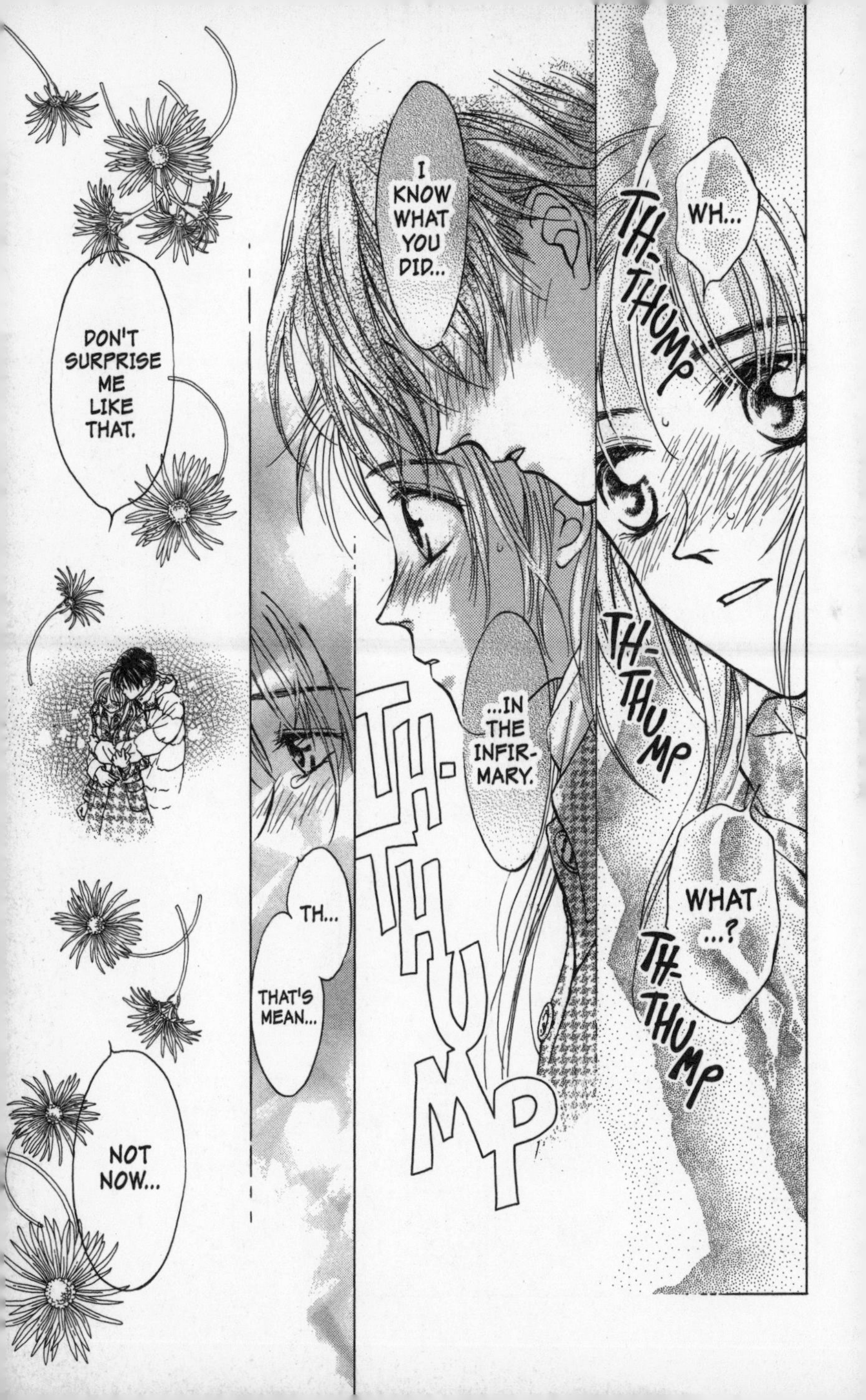
WH...
TH-THUMP
TH-THUMP
WHAT ...?
TH-THUMP
I KNOW WHAT YOU DID...
...IN THE INFIRMARY.
TH-THUMP
TH...
THAT'S MEAN...
DON'T SURPRISE ME LIKE THAT.
NOT NOW...

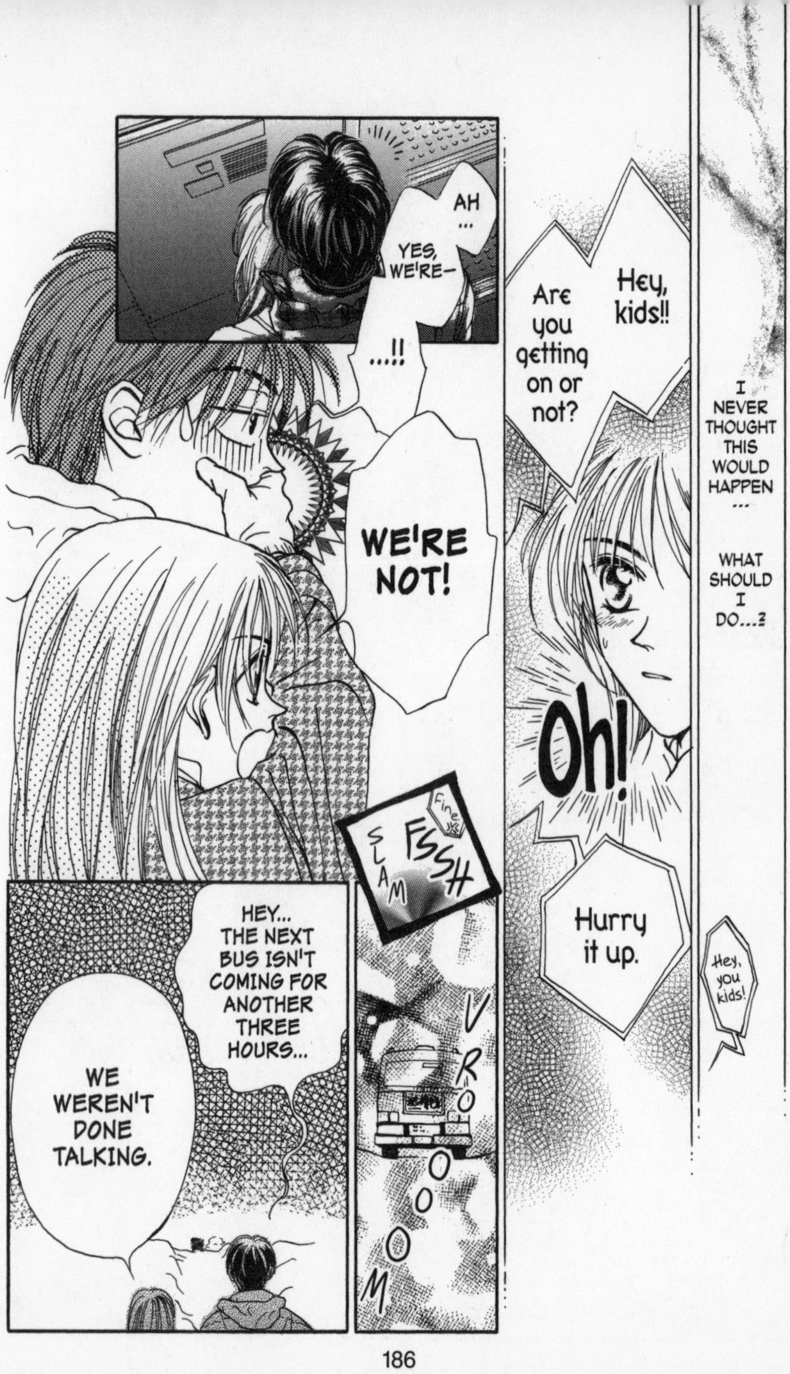
I NEVER THOUGHT THIS WOULD HAPPEN...
WHAT SHOULD I DO...?
Hey, you kids!
Hey, kids!!
Are you getting on or not?
Oh!
Hurry it up.
AH... YES, WE'RE—
...!!
WE'RE NOT!
Fine.
FSSH
SLAM
VROOOOOOM
HEY... THE NEXT BUS ISN'T COMING FOR ANOTHER THREE HOURS...
WE WEREN'T DONE TALKING.

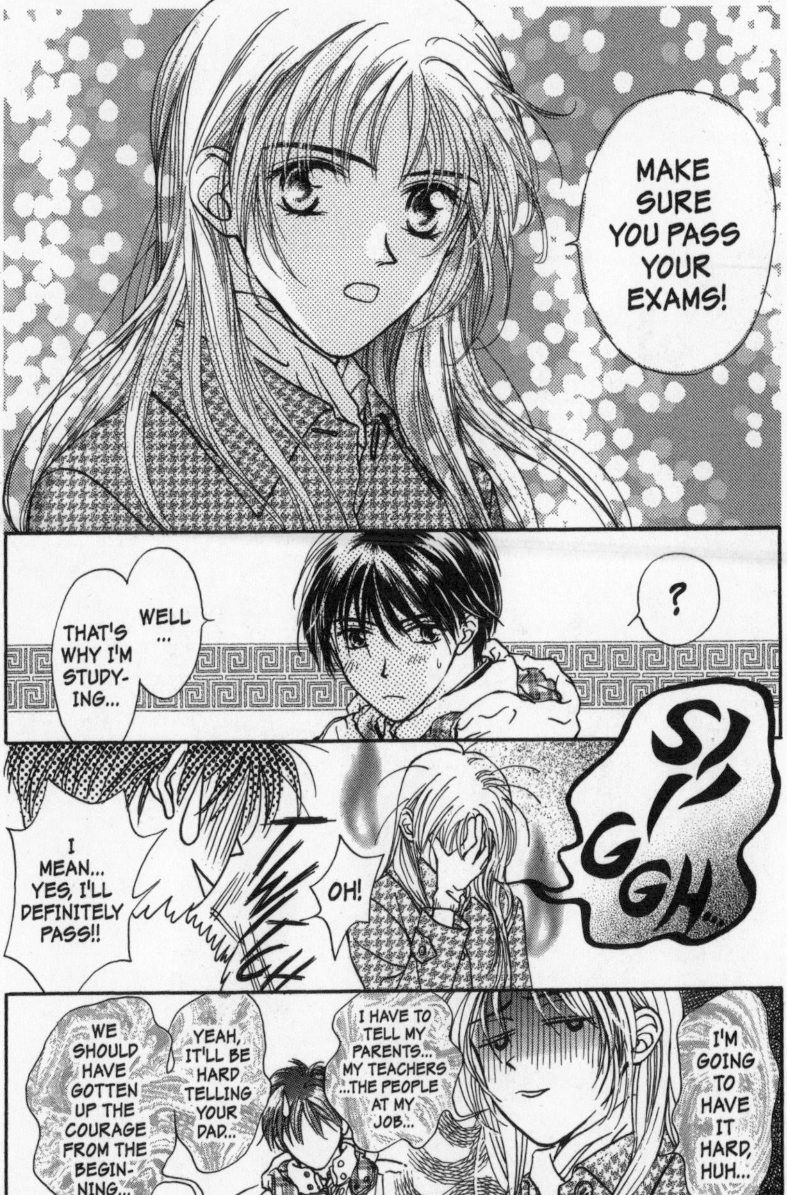
MAKE SURE YOU PASS YOUR EXAMS!
?
WELL...
THAT'S WHY I'M STUDYING...
SIGGH...
OH!
TWITCH
I MEAN... YES, I'LL DEFINITELY PASS!!
I'M GOING TO HAVE IT HARD, HUH...
I HAVE TO TELL MY PARENTS... MY TEACHERS ...THE PEOPLE AT MY JOB...
YEAH, IT'LL BE HARD TELLING YOUR DAD...
WE SHOULD HAVE GOTTEN UP THE COURAGE FROM THE BEGINNING...

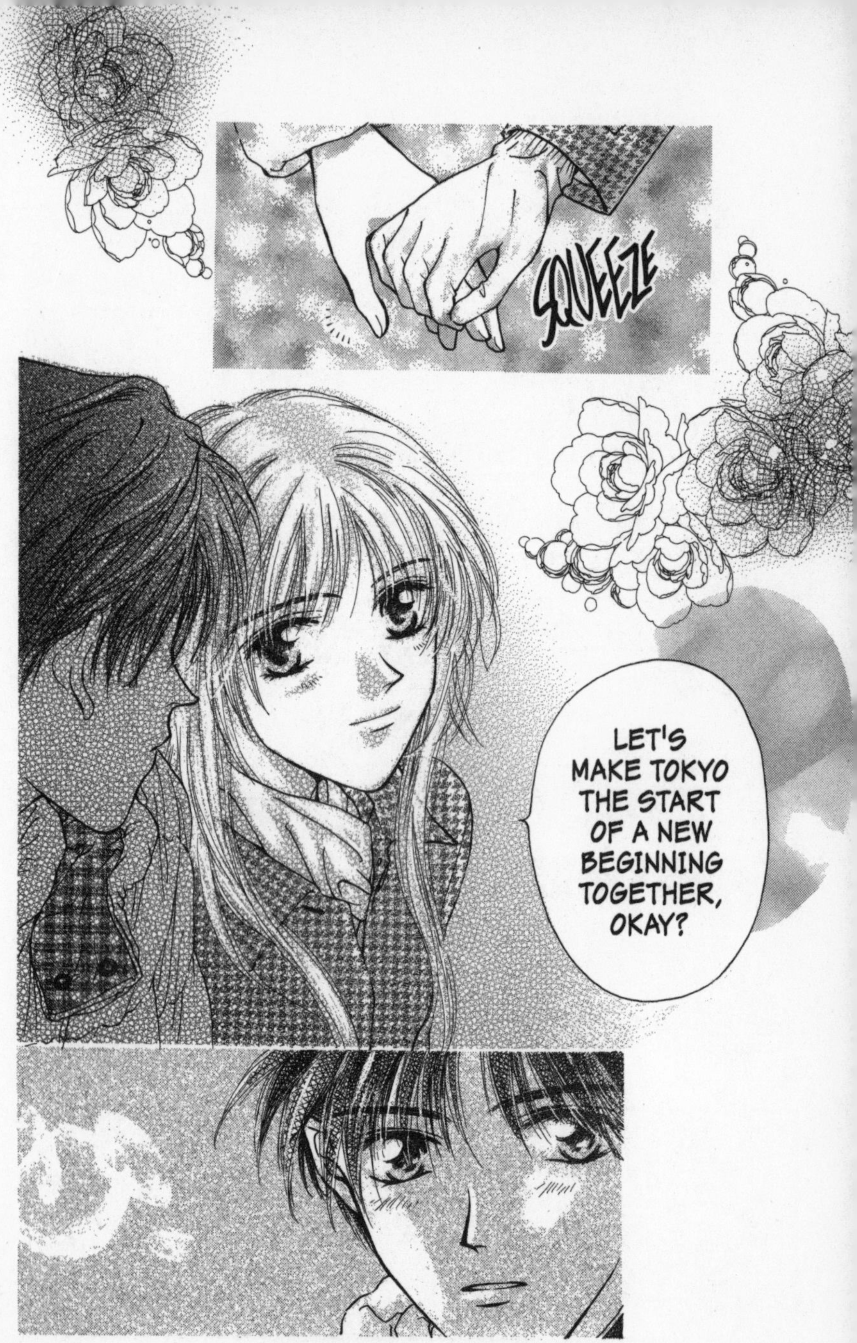
SQUEEZE
LET'S MAKE TOKYO THE START OF A NEW BEGINNING TOGETHER, OKAY?

LET TIME FREEZE / THE END

Hee hee

Thanks for reading this book. Please read the next one too!

Captive Hearts

Safety Precautions and Practical Applications

Please keep an open mind when you're reading this, okay?

CREATOR: MATSURI HINO

"CAPTIVE HEARTS" = SOMEONE IS BEING TAKEN CAPTIVE BY SOMETHING.

One day, in a bizarre, made-up setting...

In the living room
Scribble scribble
Scribble
What screentone should I use here?
Ah ha ha ha ha!
Little Brother
Waa
Ha ha!
Dad
Mom
Me

When I work in a room by myself, it gets too quiet and I feel like I'm going crazy! I like noisy rooms the best!

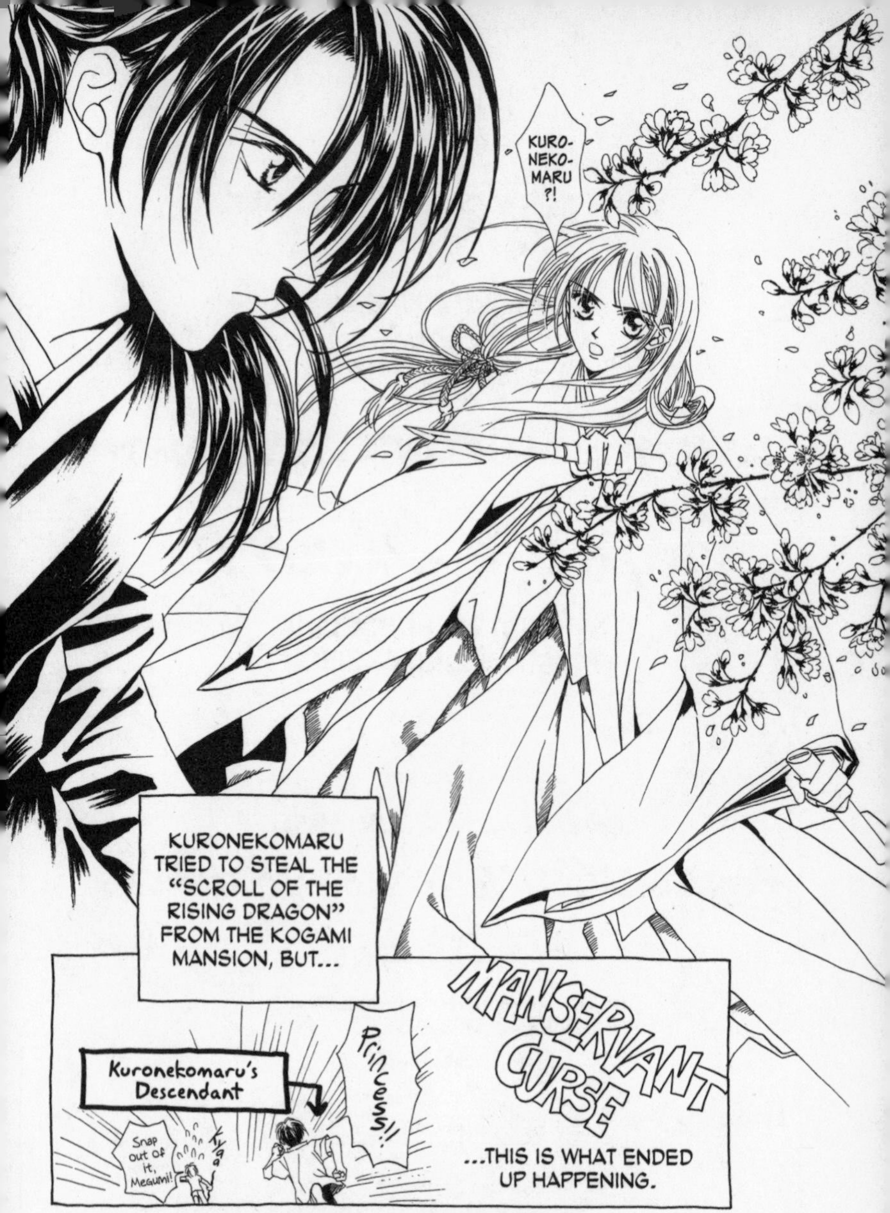
KURO-NEKO-MARU?!
KURONEKOMARU TRIED TO STEAL THE "SCROLL OF THE RISING DRAGON" FROM THE KOGAMI MANSION, BUT...
MANSERVANT CURSE
...THIS IS WHAT ENDED UP HAPPENING.
Princess!!
Kuronekomaru's Descendant
Kyaa
Snap out of it, Megumi!

WHY IS THE DRAGON GOD THE GUARDIAN DEITY OF THE KOGAMI FAMILY?
WHY DID SUZUKA'S MOM AND DAD GO ALL THE WAY TO A RURAL AREA OF CHINA?
THERE ARE MANY IMPLAUSIBLE DETAILS HERE...

Safety Precaution

DON'T TAKE CAPTIVE HEARTS TOO SERIOUSLY.

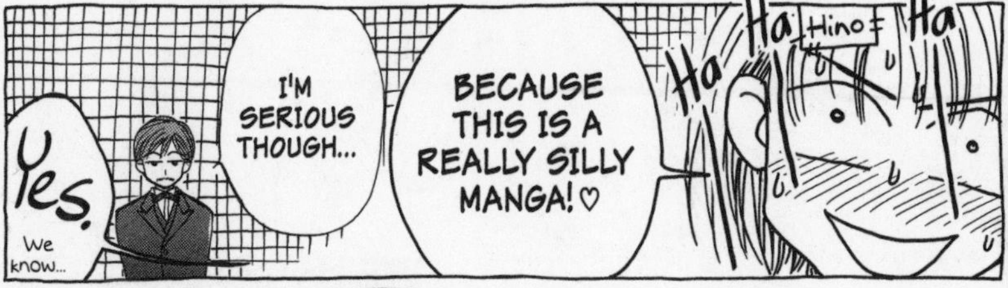
Ha Ha Ha
Hino
BECAUSE THIS IS A REALLY SILLY MANGA! ♡
I'M SERIOUS THOUGH...
Yes.
We know...

In Hino's own way...

AFTER TRYING TO GIVE UP ALL WORLDLY DESIRES, THIS IS WHAT HAPPENED.

Casualty. →

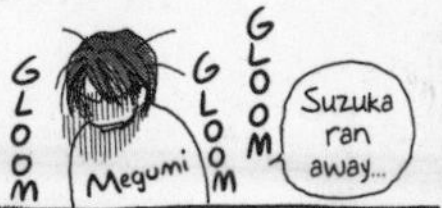
GLOOM
GLOOM
GLOOM
Megumi
Suzuka ran away...

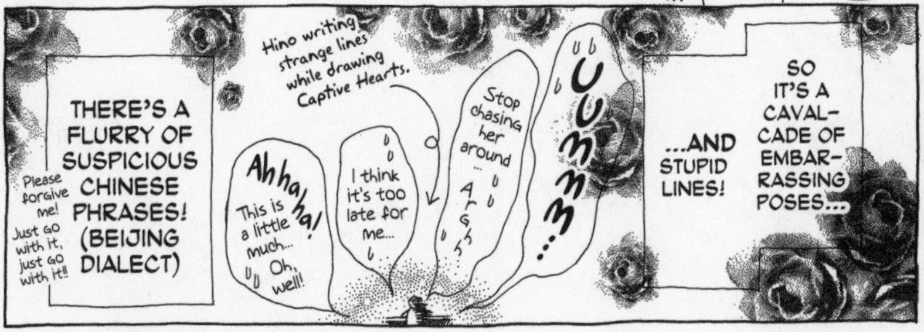
SO IT'S A CAVALCADE OF EMBARRASSING POSES...
...AND STUPID LINES!
Uuummm...
Stop chasing her around... Argh
I think it's too late for me...
Ahhaha!
This is a little much... Oh, well!
Hino writing strange lines while drawing Captive Hearts.
THERE'S A FLURRY OF SUSPICIOUS CHINESE PHRASES! (BEIJING DIALECT)
Please forgive me! Just go with it, just go with it!!

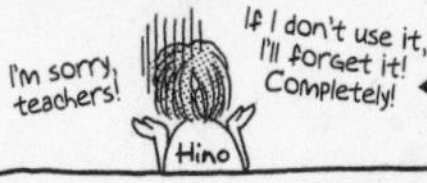
If I don't use it, I'll forget it! Completely!
I'm sorry, teachers!
Hino

← STUDIED CHINESE FOR TWO YEARS, BUT...

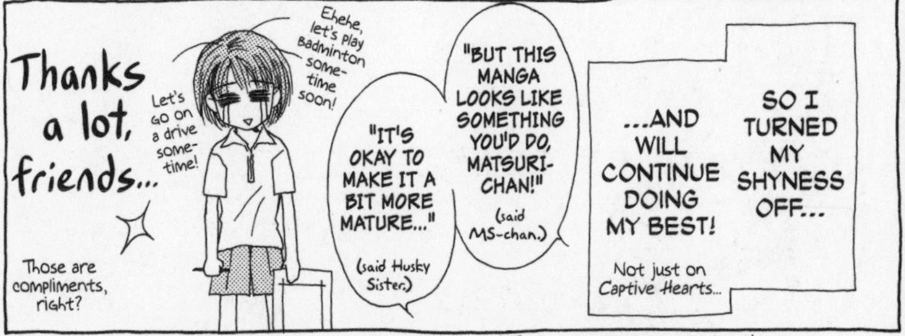
SO I TURNED MY SHYNESS OFF...
...AND WILL CONTINUE DOING MY BEST!
Not just on Captive Hearts...
"BUT THIS MANGA LOOKS LIKE SOMETHING YOU'D DO, MATSURI-CHAN!" (said MS-chan.)
"IT'S OKAY TO MAKE IT A BIT MORE MATURE..." (said Husky Sister.)
Ehehe, let's play Badminton sometime soon!
Let's go on a drive sometime!
Thanks a lot, friends...
Those are compliments, right?

Husky Sister, good luck on your submissions! MS-chan, congrats on your debut!

Practical Applications

...How?

NOW THAT HINO HAS TURNED OFF HER SHYNESS, THERE'S NOTHING SHE'S AFRAID OF!

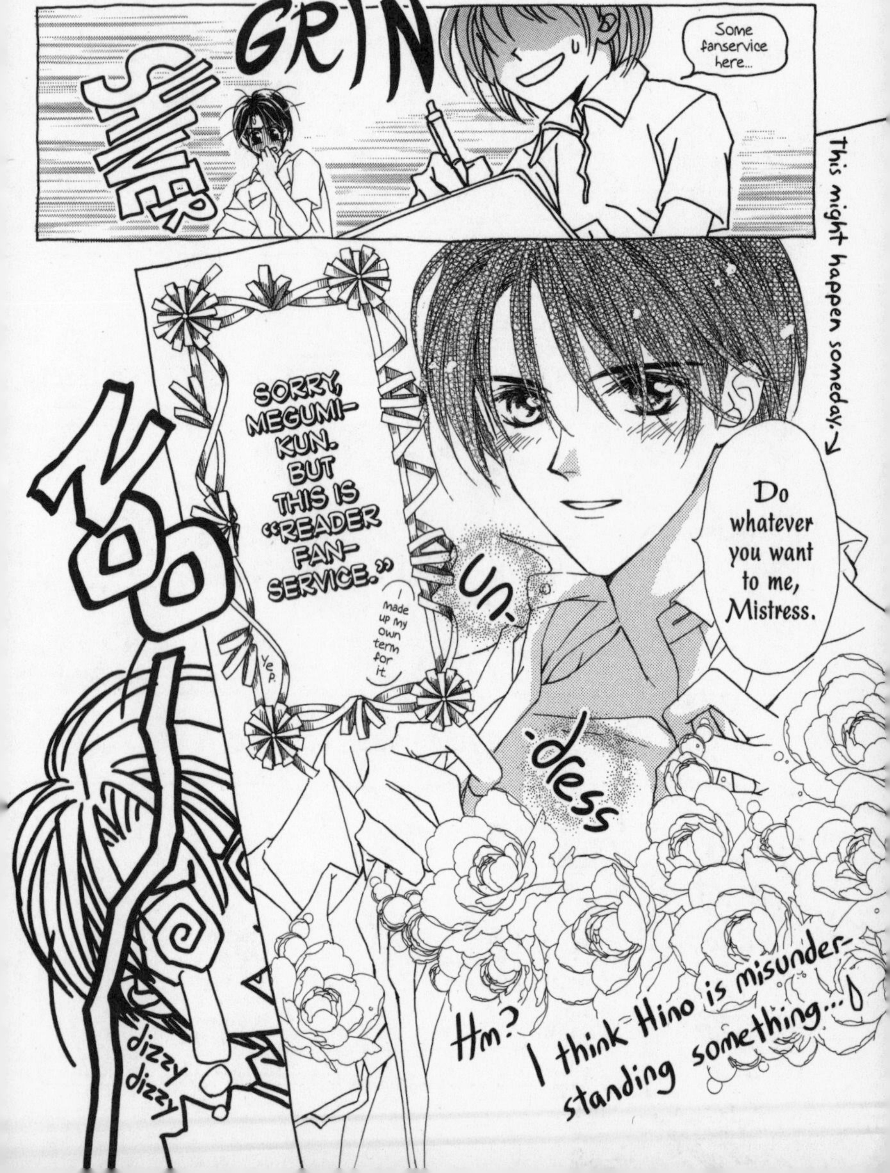
Some fanservice here...
GRIN
SHIVER
This might happen someday.
Do whatever you want to me, Mistress.
SORRY, MEGUMI-KUN. BUT THIS IS "READER FAN-SERVICE."
I made up my own term for it.
Yep.
UN-
-dress
NOO
Hm?
I think Hino is misunder-standing something...
dizzy dizzy

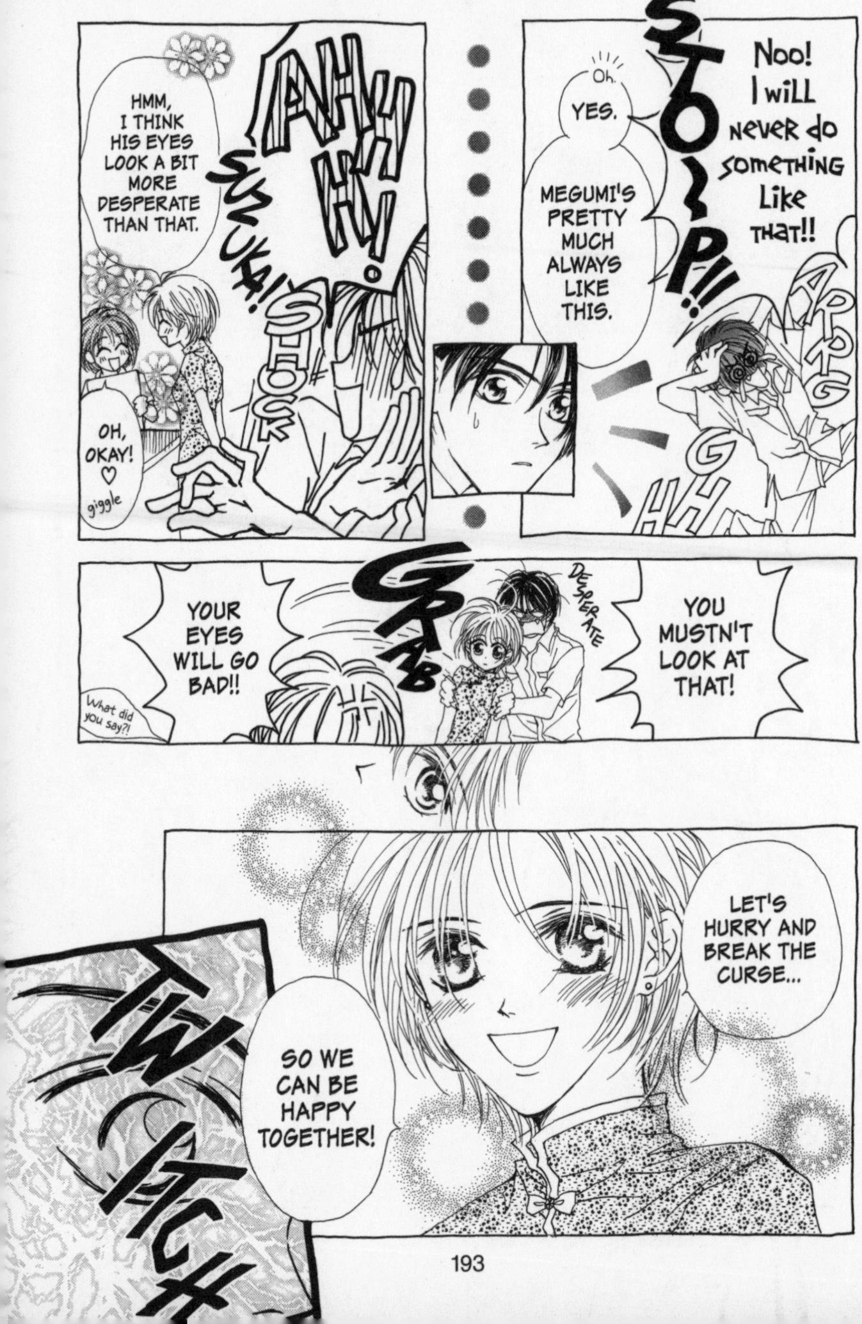
STOP!!
Noo! I will never do something like that!!
Oh.
YES.
MEGUMI'S PRETTY MUCH ALWAYS LIKE THIS.
ARGH
GHH
AHHH!
SUZUKA!!
SHOCK
HMM, I THINK HIS EYES LOOK A BIT MORE DESPERATE THAN THAT.
OH, OKAY! ♡
giggle
YOU MUSTN'T LOOK AT THAT!
DESPERATE
GRAB
YOUR EYES WILL GO BAD!!
What did you say?!
LET'S HURRY AND BREAK THE CURSE...
SO WE CAN BE HAPPY TOGETHER!
TWITCH

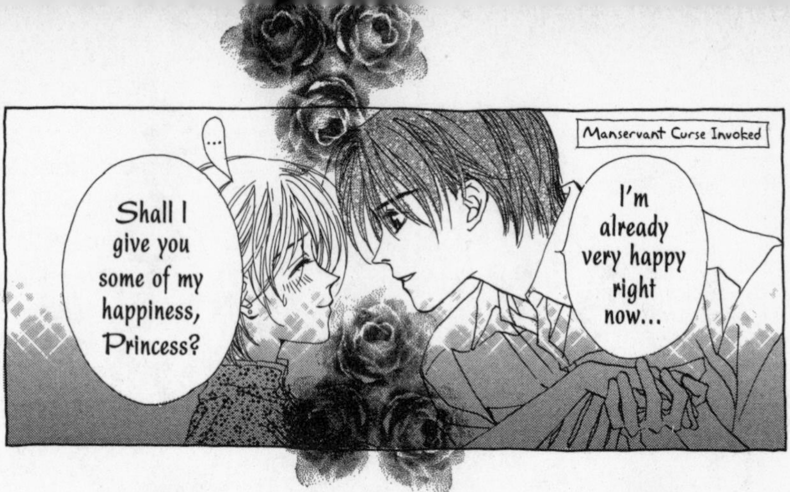
Manservant Curse Invoked
Shall I give you some of my happiness, Princess?
...
I'm already very happy right now...

WILL THERE EVER BE A DAY
WHEN THE CURSE IS BROKEN?
SEEMS DOUBTFUL.

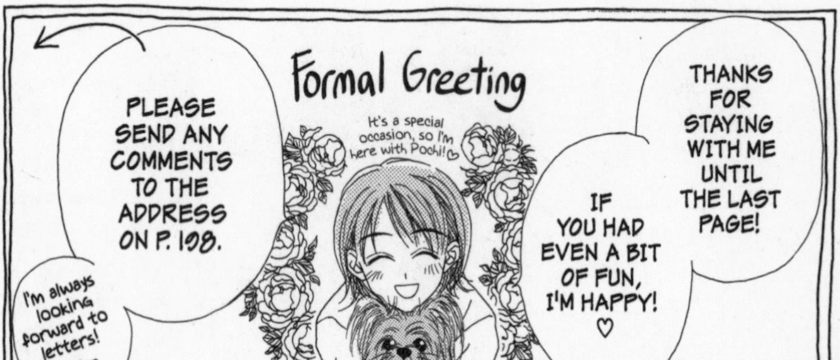
Formal Greeting
THANKS FOR STAYING WITH ME UNTIL THE LAST PAGE!
IF YOU HAD EVEN A BIT OF FUN, I'M HAPPY! ♡
It's a special occasion, so I'm here with Pochi! ♡
PLEASE SEND ANY COMMENTS TO THE ADDRESS ON P. 198.
I'm always looking forward to letters! And fan art! ♡

Z. An 18-year-old who loves cats! (I'm talking about the dog.)

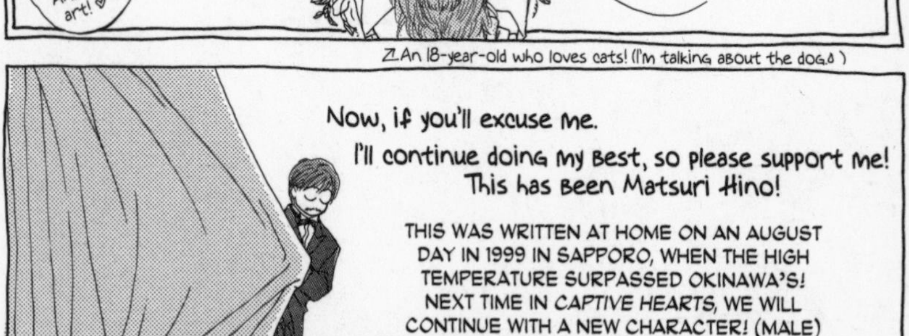
Now, if you'll excuse me.
I'll continue doing my best, so please support me!
This has been Matsuri Hino!
THIS WAS WRITTEN AT HOME ON AN AUGUST DAY IN 1999 IN SAPPORO, WHEN THE HIGH TEMPERATURE SURPASSED OKINAWA'S!
NEXT TIME IN *CAPTIVE HEARTS*, WE WILL CONTINUE WITH A NEW CHARACTER! (MALE)

Safety Precautions and Practical Applications / The End

Captivated by the story but confused by some of the terms? Here are some cultural notes to help you out!

Honorifics

Chan – an informal version of *san* used to address children and females. *Chan* can be used as a term of endearment between women who are good friends.

Kun – an informal honorific used primarily for males; it can be used by people of more senior status addressing those junior to them or by anyone in addressing male children.

San – the most common honorific title; it is used to address people outside one's immediate family and close circle of friends.

Sensei – honorific title used to address teachers as well as professionals such as doctors, lawyers and artists.

MEGUMI-KUN.
TWITCH
TAKE GOOD CARE OF HER, OKAY?

Notes

Page 19, panel 1 – **Muromachi Era**
A period of Japanese history that ran from approximately 1336 to 1573. The era ended when the last shogun Ashikaga Yoshiaki was driven out of the capital of Kyoto by Oda Nobunaga.

NOTES cont.

Page 19, panel 1 – Kuronekomaru
Kuro means "black," *neko* means "cat," and *maru* means "round" or "circle."

Page 29, panel 4 – Showa Era
This period corresponds to the reign of Emperor Showa, from December 25, 1926 to January 7, 1989.

Page 32, panel 2 – Kanji
Chinese characters that are used in the modern Japanese writing system.

Page 58, panel 3 – Shitajiki
A thin board placed underneath paper for writing.

Page 60, panel 3 – Kikoku Shijo
A Japanese person who grew up abroad but then returned home to Japan to go to school.

Page 171, panel 6 – Hokkaido and Sapporo
Hokkaido is Japan's second largest island and is located in the northeast. Sapporo is the capital of Hokkaido and its largest city.

Page 171, panel 6 – Matagi
A group of hunters that live in the Tohoku region and Hokkaido. They do not use modern technology.

Page 194, panel 4 – Okinawa
Okinawa is the second largest city in Okinawa prefecture. It has a subtropical climate with warm winters and hot summers.

MATSURI HINO burst onto the manga scene with her title
Kono Yume ga Sametara (When This Dream Is Over), which was published
in *LaLa DX* magazine. Hino was a manga artist a mere nine months after
she decided to become one.

With the success of her popular series *Captive Hearts* and *MeruPuri*, Hino
has established herself as a major player in the world of shojo manga.
Vampire Knight is currently serialized in *LaLa* and *Shojo Beat* magazines.

Hino enjoys creative activities and has commented that she would
have been either an architect or an apprentice to traditional
Japanese craft masters if she had not become a manga artist.

Captive Hearts
Vol. 1

The Shojo Beat Manga Edition

This manga volume contains material that was originally published in English in Shojo Beat magazine, October 2008 issue. Artwork in the magazine may have been altered slightly from what is presented in this volume.

STORY & ART BY
Matsuri Hino

Translation & Adaptation/Andria Cheng
Touch-up Art & Lettering/Sabrina Heep
Design/Amy Martin
Editor/Amy Yu

Editor in Chief, Books/Alvin Lu
Editor in Chief, Magazines/Marc Weidenbaum
VP, Publishing Licensing/Rika Inouye
VP, Sales and Product Marketing/Gonzalo Ferreyra
VP, Creative/Linda Espinosa
Publisher/Hyoe Narita

Toraware no Minoue by Matsuri Hino
© Matsuri Hino 1998
All rights reserved.
First published in Japan in 1999 by HAKUSENSHA, Inc., Tokyo.
English language translation rights arranged with HAKUSENSHA, Inc., Tokyo.
The stories, characters and incidents mentioned in this publication are entirely fictional.

Printed in Canada

Published by VIZ Media, LLC
P.O. Box 77010
San Francisco, CA 94107

Shojo Beat Manga Edition
10 9 8 7 6 5 4 3 2 1
First printing, November 2008

store.viz.com

High School DEBUT

SB

By Kazune Kawahara

When Haruna Nagashima was in junior high, softball and comics were her life. Now that she's in high school, she's ready to find a boyfriend. But will hard work (and the right coach) be enough?

Find out in the *High School Debut* manga series—available now!

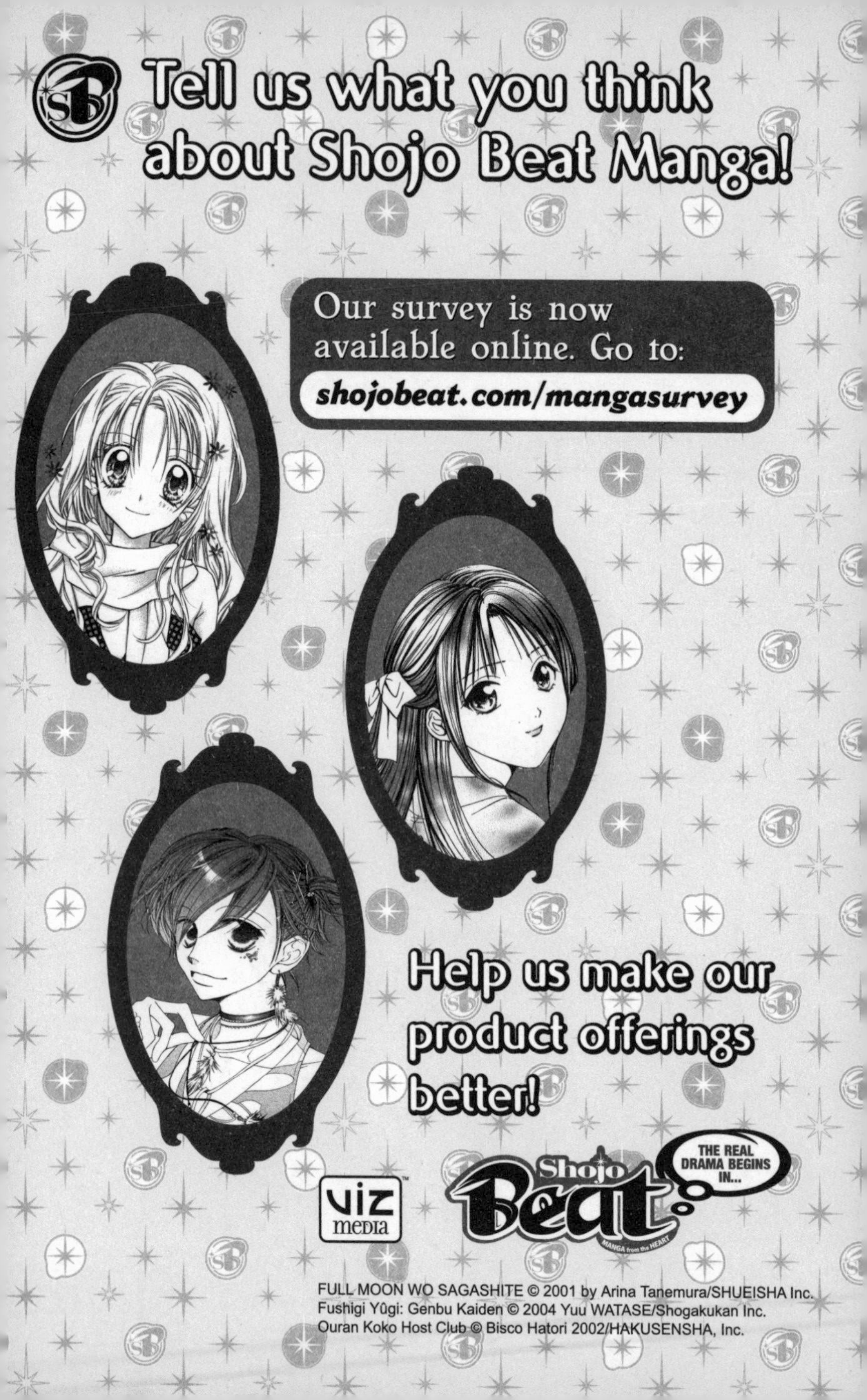

Tell us what you think about Shojo Beat Manga!
Our survey is now available online. Go to:
shojobeat.com/mangasurvey
Help us make our product offerings better!
VIZ media
THE REAL DRAMA BEGINS IN...
Shojo Beat
MANGA from the HEART
FULL MOON WO SAGASHITE © 2001 by Arina Tanemura/SHUEISHA Inc.
Fushigi Yûgi: Genbu Kaiden © 2004 Yuu WATASE/Shogakukan Inc.
Ouran Koko Host Club © Bisco Hatori 2002/HAKUSENSHA, Inc.

Find the Beat online!
Check us out at
www.shojobeat.com!